Tropical Ornamentals

Tropical Ornamentals

A GUIDE

W. Arthur Whistler

TIMBER PRESS • Portland, Oregon

Published in 2000 by

Timber Press, Inc.
The Haseltine Building
133 S.W. Second Avenue, Suite 450
Portland, Oregon 97204, U.S.A.

All photographs by the author
Book and jacket designed by Susan Applegate
Half title page photograph: *Strelitzia reginae.*
Title page photograph: Papeari Botanical Garden on Tahiti.
Printed in Hong Kong

Library of Congress Cataloging-in-Publication Data

Whistler, W. Arthur.
  Tropical ornamentals: a guide/W. Arthur Whistler.
    p.   cm.
  ISBN 0-88192-448-2 (hardback)—ISBN 0-88192-475-X (paperback)
    1. Plants, Ornamental. 2. Tropical plants. I. Title.
  SB407.W54 2000
  635.9'523—dc21   99-057321

Dedicated to the memory of my father,
Ralph Edward Whistler,
1911–1995,
generous and humble,
who did not know how much he was appreciated.
My sister Patricia and I miss him very much
and wish we had known him better.
I hope that I learned enough from Dad
that I can pass on something from him
to his grandson Sean Whistler.

Contents

Preface

Tropical Ornamentals is about plants that are cultivated in the tropics, the area between the Tropic of Cancer and the Tropic of Capricorn, which are 23.5° north and south, respectively, of the Equator. This area includes Central America (including the Caribbean), northern South America, central Africa, southern and Southeast Asia, northern Australia, and most of Oceania (Polynesia, Micronesia, and Melanesia, island clusters in the Pacific Ocean). The climates of the tropics may be wet or dry but they all have in common year-round warm weather, except for montane areas. Plants included in this book are all cultivated in the tropics and are grown for their appearance rather than their use for food, clothing, shelter, or medicine, although some are grown for more than one purpose.

Most of the featured plants are native to the tropics but some are temperate species that can be grown in warmer climates as well. Likewise, many tropical plants can be grown in temperate areas, especially in the zones between the tropics and temperate regions, which are usually known as the subtropics or warm temperate regions. These zones include the southern United States (southern California, southern Texas, Florida), the Mediterranean region, southern Africa, much of Australia, and southern South America. Most tropical plants, with the notable exception of those native to high elevations, are adapted to warm growing conditions and are killed by the cold temperatures of a temperate climate winter. However, many of these fragile tropical plants are

9

still grown in temperate regions—in greenhouses or as house plants that are protected from the cold and are able to endure the low-light conditions of winter.

The two main sources of tropical ornamentals are tropical America between Mexico and Brazil, and the islands and mainland of southeastern Asia, an area that used to be called Indo-Malaya. Whatever their origin, tropical ornamentals tend to be distributed widely and a fancier of the plants would be almost as familiar with the ornamental plants in the Caribbean as with those in Hawaii or Singapore. *Tropical Ornamentals* features more than 400 of the most common ornamentals of the world, nearly all of which are found in Hawaii, where I live. Virtually none of these plants is native to Hawaii, however, which indicates how widespread tropical ornamentals are.

The purpose of *Tropical Ornamentals* is to aid in the identification of the most common tropical ornamentals found throughout the world and to supply general information about them. A great deal of care has been taken in the selection of the featured species in order to make the book as useful as possible. Although information about how to grow and propagate the plants is given, that is not the main aim of this book. It is instead meant to fill the need for a book in between *Tropica, Color Cyclopedia of Exotic Plants,* a larger and more comprehensive book but also much more expensive, or the revision of *In Gardens of Hawai'i,* including nearly all the plants cultivated in one part of the tropics, for example, and the smaller handbooks or pamphlets sold to travelers visiting different parts of the tropics. It is hoped that the reader armed with *Tropical Ornamentals,* with its careful selection of subjects, many color photographs, and clear plant descriptions and key, will be able to identify the majority of ornamentals that he or she encounters in the tropics.

Acknowledgments

I thank Dr. George Staples, Clyde Imada, and the other staff of the Bernice P. Bishop Museum Herbarium for their help during the preparation of this book. Their update of the herbarium collections during the revision of *In Gardens of Hawaiʻi* was of immense value to the accuracy of the present book. I also thank Anne Shovic and Beate Neher for their help and suggestions.

Introduction

Tropical Plants

Tens of thousands of plants are cultivated by humans and provide many of our most basic needs such as food, shelter, clothing, and medicine. At first, useful plants were simply harvested from forests and fields when needed, but several thousand years ago early horticulturists and farmers started taking certain useful plants out of their native habitats and purposefully growing them for the needs they fulfill. The most significant examples of this include rice *(Oryza sativa)* brought into cultivation in Southeast Asia, wheat *(Triticum)* in the Middle East, and corn or maize *(Zea mays)* in Central America. Individual plants that appeared to be better at supplying the desired qualities were selected and replanted, that is, their seeds were taken in preference to those of others that were perceived to be less useful. When this was done over many plant generations, the selective breeding often produced a plant that was different from its ancestors in ways that were beneficial to humans. Today those who study how to produce and grow plants are called horticulturists; those who study the theoretical side of plants, including their origins, identities, proper names, physiology, and anatomy, are botanists; and those who specialize in garden design with ornamental plants are landscape architects. Of course, plants can be grown for pleasure by anyone.

In previous times most selective breeding involved food plants. Corn, for example, has changed so much by this process that it looks nothing like its ancestors, which have virtually disappeared. The process has accelerated in recent times and scientific principles have been incorporated into it. Much of the more recent selective breeding has been on ornamental plants, and this, along with hybridization between different species or different variations of a species, has produced many new plants called cultivars. A good example may be found in the variety of colors that some ornamental plants exhibit, some of which are not found in nature.

Ornamental Plants

It is fair to ask, What is an ornamental plant? It is a plant grown for its beauty, that is, its attractive flowers or leaves, pleasing form, or novel appearance rather than for its use in fulfilling basic human needs. Ornamentals are not a necessary part of human existence—they are the dessert rather than the main course at the table of life. They are grown to enhance the aesthetic quality of life and appear in almost every culture. There are more than 200,000 species of flowering plants in the tropics but only a small percentage of these are actually cultivated.

Plants are chosen as ornamentals for a variety of characteristics. The art of choosing and arranging ornamental plants is included in the fields of garden design and landscape architecture, based on scientific principles as well as imagination. It takes training and experience to be able to choose and arrange plants so as to produce the most appealing appearance, and this involves concepts such as line, form, color, texture, density, and balance. The right plants must be chosen for planting, and this is based not only on their appearance but also on how well plants will grow under the lighting and in the soils at the site. Landscape architecture is beyond the scope of this book but a brief discussion of the selection and arrangement of plants is included here to suggest possibilities involving tropical ornamental plants.

Attractive flowers are a feature of most ornamentals. Plants produce flowers as a means of reproduction. The conspicuous corollas and fragrances have evolved to attract pollinators, usually insects, to the flower so that these visitors can be dusted with pollen that is taken to the next flower where pollination occurs: pollen from the first flower is transferred to a second flower, usually one on a different plant. Insects and birds—sometimes bats and other mammals—use plants for food (pollen and nectar) and plants use the animals to accomplish long-distance sexual reproduction. Although all flowering plants produce flowers, not all are attractive, or even conspicuous. Ornamentals grown for their flowers happened to have flowers that are pleasing to the human sense of aesthetics, and many have been selectively bred to enhance these appealing qualities.

Flowers may be produced throughout the year or they may be seasonal. Many plants are between these two extremes. Plants that flower continuously are favored for hedges and shrubs since they add year-round color to the scene. Seasonal flowering is particularly common in trees and has the advantage, for humans, of producing an overwhelming display of color when in season. A good example is prima vera *(Tabebuia donnell-smithii)*, which drops its leaves and becomes completely covered with large yellow flowers during its flowering season. Colorful leaves, however, are less common and the use of this trait to the plant is less obvious. Some leaves, such as those on the upper parts of poinsettia *(Euphorbia pulcherrima)*, attract pollinators. But most colorful leaves are probably a result of mutations that would not survive except for human intervention since less green chlorophyll generally means less photosynthetic capacity for the plant. Some plants are cultivated for their colorful or unusual bark, such as Mindanao gum *(Eucalyptus deglupta)* and paper bark tree *(Melaleuca quinquenervia)*.

Shade, park, and street trees make a natural grouping since their functions overlap. Shade is an important part of human comfort, especially in the tropics. People, their animals, and their dwellings need protection from the hot and harmful rays of the sun, and certain trees are ideal for this. Shaded houses have lower temperatures inside. Trees that shade parks, where people gather and relax, and pastures, where animals graze, also lower the temperature through transpiration. Water evaporating from the leaves cools the air. Trees with full crowns such as yellow poinciana *(Peltophorum pterocarpum)* and monkeypod tree *(Samanea saman)* are particularly popular as shade trees. The pea family Fabaceae includes many other useful shade trees such as shower trees *(Cassia)* and Burmese rosewood *(Pterocarpus indicus)*. Banyan trees such as Indian banyan *(Ficus benghalensis)* and Indian rubber tree *(F. elastica)* are also popular as shade trees but can become immense because of their spreading habit.

Trees have traditionally been planted along streets and avenues to soften the harshness of the pavement, and common street names such as Elm Street and Oak Street, even on streets where these trees no longer grow, testify to this type of planting. Trees planted at regular intervals along streets are called street trees, and they may or may not bear showy flowers. In the tropics, perhaps the most attractive street trees are shower trees *(Cassia* spp.), royal poinciana *(Delonix regia)*, *Jacaranda mimosifolia,* queen's crape myrtle *(Lagerstroemia speciosa),* and royal palm *(Roystonea regia)*. Park trees are similar to street trees but are usually planted by themselves or in small groves surrounded by areas of lawn. Popular park trees include shower trees *(Cassia)*, Burmese rosewood *(Pterocarpus indicus),* African tulip tree *(Spathodea campanulata),* and tamarind *(Tamarindus indica)*.

Hedge plants are shrubs, or small trees or vines trimmed to be shrubs, that serve as a physical barrier or fence. Hedge plants can have colorful leaves, such as beefsteak plant *(Acalypha wilkesiana)*, snowbush *(Breynia disticha),* and caricature plant *(Graptophyllum pictum)*, or may be covered with colorful flowers, such as *Bougainvillea,* golden dewdrop *(Duranta erecta),* or Chinese hibiscus *(Hibiscus rosa-sinensis)*. Others may have neither colorful leaves nor flowers but have dense, attractive green foliage that produces a desirable form, such as Japanese privet *(Ligustrum japonicum)* and orange jessamine *(Murraya paniculata)*. The presence of thorns is also sometimes a desirable quality of hedge plants, particularly if the hedge is meant to inhibit passage, and plants such as *Bougainvillea,* pride of Barbados *(Caesalpinia pulcherrima),* and Natal plum *(Carissa macrocarpa)* are popular for that.

Screen plants are similar to hedge plants but are more of a visual barrier than a physical barrier, for example, blocking the view of an unsightly building or lights from traffic. Popular plants for this include butterfly palm *(Chrysalidocarpus lutescens),* peregrina *(Jatropha integerrima),* oleander *(Nerium oleander),* and *Sanchezia speciosa.*

Foundation plants are similar to hedges and screens but are planted at the bases of buildings to blend them into their surroundings. Popular foundation plants include variegated croton *(Codiaeum variegatum),* Tahitian gardenia *(Gardenia taitensis), Pseuderanthemum carruthersii,* and crape jasmine *(Tabernaemontana divaricata).* Border plants are similar in function but are usually lower in stature and are planted along the edge of another kind of plant such as a hedge, covering the often relatively barren shrub bases. Borders around areas of ground cover or flower beds provide a contrasting boundary. Popular border plants include lily of the Nile *(Agapanthus praecox),* red ginger *(Alpinia purpurata),* crinum lily *(Crinum asiaticum),* white ginger *(Hedychium coronarium),* red ixora *(Ixora coccinea),* and coleus *(Solenostemon scutellarioides).*

Ground cover plants are herbs or low shrubs usually less than 50 cm high (20 in) used to cover an area, either for providing attractive, low, dense vegetation or to inhibit weed growth. Ground covers may have beautiful foliage, or if color is desired, then species with attractive flowers or colorful leaves are used. Popular ground cover plants include calico plant *(Alternanthera tenella),* pothos *(Epipremnum pinnatum),* metal leaf *(Hemigraphis alternata),* mondo grass *(Ophiopogon japonicus),* and *Wedelia trilobata.* Some ground covers are particularly useful on rocks, such as climbing fig *(Ficus pumila).* Popular herbaceous ground cover or low border plants include canna lily *(Canna ×generalis),* yellow cosmos *(Cosmos sulphureus),* sultan's flower *(Impatiens wallerana),* African marigold *(Tagetes erecta),* and *Zinnia violacea.*

Some plants are usually grown in containers, which may be called planters, tubs, or if smaller, pots. Potted plants are particularly popular as houseplants. Tubs are larger and are often planted around pools and other places lacking soil. Popular potted plants include *Chrysanthemum ×morifolium* and zonal geranium *(Pelargonium ×hortorum)*. Tropical ornamentals grown as container plants in temperate areas can be brought indoors or into greenhouses in the fall to survive the cold winter. Hanging baskets are another kind of pot but hang rather than sit on a surface. Particularly popular hanging basket plants have cascading herbaceous stems, such as spider plant *(Chlorophytum comosum)* and wandering Jew *(Tradescantia zebrina)*.

Vines or plants that can be trained as vines can be used to cover fences, walls, trellises, and arches. The difference between a shrub and a vine is not always clear. If a shrub tends to have weak, spreading branches it is referred to as scandent. Woody vines are called lianas and have the advantage over herbaceous vines, especially annual herbaceous vines, of growing higher and being longer lived. Some vines climb by means of their stem's tip growing in a twining motion and wrapping around other plants or structures. Other plants have specialized clinging structures called tendrils, which may be modified leaves, stems, or other plant parts. Still other plants climb by means of adventitious roots that form along the stem and adhere to surfaces they contact. Popular vines for covering structures include Japanese honeysuckle *(Lonicera japonica)*, wood rose *(Merremia tuberosa)*, Madagascar jasmine *(Stephanotis floribunda)*, Cape honeysuckle *(Tecomaria capensis)*, and skyflower vine *(Thunbergia grandiflora)*.

A specimen plant is a plant that is grown by itself, usually because of its colorful leaves or flowers, and that can stand alone rather than being part of a larger planting. Specimen plants may be trees or shrubs. Popular specimen shrubs include chenille plant *(Acalypha hispida)*, yellow allamanda *(Allamanda cathartica)*, pink *Mussaenda* 'Queen Sirikit', and sandpaper vine *(Petraea volubilis)*. Popular specimen trees include pride of Burma *(Amherstia nobilis)*, rainbow shower *(Cassia ×nealii)*, buttercup tree *(Cochlospermum vitifolium)*, frangipani *(Plumeria rubra)*, and prima vera *(Tabebuia donnell-smithii)*. A variation on the specimen plant is the novelty plant or oddity, grown for some unusual characteristic rather that intrinsic beauty. Such plants include the cannonball tree *(Couroupita guianensis)* with large, cannonball-like fruits, pencil tree *(Euphorbia tirucalli)* with pencil-like, leafless stems, ribbon bush *(Homalocladium platycladum)* with flat, ribbon-like stems, sausage tree *(Kigelia africana)* with hanging, sausage-like fruits, and skunk tree *(Sterculia foetida)* whose flowers produce an unpleasant odor.

Two uses of ornamental plants involve extensive pruning or trimming. One is topiary, the formation of geometric or other shapes such as animals by artistic pruning. Plants ideally suited to topiary pruning are typically shrubs or small trees that produce dense foliage such as *Bougainvillea ×buttiana, B. glabra,* orange jessamine *(Murraya paniculata)*, and tobira *(Pittosporum tobira)*. The other use involving pruning is bonsai, the Japanese horticultural art of growing dwarfed trees or shrubs in small, shallow pots. Tropical plants used for bonsai include heavenly bamboo *(Nandina domestica)* and dwarf umbrella tree *(Schefflera arboricola)*.

Rock gardens, water-conserving gardens, and ponds require careful choice of ornamentals. Rock gardens are landscapes featuring rocks and soil in addition to plants, and the plant forms should complement or contrast with the rocks. Tropical rock garden plants include leopard lily *(Belamcanda chinensis)*, *Cycas circinalis*, crown of thorns *(Euphorbia milii)*, flaming Katie *(Kalanchoe blossfeldiana)*, pepper face *(Peperomia obtusifolia)*, rose moss *(Portulaca grandiflora)*, coral plant *(Russelia equisetiformis)*, and society garlic *(Tulbaghia violacea)*. Water-conserving gardens, sometimes called Xeriscape gardens, are similar but feature plants adapted to dry habitats. Such gardens are consequently popular in dry areas of the tropics since they are planted with shrubs or trees and require less water than those planted with herbaceous vegetation. Popular water-conserving garden plants in the tropics include desert rose *(Adenium obesum)*, century plant *(Agave americana)*, air plant *(Kalanchoe pinnata),* and cochineal cactus *(Opuntia cochinellifera).* Plants used in and around ponds are aquatic if they grow in the water or waterlogged soil. Popular aquatic plants include papyrus *(Cyperus papyrus),* water hyacinth *(Eichhornia crassipes),* and blue waterlily *(Nymphaea capensis).*

One final use of ornamental plants should also be mentioned: leaves and flowers may be fashioned together into attractive bouquets or other decorative arrangements, an example of which is the Hawaiian lei.

Organization of the Information in *Tropical Ornamentals*

How should the more than 400 featured plants be arranged to facilitate usage of this book? Should they be arranged by flower color? Such an arrangement presents several problems. First, flower colors constitute a continuum, just as colors of the light spectrum or the rainbow grade into each other with no clearly defined boundaries. Second, many species have cultivars in a variety of flower colors and such species would have to be placed in more than one category. Third, many ornamentals are grown for their colorful or variegated leaves rather than flowers and some of these do not produce flowers in cultivation.

Should plants be arranged by longevity or life form, with trees, shrubs, vines, herbs, and so on constituting the first division? Again, plants often do not clearly fall into only a single category. For example, a plant such as *Allamanda cathartica* could be judged to be a shrub when it is freestanding, but it looks more like a vine when it is trained on an arch. Like flower color, unrelated plants would be grouped together, and what would be the second criterion for arrangement within each life form? Even herbs, which could be divided into annuals, biennials, and perennials, and the latter by method of perennation (bulb, corm, tuber, for example), would require a further method of arrangement.

Should plants be arranged in taxonomic order, first by family, then by genus, then by species, keeping related families, genera, and species together? There are various systems by which plants can be arranged into such a sequence, but these are familiar only to botanists studying classification and a problem with any such linear arrangement is that some related families, genera, and species end up being separated from each other.

Should plants be arranged in alphabetical order by common name? This is an entirely unworkable system for several reasons. For example, some plants have more than one common name, others none, and there is no universal agreement on the common names of plants.

The arrangement settled on for this book is by alphabetical order of scientific name—by genus and species. In this arrangement closely related plants, plants in the same genus, are placed together for easier comparison. Genera in the same family are usually widely separated, but an appendix, Twenty Common Plant Families, has been provided, characterizing the families that account for about two-thirds of all the plants included in this book. Also, cross-references from family name to the names of all genera included in the book are provided in the Index.

The index also includes cross-references from the common names for those plants that have them to the accepted scientific name by which plants are alphabetized in the main body of the text, and cross-references from synonyms to the accepted names. In addition to the descriptions and photographs, another appendix, the Identification Key, is provided to facilitate identification. A glossary is provided that briefly defines the various special terms that are unavoidable when plants need to be described in detail sufficient to ensure their correct identification.

The descriptions and their accompanying photographs in the main portion of the book, The Tropical Ornamental Plants, are organized into the following sequence:

Genus and family. The genus and the family to which it belongs are followed by a short discussion of the genus. The appendix, Twenty

Common Plant Families, has additional information on the most important families of tropical ornamental plants.

Scientific name and authority. Scientific names are binomials, literally two names, composed of the name of the genus followed by a specific epithet, *Abelmoschus rugosus,* for example. This is followed by what is called the authority, a kind of bibliographic citation referring to the original description of the plant, Wight & Arnott for *A. rugosus,* for example, meaning the plant was originally described by Robert Wight and George Arnott in their *Prodromus Florae Peninsulae Indiae Orientalis,* published in 1834. Although it is outside the purposes of the present book, this information may help lead to additional information about the plant in other books through use of various taxonomic indexes. Occasionally the same binomial may have been published for two different species by different authors, and the authority has been included here for accuracy. Sometimes the authority given is "of gardens," meaning the name is commonly used in horticulture but has not been validly published. This authority is often given in other books as "Hort.," for *hortus* or *hortorum,* garden or of gardens.

Species that are known to be the result of hybridization are designated with the multiplication sign ×, *Arachnis ×maingayi,* for example, the result of a cross between *A. flos-aeris* and *A. hookeriana.* The multiplication sign is ignored in alphabetizing. In a couple of instances plants are included that are the result of hybridization, intentional or unintentional, in the garden, sometimes not between naturally occurring species. For example, *Mussaenda* 'Queen Sirikit' is a hybrid, resulting from the cross, *M. erythrophylla* × *M. philippica* 'Aurorae', that latter parent a cultivar of the species *M. philippica.* Generally such hybrids are not themselves given specific epithets but are described as cultivars, in this case the lack of a specific epithet indicating that an interspecific cross has been involved. Species may be divided, in descending order of rank, into subspecies (abbreviated subsp.), variety (var.), and form (f.).

Synonyms. Synonyms are scientific names that for various reasons are no longer valid for a plant. This may happen because an earlier valid name has been found that takes precedence over a later, more widely used one, or because what were thought to be two or more species have been reconsidered to be a single species with a single name. Usually the earliest name is chosen and the later ones are relegated to synonymy. A plant may have been described under one genus, then moved to another in an effort to reflect relationships more accurately. Thus a species may become known under different names. For example, *Hibiscus rugosus* (Wight & Arnott) Roxburgh is a synonym of *Abelmoschus rugosus*, indicating that William Roxburgh later moved the species originally described by Wight & Arnott to the genus *Hibiscus*. In addition to synonyms there may be additional notes concerning misidentification of the plants in the literature. All of these more important synonyms are provided, when they occur, so that more information on the plant may be found in other books. Synonyms are cross-referenced to the accepted names in the Index.

Distinguishing characteristics. Characteristics are provided that are useful for differentiating the species from other, similar looking species. Some of these other species are also illustrated.

Description. The description begins with the plant's scientific name followed by common names, if any. The native range is given along with ornamental and other uses. If a plant or parts of it are poisonous, that is mentioned. The plant description is divided into certain features that are highlighted, beginning with the life form, tree, shrub, vine, or herb, for example. Some distinctive life forms such as palm, liana, and epiphyte are also used to describe the plants. The more specialized terms used in the descriptions are defined in the Glossary. Descriptions of the leaves, flowers, and fruit, or for the nonflowering seed plants, the gymnosperms, the leaves, cones, and seeds, are also highlighted.

Flowering time is described under flowers. Most tropical plants flower throughout the year because they are native to areas where there is little seasonal variation in rainfall, sunlight, or pollinators. If favorable conditions are present throughout the year it is advantageous for the plant to utilize these environmental factors year-round. There is much variation in flowering times and it is not always clear for such nonseasonally flowering species if they flower more or less continuously or instead flower anytime. If it appears that flowering is nonseasonal but not continuous in an individual plant, it is referred to as flowering anytime. Plants flowering at irregular or long intervals are described as intermittently or rarely flowering, respectively. Such plants are often found without flowers.

Most seasonally flowering tropical ornamentals are native to areas with a dry season, which affects the pollinators as well as the growing conditions for seedlings. Such plants, often trees, flower at the optimal time for reproduction. Even when they are cultivated in climates suited for year-round flowering, they may still flower seasonally in response to day length (actually the length of night) or temperature, for example. Some plants can detect a difference in the length of night and when it reaches a critical short time (when the days are getting longer) flowering is initiated since favorable reproductive times should be coming —spring or summer. The flowering of such plants is described in terms of seasons—winter, spring, summer, fall—but that is not always reliable since flowering may vary with the climate where the plant is grown.

Propagation method is followed by a general description of the optimal conditions for growing the plant, whether it tends to do best in wet or dry soils and sunny or shaded places. Additional cultivation information is provided, for example, how the plant is used in particular garden situations, whether it has a tendency to escape and become weedy, or distinctive characteristics of cultivars.

The Tropical Ornamental Plants

Abelmoschus MALVACEAE

Abelmoschus is a genus of 15 Old World tree and shrub species, but some authors include them in the genus *Hibiscus*. Some are cultivated as food plants, okra, *A. esculentus* (Linnaeus) Moench, and tree spinach, *A. manihot* (Linnaeus) Medikus, for example, and a few as ornamentals for their flowers.

Abelmoschus rugosus Wight & Arnott

Synonym, *Hibiscus rugosus* (Wight & Arnott) Roxburgh and sometimes identified as a cultivar, 'Pacific Orange', or 'Mischief' or 'Mischief Pink', of *Abelmoschus moschatus* Medikus but that species is quite different, a yellow-flowered, wild-growing subshrub with the petals not reflexed. DISTINGUISHABLE from the countless varieties of the related *Hibiscus rosa-sinensis* by the subshrub habit, deeply lobed leaves, red petals white at the base, and ovoid, pod-like fruit.

Abelmoschus rugosus, which lacks a well-known common name though it may be called red musk mallow, is native to India and is cultivated for its striking red and white flowers. It is relatively new to gardens and is grown by itself in pots or as a border plant. Fertile, well-drained soils in sunny places are preferred. SUBSHRUB to 50 cm high (20 in) or more, with hairy stems and petioles. LEAVES simple, alternate, blade generally round in outline but deeply three- to five-lobed, mostly

Abelmoschus rugosus with fuzzy capsule fruit

5–12 cm long (2–5 in). **FLOWERS** continuously through the year; flowers solitary, axillary, on a long peduncle. Corolla of five free, reflexed, obovate petals 3–5 cm long (1¼–2 in), red with white at the base, surrounding the yellow, drooping staminal column. **FRUIT** a hispid, spindle-shaped, five-angled capsule. **PROPAGATE** by seeds.

Acacia FABACEAE

Acacia is a genus of about 1200 woody species found throughout the tropics and subtropics, especially in Australia and Africa, with many species important for timber, gum arabic, dyeing, and tanning chemicals as well as ornamentals. Some unusual species produce special food for ants that live on the tree and discourage grazing animals from feeding on the plant and vines from climbing on it.

Acacia confusa Merrill

DISTINGUISHABLE from most trees by the phyllode leaves and small heads of prominent yellow stamens. A similar cultivated species, *Acacia spirorbis* Labillardière, differs in having flowers in long spikes rather than heads, and the fruits coiled rather than straight.

Acacia confusa, Formosan koa, is native to the northern Philippines and perhaps Taiwan but is widely cultivated for timber and as an ornamental and is naturalized in some places, such as Hawaii. It is typically planted as a street tree or as a border around buildings and is something of a novelty because of its phyllode leaves. **TREE** to 15 m high (50 ft). **LEAVES** bipinnately compound when juvenile; adult leaves simple, alternate, subsessile, blade actually a phyllode consisting of a blade-like

Acacia confusa with straight pods and flowers in heads

Acacia spirorbis with coiled pods and flowers in spikes

petiole, narrowly elliptic and somewhat curved, 6–13 × 0.5–1.3 cm (2½–5 × ¼–½ in) with parallel veins. **FLOWERS** continuously through the year; flowers many in globose heads 6–10 mm in diameter (¼–⅜ in). Corolla of four or five tiny, free, yellow petals surrounding the numerous prominent yellow stamens. **FRUIT** a flattened, narrowly oblong pod 3–12 cm long (1¼–5 in), two- to eight-seeded. **PROPAGATE** by scarified seeds or cuttings. Dry to moist soils in sunny places are preferred.

Acalypha EUPHORBIACEAE

Acalypha comprises 400 to 450 herb, shrub, and small tree species native throughout the tropics and subtropics, with some occurring in temperate regions. Many weedy and ornamental species belong to this genus, and three of the most common hedge plants are included here.

Acalypha godseffiana Masters

Sometimes considered a synonym of *Acalypha wilkesiana* but the taxonomy of the two species is confusing and *A. godseffiana* seems to be distinct. **DISTINGUISHABLE** from other colorful shrubs by the alternate leaves, flat and ovate to linear blades with white margins, and inconspicuous unisexual flowers in separate male and female spikes.

Acalypha godseffiana, copper leaf, is perhaps native to New Guinea or Malaysia but its origin is uncertain and it is widely cultivated in the tropics for its variegated foliage. A narrow-leaved cultivar, 'Heterophylla', also called variety *heterophylla,* is probably more common than the normal one, 'Marginata', which has dark leaves with pink margins. These shrubs are often used when a tall colorful hedge is desired, one that requires periodic pruning. **SHRUB** to 4 m high (13 ft). **LEAVES** simple, alternate, blade ovate or, in 'Heterophylla', narrowly elliptic, 6–20

Acalypha godseffiana 'Marginata' with pink-fringed leaves, ovate as in wild plants

Acalypha godseffiana 'Heterophylla' with narrow, white-fringed leaves

cm long (2½–8 in), usually with white or pink, wavy or toothed margins and sometimes the rest suffused with red or mottled with other colors. **FLOWERS** anytime during the year but the flowers are inconspicuous, unisexual, in axillary spikes to 18 cm long (7 in), the male spikes with numerous flowers, the female spikes with several, each of which is borne in a bract. Corolla absent, the calyx of small, inconspicuous sepals. **FRUIT** a small capsule, infrequently formed in cultivation. **PROPAGATE** by cuttings. Well-drained soils in partially shaded places are preferred.

Acalypha hispida N. L. Burman

DISTINGUISHABLE by the long, red, rarely white, hanging spikes that look like cats' tails.

Acalypha hispida, chenille plant, is possibly native to Melanesia or Malaysia but its origin is uncertain and only female plants are known. Unlike most of the other species of the genus it has plain green leaves and is cultivated instead for its spectacular long, prominent red catkin-like inflorescence and is sometimes called cat's tail or red-hot cat's tail. It is often grown by itself or sometimes in hedges in the tropics, and in the greenhouse in temperate regions. **SHRUB** to 3 m high (10 ft). **LEAVES** simple, alternate, blade ovate, 8–27 cm long (3½–11 in), green with toothed margins. Corolla absent, the calyx of tiny, inconspicuous sepals. **FLOWERS** continuously through the year; flowers unisexual, males unknown, females with conspicuous red styles, rarely white as in 'Philippine Medusa', borne in axillary

Acalypha hispida

spikes 10–50 cm long (4–20 in). **FRUIT** unknown. **PROPAGATE** by cuttings. Moist but well-drained soils in sunny or partially shaded places are preferred.

Acalypha wilkesiana Müller Argoviensis

Synonym, *Acalypha amentacea* subsp. *wilkesiana* (Müller Argoviensis) Fosberg. **DISTINGUISHABLE** by the alternate, ovate or kidney-shaped leaves with either a mottled red surface or white-toothed margins, and inconspicuous unisexual flowers in separate male and female spikes.

Acalypha wilkesiana, beefsteak plant, is possibly native to Malaysia or Melanesia but its origin is uncertain. It has long been cultivated for its colorful leaves, no two of which are alike, that develop colors best in full sun, hence it is sometimes called match-me-if-you-can or Jacob's coat. It is often used where a tall colorful hedge is desired and is able to

Acalypha wilkesiana f. *wilkesiana* with mottled ovate leaves

Acalypha wilkesiana f. *circinata* with green, cupped leaves with toothed white margins

withstand drought and poor soil. **SHRUB** to 4 m high (13 ft). **LEAVES** simple, alternate, blade usually ovate (f. *wilkesiana*) or nearly round to kidney-shaped (f. *circinata*), 8–35 cm long (3½–14 in), often mottled with red, white, bronze, or purplish areas and the margins toothed (f. *wilkesiana*) or the surfaces green but three-dimensionally cupped and the margins white with numerous finger-like lobes (f. *circinata*). **FLOWERS** anytime during the year but the flowers are inconspicuous, unisexual, in separate axillary spikes, the male spikes with numerous flowers, the females with only several flowers, the spikes surrounded by bracts. Corolla absent, the calyx of tiny, inconspicuous sepals. **FRUIT** a capsule, infrequently formed in cultivation. **PROPAGATE** by cuttings, which is easily done. Light, well-drained soils in partially shaded to sunny places are preferred.

Adenium APOCYNACEAE

Adenium is a genus of five or six thick-stemmed shrubs adapted to living in dry places and found in semiarid regions of Africa and the Arabian Peninsula. They contain sap that is used as fish poison and to coat arrowheads in their native range. Some authors recognize only one species with a number of subspecies.

Adenium obesum (Forsskål) Roemer & J. A. Schultes

Synonym, *Adenium coetaneum* Stapf. **DISTINGUISHABLE** by the succulent habit, milky sap, leaves crowded at the stem tips, and prominent reddish flowers with five fuzzy, protruding stamens. Its flowers are similar to those of *Nerium oleander,* a much larger shrub with narrower leaves, but lack the fringe of filaments, the corona, conspicuous in the throat of the *N. oleander.*

Adenium obesum, desert rose, a misnomer since it is not related to roses, and sometimes called mock azalea, is native to East Africa but is widely cultivated for its succulent habit and prominent flowers. The sap is poisonous and in the native range of the plant it has been used to coat arrowheads. **SHRUB** to 2 m high (6½ ft) but usually much less, with

Adenium obesum

succulent, pale gray stems clustered at the base and a poisonous milky sap. LEAVES simple, opposite, crowded at the branch tips, oblong, 4–12 cm long (1⅝–5 in) with a broad, somewhat squared or rounded tip. FLOWERS continuously through the year though the leaves may fall seasonally; flowers one to several in terminal clusters. Corolla of fused petals, narrowly bell-shaped, 6–8 cm long (2½–3½ in), divided less than halfway into five spreading elliptic lobes, pink to rose-colored with a white or yellow throat. FRUIT a capsule, infrequently formed in cultivation. PROPAGATE by cuttings. Well-drained sandy soils in partially shaded places are preferred. It is often grown as a potted plant and in water-conserving gardens in the dry tropics.

Agapanthus AMARYLLIDACEAE

Agapanthus is a genus of nine herbaceous perennial African species that are important as ornamentals. Hybrids are readily made, however, and some authors suggest the genus may comprise only one variable species.

Agapanthus praecox Willdenow

Synonym, *Agapanthus orientalis* F. M. Leighton and sometimes mis-identified as *A. africanus* (Linnaeus) Hoffmannsegg. DISTINGUISHABLE by the strap-shaped leaves in two rows and many-flowered umbels of white, purple, or blue flowers. The related but less commonly cultivated *A. africanus*, also called lily of the Nile and with many cultivars, has leaves only about half as big, 10–35 × 0.8–2 cm (4–14 × ¼–¾ in).

Agapanthus praecox, lily of the Nile, sometimes called African lily, is native to South Africa, not the area of the Nile in northern Africa as the name would imply, but is widely cultivated in temperate climates and the higher elevation tropics for its umbels of prominent lavender, blue, or white flowers. This slowly growing plant is often grown as a border plant or in tubs, planters, or beds, and the long-lasting blossoms are sometimes sold as cut flowers. There are several cultivars, some with variegated leaves. **HERB**, perennial, to 1 m high (3¼ ft), arising from a thick underground rhizome, sap sticky. **LEAVES** simple, almost basal, in two rows, blade strap-shaped, usually 30–70 × 1.5–5 cm

Agapanthus praecox

(12–28 × ⅝–2 in). **FLOWERS** anytime during the year in the tropics but most abundantly in spring and summer; flowers many, to more than 100, on stalks 3–10 cm long (1¼–4 in) in a large umbel atop a leafless stalk 60–80 cm high (24–32 in). Corolla with fused petals, tubular, 4–6 cm long (1⅝–2½ in), divided about two-thirds of its length into six oblanceolate segments, blue to pale purple or sometimes white. **FRUIT** an oblong, three-angled capsule. **PROPAGATE** by rhizome division, offsets, or seeds. Fertile, moist, but well-drained soils in sunny to partially shaded places are preferred.

Agave AGAVACEAE

Agave comprises 250 to 300 robust, subwoody herbs from dry places of the southern United States to tropical South America. Some are used for fiber (sisal), fermented for alcoholic beverages (pulque and tequila), and cultivated as dryland ornamentals. Two of the most commonly cultivated tropical ornamental species are included here.

Agave americana Linnaeus

DISTINGUISHABLE by the large basal erect leaves with black marginal prickles, a sharp black spine at the leaf tip, typically yellowish white leaf margins, and a large woody inflorescence that appears near the end of the plant's life. *Agave sisalana* Perrine, sisal, a related species widely cultivated, often naturalized, for its fibers and sometimes cultivated as an ornamental, differs in having blue-green leaves mostly lacking prickles on the margins. Another related species, *Furcraea foetida* (Linnaeus) Haworth, differs in having a green rather than a black spine at the leaf tip.

    Agave americana, century plant, is native to Mexico but is widely cultivated for its attractive foliage and as a novelty. In Mexico it is grown in plantations for its leaves, which are used for making a beer called pulque. It also has medicinal uses as a diuretic, laxative, and antiseptic. The most commonly planted cultivars are variegated, with leaves with yellowish white margins ('Marginata'), a yellowish white midrib ('Mediopicta'), or with yellow and green, twisted leaves ('Variegata'). The plant is monocarpic, that is, it dies after flowering, though basal offsets may be produced first. **SUCCULENT**, large, stemless, subwoody, to 2 m high (6½ ft) before flowering. **LEAVES** simple, spirally arranged in a basal rosette, blade lanceolate, 100–200 × 12–25 cm (40–80 × 5–10 in), margins with black prickles 7–10 mm long (¼–⅜ in) and a black terminal spine 3–5 cm long (1¼–2 in), surface waxy white, in cultivars often variegated with cream stripes. **FLOWERS** infrequently, after 15 to 30 years of growth, not a century as the name would imply; flowers many and fetid in a panicle to 10 m high (33 ft). Corolla with fused tepals, funnel-shaped, divided about halfway into six wrinkled, linear-lanceolate segments 2.5–3.5 cm long (1–1⅜ in), greenish yellow. **FRUIT** an oblong capsule 5–6 cm long (2–2½ in). **PROPAGATE** by division, basal offsets, or seeds. Very well drained soils in sunny places are preferred. It is

Agave americana 'Marginata' with leaves with yellowish white margins

typically grown in water-conserving gardens and is best kept away from foot traffic because of the spiny leaf margins. The sharp tip may be clipped to prevent injury.

Agave attenuata Salm-Dyck

DISTINGUISHABLE by the attractive rosettes of gray-green leaves, lack of a terminal spine, and the large, unusual, drooping inflorescence.

Agave attenuata, swan's-neck agave, is native to Mexico. Unlike most other members of the genus it does not die after flowering; it is perennial rather than monocarpic. HERB, large, perennial, succulent, subwoody. LEAVES simple, in a basal rosette, sessile, blade lanceolate, usually 40–70 × 6–15 cm (16–28 × 2½–6 in), surface gray-green, margins entire to finely serrate, tip without a dark, terminal spine. FLOWERS anytime during the year; flowers many in a narrow panicle to 3 m high (10 ft) and drooping at maturity. Corolla with fused tepals, funnel-shaped, divided about halfway into six ovate segments mostly 1.5–2 cm long (⅝–¾ in), greenish yellow. FRUIT a many-seeded, spindle-shaped capsule about 2 cm long (¾ in). PROPAGATE by offsets, seeds, or basal suckers. Well-drained soils in sunny places are preferred. The plant is drought and frost resistant and is often grown in pots or in water-conserving gardens. It makes an attractive low border plant even when not flowering.

Aglaonema ARACEAE

Aglaonema is a genus of about 21 herbaceous, rhizomatous species found on the islands and mainland of southeastern Asia, an area that used to be called Indo-Malaya. Many of the species are cultivated as ornamentals for their attractive and often colorful leaves.

Aglaonema commutatum Schott

DISTINGUISHABLE by the erect elliptic to lanceolate, often variegated leaves, the inflorescence a white spathe and spadix, and red to orange berries. *Aglaonema modestum* Schott, also commonly cultivated and called Chinese evergreen, has larger green leaves with a long acuminate tip.

Agave attenuata

Aglaonema commutatum, Chinese evergreen, is native to tropical Asia and the Philippines but is widely cultivated for its variable, colorful leaves. **HERB**, erect to decumbent, perennial, to 1.5 m high (5 ft). **LEAVES** simple, alternate, blade elliptic to lanceolate, usually 12–35 × 3–8 cm (5–14 × 1¼–3½ in) and spotted, striped, or blotched with light green. **FLOWERS** intermittently during the year; flowers many, tightly packed in one to six axillary spadices 2–6 cm long (¾–2½ in) with a pale green ovate spathe attached at the base, 3.5–6 cm long (1⅜–2½ in). **FRUIT** an orange to red obovoid berry. **PROPAGATE** by cuttings or division of basal shoots. It is a hardy plant in outdoor beds, borders, or when grown as a ground cover in shady places in the tropics, and is grown as a houseplant in pots in temperate climates. It needs periodic trimming or it will become scraggly. There are many cultivars that differ mostly in leaf color and patterning. Fertile, moist, but well-drained soils in partially shaded places are preferred.

Aglaonema commutatum, a white-leaved plant in flower

Aglaonema commutatum, a mostly green-leaved plant with red fruits

Albizia FABACEAE

Albizia is a genus of about 150 species found throughout the tropics and subtropics, many cultivated for timber or as ornamentals, especially as street and shade trees, because of their graceful, finely pinnate foliage and attractive flowers. Some authors include the genus *Samanea* in *Albizia*.

Albizia lebbeck (Linnaeus) Bentham

DISTINGUISHABLE by the bipinnately compound leaves, flowers with long, prominent white stamens, and tan, flattened, oblong pod. It is most easily confused with trees in the genera *Acacia* and *Paraserianthes,* also members of the legume family Fabaceae.

Albizia lebbeck, siris tree, is native to tropical Asia but is widely cultivated in the tropics as an ornamental or timber tree or both, often becoming naturalized. Another common name, woman's tongue, comes from the rattling sound of the seeds in the pods, fancifully likened to the clatter of women's tongues. TREE to 15 m high (50 ft) or more, often deciduous in winter and spring. LEAVES bipinnately compound, alternate, mostly with four or five pairs of pinnae, each pinna with 3 to 11 pairs of oblong leaflets 1.5–5.5 cm long (⅝–2¼ in). FLOWERS usually in the dry season in areas with such a climate; flowers many in subglobose axillary heads on peduncles 3–10 cm long (1¼–4 in). Corolla of five petals united at the base, funnel-shaped, 5–9 mm long (¼–⅜ in), greenish yellow, with numerous white to green stamens 2–4 cm long (¾–1⅝ in). FRUIT a flattened oblong pod 15–

Albizia lebbeck

33 cm long (6–13 in). **Propagate** by seeds. Well-drained soils in sunny places are preferred. It is most often planted as a shade or street tree but the conspicuous flowers are seasonal and absent most of the year.

Allamanda APOCYNACEAE

Allamanda comprises 12 tree, shrub, and vine-like shrub species, or as many as 25 according to some authors, found in warm temperate and tropical America. Several are cultivated for their large flowers, but most have somewhat poisonous sap as do many members of the dogbane family Apocynaceae. Three widespread ornamental species are included here.

Allamanda blanchetii A. L. P. P. de Candolle

Synonym, *Allamanda violacea* Gardner & Fielding, a name used by some authors. **Distinguishable** by the milky sap, whorled leaves, large

yellow, bell-shaped flowers, and burr-like fruit. It differs from the much more common *A. cathartica* by the duller, often pubescent leaves, generally smaller flowers, and the more frequent production of fruit.

Allamanda blanchetii, purple allamanda, is native to Brazil but is widely cultivated for its large purple to pink flowers. Like other allamandas it has a somewhat poisonous sap that can also be irritating to the skin. **Vine-like shrub** to 2 m high (6½ ft) or more, sap milky. **Leaves** simple, in whorls of three or four or sometimes opposite, blade oblanceolate to elliptic, usually 4–11 cm long (1⅝–4½ in), hispid on both surfaces. **Flowers** continuously

Allamanda blanchetii

through the year; flowers several in terminal clusters. Corolla of fused petals, bell-shaped from a narrow tube, 6–8 cm long (2½–3½ in), limb 5–6.5 cm in diameter (2–2⅝ in) with five rounded lobes, reddish purple to rose-pink. FRUIT a spiny, subglobose capsule, infrequently formed in cultivation. PROPAGATE by cuttings; sometimes grafted to the rootstock of *A. cathartica*. Fertile, moist, but well-drained soils in partially shaded places are preferred. It is often used as a hedge plant in the tropics and indoors in cooler climates. Without pruning it can become quite scraggly since it is halfway between a vine and a shrub.

Allamanda cathartica Linnaeus

Synonym, *Allamanda hendersonii* Bull ex Dombrain. DISTINGUISHABLE by the milky sap, leaves that are whorled, shiny green, and glabrous, and relatively large, bell-shaped flowers.

Allamanda cathartica, yellow allamanda, sometimes called common allamanda or golden trumpet, is native to South America but is widely cultivated for its large yellow flowers and is one of the most popular and attractive tropical ornamental shrubs. Though somewhat poisonous it has been used in small quantities as a purge, hence the name *cathartica*. VINE-LIKE SHRUB, climbing to 5 m high (16½ ft), sap milky. LEAVES simple, opposite or more commonly in whorls of three to five, blade elliptic to oblanceolate, 10–15 cm long (4–6 in), upper surface glossy green, tip attenuate. FLOWERS continuously through the year; flowers several in loose clusters at the tips of the stems. Corolla of fused petals, bell-shaped, 7–15 cm

Allamanda cathartica 'Hendersonii'

Allamanda cathartica 'Stansill's Double'

Allamanda schottii with hispid leaves and, un-like most other common allamandas, bearing fruit in cultivation

long (3–6 in) from a narrow tube with a limb of five spreading, rounded lobes, or double-flowered, 7–15 cm wide (3–6 in), bright yellow. **FRUIT** a subglobose capsule covered with soft spines but is infrequently formed in cultivation. **PROPAGATE** by cuttings. Fertile, moist, but well-drained soils in sunny places are preferred. Full sun is needed for optimal flowering. It can be grown by itself as a specimen plant but it also tolerates heavy pruning and is often grown in hedges or is trained as a vine on fences, arches, pergolas, or trellises. There are several cultivars, including the large-flowered 'Hendersonii' and the less common double-flowered 'Stansill's Double'.

Allamanda schottii Pohl

Synonyms, *Allamanda cathartica* var. *schottii* (Pohl) L. H. Bailey & Raffill, *A. neriifolia* W. J. Hooker, sometimes misidentified as *A. oenotherifolia* Pohl. **DISTINGUISHABLE** by the milky sap, flowers that are large, yellow, and bell-shaped, and burr-like fruit. The flowers are typically smaller than those of *A. cathartica* and the dull-surfaced leaves are hispid rather than glabrous.

Allamanda schottii, bush allamanda, is native to Brazil but is widely cultivated for its large yellow flowers, though not as commonly as *A. blanchetii* or *A. cathartica*. Like other allamandas, the sap is poisonous. VINE-LIKE SHRUB, spreading, to 3 m high (10 ft) or more, sap milky. LEAVES simple, mostly in whorls of three to five, blade elliptic to oblanceolate or obovate, usually 5–10 cm long (2–4 in), surface dull green, midvein of lower surface pubescent. FLOWERS continuously through the year; flowers several in short terminal clusters. Corolla of fused petals, bell-shaped, 5–7 cm long (2–3 in) with five rounded lobes, yellow with purple to brown striations inside. FRUIT a spiny, globose capsule to 7 cm in diameter (3 in). PROPAGATE by cuttings or seeds. Moist soils in sunny places are preferred. It is often grown in low hedges or in mass plantings for its yellow flowers.

Alocasia ARACEAE

Alocasia is a genus of 50 to 70 rhizome-bearing perennial herbs from the islands and mainland of southeastern Asia, an area that used to be called Indo-Malaya. Some are cultivated for their edible rhizomes, giant taro, *A. macrorrhiza* (Linnaeus) G. Don, for example, and some as ornamentals.

Alocasia cucullata
(Loureiro) G. Don

DISTINGUISHABLE by the erect, green, heart-shaped leaves in a dense cluster and the periodically forming spathe-and-spadix inflorescence characteristic of the aroid family Araceae.

Alocasia cucullata, Chinese taro, is probably native to China, where it has long been grown as an ornamental, and is no longer known to occur in its wild state. Most other aroids have col-

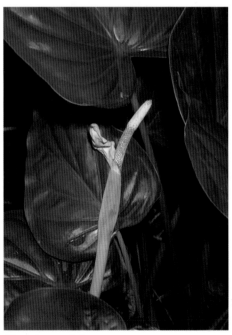

Alocasia cucullata

orful or dissected leaves (for example, *Caladium* and *Monstera*) or prominent spathes *(Anthurium)* but *Alocasia cucullata* is grown for its attractive dark green, heart-shaped leaves. HERB, perennial, erect, to 1.5 m high (5 ft), arising from a short thick stem. LEAVES simple, alternate, blade heart-shaped, usually 8–40 cm long (3½–16 in), leathery and smooth, slightly peltate on a petiole that is one to three times as long as the blade. FLOWERS intermittently during the year; flowers many, tightly packed in a cylindrical spadix usually 8–12 cm long (3½–5 in) with a greenish corrugated tip, surrounded by a lanceolate bluish green spathe 10–15 cm long (4–6 in). FRUIT a red subglobose berry, infrequently formed in cultivation. PROPAGATE by division. Highly organic, moist soils in shaded places are preferred. It is often used as a low border or ground cover plant and does well in tubs and planters.

Aloe AGAVACEAE

Aloe is a genus of about 200 succulent or tree-like species, or as many as 325 according to some authors, found throughout the tropics but concentrated in Africa, the Arabian Peninsula, and Madagascar. Some authors put the genus into a separate family, Aloeaceae, or include it in the lily family Liliaceae.

Aloe vera Linnaeus

Synonym, *Aloe barbadensis* Miller. DISTINGUISHABLE by the basal rosette of succulent, gray leaves, soft spines on the leaf margins, and erect racemes of drooping, red to orange flowers. A related, commonly cultivated species, *A. arborescens* Miller, candelabra plant, differs in having a distinct trunk and narrow, often curved or curled leaves.

Aloe vera, aloe vera or aloe, is native to North Africa but is widely cultivated in the tropics for its commercial use in shampoos and as an ornamental. Its use as a purge dates back to before the time of Alexander the Great, 356–323 B.C. In a well-known contemporary folk remedy, the sap is applied to burns. HERB, perennial, succulent, to 1 m high (3¼ ft) with a short thick stem. LEAVES simple, arranged in a basal rosette,

Aloe vera

Aloe arborescens

succulent, sessile, blade lanceolate, 20–60 cm long (8–24 in), gray to purplish green or mottled white and green, margins spiny. **Flowers** anytime during the year; flowers many in an erect basal raceme to 1 m high (3¼ ft). Corolla with fused tepals, tubular, 2–3.3 cm long (¾–1¼ in), divided about halfway into six segments, the outer three red to orange, the inner three commonly yellow. **Fruit** an ovoid, many-seeded capsule 1.5–2.5 cm long (⅝–1 in). **Propagate** by seeds, stem cuttings, or offsets. Fertile, well-drained soils in sunny or partially shaded places are preferred. It is commonly cultivated around houses, in water-conserving gardens, or especially in temperate climates, indoors in pots.

Alpinia ZINGIBERACEAE

Alpinia comprises about 200 to 300 rhizomatous herbaceous species native from tropical Asia to Japan and eastward to Polynesia. Many are cultivated for their attractive inflorescences or leaves or both and, less commonly, for essential oils and for rhizomes used as a condiment. Three of the most common ornamental species are included here.

Alpinia purpurata (Vieillard) K. Schumann

DISTINGUISHABLE by the large inflorescence of inconspicuous white flowers among spreading red, purple, pink, or white bracts.

Alpinia purpurata, red ginger, is native to Melanesia from New Caledonia to Vanuatu but is widely cultivated for its red-purple or pink, rarely white (as in 'Jungle Queen') inflorescence. It is one of the most common ornamental plants in the tropics and sometimes becomes naturalized in shady places. **HERB**, perennial, coarse, unbranched, erect, to 4 m high (13 ft), arising from an underground rhizome. **LEAVES** simple, alternate, two-ranked, subsessile atop a sheath, blade oblong, usually 15–70 × 5–20 cm (6–28 × 2–8 in). **FLOWERS** continuously through the year; flowers many, enclosed in groups of one to five between red-purple or pink, rarely white, obovate to narrowly oblong bracts 2.5–6 cm long (1–2½ in) in a narrow, dense, terminal, raceme-like panicle 15–30 cm long (6–12 in) or more. Corolla with fused petals, tubular, 2.5–3.5 cm long (1–1⅜ in), divided about halfway into three subequal lobes, white, labellum about as long as corolla. **FRUIT** a globose many-seeded capsule 2–3 cm in diameter (¾–1¼ in), infrequently formed in cultivation. **PROPAGATE** by rhizome division and by the bulbils that are produced in the axils of the lowest inflorescence bracts. Fertile,

Alpinia purpurata, the lower one with pink bracts, less commonly grown than plants with red bracts

moist, but well-drained soils in sunny or partially shaded places are preferred. Often grown as a border plant in the tropics and in the greenhouse in temperate climates and it is advisable to cut back the stalks that have finished flowering. Its long-lasting colorful bracts makes this ginger a favorite in cut flower arrangements.

Alpinia vittata Bull

Synonym, *Alpinia sanderae* of gardens. DISTINGUISHABLE by the variegated leaves and small raceme-like panicles of unspectacular white flowers.

Alpinia vittata, variegated ginger, is native to Melanesia and perhaps is only a cultivar of a green-leaved species of the Solomon Islands, *A. oceanica* of gardens. Its flowers and bracts are not particularly attractive, especially among the alpinias, but the plant is widely cultivated for its handsome variegated foliage. HERB, perennial, coarse, unbranched, erect, to 2.5 m high (8¼ ft) or more, arising from a rhizome. LEAVES simple, alternate, two-ranked, attached atop a sheath, blade narrowly elliptic, usually 20–50 × 4–10 cm (8–20 × 1⅝–4 in), variegated green and white. FLOWERS anytime during the year; flowers many, enclosed in groups of one to five in pink elliptic bracts in a loose, narrow, terminal, hanging, raceme-like panicle 3–20 cm long (1¼–8 in). Corolla with fused petals, tubular, 3–4 cm long (1¼–1⅝ in), divided about halfway into three lobes, white. FRUIT a many-seeded capsule. PROPAGATE by rhizome cuttings. Fertile, moist, but well-drained soils in sunny or partially shaded places are preferred. It is

Alpinia vittata

often grown as a border plant in the tropics and as a potted plant in the greenhouse in temperate climates.

Alpinia zerumbet (Persoon) Burtt & R. M. Smith

Synonym, *Alpinia speciosa* (J. C. Wendland) K. Schumann and sometimes misidentified as *A. nutans* Roscoe, a synonym for torch ginger, *Etlingera elatior*. DISTINGUISHABLE by the ginger-like leaves and pink bracts surrounding the red and yellow flowers. Two similar species, *A. calcarata* Roscoe and *A. mutica* Roxburgh, differ in having smaller leaves, bracts, and flowers, and more or less erect rather than drooping panicles.

   Alpinia zerumbet, shell ginger, also called shell flower or pink porcelain lily, is native to New Guinea or nearby Malaysia but is widely cultivated for its yellow flowers delicately marked with red lines. HERB, perennial, coarse, unbranched, erect, to 3 m high (10 ft), arising from a rhizome. LEAVES simple, alternate, two-ranked, subsessile atop a sheath, blade narrowly lanceolate, usually 25–70 × 5–13 cm (10–28 × 2–5 in) with hairy margins. FLOWERS anytime during the year; flowers many, enclosed in groups of one or more in pink to white bracts 2–2.5 cm long (¾–1 in) in a terminal, fuzzy, drooping, raceme-like panicle 25–40 cm long (10–16 in). Corolla with fused petals, 3–5 cm long (1¼–2 in), divided about halfway into three lobes, labellum cup-shaped, yellow with red in the center. FRUIT a red, globose, many-seeded capsule 1.5–2 cm in diameter (⅝–¾ in). PROPAGATE by rhizome division or seeds. Fertile, moist, but well-drained soils in sunny or partially shaded places are pre-

Alpinia zerumbet

ferred. It is one of the most beautiful and popular of the gingers and is grown outdoors by itself or as a border plant in the tropics and in the greenhouse in temperate climates. It grows best in protected places since excessive wind tends to shred the leaves.

Alternanthera AMARANTHACEAE

Alternanthera comprises 80 to 200 herbaceous species found throughout the tropics and subtropics, especially in the Americas. Some are cultivated as ornamentals for their colorful leaves and many others are naturalized as weeds of disturbed places. Two ornamental species are included here.

Alternanthera brasiliana (Linnaeus) Kuntze

DISTINGUISHABLE by the opposite purple leaves and long-stalked, subglobose heads of white bracts.

Alternanthera brasiliana, without a well-known common name but sometimes called purple alternanthera, is native to Brazil but is cultivated for its dark purple foliage and white heads. It is much larger and darker than other ornamental alternantheras but is also much less commonly grown. HERB, perennial, to 1.5 m high (5 ft). LEAVES simple, opposite, blade elliptic to ovate, 3–12 cm long (1¼–5 in), purple to dark red. FLOWERS anytime during the year; flowers many in white, long-stalked, terminal and upper axillary subglobose heads 7–15 cm in diameter (3–6 in). Corolla of five tiny, free tepals borne among white chaffy bracts. FRUIT a tiny, one-seeded utricle. PROPAGATE by

Alternanthera brasiliana

seeds. Moist but well-drained soils in partially shaded places are preferred. It is often planted in borders and sometimes escapes from cultivation to become somewhat weedy.

Alternanthera tenella Colla

Synonyms, *Alternanthera amoena* (Lemaire) Regel, *A. bettzickiana* (Regel) Voss, a name used by many authors, *A. ficoidea* var. *bettzickiana* (Regel) Backer, and *A. versicolor* (Lemaire) Seubert. DISTINGUISHABLE by the low habit, leaves that are small, opposite, colorful, and variegated, and tiny flowers borne among chaffy bracts in inconspicuous sessile heads. Some authors consider *A. tenella* to differ from *A. bettzickiana* in having narrow green leaves rather than wider, often red or yellow ones, and entire rather than notched flower bracts.

Alternanthera tenella, calico plant, is native to Brazil but is widely cultivated for its colorfully variegated foliage. Other names include joy-

Alternanthera tenella 'Bettzickiana'

Alternanthera tenella, a less commonly grown plant, white variegated weed, Jacob's coat, and parrot leaf. **HERB**, perennial, to 50 cm high (20 in). **LEAVES** simple, opposite, blade variable in shape but usually ovate, obovate, or round, usually 1–6 cm long (⅜–2½ in), usually with a distinct petiole, usually variegated with white, yellow, or red. **FLOWERS** anytime during the year; flowers many, in white, sessile, axillary, subglobose to ovoid heads 4–8 mm in diameter (about ¼ in). **FRUIT** a tiny, one-seeded utricle. **PROPAGATE** by cuttings. Fertile, moist, but well-drained soils in sunny places are preferred. It is often grown as a garden border or low hedge, and sometimes a red variety and a green variety are planted together in a pattern to produce a word (for example, the name of a college or high school), emblem, or even a clock. Regular trimming is needed to maintain the height. Full sun is required for the best color; the plant may remain green if grown in the shade. There is much confusion on how the various cultivars should be named. One of the most common is 'Bettzickiana'.

Amaranthus AMARANTHACEAE

Amaranthus is a genus of about 60 species of annual or short-lived perennial plants found throughout the tropics and temperate regions. Some are or have been cultivated as a food crop for their leaves or seeds, and some are cultivated as ornamentals for their leaves or inflorescences or both.

Amaranthus tricolor Linnaeus

Synonym, *Amaranthus melancholicus* Linnaeus. **DISTINGUISHABLE** by the red upper leaves and small green fruit that contains a single shiny black seed.

Amaranthus tricolor, Joseph's coat, is native to tropical Asia and was originally named from India but is widely cultivated as a potherb (the drab type, known as Chinese spinach) or as an ornamental (the colorful cultivars) throughout the year in the tropics and in the warm season in temperate regions. There has been much taxonomic confusion in the literature, with some authors recognizing the two extremes as separate

Amaranthus tricolor

species. There is also some confusion concerning common names, with some authors referring to *A. tricolor* as Jacob's coat. Another name that has been used is tampala. **HERB**, annual, to 1.5 m high (5 ft). **FLOWERS** anytime during the year after maturity; flowers many in terminal and axillary clusters or spikes or both. **LEAVES** simple, alternate, blade ovate to lanceolate or elliptic, 6–25 cm long (2½–10 in), green in forms that are not ornamental, typically red or variegated with red, green, and yellow in ornamental cultivars. Corolla absent, the three green sepals long-acuminate, 2–6 mm long (about ¹⁄₁₆–¼ in) with a green or purple medial band. **FRUIT** a utricle about 2 mm long (about ¹⁄₁₆ in), the cap splitting off to release the single shiny black seed. **PROPAGATE** by seeds. Fertile, moist soils in sunny places are preferred.

Amherstia FABACEAE

Amherstia is a genus with a single species from Myanmar (Burma), found only twice in the wild and named in honor of William Pitt Amherst, British governor general of India who waged an unsuccessful war on the king of Burma, 1824–1826.

Amherstia nobilis Wallich

DISTINGUISHABLE by the pinnately compound leaves and hanging racemes bearing paired pink bracts, and pink flowers with two twisted petals and one larger flat petal, each with a yellow blotch.

Amherstia nobilis, pride of Burma, with its pink and yellow flowers, is considered one of the most beautiful trees in the world but has flowers only a few months a year, most spectacularly in areas with a pronounced dry season. Because it is delicate and difficult to grow and rarely sets seeds, it is typically found only in tropical botanical gardens where it is grown as a specimen plant. TREE to 18 m high (59 ft). LEAVES pinnately compound, alternate, leaflets in five to eight pairs, blades oblong to lanceolate, 12–34 cm long (5–13 in), long-acuminate, lower surface somewhat gray-green. FLOWERS once a year, usually in the dry season if there is one; flowers many, borne loosely in terminal, hanging racemes to 80 cm long (32 in) with two

Amherstia nobilis

pink to red lanceolate bracteoles below each flower. Corolla of three free, unequal, pink to red petals (plus two rudimentary ones) 6–10 cm long (2½–4 in), the lateral two narrow and twisted, the center one spoon-shaped with a yellow blotch at the tip, surrounding the five long and four short up-curving stamens. FRUIT a pod 13–20 cm long (5–8 in). PROPAGATE by cuttings. Moist, fertile soils in humid, sunny to partially shaded places are preferred. The young leaves and flowers are edible.

Angelonia SCROPHULARIACEAE

Angelonia comprises 25 to 30 tropical American subshrub species, many cultivated as garden ornamentals or potted plants. The taxonomy of the genus is confusing, however, making identification of species difficult. Two of the most common ornamental species are included here.

Angelonia biflora with pink flowers

Angelonia biflora Bentham

May be the same plant that some call *Angelonia gardneri* W. J. Hooker. DISTINGUISHABLE by the opposite, narrow, sticky-pubescent leaves and typically paired, pink or purple flowers with the lateral corolla lobes folded back.

Angelonia biflora, which lacks a distinctive common name, is native to South America and was first collected in Brazil but is widely cultivated in gardens and containers for its long inflorescences of colorful flowers. Several color forms exist and the plant is often grown with *A. salicariifolia,* leading to confusion in the identification of species. HERB, perennial, erect, to 1 m high (3¼ ft), covered with sticky hairs. LEAVES simple, opposite, blade narrowly oblong to lanceolate, subsessile, to 10 cm long (4 in) with toothed margins. FLOWERS continuously through the year; flowers paired or solitary in the leaf axils on pedicels with sticky hairs, the top of the plant appearing like a leafy raceme. Corolla with fused petals, cup-shaped, two-lipped, with a somewhat reflexed, spreading, five-lobed limb 2–2.8 cm across (¾–1⅛ in) top to bottom, pink, sometimes dark purple, with dark red spots within. FRUIT a subglobose capsule. PROPAGATE by cuttings or seeds. Fertile, moist, but well-drained soils in sunny places are preferred.

Angelonia salicariifolia Humboldt & Bonpland

May be the same plant some authors call *Angelonia angustifolia* Bentham. DISTINGUISHABLE by the narrow, opposite, sticky-haired leaves, toothed leaf margins, and most obviously from *A. biflora* in flower color—blue to purplish, or white, sometimes both—the flowers typically solitary, the corolla two-lipped with the lateral lobes not folded back.

Angelonia salicariifolia, which lacks a distinctive common name, is native to tropical America but is widely cultivated in gardens and containers in tropical to temperate regions for its flowers. **HERB**, perennial, erect, to 60 cm high (24 in), covered with sticky hairs. **LEAVES** simple, opposite, blade narrowly oblong to lanceolate, subsessile, 2–10 cm long (¾–4 in) with toothed margins. **FLOWERS** continuously through the year after maturity; flowers solitary or sometimes paired in the leaf axils, the top of the plant appearing like a leafy raceme. Corolla

Angelonia salicariifolia

with fused petals, cup-shaped, two-lipped, with a spreading limb 1.5–2.7 cm across (⅝–1⅛ in) top to bottom, blue or purple with white margins or all white. **FRUIT** a subglobose capsule. **PROPAGATE** by cuttings or seeds, the latter especially in temperate areas. Fertile, moist, but well-drained soils in sunny places are preferred.

Anthurium ARACEAE

Anthurium is a tropical American genus of 700 to 750 or more terrestrial and climbing herbaceous species, many cultivated for their distinctive inflorescences or leaves or both. Many of the cultivated plants are hybrids, sometimes involving more than two parental species. They are favorites in greenhouses because of their colorful, long-lasting spathes.

Anthurium andraeanum Linden ex André

DISTINGUISHABLE by the heart-shaped green leaves and prominent shield-like spathe at the base of the drooping yellow spadix.

Anthurium andraeanum, sometimes called flamingo flower or lily, is native to Colombia, where it was discovered in the 1870s and soon thereafter became popular in cultivation. It is now widely grown throughout the tropics and cooler regions for it prominent inflorescence. The flowers constitute the yellow spadix and the spathe is the waxy, red, leaf-like structure at its base. **HERB**, perennial, nearly stemless, to 60 cm high (24 in) from a short erect stem. **LEAVES** simple, alternate, blade heart-shaped, usually 12–30 cm long (5–12 in) on a petiole one to two times as long. **FLOWERS** continuously through the year; flowers many, tightly packed in a curved, typically yellow spadix 7–11 cm long (3–4½ in) with a white ring in the zone with fertile stigmas, sub-

Anthurium andraeanum

tended by a leathery, persistent, waxy, red or occasionally white or yellow, heart-shaped spathe 6–15 cm long (2½–6 in). **FRUIT** a fleshy ovoid berry, infrequently formed in cultivation. **PROPAGATE** by division. Fertile, moist, but well-drained soils in partially shaded places are preferred. Anthuriums are an important commercial crop for their cut flowers and are often grown in greenhouses, especially in temperate climates. The plant has been used extensively in hybridization, resulting in plants with spathes of varying colors. It is grown outdoors in the tropics as a border plant or epiphyte. All parts of the plant may cause stomach problems, and contact with the sap may irritate the skin.

Antigonon POLYGONACEAE

Antigonon is a genus of two to eight tendril-bearing vine species of tropical America, at least two of which are cultivated as ornamentals because of their colorful sepals.

Antigonon leptopus Hooker & Arnott

DISTINGUISHABLE by the viny habit, tendrils, coarse, alternate, arrowhead-shaped leaves, and pink flowers.

Antigonon leptopus, coral vine, was originally named from Mexico but is widely cultivated in the tropics and subtropics for its large clusters of pink flowers. Among its many other common names are chain of love, Mexican creeper, and corallita. VINE, herbaceous, climbing, growing from a tuberous root, with tendrils at the end of the inflorescences. LEAVES simple, alternate, blade broadly ovate to heart-shaped, 3–10 cm long (1¼–4 in) with a heart-shaped base and shallowly, irregularly lobed margins. FLOWERS con-

tinuously through the year; flowers many in axillary and terminal racemes and panicles. Corolla absent but with five free elliptic to obovate, pink or sometimes white petal-like sepals 8–16 mm long (¼–⅝ in). FRUIT a short conical nut surrounded by the persistent, enlarged, heart-shaped sepals. PROPAGATE by seeds or cuttings. Fertile, well-drained soils in sunny places are preferred. Often pruned and grown on fences, walls, arches, and trellises, it can even be used as a ground cover. It sometimes becomes naturalized and weedy. The roots are eaten in Mexico. There is also a cultivar with white bracts, 'Album'.

Antigonon leptopus

Aphelandra ACANTHACEAE

Aphelandra comprises about 170 tropical American herb and shrub species. Many are cultivated, especially as houseplants, for their brilliantly colored inflorescences or attractive, often variegated leaves. Two of the most common and attractive ornamental species are included here.

Aphelandra aurantiaca (Scheidweiler) Lindley

Synonym, *Aphelandra facinator* Lindley & André. DISTINGUISHABLE by the opposite leaves, silvery veins, terminal spikes with the flowers borne among overlapping, greenish, toothed-margin bracts, and orange to red two-lipped corolla.

Aphelandra aurantiaca, fiery spike, is native from Mexico to Bolivia but is widely if not commonly cultivated for its dense racemes of spectacular red to orange flowers as well as for its attractive leaves whose secondary veins are highlighted by gray or silver margins. SUBSHRUB, glabrous, to 75 cm high (30 in) or more. LEAVES opposite, simple, blade ovate to elliptic, 5–18 cm long (2–7 in), the main veins bordered by a silver or gray margin. FLOWERS anytime during the year; flowers many in terminal four-sided spikes to 18 cm long (7 in), each flower borne above an overlapping, ovate, acuminate, greenish bract with toothed margins. Corolla of fused petals, two-lipped, orange, vermilion, or scarlet, the tube 3.5–5 cm long (1⅜–2 in), the lower lip with three unequal ovate to elliptic lobes 1.2–2 cm long (½–¾ in), the upper enclosing the stamens. FRUIT a four-seeded capsule. PROPAGATE by seeds or cuttings. Moist, well-drained soils in partially shaded places are pre-

Aphelandra aurantiaca var. *aurantiaca*

ferred. The beauty of this plant makes

it a favorite for growing in gardens as a border plant in the tropics, and as a houseplant or greenhouse plant in temperate areas.

Aphelandra sinclairiana Nees

DISTINGUISHABLE by the opposite leaves, long dense spikes covered with overlapping orange bracts, and two-lipped pink to rose-colored corollas.

Aphelandra sinclairiana, coral aphelandra, is native to Panama but is widely if not commonly cultivated for its inflorescence, which unlike that of *A. aurantiaca* has orange bracts and pink to rose-colored flowers.

Aphelandra sinclairiana

SHRUB to 4 m high (13 ft) with downy young stems. **LEAVES** simple, opposite, blade elliptic, 8–35 cm long (3½–14 in), base attenuate, surfaces pubescent. **FLOWERS** continuously through the year; flowers in several dense spikes clustered at the top of the plant and borne between prominent, overlapping, orange, obovate bracts. Corolla of fused petals, tubular, two-lipped, 5–6 cm long (2–2½ in), pink to rose-colored. **FRUIT** an ovoid four-seeded capsule. **PROPAGATE** by cuttings. Moist soils in partially shaded places are preferred. It is usually planted by itself or sometimes as a border plant but it does not make a good hedge plant.

Arachnis ORCHIDACEAE

Arachnis is a genus of seven terrestrial or epiphytic orchid species found from Southeast Asia to Malaysia, some cultivated for their flowers. The name *Arachnis* is from the Greek word for spider, referring to the appearance of the flowers.

Arachnis ×maingayi (J. D. Hooker) Schlechter

DISTINGUISHABLE by the vine-like habit and pale yellow, spider-like flowers mottled with interrupted bands of reddish brown.

Arachnis ×maingayi, spider orchid, sometimes called scorpion orchid, is a hybrid that is found in nature but that also has been reproduced artificially. It is the result of a cross between two similar species, *A. flos-aeris* (Linnaeus) Reichenbach fil. and *A. hookeriana* (Reichenbach fil.) Reichenbach fil., and is widely cultivated and sold commercially as cut flowers and potted plants. HERB, terrestrial, vine-like, with stems to 2 m long (6½ ft) or more. LEAVES simple, alternate, sessile, narrowly oblong, 7–14 × 1.5–3 cm (3–6 × ⅝–1¼ in), two-lobed at the tip. FLOWERS continuously through the year; flowers several in erect racemes mostly 30–60 cm long (12–24 in), arising from the node and piercing the leaf sheath. Corolla of five free, curved, narrowly spoon-shaped to oblanceolate tepals 3–6 cm long (1¼–2½ in), pale yellow mottled with reddish brown spots, with a shorter labellum. FRUIT a capsule, infrequently formed in cultivation. PROPAGATE by division. Fertile, moist, but well-drained soils or compost in partially shaded or sunny places are preferred, but full sunlight is required for maximum flowering. The plants are popular for growing on tree-fern posts in the tropics, and in warm greenhouses in temperate climates.

Arachnis ×maingayi

Araucaria ARAUCARIACEAE

Araucaria is a genus of 18 or 19 tree species found from New Guinea to New Zealand and in Brazil and Chile, an interesting southern hemisphere, Old and New World distribution. Many are valuable as timber and also as ornamentals, and some have edible seeds.

Araucaria heterophylla (Salisbury) Franco

Synonym, *Araucaria excelsa* (Lamarck) R. Brown. DISTINGUISHABLE by the tall pine-like habit, conical form, awl-shaped juvenile leaves, and large cones. A similar species native to New Caledonia, *A. columnaris* (J. G. A. Forster) W. J. Hooker, Cook pine, differs in having a columnar shape and narrower, triangular to lanceolate juvenile leaves.

Araucaria heterophylla, Norfolk Island pine, a misnomer since it is not a pine, is native to Norfolk Island east of Australia but is widely cultivated as an ornamental and timber tree. TREE, dioecious, to 25 m high (82 ft), conical, symmetrical with spirally arranged, horizontal or drooping branches, with a trunk to 1 m in diameter (3¼ ft). LEAVES whorled, crowded and covering the stem, evergreen, dimorphic, juvenile leaves awl-shaped, 5–12 × 2–3 mm (¼–½ × about ¹⁄₁₆–⅛ in), adult leaves ovate, concave, waxy white on the upper, inner surface, 6–9 × 4–8 mm (¼–⅜ × about ¼ in), in several spiral rows on branchlets that are drooping to ascending from the stem. CONES produced intermittently during the year. Male cone oblong, 3.5–7 cm long (1⅜–3 in). Female cone ovoid, 10–13 cm long (4–5 in), composed of tightly overlapping scales with a recurved acuminate tip. SEEDS borne beneath and attached to the cone scales, to 3 cm long (1¼ in). PROPAGATE by seeds; sometimes can be propagated by cuttings. Fertile, moist, but well-drained soils in sunny but

Araucaria heterophylla

Araucaria heterophylla

protected places are preferred, but it does best when grown in the shade when young. It makes a nice tub plant when young, and in the tropics it is often used as a Christmas tree in place of the expensive, cut, imported conifers. Trees may be grown by themselves as specimens, or in rows along roadsides or borders. In temperate areas they are often grown in tubs in greenhouses because of their attractive fern-like needles.

Argyreia CONVOLVULACEAE

Argyreia is a genus of 90 liana species, ranging from India to Australia. Some are used medicinally, and a few are cultivated as ornamentals because of their attractive flowers and viny habit.

Argyreia nervosa (N. L. Burman) Bojer

DISTINGUISHABLE by the viny habit, heart-shaped leaves covered with downy white pubescence, and funnel-shaped, lavender corolla with a darker center.

Argyreia nervosa, woolly morning-glory, sometimes called silver morning glory or elephant climber, is native to India but is widely cultivated for its attractive foliage and funnel-shaped lavender flowers, which, however, are less visible surrounded by the silvery leaves. **VINE**, twining, with downy white stems to 10 m long (33 ft). **LEAVES** simple, alternate, blade heart-shaped, usually 10–25 cm long (4–10 in), densely downy white on the lower surface. **FLOWERS** anytime during the year; flowers several, mostly three to six in axillary cymes on a

Argyreia nervosa

peduncle 5–15 cm long (2–6 in). Corolla of fused petals, funnel-shaped, 6–9 cm long (2½–3½ in), limb shallowly five-lobed, 7–8 cm across (3–3½ in), lavender with a darker throat. FRUIT a subglobose four-seeded capsule 1–1.8 cm in diameter (⅜–¾ in). PROPAGATE by seeds or cuttings. The vine is often grown on trellises or fences, with a vigorous growth that can entirely cover them. Moist, well-drained soils in sunny places are preferred.

Aristolochia ARISTOLOCHIACEAE

Aristolochia is a genus of about 300 species found throughout the tropics and warm temperate regions. Many are grown as ornamental vines because of their unusual, attractive flowers, often foul smelling to attract insects needed for pollination. Many species are somewhat poisonous but have medicinal uses.

Aristolochia littoralis Parodi

Synonym, *Aristolochia elegans* Masters. DISTINGUISHABLE by the viny habit, heart- or kidney-shaped leaves, and mottled purple and yellow, pipe-like flowers. A related species common in cultivation, *A. grandiflora* Swartz, pelican flower, differs most obviously in having a petal-like calyx with a long-attenuate tip.

Aristolochia littoralis, calico flower, sometimes called Dutchman's pipe, is probably native to Brazil and Argentina but is widely cultivated as a novelty for its unusual, attractive flowers. Unlike the flowers of most members of the genus, those of *A. littoralis* are not particularly foul smelling but their carrion color attracts flies needed for pollination. The flies are temporarily trapped inside the oddly shaped flowers by downward-pointing hairs. These hairs soon wither, however, and the flies, dusted with the pollen needed to pollinate the next flower they visit, escape. VINE, perennial, slender. LEAVES alternate, simple, blade heart- or kidney-shaped, wider than long, 4–10 cm across (1⅝–4 in), palmately veined from the base. FLOWERS anytime during the year; flowers solitary, axillary on a long stalk. Corolla absent but the petal-

Aristolochia littoralis

Aristolochia grandiflora with distinctive long-attenuate calyx tip

like calyx modified into a long, curved, pipe-shaped tube with an expanded oval, concave limb 5–9 cm in diameter (2–3½ in), mottled white or yellow and dark purple with a white throat. FRUIT a black, ribbed capsule 3–5 cm long (1¼–2 in), oblong in outline. PROPAGATE by seeds. Fertile, moist soils in partially shaded places are preferred.

Artabotrys ANNONACEAE

Artabotrys is a genus of about 100 species widespread in the Old World tropics.

Artabotrys hexapetalus (Linnaeus fil.) Bhandari

Synonym, *Artabotrys uncinatus* (Lamarck) Merrill. DISTINGUISHABLE by the vine-like habit, hook-like structure on the flower stalk, and the fragrant yellow flowers with many stamens and ovaries.

Artabotrys hexapetalus

Artabotrys hexapetalus, climbing ylang-ylang, is native to India but is cultivated as a novelty because of its unusual hooked flower stalks, glossy, dark green foliage, and fragrant flowers. LIANA or vine-like shrub, climbing by means of a woody hook-like structure formed in the middle of the flower stalk. LEAVES simple, alternate, blade elliptic to oblanceolate, 7–22 cm long (3–9 in), glossy green. FLOWERS intermittently during the year; flowers one to four, borne on the hook-like branch. Corolla of six free, ovate, yellow to yellow-green petals 2–3.5 cm long (¾–1⅜ in), folded over the disk that contains the ovaries and numerous stamens. FRUIT a cluster of several yellow globose berries 2.5–3.5 cm long (1–1⅜ in) formed from the same flower. PROPAGATE by seeds. Moist soils in partially shaded places are preferred. It is often grown on trellises or fences but is sometimes left freestanding as a shrub. The flowers are not nearly as numerous or as attractive as the true ylang-ylang, *Cananga odorata,* which is a tree instead of a vine or shrub.

Arundina ORCHIDACEAE

Arundina is a genus of five terrestrial orchid species found in Asia, at least two of which are cultivated for their large, attractive flowers. The name *Arundina* is derived from the Latin word *arundo,* meaning reed, referring to the tall, narrow habit of the plants.

Arundina graminifolia (D. Don) Hochreutiner

Synonym, *Arundina bambusifolia* (Roxburgh) Roxburgh ex Lindley.

DISTINGUISHABLE by the erect habit, linear-lanceolate leaves, and the pink to rose-colored labellum and pink tepals below it. It can be confused with the similarly colored vanda orchids, *Papilionanthe* 'Agnes Joaquim', for example, which has cylindrical leaves and broader tepals.

Arundina graminifolia

Arundina graminifolia, bamboo orchid, is native from India to Malaysia but is widely cultivated in the tropics for its attractive flowers. It is frequently grown in planters or in gardens, often mixed with other flowers. Most natural orchids, that is, ones that are not artificial hybrids, are pollinated by a specific insect and when they are introduced into a new area they do not usually spread because the specific pollinator does not arrive with them. However, bamboo orchid is not so picky and is fertile over most of its range. It sometimes becomes naturalized, as in Hawaii, but has not been reported as a problem weed. **HERB**, terrestrial, tufted, to 2.5 m high (8¼ ft) or more, arising from a horizontal rhizome. **LEAVES** simple, alternate and distichous, blade sessile, linear-lanceolate, stiff, 8–30 cm long (3½–12 in). **FLOWERS** continuously through the year; flowers several in terminal racemes 10–70 cm long (4–28 in), fragrant, short-lived, two or three open at a time. Corolla of five pink unequal tepals 2.5–4.5 cm long (1–1¾ in) with a slightly longer labellum that is pale pink to rose-colored with yellow in the center. **FRUIT** a cylindrical capsule 3.5–5.5 cm long (1⅜–2¼ in). **PROPAGATE** by division or seeds. Fertile, moist, but well-drained soils in shaded places are preferred.

Arundo POACEAE

Arundo is a genus of three rhizomatous perennial grasses ranging from the Mediterranean region to Asia, at least two of which are cultivated as ornamentals. The name *Arundo* aptly means reed in Latin.

Arundo donax Linnaeus

DISTINGUISHABLE by it large habit, often variegated green and white leaves, and a large panicles of silky spikelets.

Arundo donax, Spanish reed, sometimes called giant reed, is native to the western Mediterranean region but is widely cultivated and naturalized in areas with warm climates. It is the cane mentioned in the Bible, and its stems are used for musical instruments, fishing poles, walking sticks, fiber, and even in light construction. **GRASS**, clump forming, to 6 m high (20 ft) or more, arising from a thick, scaly rhizome. **LEAVES** simple, linear, blade 45–70 × 3–6 cm (18–28 × 1¼–2½ in), green or striped

Arundo donax var. *versicolor*

with white. **FLOWERS** seasonally, late summer to early winter; flowers many in spikelets borne in an ovoid panicle 40–90 cm long (16–36 in). Spikelets lanceolate, 1.3–1.7 cm long (½–¾ in), three- to five-flowered, surrounded by many silky bristles. **PROPAGATE** by seeds or cuttings. Moist but well-drained soils in sunny places are preferred. It is often grown by itself in large clumps or as a border plant in the tropics, and in greenhouses or conservatories in temperate climates. *Arundo donax* var. *versicolor* (Miller) Stokes, variegated with white lines and margins, is commonly cultivated for its attractive foliage.

Asclepias ASCLEPIADACEAE

Asclepias is a genus of about 120 tropical and subtropical American species, some weedy and harmful to livestock because they are poisonous, and some cultivated as ornamentals because of their attractive flowers. The name *Asclepias* is derived from that for the Greek god of medicine, Asklepios, referring to the medicinal properties of the plants.

Asclepias curassavica Linnaeus

DISTINGUISHABLE by the milky sap, opposite leaves, umbels of orange and red flowers, and pods filled with silky seeds.

Asclepias curassavica, blood flower, is native to tropical America and was originally named from Curaçao in the Caribbean. It is widely cultivated for its colorful red and orange flowers, often as an annual in cooler climates. Often grown in borders or around houses, it is more commonly found as a weed in disturbed habitats in the tropics and can become noxious in pastures because it is poisonous to livestock and may irritate the skin of humans. It can rapidly spread by means of silky-tufted seeds that float on the wind. **SUBSHRUB**, perennial, or annual in temperate areas, to 1.5 m high (5 ft), sap milky. **LEAVES** simple, opposite, blade oblong to lanceolate, 5–18 cm long (2–7 in). **FLOWERS** continuously through the year; flowers four to ten in long-stalked axillary umbels. Corolla of fused petals, deeply divided into five reflexed lobes 7–9 mm long (¼–⅜ in), red, with the stamens united into an orange corona of five hood-like structures. **FRUIT** a spindle-shaped follicle 5–7.5 cm long

Asclepias curassavica

(2–3 in), splitting along one side to release the silky-tufted seeds. **PROP-AGATE** by seeds. Light, fertile soils in sunny places are preferred.

Asparagus LILIACEAE

Asparagus comprises about 300 subshrub and climber species and is sometimes separated from the lily family Liliaceae into the family Asparagaceae. The genus includes the edible asparagus, *A. officinalis.* Many species are cultivated as ornamentals for their fern-like foliage, and two of the most common asparagus ferns, of course not ferns at all, are included here.

Asparagus densiflorus (Kunth) Jessop

Synonym, *Asparagus sprengeri* Regel. **DISTINGUISHABLE** by the drooping stems, linear, leaf-like branchlets, short spines, and short axillary racemes of small white flowers. It differs from *A. setaceus,* which has smal-

Asparagus densiflorus

ler, flat rather than spirally arranged branchlets and solitary flowers.

Asparagus densiflorus, sometimes called coarse asparagus fern, is native to southern Africa but is widely cultivated for its fern-like foliage. **HERB,** perennial, coarse, with weak, drooping stems to 2 m long (6½ ft) and short spines below the axils on the main stem. **LEAVES** reduced to scales but leaf-like, solitary or with clusters of two or three linear branchlets called cladophylls, mostly 1–2.5 × 0.1–0.2 cm (⅜–1 × about ⅛ in), arising from their axils. **FLOWERS** anytime during the year; flowers many, fragrant, in short axillary racemes 1–3 cm long (⅜–1¼ in). Corolla of six free elliptic tepals 1.5–3 mm long (to about ⅛ in), pinkish white. **FRUIT** a small, red, one- to three-seeded, globose berry 6–12 mm in diameter (¼–½ in). **PROPAGATE** by seeds or division. Fertile, moist soils in shaded or partially shaded places are preferred. It is commonly grown as a border plant, and often in pots or hanging baskets, especially in greenhouses in temperate climates. Its dense growth also makes it ideal as a ground cover, especially on embankments. Several cultivars are recognized based on differences in branching and habit. 'Sprengeri', Sprenger asparagus, is favored by florists, who use its fern-like foliage in flower arrangements.

Asparagus setaceus (Kunth) Jessop

Synonym, *Asparagus plumosus* Baker. **DISTINGUISHABLE** by the foliage arranged in one plane, tufts of tiny filamentous branchlets, and tiny, white, solitary flowers.

This so-called asparagus fern, *Asparagus setaceus*, is native to southern Africa but is widely cultivated, often as a potted plant, for its feathery foliage. **SHRUB**, woody, with slender, spreading, thorny stems to 3 m long (10 ft). **LEAVES** reduced to minute scales but tufts of 5 to 20 filamentous branchlets called cladophylls, 3–10 mm long (about ⅛–⅜ in), arising from their axils, arranged like a fern frond in one plane on the branches. **FLOWERS** anytime during the year; flowers solitary, borne at the top of short branches surrounded by tufted cladophylls. Corolla of six free obovate tepals 2–3 mm long (to about ⅛ in), white. **FRUIT** a small, black, globose, one- to three-seeded berry 5–7 mm in diameter (about ¼ in). **PROPAGATE** by seeds or division. Moist soils in partially shaded places are pre-

Asparagus setaceus

ferred. It is usually grown outdoors in the tropics and in greenhouses or as a houseplant in temperate climates. Unlike *A. densiflorus* it is not suitable as a ground cover with its delicate foliage and erect habit. The foliage is often used in flower arrangements and corsages.

Aster ASTERACEAE

Aster, the name of the genus from the Greek word for star, comprises about 250 species found mostly in the cooler temperate zone of both hemispheres. Many are cultivated for their attractive flower heads, with many cultivars named.

Aster laevis Linnaeus

DISTINGUISHABLE by the basal, oblanceolate, often white-waxy leaves and panicles of heads with pink to blue-violet ray florets and yellow disk florets. It is very similar to, and difficult to distinguish from, an-

other ornamental herb, *Aster nova-belgii* Linnaeus, which differs in its oblong to linear-lanceolate leaves that are glabrous but not white-waxy.

Aster laevis, Michaelmas daisy, sometimes called smooth aster, is basically a temperate plant that is native to the northwestern United States but is widely cultivated in warm regions, including the tropics, for its flower heads. HERB, perennial, clump forming, to 50 cm high (20 in) or more with glabrous stems. LEAVES simple, alternate, the lower ones almost in a rosette, blade elliptic to oblanceolate, 2–15 cm long (¾–6 in), smaller on the upper part of the plant, surfaces somewhat white-waxy. FLOWERS continu-

Aster laevis

ously through the year; flowers in terminal and axillary panicles of heads, each head surrounded by lanceolate bracts. Ray florets many, linear-oblanceolate, 8–12 mm long (¼–½ in), pink to blue-violet. Disk florets many, yellow. **FRUIT** an achene with narrow bristles on the top. **PROPAGATE** by division of the rhizomes. Moist but well-drained soils in partially shaded places are preferred. It is often grown as a low border plant or in pots or planters.

Asystasia ACANTHACEAE

Asystasia comprises 40 to 70 perennial herb or low shrub species widely distributed in the Old World tropics. Some of them are cultivated for their flowers or as ground covers, two of which are included here.

Asystasia gangetica (Linnaeus) T. Anderson

Synonym, *Asystasia coromandeliana* Nees. **DISTINGUISHABLE** by the weak-stemmed habit, prominent funnel-shaped lavender or white flowers, and club-shaped capsule.

Asystasia gangetica, coromandel, is native to India, not China as another name, Chinese violet, would imply, but is widely cultivated for its lavender or white flowers. In some places, Hawaii, for example, it is naturalized in disturbed forest communities. **HERB**, perennial, weak stemmed, to 1 m high (3¼ ft) or more. **LEAVES** simple, opposite, blade ovate, 2.5–8 cm long (1–3½ in). **FLOWERS** continuously through the year; flowers several in a one-sided terminal raceme. Corolla of fused petals, funnel-shaped, 3–5.5 cm long (1¼–2¼ in), somewhat two-lipped with five rounded spreading lobes, pale lavender

Asystasia gangetica with purple to lavender flowers

to purple with a yellow throat or all white. **Fruit** a club-shaped capsule 2–3 cm long (¾–1¼ in). **Propagate** by seeds or cuttings; it is easily grown. Relatively dry soils in sunny or partially shaded places are preferred. It can withstand drought and makes a good ground cover, especially on slopes that need protection from erosion. It can even be made into a lawn plant since it is able to withstand frequent cutting. If established underneath a hedge it often comes up through the hedge by leaning its weak stems on the shrub's branches.

Asystasia salicifolia Craib

Distinguishable by the low shrubby habit, narrowly elliptic leaves, and lavender flowers with a dark purple throat, or occasionally all white.

Asystasia salicifolia, without a well-known common name, is native to Thailand but is cultivated elsewhere, though not commonly, for its white or lavender flowers. It is much less frequently grown than the lar-

Asystasia salicifolia

ger flowered *A. gangetica* and does not become weedy. **Herb**, perennial, spreading, to 1 m high (3¼ ft) or more with pubescent stems. **Leaves** simple, opposite, blade narrowly elliptic, usually 4–11 cm long (1⅝–4½ in). **Flowers** continuously through the year; flowers several in long, terminal racemes that may branch at the base. Corolla of fused petals, bell-shaped, somewhat two-lipped, 3–5 cm long (1¼–2 in) with five short, rounded lobes, lavender with darker purple inside or all white. **Fruit** a club-shaped capsule, infrequently formed in cultivation. **Propagate** by cuttings. Relatively dry soils in sunny or partially shaded places are preferred. It is usually planted by itself to form small clumps.

Bambusa POACEAE

Bambusa is a genus of 70 to 100 robust grasses native to tropical and subtropical America and Asia. *Bambusa* and other related woody grasses are collectively called bamboos. They are grown for timber, pulp, fishing poles, and as ornamentals, and some species have edible shoots.

Bambusa vulgaris Schrader ex J. C. Wendland

DISTINGUISHABLE by the bamboo habit and stems often yellow with vertical green stripes.

Bambusa vulgaris, common bamboo, is native to somewhere between India and Indonesia but is widely and commonly cultivated in tropical and subtropical regions for use in construction, as fishing poles, and for making artifacts. It is also commonly planted as an ornamental, especially 'Vittata', golden or golden-stemmed bamboo, which has yellow stems with vertical green striations. GRASS, robust, hard stemmed, to 20 m high (66 ft) or more with hollow stems, but solid internodes, to 10 cm in diameter (4 in), green or yellow with vertical green stripes. LEAVES simple, on numerous spreading branches arising from the internodes, blade linear-lanceolate, 9–30 × 1–4 cm (3½–12 × ⅜–1⅝ in). FLOWERS only at intervals of several decades when the whole population in an area flowers at once; flowers many in spikelets borne in sessile clusters in large panicles arising from the internodes. Spikelets lanceolate, 2–3.5 cm long (¾–1⅜ in). PROPAGATE by division. Fertile, moist soils in cool places are preferred. A stand of this bamboo gives a particularly tropical forest ap-

Bambusa vulgaris 'Vittata'

pearance where it is planted, but because it tends to form large clumps it is not very suitable for small yards.

Barleria ACANTHACEAE

Barleria is a genus of about 80 species, or as many as 250 according to some authors, widespread in the tropics, especially in Africa and Asia. At least three are cultivated for their attractive flowers.

Barleria cristata Linnaeus

DISTINGUISHABLE by the shrubby habit, opposite leaves, and pale violet, blue, or white, funnel-shaped flowers enclosed within a pair of spiny-edged bracts.

    Barleria cristata, Philippine violet, which is native to India, not the Philippines, is not a member of the violet family. It is widely cultivated for its pale blue or violet flowers, being grown often as a hedge or by it-self as a small specimen plant. It must be pruned occasionally to keep its shape and is sometimes clipped into geometrical shapes. SHRUB to 1.5 m high (5 ft). LEAVES simple, opposite, blade usually elliptic, 3–10 cm long (1¼–4 in). FLOWERS continuously through the year; flowers sessile, borne in axillary fascicles of one to three enclosed by a pair of spiny-edged bracts. Corolla of fused petals, funnel-shaped, 5–7 cm long (2–3 in) with five rounded lobes, pale violet or blue, rarely white. FRUIT a flattened ovoid capsule, infrequently formed in cultivation. PROPAGATE by seeds or cuttings. Well-drained soils in sunny or partially shaded places are preferred. Full sun-

Barleria cristata

light is needed for optimal flowering. It becomes naturalized in some places but does not readily spread to become a nuisance.

Bauhinia FABACEAE

Bauhinia comprises about 250 shrub and small tree species native throughout the tropics but not east of Malaysia in the Pacific. Its members are characterized by the simple leaves formed by the partial or complete fusion of two leaflets. Many species are cultivated for their large, colorful, often orchid-like flowers, three of the most common of which are included here.

Bauhinia galpinii N. E. Brown

Synonym, *Bauhinia punctata* Bolle. **DISTINGUISHABLE** by the notched leaves, red flowers with long-stalked petals, and woody pods.

Bauhinia galpinii, pride of the Cape, is native to southern Africa, the Cape in its name referring to the Cape of Good Hope, the southern tip of Africa, but is widely cultivated in the tropics and subtropics for its large red flowers. It is sometimes called red butterfly tree or red bauhinia. **SHRUB** or small tree to 9 m high (30 ft) but usually much shorter. **LEAVES** simple, alternate, blade broadly ovate, 2–8 cm long (¾–3½ in) and somewhat wider, notched at the tip one-fourth or less of the length into two rounded lobes. **FLOWERS** anytime during the year; flowers several in axillary racemes. Corolla of five free petals 3–5 cm long (1¼–2 in), clawed for half their length into an ovate to round tip, red to red-orange, with tiny yellow glands on

Bauhinia galpinii

the outside and three long fertile stamens (and two infertile ones) in the center. FRUIT a linear pod 9–13 cm long (3½–5 in). PROPAGATE by seeds or air layering. Well-drained soils in sunny places are preferred. Though it can grow to be a tree it is often maintained as a scrambling shrub. It is often planted by itself or to form a hedge in the tropics, and in temperate areas it may be grown in the greenhouse.

Bauhinia monandra Kurz

DISTINGUISHABLE by the deeply notched leaves with palmate venation, orchid-like flowers of stalked, white to pink petals spotted with red, one fertile stamen, and woody pods. A similar, widely cultivated species, *Bauhinia variegata* Linnaeus, called orchid tree, differs in having pale purple to white flowers with five fertile stamens. *Bauhinia* ×*blakeana* Dunn, a hybrid, perhaps *B. variegata* × *B. purpurea* Linnaeus, differs in having pink flowers and five fertile stamens.

Bauhinia monandra with white to pink flowers having one fertile stamen

Bauhinia variegata with five fertile stamens

Bauhinia monandra, pink orchid tree, is native to tropical America and was originally named from Venezuela but is widely cultivated in the tropics for its large pink flowers. It is sometimes called butterfly flower, pink butterfly tree, pink bauhinia, or like *B. tomentosa,* St. Thomas tree. TREE to 10 m high (33 ft) or more. LEAVES simple, alternate, blade ovate to nearly round, 7–16 cm long (3–6 in), notched from the tip half of its length, usually 11- to 13-veined from the base. FLOWERS continuously through the year; flowers several in upper axillary and terminal racemes. Corolla of five free oblanceolate petals 4–6 cm long (1⅝–2½ in), white to pink, often spotted red, with one fertile stamen (and four infertile

Bauhinia ×blakeana with pink flowers and five fertile stamens

ones). FRUIT a flattened, linear-oblong pod 15–25 cm long (6–10 in) with the persistent long style at the tip. PROPAGATE by scarified seeds. Fertile, well-drained soils in sunny places are preferred. It is one of the most commonly grown species of the genus and is typically planted around houses or along roads but has escaped and become naturalized in some places. It is also ideal as a free-standing specimen plant because of the pink, orchid-like flowers that cover the tree.

Bauhinia tomentosa Linnaeus

DISTINGUISHABLE by the notched leaves, yellowish bell-shaped flowers that scarcely open at maturity, and woody pods.

Bauhinia tomentosa, yellow bauhinia, is native from tropical Africa to Southeast Asia but is widely cultivated for its yellow flowers. It is sometimes called, like *B. monandra,* St. Thomas tree. Though its flowers, which scarcely open, differ from those of most other species in the

Bauhinia tomentosa

genus, the leaves, which are formed from two fused leaflets, are like those of other bauhinias. TREE to 4 m high (13 ft) or more. LEAVES simple, alternate, blade broadly ovate, 2–9 cm long (¾–3½ in), deeply notched at the tip, 7- to 11-veined from the base. FLOWERS continuously through the year; flowers one to several in short terminal racemes. Corolla bell-shaped because the petals do not open fully, with five free, nearly round, short-stalked petals 2.5–6 cm long (1–2½ in), pale yellow, sometimes one or more blotched purple, and ten fertile stamens. FRUIT a linear-oblong pod usually 8–12 cm long (3½–5 in). PROPAGATE by scarified seeds, air layering, or cuttings. Moist but well-drained soils in sunny places are preferred. It is grown by itself as a specimen tree or as a relatively short street tree.

Beaumontia APOCYNACEAE

Beaumontia, herald's trumpet, is a genus of eight to ten species found in tropical Asia and Malaysia. There has been some confusion in the identification of species of this genus, but apparently at least three species are cultivated for their large, attractive flowers.

Beaumontia multiflora Teijsmann & Binnendijk

Sometimes misidentified as *Beaumontia grandiflora* Wallich or *B. jerdoniana* Wight. DISTINGUISHABLE by the viny habit, milky sap, glossy green, opposite leaves, and large, white, widely opening flowers. *Beaumontia grandiflora,* with larger flowers and leaves, is perhaps more common in cultivation.

Beaumontia multiflora, a herald's trumpet, is native to Java but is widely if not commonly cultivated for its large white flowers. LIANA or vine-like shrub, often climbing into trees, sap milky. LEAVES simple, opposite, blade elliptic to oblanceolate, usually 10–25 cm long (4–10 in). FLOWERS anytime or continuously through the year; flowers several in dense terminal clusters. Corolla of fused petals, rotate, 8–14 cm across (3½–6 in), divided about halfway into five broad lobes, white, tinged green in the center. FRUIT a pair of capsule-like segments, infrequently formed in cultivation. PROPAGATE by cuttings. Fertile, moist soils in sunny places are preferred. It is

Beaumontia multiflora

often seen as a vigorous climber that ascends high into trees, in which case the attractive flowers cannot easily be viewed except when they fall to the ground, so trellises or fences are more suitable sites for it. It can also be trained as a shrub.

Begonia BEGONIACEAE

Begonia is a genus of 800 to 900 perennial and annual herbaceous species found throughout the tropics and subtropics, many cultivated as indoor or shade plants for their flowers or foliage. Begonias form one of the largest group of cultivated plants and extensive hybridization within the genus has led to many more cultivars and hybrids.

Begonia ×semperflorens-cultorum of gardens

Sometimes misidentified as *Begonia semperflorens* Link & Otto. DISTIN-GUISHABLE by the small habit, unequally sided leaves, unisexual flowers

Begonia ×semperflorens-cultorum

that have four pink petal-like sepals on the male and five on the female, and three-winged capsule.

Wax begonia, sometimes called bedding begonia, is thought actually to be a group of hybrids, many of them sterile triploids, derived from crosses between two Brazilian begonias, *B. cucullata* var. *hookeri* (A. L. P. P. de Candolle) L. B. Smith & Schubert, and *B. schmidtiana* Regel. Because of the hybridization there is much confusion about the correct names of the species. **HERB**, perennial, semisucculent, to 50 cm high (20 in). **LEAVES** simple, alternate, blade ovate, 4–11 cm long (1⅝–4½ in), unequally sided, base oblique, surfaces green or variegated with white. **FLOWERS** continuously through the year; flowers unisexual, several, borne in axillary cymes. Corolla absent but calyx of four (male flowers) or five (female flowers) free, unequal, petal-like sepals mostly 5–15 mm long (¼–⅝ in), pink or white, the male flowers with many yellow stamens in the center, the female ones with about six yellow irregular stigma lobes. **FRUIT** a three-winged capsule. **PROPAGATE** by cuttings and seeds. Fertile, moist soils in partially shaded places are preferred. Wax begonias are usually grown in pots around houses and sometimes escape to become weedy.

Belamcanda IRIDACEAE

Belamcanda is a genus of two rhizomatous perennial Asian species, one of which is cultivated for its attractive flowers, which are spotted, hence the name leopard lily.

Belamcanda chinensis

(Linnaeus) A. P. de Candolle

DISTINGUISHABLE by the equitant leaves and long panicles of flowers with six pale red-orange, red-spotted tepals, cream-colored in the center.

Belamcanda chinensis

Belamcanda chinensis, leopard lily, sometimes called blackberry lily, misnomers since it is a member of the iris rather than lily family, is native from northern India to Japan but is widely cultivated in temperate and subtropical climates, less frequently in the tropics, for its orange flowers. The leaves are overlapping in two ranks, a condition called equitant that is characteristic of the iris family. HERB, perennial, erect, to 1 m high (3¼ ft) or more, arising from a rhizome. LEAVES simple, basal, equitant, blade linear-lanceolate, the two sides folded together the whole length and fused toward the tip, the lower leaves mostly 20–60 × 1–3 cm (8–24 × ⅜–1¼ in). FLOWERS anytime during the year; flowers 6 to 12, borne 2 at a time in an open, branching panicle 30–50 cm long (12–20 in). Corolla with fused tepals, deeply split into six elliptic to oblanceolate segments 1.8–3 cm long (¾–1¼ in), light red-orange with the center cream-colored, spotted with red. FRUIT a many-seeded, obovoid, three-angled capsule 1.5–3 cm long (⅝–1¼ in). PROPAGATE by rhizome division or seeds. Fertile, well-drained soils in sunny places are preferred. It is often grown as a border plant or in rock gardens.

Bixa BIXACEAE

Bixa is a genus with only one species.

Bixa orellana Linnaeus

Synonym, *Bixa arborea* Huber. **DISTINGUISHABLE** by the alternate leaves palmately veined from the base, large pink flowers, and soft-spiny capsule that opens to expose the greasy red seeds.

Bixa orellana, annatto, is native to tropical America and the West Indies but is widely cultivated for its fruit, which yields numerous seeds coated in a red substance once used as a tasteless dye for food products such as butter, cheese, and chocolate. This coloring has also been used in Polynesia and Melanesia for dying tapa cloth, and widely for personal decoration, lipstick, for example, hence the name lipstick tree for the plant. **TREE** or shrub to 5 m (16½ ft) high. **LEAVES** simple, alternate, blade ovate to heart-shaped, 6–18 cm long (2½–7 in), palmately veined from the base, on a long petiole. **FLOWERS** mostly in late spring to summer with the fruits opening in winter; flowers many, borne in terminal panicles. Corolla of five free, obovate, pink petals 2–4 cm long (¾–1⅝ in), surrounding the numerous pink stamens. **FRUIT** a red, ovoid, soft-spiny capsule 3–5 cm long (1¼–2 in), opening at the tip to expose the numerous greasy, red seeds. **PROPAGATE** by seeds or cuttings. Moist but well-drained soils in sunny places are preferred. Synthetic dyes have largely replaced the main uses of the plant and it is mostly cultivated for its attractive pink flowers, or perhaps more as a novelty because of its unusual looking, attractive red fruits that are sometimes used in dried flower arrangements. As an ornamental, the tree is usually grown by itself as a specimen plant, or it can be pruned into a hedge.

Bixa orellana

Bougainvillea NYCTAGINACEAE

Bougainvillea comprises 14 to 18 tropical American shrubby, climbing species, many cultivated for their inflorescences. The genus is named after the French navigator and explorer Louis-Antoine de Bougainville, 1729–1811, who discovered the plants in Brazil during one of his voyages. There is much hybridization in the genus, making the identification of some of the species and cultivars difficult. Two ornamental species, each sometimes called paper flower, one of them of hybrid origin, are included here.

Bougainvillea ×buttiana Holttum & Standley

Often misidentified as *Bougainvillea spectabilis* Willdenow. DISTIN-GUISHABLE by the scrambling shrubby habit, nasty spines, dull green leaves, and clusters of small white flowers, each attached to a prominent purple, red, orange, or white bract. It is very similar to *B. glabra*, which has relatively narrower, shiny green leaves with a longer tip

Bougainvillea ×buttiana is apparently a hybrid between two other species, one of which is possibly *B. spectabilis*, with which it is often confused. VINE-LIKE SHRUB, scrambling, sometimes climbing into trees, and bearing stout axillary spines mostly 6–40 mm long (¼–1⅝ in). LEAVES simple, alternate, blade broadly ovate, 3–11 cm long (1¼–4½ in), dull green, glabrous, with an acute tip. FLOWERS continuously through the year; flowers borne in one to three clusters of three each or in panicles atop a stalk that becomes a spine, each flower attached to an elliptic purple, red, orange, or white bract

Bougainvillea ×buttiana

2–4 cm long (¾–1⅝ in). Corolla absent but calyx tubular, corolla-like, 1.5–2 cm long (⅝–¾ in), white, with a spreading 5-lobed (but appearing 15-lobed) limb. **FRUIT** dry, one-seeded, called an anthocarp, infrequently formed in cultivation. **PROPAGATE** by cuttings. Fertile, well-drained soils in sunny places are preferred. It is one of the most spectacular ornamental shrubs and is often grown by itself or in hedges. Vigorous growth of the stems requires frequent trimming. Because of its dense growth, it can be pruned into the shapes of animals, an art known as topiary. Its spiny stems, like those of the other bougainvilleas, can be a drawback, especially when the plant needs to be trimmed, so it is not advisable to situate the plants too close to foot traffic. There are many cultivars, differing mostly in the color of the bracts.

Bougainvillea glabra Choisy

DISTINGUISHABLE by the scrambling shrubby habit, shiny green leaves, nasty spines, and clusters of small white flowers, each attached to a typically magenta bract. It is sometimes confused with *Bougainvillea ×buttiana,* which is more common and differs in having a duller upper leaf surface and an acute rather than attenuate leaf tip.

Bougainvillea glabra

Bougainvillea glabra, sometimes called lesser bougainvillea, is native to South America, possibly to Brazil, but is widely cultivated for its colorful flowers bracts though its spiny stems are a drawback. *Bougainvillea glabra* and *B. ×buttiana* hybridize, leading to further difficulty in identification. **VINE-LIKE SHRUB,** scrambling, sometimes climbing up into trees, and bearing axillary spines to 1.5 cm long (⅝ in). **LEAVES** simple, alternate, blade elliptic to ovate, usually 3–7 cm long (1¼–3 in), glabrous, dark shiny green and typically with a somewhat attenuate tip. FLOWERS continuously through the year; flowers typically borne in three clusters of three each atop a stalk that becomes a spine, each flower attached to an ovate magenta bract, sometimes white or other colors, 2.5–4.5 cm long (1–1¾ in). Corolla absent but the calyx tubular, petal-like, white, 1.5–2.2 cm long (⅝–⅞ in) with a spreading 5-lobed (but appearing 15-lobed) limb. FRUIT dry, one-seeded, called an anthocarp, infrequently formed in cultivation. PROPAGATE by seeds. Fertile, moist, but well-drained soils in sunny places are preferred. The plant is typically grown as a thorny hedge or by itself. Regular pruning is needed to trim the vigorous growth but this can be a painful experience. Like other bougainvilleas, it can be trimmed into the shape of animals, topiary. There are many cultivars, of which one of the best known is 'Sanderiana', with magenta bracts.

Brachychiton STERCULIACEAE

Brachychiton is a genus of 31 species found in Australia and Papua New Guinea, some cultivated especially for their attractive, seasonal flowers. Many are called bottle trees, and some are cultivated for fodder in eastern Australia.

Brachychiton acerifolius A. Cunningham ex F. von Mueller

DISTINGUISHABLE by the bottle-shaped trunk, leaves deeply lobed, deciduous, and large, loose panicles of small red flowers that seasonally cover the tree when it is nearly barren of leaves.

Brachychiton acerifolius, Australian flame tree, is native to subtropical Queensland and New South Wales, eastern Australia, but is widely cultivated as a deciduous, seasonally flowering tree in warm places, somewhat more commonly in the subtropics and warm temperate regions than in the tropics. Its red flowers cover the nearly leafless branches during its spectacular flowering season, making it one of Australia's most beautiful trees. Fibers from the bark have been used for weaving

Brachychiton acerifolius

baskets in Australia, and a dye is produced from the seeds. TREE to 30 m high (100 ft) but usually much less, with a bottle-shaped trunk, deciduous for part of summer. LEAVES alternate, simple, blade ovate, palmately lobed to varying degrees, especially when young, 9–25 cm long (3½–10 in), glabrous, glossy, on a petiole 2–24 cm long (¾–9 in). FLOWERS seasonally, mostly in late spring and early summer; flowers in loose, axillary, many-flowered panicles with reddish branches. Corolla absent but calyx bright red, bell-shaped, shallowly five- or six-lobed, 1.5–2.3 cm long (⅝–⅞ in). FRUIT of one to five long-stalked follicles 9–12 cm long (3½–5 in). PROPAGATE by seeds or cuttings. Dry, well-drained, moderately fertile soils in sunny places are preferred. It is grown as a street tree or by itself as a specimen tree.

Breynia EUPHORBIACEAE

Breynia is a genus of about 25 species found from China to Melanesia, several cultivated for their attractive leaves or as hedge shrubs.

Breynia disticha J. R. Forster & J. G. A. Forster

Synonym, *Breynia nivosa* (W. G. Smith) Small. DISTINGUISHABLE by the small, alternate, ovate to oblong, variously colored leaves and inconspicuous axillary, solitary female flowers that hang from the lower surface of the branches.

Breynia disticha, snowbush, sometimes called leaf flower, is native to the Melanesia but is widely cultivated for its variegated foliage. SHRUB

to 2 m high (6½ ft) with zigzag
branches. LEAVES simple, alternate,
blade ovate to oblong, 1.5–6 cm long
(⅝–2½ in), often mottled with white,
red, purple, or pink or all three colors.
FLOWERS anytime during the year but
the flowers are inconspicuous, unisexual, the male flowers few, borne in
clusters in the lower leaf axils, the female flowers solitary in the upper leaf
axils. Corolla absent but the calyx of
the female flowers deeply six-lobed,
2–4 mm long (about 1/16–1/4 in), greenish yellow or white. FRUIT a globose
capsule, infrequently formed in cultivation. PROPAGATE by cuttings and
suckers. Fertile, moist soils in partially
shaded places are preferred, but bright

Breynia disticha 'Roseopicta'

light brings out the best colors. It is typically grown in hedges where the
relatively small leaves provide a wealth of color but it can also be grown
alone as a small specimen plant. The common cultivar is 'Roseopicta'.

Brownea FABACEAE

Brownea is a genus of about 25 tropical American species, some cultivated as flowering trees for their spectacular inflorescences, colored
various shades of red, and for their unusual, colorful young leaves.

Brownea macrophylla Linden

This genus is still poorly understood and is in need of revision so the
name used here may not be correct. DISTINGUISHABLE by the spreading,
weak branches, pinnately compound leaves, large leaflets, and dense
sessile clusters of red-orange flowers and bracts that form on the trunk
and branches.

Brownea macrophylla

Brownea macrophylla, Panama flame, sometimes called rouge puff, is native to Panama and Colombia but is widely if not commonly cultivated for its large compact clusters of seasonal red-orange flowers that adorn the branches and make it one of the most attractive tropical flowering trees, though the shape of the tree is not that pleasing. The young leaves are also attractive for the pink to red color they exhibit before they mature. TREE to 10 m high (33 ft) with somewhat weak branches that sometimes lean on nearby trees. LEAVES alternate, pinnately compound, leaflets in three to nine pairs, blades elliptic, the longest mostly 12–30 cm long (5–12 in), reddish when young. FLOWERS seasonally, mostly in late fall to spring; flowers 30 to 50, borne among red-orange bracts in a tightly packed, globose head 10–25 cm in diameter (4–10 in), arising from the branches and trunk. Corolla of four or five stalked, elliptic, red-orange petals 3–4 cm long (1¼–1⅝ in), surrounding the four or five yellowish, long, and protruding stamens. FRUIT a flattened, pubescent, few-seeded pod to 20 cm long (8 in) or more. PROPAGATE by scarified seeds. Moist soils in partially shaded places are preferred. The tree is grown in the tropics as a specimen tree in gardens or yards, often under other taller trees, and in the greenhouse in temperate areas.

Brugmansia SOLANACEAE

Brugmansia is a genus of five or six shrub species found in the mountains of South America. They contain alkaloids, especially scopolamine, that were used as hallucinogens by American Indians. Several species are cultivated for their large, pendulous flowers in spite of their toxicity.

Brugmansia ×candida Persoon

Synonym, *Datura candida* (Persoon) Stapf. **DISTINGUISHABLE** by the shrubby habit, leaves that are downy and alternate, flowers that are large, hanging, funnel-shaped, and white, often double-flowered, and acute, unlobed calyx. The similar *Brugmansia suaveolens* (Willdenow) Berchtold & Presl (synonym, *D. arborea* of some authors, not Linnaeus), called angel's trumpet, can be distinguished by its shorter habit, smaller flowers, and three- to five-lobed calyx.

Brugmansia ×candida, angel's trumpet, is a hybrid between two tropical Andean species, *B. aurea* Lagerheim and *B. versicolor* Lagerheim, and is widely cultivated for its large, hanging, trumpet-shaped, white flowers that make the plant a striking garden ornamental. The flowers emit a musky scent in the evening. The whole plant is poisonous because it contains a potent narcotic, scopolamine, which in minute quantities is used in skin patches to control motion sickness but can be fatal if ingested. **SHRUB** to 1.8 m high (6 ft). **LEAVES** simple, alternate, blade ovate to elliptic, usually 15–30 cm long (6–12 in), surfaces downy. **FLOWERS** continuously through the year; flowers solitary, axillary, hanging. Corolla with fused petals, narrowly funnel-shaped, 25–45 cm long (10–18 in), white, shallowly five-lobed or often double-flowered, surrounded at the base by an acute, unlobed calyx. **FRUIT** an ellip-

Brugmansia ×candida

soidal or cylindrical capsule 12–18 cm long (5–7 in). PROPAGATE by cuttings, the technique most frequently used. Fertile, moist, but well-drained soils in sunny to partially shaded places are preferred. It is usually planted in borders or by itself as a specimen plant and can be trimmed to form a small tree. There are a number of cultivars, some double-flowered.

Brunfelsia SOLANACEAE

Brunfelsia comprises about 40 tropical American tree and shrub species, several of which are cultivated for their colorful flowers that often change color with age. Two of the most common ornamental species are included here.

Brunfelsia americana Linnaeus

DISTINGUISHABLE by the small alternate leaves and fragrant white flowers with a long tube and spreading five-lobed limb.

Brunfelsia americana

Brunfelsia americana, lady of the night, is native to the West Indies but is widely if not commonly cultivated for its white flowers, which are fragrant at night, hence the common name. It differs from most other species of *Brunfelsia* in having a much longer, white rather than violet, corolla tube. The fruits are reported to be poisonous. SHRUB to 3 m high (10 ft) or more. LEAVES simple, alternate, blade elliptic to obovate or oblanceolate, 3–11 cm long (1¼–4½ in). FLOWERS continuously through the year; flowers solitary, terminal on the end of a short lateral shoot. Corolla with fused petals, salverform, tube 4–9 cm long (1⅝–3½ in), limb spreading, shallowly five-lobed, 4–5.5 cm across (1⅝–2¼ in), white fading to pale yellow, fragrant at night. FRUIT a subglobose capsule 1–2 cm long (⅜–¾ in). PROPAGATE by cuttings; sometimes propagated by seeds. Fertile, moist, but well-drained soils in sunny places are preferred. It is often planted by itself as a specimen plant because of the flowers.

Brunfelsia pauciflora (Chamisso & Schlechtendal) Bentham

Synonym, *Brunfelsia calycina* Bentham. DISTINGUISHABLE by the alternate leaves and salverform corolla that starts out violet but ages to pale violet or white in a few days. Two related, commonly cultivated species, *Brunfelsia latifolia* (W. J. Hooker) Bentham and *Brunfelsia uniflora* (Pohl) D. Don, have generally smaller corollas. The latter also has mostly solitary or paired flowers.

Brunfelsia pauciflora, yesterday-today-and-tomorrow, is native to Brazil but is widely cultivated for its prominent, fragrant flowers that when young are violet with a white throat but that age in a few days to pale violet or white. The taxonomy of the genus is difficult and it is not easy distinguish *B. pauciflora* from several other similar species with violet flowers that fade to white that are also widely cultivated and called yesterday-today-and-tomorrow. SHRUB to 2 m high (6½ ft) or more. LEAVES simple, alternate, blade elliptic to lanceolate, 7–15 cm long (3–6 in), acute at the tip. FLOWERS continuously through the year; flowers one to ten, terminal on short lateral shoots. Corolla with fused petals, salverform, tube 3–4 cm long (1¼–1⅝ in), limb shallowly five-

Brunfelsia pauciflora

lobed, 3–7 cm across (1¼–3 in), violet with a white center, fading to pale violet or white, not noticeably fragrant. **FRUIT** an ovoid capsule 9–12 mm long (⅜–½ in). **PROPAGATE** by cuttings. Fertile, well-drained soils in sunny or partially shaded places are preferred. It is usually planted by itself as a specimen plant that is both unusual and attractive, with all three colors often found simultaneously on the same branch.

Caesalpinia FABACEAE

Caesalpinia is a genus of about 100 tree, shrub, and liana species found throughout the tropics and subtropics, some of which are used for timber and tannin, and a few are cultivated as ornamentals. Many are thorny, however, limiting their value as ornamentals.

Caesalpinia pulcherrima (Linnaeus) Swartz

Synonym, *Poinciana pulcherrima* Linnaeus. **DISTINGUISHABLE** by the thorny stems, bipinnately compound leaves, and yellow or red flowers

with crinkled petal margins and long, protruding stamens. A related species sometimes cultivated as an ornamental, *Caesalpinia coriaria* (Jacquin) Willdenow, Mysore thorn, differs in having smaller leaflets 4–9 mm long (about ¼–⅜ in) and smaller petals 3–6 mm long (about ⅛–¼ in).

Caesalpinia pulcherrima, pride of Barbados or Barbados pride, is native to tropical America but is widely cultivated for its continuous display of red and yellow flowers and is one of the best known tropical ornamental plants; *pulcherrima* is from the Latin word for beautiful. It is sometimes called Barbados flower fence, dwarf poinciana, or

Caesalpinia pulcherrima with the yellow flowers of *C. pulcherrima* 'Flava'

peacock flower. SHRUB to 4 m high (13 ft), sometimes with thorny stems and leaves. LEAVES bipinnately compound, alternate, divided into 4 to 9 pairs of pinnae, each pinna with 5 to 12 pairs of leaflets, blades oblong to obovate, 1–3 cm long (⅜–1¼ in). FLOWERS continuously through the year; flowers many, borne on long stalks in terminal racemes. Corolla of five free obovate petals 1.5–2.5 cm long (⅝–1 in), red to yellow, with crinkled, often orange margins, with ten long, protruding, red stamens. FRUIT a flattened, narrowly oblong pod 8–12 cm long (3½–5 in). PROP-AGATE by scarified seeds or cuttings. Fertile soils in sunny or partially shaded places are preferred. The plant is grown in colorful hedges or by itself as a specimen plant but its thorny stems can be a drawback. Prun-ing is needed to keep it in shape, and this promotes flowering. It is re-ported to escape from cultivation sometimes to become a weed in cer-tain places but it does not spread readily since the seeds are not easily dispersed. In temperate areas it can be grown in the greenhouse. A cul-tivar with all-yellow flowers, 'Flava', is also commonly cultivated.

Caladium ARACEAE

Caladium is a genus of 7 to 20 herbaceous tropical American species, some cultivated for their colorful leaves, variously marked with red, white, and pink. Many of the plants are of hybrid origin.

Caladium bicolor (Aiton) Ventenat

Synonym, *Caladium hortulanum* Birdsey. DISTINGUISHABLE by the mul-ticolored, shield-shaped leaves and inconspicuous spathe-and-spadix inflorescences.

Caladium bicolor is native to the Amazon region of Brazil but is wide-ly grown for its colorful leaves. It has been given many common names, including fancy-leaved caladium, angel wings, elephant's ear, and heart of Jesus. The taxonomy of this species, perhaps a group of species, is confusing and hundreds of cultivars have been named, dif-fering widely in the color and patterns on the leaves. HERB, perennial, stemless, to 50 cm high (20 in) or more, arising from a globose rhizome.

Caladium bicolor, a cultivar with white flecks on the leaf

Caladium bicolor, a cultivar with leaves red in the center

LEAVES simple, alternate, blade peltate, arrowhead- or heart-shaped, usually 20–40 cm long (8–16 in), variously colored with spots and blotches of red, pink, or white or all three colors. FLOWERS infrequently during the year; flowers many, borne tightly packed in a cylindrical spadix usually 6–10 cm long (2½–4 in) on a short stalk, surrounded by a slightly longer, ovate, whitish spathe attached at the base. FRUIT a pear-shaped white berry, infrequently formed in cultivation. PROPAGATE by tuber division. Fertile, moist, but well-drained soils in partially or fully shaded places are preferred. It is grown in the garden, often as a border plant as well as a potted plant in the tropics, and as a potted plant in the greenhouse in temperate climates. It is most attractive when a single cultivar or clone is grown in an area rather than a mixture of different ones. The plant may die back during the dry season.

Calliandra FABACEAE

Calliandra, the name of the genus from the Greek words meaning beautiful and male, referring to the stamens, comprises about 200 shrub or small tree species found throughout the tropics, some cultivated for their prominent, often red flowers. Two of the most common ornamental species are included here.

Calliandra haematocephala Hasskarl

Synonym, *Calliandra inequilatera* Rusby. DISTINGUISHABLE by the shrubby habit, bipinnately compound leaves with two spreading pinnae, each pinna bearing unequally sided leaflets, and large heads composed of long red or white stamens.

Calliandra haematocephala, red powder puff, is native to Brazil and Bolivia but is widely cultivated for its large heads of red flowers that resemble powder puffs. The name *haematocephala* is from the Greek words meaning (blood-) red head. The heads of flowers look somewhat like those of bottlebrushes *(Callistemon),* which also have prominent red stamens but simple opposite leaves rather than compound alternate ones. SHRUB to 3 m high (10 ft) or more. LEAVES bipinnately compound, alternate, with two spreading pinnae, each pinna bearing five to eight pairs of leaflets, blades elliptic to lanceolate or ovate, 1–5.5 cm long (⅜–2¼ in), unequally sided. FLOWERS continuously through the year; flowers many, borne in dense axillary heads

Calliandra haematocephala with red flowers, and white flowers from the less commonly grown plant

5–9 cm in diameter (2–3½ in). Corolla funnel-shaped, five fused petals 5–8 mm long (about ¼ in) surrounding the numerous red (white in one cultivar) stamens to 4 cm long (1⅝ in). FRUIT a flattened, narrowly ellipsoidal pod usually 9–10 cm long (3½–4 in) with thickened seams. PROPAGATE by scarified seeds. Fertile, moist, but well-drained soils in sunny places are preferred. These plants are often grown in hedges or as a shrub border, or by themselves as specimen plants. A less common white-flowered "red" powder puff is also cultivated.

Calliandra surinamensis Bentham

DISTINGUISHABLE by the bipinnately compound leaves with two spreading pinnae, each pinna bearing narrowly oblong leaflets, and heads of white, red-tipped stamens.

Calliandra surinamensis, pink powder puff, is native to northern South America and was originally named from Dutch Guiana, now called Suriname, but is widely cultivated for its attractive heads of red and white flowers, resembling powder puffs. SHRUB to 4 m high (13 ft) or more with spreading branches. LEAVES bipinnately compound, alternate, with two spreading pinnae, each pinna bearing 8 to 12 pairs of leaflets, blades narrowly oblong to lanceolate, 6–25 mm long (¼–1 in), unequally sided. FLOWERS continuously through the year; flowers many, borne in short-stalked axillary heads. Corolla funnel-shaped, of five partly fused, yellow to green or red-tipped petals 5–7 mm long (about ¼ in), stamens many, prominent, fused at the base into a white staminal tube, red at the tips, to

Calliandra surinamensis

3 cm long (1¼ in). FRUIT a linear-oblong pod 6–10 cm long (2½–4 in), with thickened margins. PROPAGATE by scarified seeds or cuttings. Fertile, moist, but well-drained soils in sunny places are preferred. It is often planted in rows and trimmed to make low hedges, or is planted alone and not trimmed to form a large attractive shrub with drooping branches covered with the red and white flowers.

Callistemon MYRTACEAE

Callistemon is a genus of about 25 tree and shrub species found in Australia and New Caledonia, many grown as ornamentals. Most have red, bottlebrush-like inflorescences and are pollinated by birds. The name *Callistemon* is from the Greek words meaning beautiful stamens.

Callistemon citrinus (Curtis) Skeels

Synonym, *Callistemon lanceolatus* (Smith) A. P. de Candolle. DISTINGUISHABLE by the opposite, narrowly elliptic leaves, pubescent leaf margins, erect, bottlebrush-like inflorescences with prominent red stamens, and woody, cup-like fruits. A similar, very commonly cultivated species, *C. viminalis* (Solander ex Gaertner) G. Don ex Loudon, weeping bottlebrush, that is native to New South Wales, Australia, differs in having linear leaves less than 8 mm wide (¼ in) and hanging rather than erect bottlebrush-like inflorescences.

Callistemon citrinus, red bottlebrush, is native to eastern Australia but is widely cultivated in tropical to warm temperate regions for its red flowers. The name *Callistemon* is from the Greek words meaning beautiful stamens, aptly describing the inflorescences. It is sometimes called crimson bottlebrush or lemon bottlebrush. The hard, heavy wood is useful but is not utilized in cultivation. SHRUB or tree to 8 m high (26 ft) or more with furrowed bark. LEAVES simple, opposite, blade narrowly elliptic, usually 4–7 × 0.6–1.5 cm (1⅝–3 × ¼–⅝ in), pinnately veined with a distinct marginal vein, pubescent on the margins. FLOWERS intermittently during the year; flowers many, borne in erect, terminal,

Callistemon citrinus with erect spikes

Callistemon viminalis with hanging spikes and narrower leaves

cylindrical spikes, the axes of which later become leafy beyond the spike. Corolla of five small red petals falling soon after the flower opens, with numerous red, bristle-like stamens 1.8–3 cm long (¾–1¼ in) and giving the inflorescence its bottlebrush shape. FRUIT a small, sessile, woody, subglobose capsule 5–7 mm long (about ¼ in), densely packed on the stem. PROPAGATE by seeds, usually, or by cuttings or air layering. Fertile, well-drained soils in sunny places are preferred. It is typically pruned to form a hedge or is left untrimmed and used as a specimen or screen plant. In cooler climates, it is often grown in the greenhouse.

Calotropis ASCLEPIADACEAE

Calotropis is a genus of six species, two according to some authors, of tropical Asia and Africa. Some are used as a source of fiber, from the seed floss and bark, or as ornamentals.

Calotropis gigantea (Linnaeus) Aiton

Distinguishable by the large erect habit, milky sap, white-powdery, opposite leaves, and axillary umbels of white to pale purple, crown-like flowers. A related ornamental, *Calotropis procera* (Aiton) Aiton fil., small crown flower, differs in being a smaller shrub with erect corolla lobes, each lobe usually with a spot at the base.

Calotropis gigantea, crown flower, is native to India and Southeast Asia but is widely cultivated in the tropics for its attractive powdery white foliage and unusual waxy white, crown-like flowers. It has been grown for bark fibers that are used in weaving, for medicinal purposes, for its long-lasting flowers used in leis, and for the silky kapok-like material on the seeds that is used to stuff pillows, but over most of its cultivated range it is an ornamental plant. The sap is somewhat poisonous, which is typical of many other plants in the milkweed family Asclepiadaceae. The plant is also a favorite for monarch butterflies who use it during all stages of their development. The flowers have an interesting adaptation to insect pollination—the two parts of the anthers are attached together by a loop of tissue that forms a stirrup that is snagged by the leg of the pollinating insect, who then carries away the whole apparatus to another flower. **Shrub** to 4 m high (13 ft) with milky sap. **Leaves** simple, opposite, blade elliptic to obovate, 8–23 cm long (3½–9 in), subsessile with a heart-shaped base, surface powdery white. **Flowers** continuously through the year; flowers several, borne in stalked clusters arising between the petiole pairs. Corolla of fused petals, rotate, 3–4 cm in diameter (1¼–1⅝

Calotropis gigantea

in), deeply split into five spreading, acute lobes, waxy white or tinted purple, with the stamens fused to the discoid stigma to form a conspicuous corona. **FRUIT** an oblong to ovoid follicle 7–10 cm long (3–4 in) with silky-tufted seeds but infrequently formed in cultivation. **PROPAGATE** by cuttings, the usual method. Well-drained soils in sunny places are preferred. It is usually planted in hedges, often in seaside areas since it is a hardy, relatively salt-tolerant plant, but it can also be trimmed to form a small tree.

Cananga ANNONACEAE

Cananga is a genus of two species found from tropical Asia to Australia, one of which is widely grown in Asia and the Pacific for its attractive, fragrant flowers.

Cananga odorata (Lamarck) J. D. Hooker & Thomson

Synonym, *Canangium odoratum* (Lamarck) Baillon ex King. **DISTINGUISHABLE** by the alternate leaves arranged in one plane on horizontal branches, and dense clusters of fragrant yellow-green flowers with many ovaries and stamens on a central disk.

Cananga odorata, ylang-ylang, is native to Southeast Asia, possibly originally the Philippines, but was carried by ancient voyagers as far east as Polynesia. It is widely cultivated for its fragrant yellow-green flowers that are used to make leis and to scent coconut oil. The volatile oil in the flowers is distilled and used to make perfume in the Philippines, India, and the East Indies, and the plant is sometimes called perfume tree. **TREE** to 20 m high (66 ft)

Cananga odorata

with leaves in one plane on spirally arranged, horizontal branches. LEAVES simple, alternate, blade oblong to elliptic, 10–35 cm long (4–14 in). FLOWERS anytime during the year; flowers many, borne in stalked axillary clusters. Corolla of six free, linear-lanceolate, yellow-green petals 4–9 cm long (1⅝–3½ in), with several ovaries and numerous stamens forming a disk in the center. FRUIT a cluster of black globose berries 1–2 cm in diameter (⅜–¾ in), originating from the same flower. PROPAGATE by seeds or cuttings. Fertile, moist, but well-drained soils in sunny places are preferred. The tree is grown by itself or sometimes as a street tree, and is naturalized in secondary forests in some places.

Canna CANNACEAE

Canna comprises 8 to 10 herbaceous species, or as many as 50 according to some authors, found in tropical to warm temperate America. The name *Canna* is from the Greek and Latin word for a type of reed. Some produce starchy rhizomes, and many, the canna lilies, are cultivated as ornamentals for their flowers. Two ornamental species of *Canna* are included here.

Canna ×*generalis* L. H. Bailey

Often misidentified as *Canna indica* Linnaeus. DISTINGUISHABLE by the basal, banana-leaf-like foliage often somewhat waxy white on the lower surface and the large flowers that are typically red, or yellow spotted with red.

Canna ×*generalis* forms a complex group of hybrids, often with the tropical American *C. indica* as one parent, widely cultivated for their flowers. Some of the petals are actually sterile but prominent stamens. HERB, perennial, to 1 m high (3¼ ft) or more, arising from a tuberous rhizome. LEAVES simple, alternate, spirally arranged, blade oblong to elliptic, usually 20–50 cm long (8–20 in), sessile, clasping, somewhat waxy on the lower surface. FLOWERS continuously through the year; flowers in two-flowered cymes arranged in a terminal raceme or panicle. Corolla of three fused petals 7–11 cm long (3–4½ in), united at the

Canna ×generalis with yellow flowers

base, red, yellow, or yellow spotted with red, with three similarly colored, petal-like staminodes. **FRUIT** an ellipsoidal capsule. **PROPAGATE** by rhizome division, the method most used. Fertile, moist soils in sunny places are preferred. It is often planted in borders or in large beds in the tropics. In temperate climates it may be grown in greenhouses or conservatories, or outdoors if it is taken indoors in winter. The roots grow rapidly and a barrier may be necessary to keep them confined to the desired area. Old flowering stems should be cut back. Hundreds of cultivars, differing mostly in color or colors of the flowers, have been named.

Canna indica Linnaeus

DISTINGUISHABLE by the basal, banana-leaf-like foliage, terminal panicles of small red flowers, and a warty capsule filled with many black seeds.

Canna indica, Indian shot, is native to tropical America, not India. The seeds are suitable as peashooter ammunition, hence the common name, as well as being used in hula rattles in Hawaii. The plant is widely cultivated for its red or yellow flowers and is commonly naturalized in wet places. It is a parent species for many hybrids, *C. ×generalis,* for example, and its relatively small flowers are not nearly as prominent as those of the hybrids. **HERB,** perennial, to 1.5 m high (5 ft) or more, arising from a tuberous rhizome. LEAVES simple, alternate, spirally arranged, blade lanceolate to elliptic, usually 30–60 cm long (12–24 in). FLOWERS anytime during the year; flowers several, borne in a terminal raceme or panicle. Corolla of three fused lanceolate petals 3–6 cm long (1¼–2½ in), red or yellow, with three similarly colored, petal-like staminodes. FRUIT a many-seeded, ellipsoidal capsule 2.2–3 cm long (⅞–1¼ in), warty on the surface. PROPAGATE by seeds or rhizome division. Moist, fertile soils in sunny places are preferred. It is often used as a border plant to add color.

Canna indica

Carissa APOCYNACEAE

Carissa is a genus of 20 to 37 species found in warm regions between Europe and Australia. At least two are grown as hedge plants or for their attractive white flowers.

Carissa macrocarpa (Ecklon) A. L. P. P. de Candolle

Synonym, *Carissa grandiflora* (E. Meyer) A. L. P. P. de Candolle. DISTINGUISHABLE by the milky sap, two- to four-pronged thorns, leaves that are opposite, dark green, and leathery, prominent white, five-lobed flowers, and edible red drupe.

Carissa macrocarpa, Natal plum, is native to South Africa, where KwaZulu-Natal is one of the provinces, but is widely cultivated in the tropics and subtropics for its attractive foliage and flowers. The name *macrocarpa* is from the Greek words meaning large fruit, accurately describing the large, edible drupe that is used particularly to make a jelly.

Carissa macrocarpa

SHRUB or small tree to 4 m high (13 ft) with milky sap and two- to four-pronged thorns to 5 cm long (2 in), arising in the leaf axils. **LEAVES** simple, opposite, blade ovate to elliptic, 2–7 cm long (¾–3 in), leathery, dark green. **FLOWERS** continuously through the year; flowers solitary and upper axillary or several borne in short terminal clusters. Corolla of fused petals, salverform, white, the tube 1–2.5 cm long (⅜–1 in), the limb 4–7 cm wide (1⅝–3 in) with five narrow, spreading lobes. **FRUIT** a red ovoid drupe to 3 cm long (1¼ in). **PROPAGATE** by seeds or cuttings, the latter for the cultivars. Fertile, moist soils in sunny to partially shaded places are preferred. It is often planted in rows and heavily pruned to form thorny hedges, or it can be grown in tubs. The plant is tolerant of wind and salt spray and does well near the ocean. Several cultivars have been named.

Carludovica CYCLANTHACEAE

Carludovica is a genus of three tropical American palm-like shrubs with leaves that are used for thatch, brooms, and for making mats, and one species is grown as an ornamental.

Carludovica palmata Ruiz & Pavón

DISTINGUISHABLE by the stemless, palm-like habit, long-stalked, fan-shaped leaves, and cone-like inflorescence covered when young by numerous white filaments.

Carludovica palmata, Panama-hat palm, is native to Peru, where it is cultivated for the fiber. Panama hats, originally sold in Panama, are made from its fibers, which are also used to make mats. **PALM-LIKE TREE**, clump forming, to 3 m high (10 ft) or more. **LEAVES** simple, spirally arranged, basal, on a petiole to 2 m long (6½ ft) or more, blade fan-shaped, more or less round, to 80 cm in diameter (32 in), divided to the base into four sections and these further divided into sharply tipped, lanceolate lobes. **FLOWERS** anytime during the year; flowers many, separate male and female flowers mixed in a cylindrical leafless spike surrounded when young by three or four petal-like spathes. Corolla absent but the spadix covered with numerous long, white, filamentous staminodes. **FRUIT** of tightly packed red berries fused together into a syncarp 10–20 cm long (4–8 in). **PROPAGATE** by seeds. Fertile, moist, but well-drained soils in shaded places are preferred. They are widely cultivated as ornamentals because of the palm-like form that gives a tropical look to a garden and are commonly planted in clumps under trees in the tropics. In temperate climates they are grown in greenhouses or outdoors in summer.

Carludovica palmata

Caryota ARECACEAE

Caryota, the genus of fishtail palms, comprises 12 palm species ranging from the islands and mainland of southeastern Asia, an area that used to be called Indo-Malaya, to Australia. These palms are distinguished by the bipinnately compound fronds, very unusual in the palm family Arecaceae.

Caryota mitis Loureiro

DISTINGUISHABLE by the clump-forming palm habit, bipinnately compound leaves with unequally sided leaflets, and hanging panicles of numerous greenish yellow flowers. The similar fishtail palm, *Caryota urens* Linnaeus, toddy palm or wine palm, differs in being monocarpic—it dies after fruiting—and in having solitary rather than clustered trunks, larger fruits, and hanging spikes to 3 m long (10 ft).

Caryota mitis, sometimes called smaller, or lesser, or clustered fishtail palm or Burmese fishtail palm, is native from Myanmar (Burma) to Indonesia but is widely cultivated as a novelty. The fruits contain irritant oxalate crystals that can cause dermatitis and eye problems. Unlike some of the other members of its genus, it does not die after flowering and fruiting. PALM to 13 m high (43 ft) or more, clump forming, monoecious. LEAVES bipinnately compound, alternate, 1–3 m long (3¼–10

Caryota mitis

ft), leaflets unequally sided, one side straight and entire, the other angled and serrate, mostly 12–22 cm long (5–9 in). FLOWERS intermittently during the year; flowers many, separate male and female flowers borne together in axillary panicles of many narrow, hanging spikes to 30 cm long (12 in) or more. Corolla with fused petals, deeply divided into three lobes 4–6 mm long (about ¼ in), purple with yellowish green markings. FRUIT a red subglobose drupe 1.2–1.8 cm long (½–¾ in). PROPAGATE by seeds. Fertile, moist, but well-drained soils in partially shaded places are preferred. It is usually planted by itself in the tropics, forming clumps or screens, or grown as a potted plant when young, and in temperate climates it is grown as a large potted houseplant or in the greenhouse.

Cassia FABACEAE

Cassia comprises about 30 tree species native from Africa to Australia. Some authors recognize this genus as including *Senna* and another genus of the bean family Fabaceae, in which case it would number more than 500 species. *Cassia* differs from *Senna* in having at least three of the stamen filaments curved and elongate, and a pulp-filled pod that does not split open. Many species of *Cassia* are cultivated as ornamentals because of their abundant flowers. Four of the most common species, one a hybrid between two of the others, are included here.

Cassia fistula Linnaeus

DISTINGUISHABLE by the relatively large, pinnately compound leaves, long, hanging racemes of large, yellow, seasonal, five-petaled flowers, and cylindrical pod with seeds embedded in a sticky pulp.

Cassia fistula

Cassia fistula, golden shower tree, sometimes called pudding-pipe tree or Indian laburnum, is native to Southeast Asia but was an early introduction elsewhere in the tropics. It is commonly cultivated, often as an street or specimen tree, because of the hanging yellow racemes that cover the tree during the flowering season. The tree is deciduous and barren for a short period, typically just before flowering. The sticky pulp of the pods is used medicinally in Asia and elsewhere as a laxative, and the seeds are used to make leis in Hawaii. **TREE** to 10 m high (33 ft) or more with tiny linear stipules. LEAVES even-pinnately compound, alternate, with three to eight pairs of leaflets, blades ovate to elliptic, 6–15 cm long (2½–6 in), waxy white on the lower surface. FLOWERS usually seasonal in spring to early fall; flowers many, borne in hanging axillary racemes to 80 cm long (32 in). Corolla of five free, ovate to elliptic, yellow, clawed petals 1.8–4 cm long (¾–1⅝ in). FRUIT a narrow, hanging, cylindrical pod 30–60 cm long (12–24 in), filled with seeds embedded in a sticky pulp. PROPAGATE by scarified seeds. Fertile, well-drained soils in sunny to partially shaded places are preferred.

Cassia grandis Linnaeus

DISTINGUISHABLE by the bipinnately compound leaves and long, hanging racemes of white to pink, seasonal flowers. The similar *Cassia javanica* differs most obviously in its two-lobed stipules and smaller, more lanceolate leaves.

Cassia grandis

Cassia grandis, pink shower tree, is probably native to tropical America, from Brazil to the West Indies, but has long been cultivated for its racemes of pink flowers, often as a street, shade, or park tree, but perhaps less commonly than some of the other shower trees. The tree is deciduous and barren for a short period around flowering time. The sticky pulp of the pod has purgative properties, and the seeds are used for making leis in Hawaii. TREE to 10 m high (33 ft) or more with tiny awl-shaped stipules. LEAVES even-pinnately compound, alternate, mostly with 4 to 16 pairs of leaflets, blades oblong, mostly 4–8 cm long (1⅝–3½ in), fuzzy on the lower surface. FLOW-

ERS seasonally, mostly in spring, somewhat earlier than the other common *Cassia* species; flowers many, borne in hanging axillary racemes mostly 10–25 cm long (4–10 in). Corolla of five free obovate petals 3–4.5 cm long (1¼–1¾ in), pink to white. FRUIT a narrow, two-ribbed cylindrical pod usually 40–60 cm long (16–24 in) with the seeds embedded in a sticky, foul-smelling pulp. PROPAGATE by scarified seeds. Fertile, well-drained soils in sunny places are preferred.

Cassia javanica Linnaeus

Synonym, *Cassia nodosa* Roxburgh, which many have considered to be a separate species. DISTINGUISHABLE by the pinnately compound leaves, two-lobed stipules, leaflets pubescent on the lower surface, and relatively short racemes of pink and white flowers that cover the tree during the flowering season.

Cassia javanica, pink-and-white shower tree, sometimes called apple-blossom shower, is probably native to somewhere from India to New Guinea but has been widely cultivated for a long time. It is commonly cultivated, especially as a street tree, for its relatively short racemes of pink and white flowers that occur during a relatively long flowering season. The tree is sometimes deciduous just before flowering. TREE to 12 m high (40 ft) or sometimes much more, with two-lobed stipules. LEAVES even-pinnately compound, alternate, with 5 to 15 pairs of leaflets, blades oblong to ovate or lanceolate, mostly 1.5–6 cm long (⅝–2½ in), pubescent on the lower surface. FLOWERS seasonally, usually spring and summer; flowers many,

Cassia javanica

borne in relatively stiff racemes to 18 cm long (7 in), typically on short, blunt branches. Corolla of five free ovate to oblong petals 1.5–3 cm long (⅝–1¼ in), pink to white but aging red to yellowish pink, with ten unequal, yellow stamens. FRUIT a narrow cylindrical pod to 50 cm long (20 in), lacking conspicuous seams and sticky pulp. PROPAGATE by scarified seeds and cuttings. Fertile, moist soils in sunny places are preferred. Some authors recognize four varieties but these are sometimes hard to distinguish.

Cassia ×nealii Irwin & Barneby

DISTINGUISHABLE by the tree habit, bipinnately compound leaves, hanging racemes of cream, pink, or yellow petals, and pods not usually forming.

    Cassia ×nealii, rainbow shower, is a hybrid produced by applying pollen from *C. fistula* to *C. javanica* and was first produced in Hawaii about 1925, the name honoring Marie C. Neal, who wrote the classic *In Gardens of Hawai'i.* It can be grown by itself as a specimen tree but is more popular as a street tree, particularly in Hawaii, since it produces a riot or seasonal color, the flowers covering the tree during spring and summer—for a longer period and with a more prolific display than the other shower trees. TREE to 10 m high (33 ft) or more with small two-lobed stipules. LEAVES evenpinnately compound, alternate, mostly with six to nine pairs of leaflets, blades elliptic, mostly 6–12 cm long (2½–5 in). FLOWERS in spring to fall; flowers many, borne in hanging axillary racemes to 80 cm long (32 in) or more. Corolla of five free, ovate to el-

Cassia ×nealii

liptic, cream, yellow, or red petals 1.5–3.5 cm long (⅝–1⅜ in). **Fruit** a narrow, hanging, cylindrical pod but not usually forming. **Propagate** by air layering since cuttings do not readily grow and the hybrid is mostly sterile and seedless. Moist but well-drained soils in sunny places are preferred. This hybrid origin accounts for the variety of colors of the flowers. Several cultivars have been named, differing mostly in flower color.

Catalpa BIGNONIACEAE

Catalpa is a genus of 11 to 13 tree species found in temperate North America and East Asia, with several species in the West Indies. Some are used in their native range for timber, and several are planted as ornamentals.

Catalpa longissima (Jacquin) Dumont de Courset

Distinguishable by the tree habit, leaves that are simple and opposite, panicles of white, bell-shaped, two-lipped flowers, and a linear capsule containing hairy seeds.

Catalpa longissima, yokewood, is native to the Caribbean Islands but is widely cultivated for its timber, and widely if not commonly as an ornamental. **Tree** to 15 m high (50 ft) with gray, furrowed bark. **Leaves** simple, opposite, blade ovate to lanceolate, 5–14 cm long (2–6 in). **Flowers** continuously through the year; flowers several, borne in terminal or subterminal panicles. Corolla of fused petals, bell-shaped, 2.5–3.5 cm long (1–1⅜ in),

Catalpa longissima

two-lipped with five rounded lobes, white to pink with purple lines within. **FRUIT** a hanging linear capsule 30–60 cm long (12–24 in), containing many hairy seeds. **PROPAGATE** by seeds or cuttings. Moist but well-drained soils in sunny places are preferred. It is typically planted as a shade, park, or street tree for its attractive, though relatively small, white to pink flowers.

Catharanthus APOCYNACEAE

Catharanthus is a genus of eight species, all native to Madagascar and related to periwinkles (*Vinca* spp.). The genus is important medicinally, and one species is well known in cultivation. The name *Catharanthus* is from the Greek words meaning flower without blemish.

Catharanthus roseus (Linnaeus) G. Don

Synonyms, *Lochnera rosea* (Linnaeus) Reichenbach and *Vinca rosea* Linnaeus. **DISTINGUISHABLE** by the subshrub habit, milky sap, leaves that are opposite and elliptic to oblanceolate, and paired flowers with a spreading white or rose-purple corolla limb.

Catharanthus roseus

Catharanthus roseus, Madagascar periwinkle, is widely cultivated for its pink or white flowers. It is often grown in planters, as a border, and as a ground cover in the tropics, and indoors in cooler climates. The sap is poisonous, as in many other members of the dogbane family Apocynaceae, but also contains vincristine, an extract used to treat leukemia. **SUBSHRUB**, perennial, to 70 cm high (28 in) with milky sap. **LEAVES** simple, opposite, blade elliptic to oblanceolate, 3–9 cm long (1¼–3½ in), glossy green. **FLOWERS** continuously through the year; flowers in pairs at the leaf axils but appearing terminal. Corolla of fused petals, salverform, tube 2–3 cm long (¾–1¼ in), limb 3–5.5 cm wide (1¼–2¼ in) with five spreading, rounded lobes, rose-purple or white with a red throat as in 'Bright Eyes'. **FRUIT** a pair of cylindrical pod-like segments 2–3.5 cm long (¾–1⅜ in), fuzzy and longitudinally grooved. **PROPAGATE** by seeds or cuttings. Fertile, moist, but well-drained soils in sunny to partially shaded places are preferred. Its form becomes unattractive with age and replanting or pruning is sometimes required. It may become a naturalized weed, especially in dry habitats. Several cultivars have been named, some with a colorful center of the flower, the eye.

Celosia AMARANTHACEAE

Celosia is a genus of about 60 species, collectively called cockscombs, of tropical Africa and America. Many are weedy but some, mostly of hybrid origin, are grown as ornamentals.

Celosia argentea Linnaeus

DISTINGUISHABLE by the herbaceous habit, alternate leaves, and often elaborate inflorescences composed of colorful dry bracts with tiny, inconspicuous flowers between them.

Celosia argentea is probably native to tropical Africa but has long been cultivated, often in gardens, planters, or pots, for its colorful inflorescences. **HERB**, annual, to 1.8 m high (6 ft). **LEAVES** simple, alternate, blade lanceolate or ovate to narrowly elliptic, 10–16 cm long (4–6 in), sometimes with a large red blotch ('Cristata') or often suffused with purple. **FLOWERS** continuously through the year after maturity; flowers numerous, borne in narrow pink to purple spikes, rarely orange or yellow as in 'Golden Spire' and 'Flame', or these variously crested at the top. Corolla of five tiny free tepals usually white with pink at the tip. **FRUIT** a small dry utricle, containing a single shiny black seed. **PROPAGATE** by seeds. Fertile, moist, but well-drained soils in sunny places are

Celosia argentea with a simple spike

Celosia argentea 'Cristata' with a crested inflorescence

preferred. Many variations have been named and are so diverse that they hardly look like the same species. One has a narrow spike; another is plumose, variety *plumosa* (Burvenich) Voss or 'Flame'; and a third is larger and variously crested, variety *cristata* (Linnaeus) Kuntze or 'Cristata', sometimes recognized as a separate species, *C. cristata* Linnaeus.

Centratherum ASTERACEAE

Centratherum is a genus of two Old and New World tropical species, one of which is cultivated as an ornamental.

Centratherum punctatum Cassini

DISTINGUISHABLE by the alternate leaves, winged petioles, toothed leaf margins, and lavender flower heads composed of unequal bracts (the outer ones leaf-like) and light purple disk florets (the outer ones longer than the inner).

Centratherum punctatum, Brazilian button flower, is native to the Old World tropics from the Philippines to Australia, not to Brazil, but is widely if not commonly cultivated in the tropics as a garden herb for its light purple flower heads. **HERB**, erect, to 50 cm high (20 in) with pubescent stems. **LEAVES** simple, alternate, blade ovate to spoon-shaped, 2.5–8 cm long (1–3½ in) with a winged petiole and toothed margins. **FLOWERS** continuously through the year after maturity; flowers in stalked terminal heads surrounded by two types of bracts, the

Centratherum punctatum

outer larger and leaf-like, the inner small. Ray florets none. Disk florets many, light purple, mostly 9–14 mm long (⅜–½ in), the central ones distinctly shorter than the marginal ones. **FRUIT** a pale linear achene covered with upward pointing bristles. **PROPAGATE** by achenes. Moist but well-drained soils in sunny places are preferred. It is attractive in mass plantings or as a border.

Cestrum SOLANACEAE

Cestrum comprises 175 to 250 tropical American shrub and small tree species, many cultivated for their conspicuous or fragrant flowers and some ultilized for their medicinal properties. Two of the most common ornamental species are included here.

Cestrum diurnum Linnaeus
DISTINGUISHABLE by the shrubby habit, alternate leaves, rounded leaf

Cestrum diurnum

tips, racemes or panicles of tubular white corollas with the five lobes folded back, and daytime fragrance.

Cestrum diurnum, day cestrum, sometimes called day-blooming cestrum or day jessamine, is native to Central America but is widely if not commonly cultivated in the tropics for its small flowers that though not very attractive are fragrant in the daytime. The fruit is poisonous when eaten in quantity. **SHRUB** to 4 m high (13 ft) or more. **LEAVES** simple, alternate, blade elliptic to ovate, 3–13 cm long (1¼–5 in), tip rounded. **FLOWERS** most of the time through the year; flowers many, borne in axillary and terminal racemes and panicles. Corolla with fused petals, tubular, 1.1–1.5 cm long (⅜–⅝ in) with five spreading or recurved lobes 1–2 mm long (about ¹⁄₃₂–¹⁄₁₆ in), white or sometimes with purple at the tip. **FRUIT** a black to purple subglobose berry 6–10 mm in diameter (¼–⅜ in). **PROPAGATE** by seeds or cuttings. Fertile, moist, but well-drained soils in sunny places are preferred. The plant is typically grown by itself or in hedges but it is not nearly as popular as *C. nocturnum* which is more fragrant, and fragrant at the right time, nighttime.

Cestrum nocturnum Linnaeus

DISTINGUISHABLE by the alternate leaves, acute leaf tips, panicles of many tubular, pale yellow flowers with straight lobes, and powerful nighttime fragrance. It differs from *Cestrum diurnum* most obviously by the time of fragrance and the corolla lobes that are erect rather than curved back. *Cestrum elegans* Schlechter, also cultivated, differs most obviously in having pink-purple flowers.

Cestrum nocturnum, night cestrum, sometimes called night-blooming cestrum, night jessamine, or queen of the night, is native to tropical America but is widely cultivated in the tropics and warm temperate regions for its flowers, which have a strong, sometimes overpowering fragrance that pervades the night air. The fruit is somewhat poisonous to humans. **SHRUB**, erect, to 5 m high (16½ ft). **LEAVES** simple, alternate, blade elliptic or ovate to lanceolate, 6–16 cm long (2½–6 in). **FLOWERS** continuously through the year; flowers many, borne in axillary panicles. Corolla with fused petals, tu-

Cestrum nocturnum

bular, tube 1.5–1.8 cm long (⅝–¾ in) with five short, straight lobes 3–4 mm long (about ⅛–¼ in), pale yellow to greenish. **FRUIT** a white subglobose berry 6–10 mm in diameter (¼–⅜ in). **PROPAGATE** by seeds and cuttings. Fertile, moist soils in sunny to partially shaded places are preferred. It is often grown beside houses, in hedges, and along shrubbery borders. Periodic pruning is required to keep it from becoming scraggly. It can become an invasive weed in the tropics.

Chlorophytum LILIACEAE

Chlorophytum, the name of the genus from the Greek words meaning green plant, comprises 250 to 300 rhizomatous, perennial, herbaceous species distributed throughout the Old World tropics, especially in India and Africa. Their only significant uses are as ornamentals.

Chlorophytum comosum (Thunberg) Jacques

Synonym, *Chlorophytum elatum* R. Brown and sometimes misidentified as *C. capense* (Linnaeus) Voss. **DISTINGUISHABLE** by the rosette-forming, often variegated leaves, drooping inflorescences that produce roots where they touch the ground, and small flowers with six spreading white tepals.

    Chlorophytum comosum, spider plant, is native to southern Africa but is widely cultivated in subtropical and tropical areas for its attractive, often variegated foliage. **HERB,** rosette forming, from a tuberous rhizome, with plantlets on the drooping inflorescences rooting where they touch the ground. **LEAVES** simple, in tufts, linear-lanceolate, mostly 15–40 × 1–2 cm (6–16 × ⅜–¾ in), green or variegated with the margins or midline white to yellow. **FLOWERS** continuously through the year; flowers several, borne in clusters, each cluster in the axil of a bract in a raceme 15–35 cm long (6–14 in) that often has a leafy shoot near the end. Corolla of six free elliptic to oblong tepals 7–12 mm long (¼–½ in), white, sometimes fading to pink. **FRUIT** a leathery capsule, deeply three-lobed, wider than long. **PROPAGATE** by offsets, the usual method. Fertile, moist, but well-drained soils in shaded places are preferred. It is often used as a ground cover or border plant and is grown indoors in pots or hanging baskets. Several cultivars have been named based on differences in foliage colors and patterns, one of the most common of which is 'Variegatum'.

Chlorophytum comosum 'Variegatum'

Chrysalidocarpus ARECACEAE

Chrysalidocarpus, the name of the genus from the Greek words meaning chrysalis fruit, referring to the resemblance of some to butterfly pupae, comprises 20 palm species found in the Comoro Islands and Madagascar. Some have edible buds and some are cultivated as ornamental plants in tropical and subtropical gardens.

Chrysalidocarpus lutescens H. Wendland

Synonym, *Dypsis lutescens* (H. Wendland) Beentje & Dransfield, a name used by some authors. DISTINGUISHABLE by the clump-forming palm habit, yellowish petioles and midribs, and large axillary panicles of yellow to black drupes.

Chrysalidocarpus lutescens is native to Madagascar, where it is now rare, but is one of the most popular ornamental palms in the tropics, where it is widely cultivated in pots, planters, as a screen, windbreak, or by itself as a specimen plant because of its attractive stems and clump-forming habit. It has many common names, including butterfly palm, golden cane palm, yellow cane palm, yellow palm, bamboo palm, and areca palm, misleading since there is a different palm genus *Areca*. The name *lutescens* comes from the Greek word for yellow, in reference to its yellow stems. PALM to 10 m high (33 ft), clump forming, with conspicuously ringed stems to 12 cm in diameter (5 in), monoecious. LEAVES pinnately compound, in outline narrowly elliptic to 2.5 m long (8¼ ft), arching, divided into 80 to 100 linear leaflets, each with a yellow to somewhat orange petiole and midrib. FLOWERS intermittently during the year; flowers many, unisexual, in large axillary panicles to 80 cm long (32 in). Corolla of three yellow-green petals about 3 mm long (about ⅛ in). FRUIT an ovoid yellow to violet-black drupe usually 1.5–2 cm long (⅝–¾ in). PROPAGATE by seeds or division. Moist but well-drained soils in sunny or partially shaded places are preferred.

Chrysalidocarpus lutescens

Chrysanthemum ASTERACEAE

Chrysanthemum comprises various species, some of which had been considered by some authors to be part of the genus *Dendranthema*. Some are cultivated as ornamentals, forming hybrids that are difficult to classify.

Chrysanthemum ×morifolium Ramatuelle

Synonym, *Dendranthema ×grandiflorum* Kitamura. DISTINGUISHABLE by the alternate, downy gray leaves, deeply lobed leaf margins, and heads with many colorful ray florets.

    Chrysanthemum ×morifolium, chrysanthemum, sometimes called florist's chrysanthemum or just mum, is a temperate species native to eastern Asia but has been cultivated and modified for so long that the original form is unknown. HERB, perennial, coarse, to 1 m high (3¼ ft) or more. LEAVES simple, alternate, blade ovate, 4–15 cm long (1⅝–6 in), the margins deeply lobed, the surface often downy gray. FLOWERS anytime during the year in the tropics; flowers in one to several large terminal heads surrounded by two to four series of bracts. Ray florets 10 to 25, or many in some cultivars, variable in size and color: yellow, orange, red, pink, or white. Disk florets numerous, often yellowish. FRUIT an achene, infrequently formed in cultivation. PROPAGATE by cuttings or achenes. Plants are adaptable to most soils in sunny places and are grown for their variously colored flower heads in the garden or along borders, as indoor potted plants, or as cut flowers in temperate to tropical regions. Many cultivars in several dis-

Chrysanthemum ×morifolium, one of many cultivars

tinct groups are recognized. There is so much variation in this hybrid complex that the cultivars may look as though they hardly belong to the same species.

Chrysophyllum SAPOTACEAE

Chrysophyllum is a genus of 80 to 100 species found in tropical America and from Africa to New Caledonia. Many are utilized for their timber, and a few are cultivated as ornamentals because of their attractive leaves. The name *Chrysophyllum* is aptly derived from the Greek words meaning golden and leaf.

Chrysophyllum oliviforme Linnaeus

DISTINGUISHABLE by the tree habit, milky sap, leaves that are alternate and glossy green with the lower surface covered with a velvety, copper-colored pubescence, and small, oblong, purple berries. A related ornamental and commercial species, *Chrysophyllum cainito* Linnaeus, star apple, differs in having larger, round, and edible fruits and larger leaves mostly 10–16 cm long (4–6 in).

Chrysophyllum oliviforme, satin leaf, is native to the Caribbean area but is widely cultivated as an ornamental. Though its flowers and fruits are inconspicuous, the attractive leaves, covered on the lower surface by a copper-colored, velvety layer, make it attractive, especially when planted as a street or shade tree. TREE to 10 m high (33 ft) with milky sap. LEAVES simple, alternate, blade ovate to oblong, 3–10 cm long (1¼–4 in), dark glossy green on the upper surface, densely copper-

Chrysophyllum oliviforme

colored on the lower. **FLOWERS** anytime during the year but mostly in late summer to early fall with mature fruits in winter; flowers several to many, borne in axillary clusters. Corolla of five free ovate petals 4–6 mm long (about ¼ in), greenish white. **FRUIT** an oblong purple berry 1.3–2.7 cm long (½–1⅛ in), containing a hard black seed. **PROPAGATE** by seeds or cuttings. Fertile, moist, but well-drained soils in sunny places are preferred.

Chrysothemis GESNERIACEAE

Chrysothemis is a tropical American genus of seven perennial herbaceous species, at least two of which are cultivated for their attractive and colorful flowers. The genus is named after Chrysothemis, a daughter of Agamemnon, a hero of the Trojan War.

Chrysothemis pulchella (Donn ex Simms) Decaisne

DISTINGUISHABLE by the opposite, dark green leaves, toothed leaf margins, winged red calyx, and orange corolla.

Chrysothemis pulchella, dozakie, is native to Central America and the Caribbean but is widely cultivated for its red and orange flowers. The name *pulchella* is from the Latin word for beautiful, an appropriate name for this colorful herb. **HERB**, perennial, low growing, somewhat fleshy, to 90 cm high (36 in), arising from tuberous roots. **LEAVES** simple, opposite, blade ovate, 10–25 cm long (4–10 in), margins toothed, surface wrinkled and scabrous, lower surface purple. **FLOWERS** continuously through the year; flowers several, borne in short-stalked,

Chrysothemis pulchella

upper axillary umbels. Corolla with fused petals, broadly tubular, somewhat two-lipped, four-lobed, 1.6–3 cm long (⅝–1¼ in), orange, enclosed in a prominent red, five-winged calyx. **FRUIT** a capsule, infrequently formed in cultivation. **PROPAGATE** by cuttings and bulbils. Moist surfaces in shady places are preferred. It does well on rocky surfaces, such as rock walls, and is often grown as an indoor potted plant.

Citharexylum VERBENACEAE

Citharexylum comprises 70 to 100 tree and shrub species ranging from the southeastern United States to Uruguay. Some are utilized for their timber, and a few are cultivated as ornamentals. The name *Citharexylum* is from the Greek words meaning zither wood, and common names for the useful and ornamental members of the genus are zither tree or fiddlewood. Two of the most common ornamental species are included here.

Citharexylum caudatum

Citharexylum caudatum
Linnaeus

DISTINGUISHABLE by the tree habit, opposite, oblong to obovate leaves, stiff terminal racemes of small, five-lobed flowers, and small dark drupes.

Citharexylum caudatum, a fiddlewood with no specific, well-known common name, is native from Mexico to northern South America and the West Indies but is widely cultivated elsewhere in the tropics as an ornamental tree. In some places, Hawaii, for example, the fruits are readily dispersed by birds, which has led to the tree becoming weedy in wet areas in the mountains. **TREE** or shrub to 15 m high (50 ft) or more. LEAVES simple, opposite, blade oblong to obovate, 7–16 cm long (3–6 in), somewhat leathery and glossy green with a blunt tip and green petiole. FLOWERS anytime during the year; flowers many, borne in narrow, stiff, terminal racemes. Corolla with fused petals, funnel-shaped, 4–7 mm long (about ¼ in) with five rounded, spreading lobes, white. FRUIT a purplish black subglobose drupe 5–8 mm long (about ¼ in). PROPAGATE by seeds or cuttings. Relatively moist soils in sunny places are preferred. It is typically planted as a street or garden tree.

Citharexylum spinosum Linnaeus

Synonym, *Citharexylum quadrangulare* Jacquin. DISTINGUISHABLE by the tree habit, leaves that are opposite and elliptic to ovate, and hanging axillary and terminal inflorescences of small, white, fragrant flowers.

Citharexylum spinosum, a fiddlewood with no other well-known common name, is native to the West Indies and northern South America. Its flowers are small but fragrant. In some places, Fiji, for example, birds readily disperse the fruits and the tree has become an invasive weed. It apparently sometimes hybridizes with *C. caudatum*. TREE to 15 m high (50 ft). LEAVES simple, opposite or in whorls of three, blade elliptic to ovate, usually 4–20 cm long (1⅝–8 in) with an acute tip and orange petiole. FLOWERS anytime during the year; flowers many, borne in long, hanging, axillary and terminal racemes and narrow panicles 20–40 cm long (8–16 in). Corolla with fused petals, bell-shaped, 6–9 mm long (¼–⅜ in) with five rounded lobes, mostly white, fragrant. FRUIT a red to black subglobose drupe 7–10 mm long (¼–⅜ in). PROPAGATE by

Citharexylum spinosum

seeds. Fertile, moist, but well-drained soils in sunny places are preferred. It is often grown as a shade or street tree but the relatively weak wood is susceptible to breakage in strong winds.

Cleome CAPPARIDACEAE

Cleome is a genus of about 150 species found throughout the tropics, some of which are utilized medicinally or for edible seeds, and some are cultivated as ornamentals, especially for cut flowers.

Cleome speciosa Rafinesque

Synonym, *Gynandropsis speciosa* (Rafinesque) A. P. de Candolle. DISTINGUISHABLE by the alternate, palmately lobed leaves, spider-like flowers with long, white stamen filaments, and a stalked, linear capsule. A very similar tropical American species, *Cleome spinosa* Jacquin, also called spider flower, is also sometimes cultivated and differs most obviously in having glandular pubescent foliage and small spines.

Cleome speciosa

Cleome speciosa, spider flower, is native to tropical America from Mexico to Peru but is widely if not commonly cultivated for its unusual, strongly scented flowers with long stamens reminiscent of spider legs. HERB, annual, to 1.5 m high (5 ft) with glabrous stems and foliage. LEAVES palmately compound, alternate, blade with three to seven oblanceolate to elliptic lobes 2–16 cm long (¾–6 in). FLOWERS anytime during the year after maturity; flowers many, each subtended by a small leaf-like bract, borne in terminal racemes. Corolla of four free, oblanceolate, pink to white petals 2.8–3.8 cm long (1⅛–1½ in), stamens six, on filaments 3–6 cm long (1¼–2½ in), ovary long stalked. FRUIT a linear capsule to 8 cm long (3½ in) or more on a long stalk above the pedicel but infrequently formed in cultivation. PROPAGATE by seeds. Moist but well-drained soils in sunny places are preferred. It is often planted by itself in gardens, along borders, or around houses.

Clerodendrum VERBENACEAE

Clerodendrum comprises about 400 tree, shrub, and climber species found throughout warm regions but particularly in the Old World tropics, many of which, called glorybowers, are cultivated for their flowers. Seven of the most widespread and common ornamental species are included here.

Clerodendrum buchananii (Roxburgh) Walpers

Synonyms, *Clerodendrum fallax* (Lindley) Bakhuizen and *C. speciosissimum* Van Geert ex Morren. DISTINGUISH-ABLE by the opposite, fuzzy, nearly round leaves and red, funnel-shaped flowers in a loose terminal panicle. It has larger flowers than the similar *C. paniculatum,* in a loose rather than ovoid inflorescence.

Clerodendrum buchananii, Java glorybower, sometimes called red clerodendrum, is native to Malaysia but is widely cultivated for its red flowers and sometimes becomes adventive or fully naturalized in disturbed places. SHRUB, spreading, to 2 m high (6½ ft) or more. LEAVES simple, opposite or in whorls of three, blade broadly ovate or

Clerodendrum buchananii

heart-shaped to nearly round, 10–20 cm long (4–8 in), fuzzy on both surfaces. **FLOWERS** continuously through the year; flowers many, borne in loose terminal panicles. Corolla with fused petals, funnel-shaped, tube 2–3 cm long (¾–1¼ in), limb deeply divided into five oblanceolate, spreading lobes 1–1.8 cm long (⅜–¾ in), bright red, with four long, protruding stamens. **FRUIT** a four-lobed drupe 6–9 mm in diameter (¼–⅜ in), red turning to black at maturity. **PROPAGATE** by seeds or cuttings. Moist, well-drained soils in partially shaded places are preferred. It is often grown by itself or as a border plant. Some authors recognize the ornamental plant as variety *fallax*.

Clerodendrum indicum (Linnaeus) Kuntze

Synonym, *Clerodendrum siphonatus* R. Brown. **DISTINGUISHABLE** by the erect, scarcely branching habit, whorled leaves, and axillary clusters of white flowers, each with a very long, narrow, drooping, four-lobed corolla tube.

Clerodendrum indicum

Clerodendrum indicum, tube flower, is native to Southeast Asia but is widely cultivated for its long, white flowers. It is not as common as some of the other clerodendrums, perhaps because the plant does not have an attractive form to go along with its flowers. **SHRUB**, erect, scarcely branching, to 4 m high (13 ft). **LEAVES** simple, in whorls of four, blade narrowly elliptic, usually 10–23 cm long (4–9 in) on a very short petiole. **FLOWERS** continuously through the year; flowers mostly three to six in stalked clusters arising from each of the four leaf axils at a node. Corolla with fused petals, narrowly tubular, 7.5–11 cm long (3–4½ in), limb divided into five elliptic lobes 1.2–2 cm long (½–¾ in), cream with red markings in the throat, with four long, protruding stamens. **FRUIT** a metallic blue-black, four-lobed drupe 7–10 mm in diameter (¼–⅜ in). **PROPAGATE** by seeds or root suckers. Moist but well-drained soils in sunny places are preferred. It is often grown as a border or specimen plant but is not suitable for a hedge because of its scarcely branching habit.

Clerodendrum myricoides (Hochstetter) Vatke

Synonym, *Clerodendrum ugandense* Prain, a name used by some authors. **DISTINGUISHABLE** by the shrubby habit, opposite leaves, and axillary, blue, two-lipped flowers, each with four long, protruding stamens.

Clerodendrum myricoides, Ugandan glorybower, is native to tropical East Africa and was originally named from Kenya, not Uganda, but is widely cultivated for its blue flowers, reminiscent of blue butterflies. It is sometimes called blue butterfly bush or blue glorybower. **SHRUB** to 2 m high (6½ ft) or more. **LEAVES** simple, opposite or in whorls of three, blade elliptic to oblanceolate, 4–15 cm long (1⅝–6 in). **FLOWERS** continuously through the year; flowers several, borne in terminal and sometimes axillary panicles. Corolla with fused petals, salverform, 1.2–1.6 cm long (½–⅝ in), unequally two-lipped, lobes five, spreading, the upper four lobes light blue, mostly 1–1.5 cm long (⅜–⅝ in), the lower, longer one dark blue to purple, with four long, protruding stamens. **FRUIT** a black, four-lobed, subglobose drupe 8–10 mm in diameter (¼–⅜ in). **PROPAGATE** by seeds or cuttings. Well-

Clerodendrum myricoides

drained soils in partially shaded places are preferred. It is an attractive shrub planted by itself as a small specimen plant or as a border plant; it is grown as a potted plant in temperate climates. The ornamental type is called 'Ugandense' though some authors consider the species to be correctly called *C. ugandense.*

Clerodendrum paniculatum Linnaeus

DISTINGUISHABLE by the shrubby habit, opposite, lobed leaves, scaly lower leaf surface, and dense, cone-shaped axillary panicles of red flowers. It is similar to *Clerodendrum buchananii,* which differs in having unlobed fuzzy leaves and larger flowers in loose panicles.

Clerodendrum paniculatum, pagoda flower, is native from India to Malaysia but is widely cultivated in the tropics for its red flowers, arranged in large, ovoid inflorescences. It is often planted by itself or as a colorful border plant but sometimes becomes naturalized as a weed.

Clerodendrum paniculatum

Since the plant often does not form seeds, however, it usually does not spread far from where it was planted or dumped. SHRUB to 2 m high (6½ ft) or more. LEAVES simple, opposite, blade broadly ovate, usually 5–30 cm long (2–12 in), prominently three- to seven-lobed (lower leaves) to entire, with a heart-shaped base and scaly lower surface. FLOWERS seasonally, mostly in spring to early fall; flowers many, borne in large, axillary and terminal, ovoid panicles. Corolla with fused petals, salverform, tube red, 1.2–1.8 cm long (½–¾ in), limb spreading, four-lobed, red-orange, 7–8 mm long (about ¼ in), with four long, protruding stamens. FRUIT a bluish black drupe, infrequently formed in cultivation. PROPAGATE by seeds or cuttings. Moist but well-drained soils in sunny places are preferred.

Clerodendrum quadriloculare (Blanco) Merrill

DISTINGUISHABLE by the large size, leaves that are opposite and purple underneath, and dense, flat-topped panicles of white tubular flowers.

Clerodendrum quadriloculare is native to the Philippines and is sometimes called Philippine glorybower but is cultivated elsewhere in the tropics for its large clusters of beautiful, long, white, *Ixora*-like flowers as well as for its colorful foliage, purple on the lower surface, making up for flowers that appear only part of the year. This distinctive foliage is unique among the commonly cultivated glorybowers. The species has only more recently become popular in cultivation. SHRUB or small tree to 4 m high (13 ft) or more. LEAVES simple, opposite, elliptic to ovate, 9–22 cm long (3½–9 in), strongly veined and purple on the lower surface. FLOWERS seasonally, unlike most other clerodendrums, usually in winter and spring, sometimes more than once in the same season; flowers many, borne in short, dense, flat-topped, terminal panicles. Corolla with fused petals, salverform, tube narrow, 8–11 cm long (3½–4½ in), pink, limb deeply divided into five spreading, narrowly elliptic white lobes 1.5–2.4 cm long (⅝–⅞ in), with four long, protruding stamens. FRUIT a four-lobed drupe, infrequently formed in cultivation. PROPAGATE by cuttings. Moist but well-drained soils in sunny places are preferred. It is often grown by itself as a specimen plant and is taller than most other clerodendrums.

Clerodendrum quadriloculare

Clerodendrum thomsonae I. B. Balfour

DISTINGUISHABLE by the vine-like habit, leaves that are opposite and dark green, and stalked axillary clusters of flowers with red corolla and white or purplish calyx.

Clerodendrum thomsonae, bleeding heart, is native to tropical West Africa but is widely and commonly cultivated for its flowers. It differs from most other clerodendrums in its weak-stemmed habit and is often grown as a border plant, by itself, or is trained on trellises to be a vine; it is grown as a potted plant in temperate climates. VINE-LIKE SHRUB to 3 m high (10 ft). LEAVES simple, opposite, blade elliptic to ovate, 6–14 cm long (2½–6 in). FLOWERS continuously through the year; flowers many, borne in stalked axillary and terminal clusters. Corolla with fused petals, salverform, tube 1.5–2.5 cm long (⅝–1 in), limb deeply divided into five spreading elliptic lobes 7–10 mm long (¼–⅜ in), red, with four long, protruding stamens that curl up with age, and surrounded by the white or purplish, deeply four-lobed calyx. FRUIT a four-lobed, subglobose drupe 6–10 mm long (¼–⅜ in), glossy black with a red matrix connecting the four segments. PROPAGATE by seeds or cuttings. Fertile soils in sunny or partially shaded places are preferred, and the plant is drought resistant.

Clerodendrum thomsonae

Clerodendrum wallichii Merrill

Synonym, *Clerodendrum nutans* Wallich ex D. Don. DISTINGUISHABLE by the shrubby habit, opposite leaves, hanging racemes of white, two-lipped flowers, and stamens that are white, long, and protruding.

Clerodendrum wallichii, which lacks a widely recognized common name, is native to Asia from southern China to Pakistan but is widely if not commonly cultivated in warm regions for its white flowers, forming cascades. With the exception of *C. quadriloculare,* it is less common than the other ornamental clerodendrums. **SHRUB** to 2 m high (6½ ft) or more, with four-angled stems. **LEAVES** simple, opposite, blade oblanceolate to oblong, 7–25 cm long (3–10 in), usually with a long-attenuate tip. **FLOWERS** continuously through the year; flowers many, borne in hanging, loose, terminal panicles. Corolla with fused petals, salverform, tube 1–2 cm long (⅜–¾ in), limb spreading, deeply divided into five obovate to oblong lobes 2–3 cm long (¾–1¼ in), white, with four long, protruding stamens. **FRUIT** a black, four-lobed, sub-

Clerodendrum wallichii

globose drupe. **PROPAGATE** by seeds. Fertile soils in partially shaded places are preferred. It is usually grown by itself as a specimen plant to highlight the hanging racemes.

Clitoria FABACEAE

Clitoria is a genus of 30 to 70 shrub, herb, vine, or sometimes tree species found throughout the tropics and subtropics, some of which are cultivated as ornamental climbers.

Clitoria ternatea Linnaeus

DISTINGUISHABLE by the herbaceous viny habit, pinnately compound leaves, spreading, butterfly-like flowers with a rich blue corolla and yellow or white center, and flattened, linear pod.

    Clitoria ternatea, butterfly pea, is probably native to tropical America but has long been cultivated for its large, unusual, blue flowers, an un-

Clitoria ternatea

common color in tropical gardens. VINE, perennial with a woody root, climbing over low vegetation. LEAVES odd-pinnately compound, alternate, leaflets mostly five, rarely as many as nine, blades ovate to elliptic, 2–7 cm long (¾–3 in). FLOWERS continuously through the year after maturity; flowers solitary or paired on a short axillary stalk. Corolla papilionaceous, 3–6 cm long (1¼–2½ in) with four unequal petals, one of which forms an oval limb, rich blue with yellow or white at the base, surrounding the ten fused stamens. FRUIT a flattened, linear-oblong pod 8–12 cm long (3½–5 in). PROPAGATE by seeds or cuttings. Fertile, moist, but well-drained soils in sunny places are preferred. It is often grown in gardens, sometimes as a biennial, on trellises and fences but sometimes escapes from cultivation to become naturalized in disturbed places.

Clivia AMARYLLIDACEAE

Clivia, the genus of kaffir lilies, comprises four southern African stemless, herbaceous species that are cultivated for their attractive flowers.

Clivia miniata Regel

DISTINGUISHABLE by the arching, strap-shaped leaves in two opposite rows and umbels of attractive orange, funnel-shaped, seasonal flowers.

Clivia miniata is a kaffir lily that is native to warm forest habitats of KwaZulu-Natal Province, South Africa, but is widely cultivated for its orange, seasonal flowers. HERB arising from a bulb, stemless. LEAVES in two opposite ranks, strap-shaped, arching, 20–60 × 3–7 cm (8–24 ×

1¼–3 in), without a midrib. **FLOWERS** seasonally, spring and summer; flowers 12 to 20 in short-stalked umbels, each on a pedicel 2.5–5 cm long (1–2 in). Corolla of fused tepals, funnel-shaped, 6–8 cm long (2½–3½ in), orange-red with a yellow throat, with six rounded lobes. **FRUIT** an ovoid, red, three-seeded berry. **PROPAGATE** by division or seeds. Moist but well-drained soils in shaded places are preferred. It is often grown in tropical gardens as a border plant, and in pots indoors or in the greenhouse in temperate areas.

Clivia miniata

Clusia CLUSIACEAE

Clusia is a genus of about 145 tropical and subtropical American shrub and tree species, including some stranglers. Some are useful as medicinal plants, some for their resin burned as incense, and a few as ornamentals.

Clusia rosea Jacquin

Synonym, *Clusia major* (Jacquin) Linnaeus. **DISTINGUISHABLE** by the tree habit, leaves that are large and leathery, conspicuous white flowers of six to eight petals, and round fruit splitting open from the top along seven to nine seams and containing many red seeds.

Clusia rosea, autograph tree, is native to the West Indies but is widely cultivated for its flowers, attractive leaves, and unusual, crab-like fruits, which are used in dried flower arrangements. The name autograph tree comes from the fact that the leaves with, or without, names scratched on the surface last for a long time. The leaves have also been used as substitutes for playing cards. The plant is sometimes called pitch apple, copey, or Scotch attorney. **TREE** to 10 m high (33 ft) or more with yellow

Clusia rosea

sap, often beginning as an epiphyte or banyan-like strangler on other trees and forming hanging aerial roots. Leaves simple, opposite, blade obovate, 8–20 cm long (3½–8 in), thick, leathery, dark green. Flowers intermittently during the year; flowers solitary, terminal or borne in the axils. Corolla of six to eight free, obovate to nearly round petals 3–5 cm long (1¼–2 in), often notched at the tip, white aging to pink, surrounding the numerous yellow stamens. Fruit a globose green capsule 5–8 cm in diameter (2–3½ in), splitting open from the top along seven to nine or more seams, each valve with a persistent stigma lobe, to release the numerous red seeds. The opened fruit, put upside down on the ground, looks somewhat like a crab. Propagate by seeds or cuttings. Well-drained soils in sunny or partially shaded places are preferred. The plant is usually grown as a specimen or street tree and does well in exposed coastal areas because it is resistant to salt spray. In temperate areas it is grown indoors or in the greenhouse as a foliage plant.

Coccoloba POLYGONACEAE

Coccoloba is a genus of about 150 tree, shrub, and liana species found in tropical and subtropical America, some with edible fruits, a minor use, and some cultivated as ornamentals.

Coccoloba uvifera (Linnaeus) Linnaeus

Distinguishable by the tree habit, kidney-shaped or nearly round leaves with reddish veins, narrow racemes of tiny white flowers, and clusters of grape-like fruits.

Coccoloba uvifera, sea grape, sometimes called pigeon plum, is native to tropical America but is widely cultivated for its attractive, platter-like leaves. The name *uvifera* is from the Latin words meaning, bearing clusters of grapes. In tropical America the plant is useful as timber for making cabinets, as fruit for making jelly, as a dye plant, and as an ingredient in various medicines. TREE to 6 m high (20 ft) or more. LEAVES simple, alternate, blade nearly round, 6–20 cm long and wide (2½–8 in), often broader than long, thick, leathery, dark green, with reddish veins and a heart-shaped base. FLOWERS any-time during the year; flowers many,

Coccoloba uvifera

borne in clusters of four in hanging terminal and axillary racemes to 30 cm long (12 in). Corolla none, calyx of five white sepals 1.5–2.5 mm long (about ¹⁄₁₆–⅛ in). FRUIT a red obovoid nut 1–1.5 cm long (⅜–⅝ in). PROPAGATE by seeds, cuttings, or air layering. Well-drained soils in sunny places are preferred. It is often planted in seashore landscapes because of its resistance to salt spray and can be grown as a tree or pruned to form a hedge or border plant.

Cochlospermum COCHLOSPERMACEAE

Cochlospermum a genus of 15 to 30 tree and shrub species found in tropical Africa, Australia, and America, some utilized commercially for a gum and others as ornamentals for their attractive, seasonal flowers.

Cochlospermum vitifolium (Willdenow) Sprengel
DISTINGUISHABLE by the tree habit, leaves that are alternate, round, and deeply palmately lobed, toothed leaf margins, and large yellow, season-

Cochlospermum vitifolium

al flowers, often double-flowered, on the nearly leafless tree in winter and spring.

Cochlospermum vitifolium, buttercup tree, is native to tropical America from Mexico to Brazil but is widely cultivated in the tropics for its large yellow flowers, especially the double-flowered 'Plenum', which with its numerous petals formed from the stamens, and hence sterile, has flowers that look like those of a yellow peony. The name *vitifolium* is from the Latin words meaning grape leaf, an apt description of the foliage. TREE to 10 m high (33 ft) or more, deciduous. LEAVES simple, alternate, blade generally round but deeply three- to seven-lobed, 10–35 cm in diameter (4–14 in), coarsely palmately veined, margins toothed. FLOWERS mostly in winter and spring before the leaves reappear; flowers many, borne in axillary and terminal racemes. Corolla of five free, obovate, bright yellow petals, or double-flowered with many petal-like staminodes, mostly 4–6 cm long (1⅝–2½ in), notched at the tip. FRUIT a large ovoid to elliptic capsule 6–9 cm long (2½–3½ in) but not forming in the double-flowered cultivar, filled with many silky-hairy seeds. PROPAGATE by seeds, from fertile trees, or cuttings. Dry, well-drained soils in sunny places are preferred. The tree is typically deciduous during dry seasons, and during its seasonal flowering the fallen blooms may cover the ground beneath the leafless tree.

Codiaeum EUPHORBIACEAE

Codiaeum is a genus of 15 to 25 shrub or small tree species found from

Melanesia and Australia to Malaysia, one of which is grown as an ornamental.

Codiaeum variegatum (Linnaeus) A. H. L. Jussieu

DISTINGUISHABLE by the shrubby habit, leaves that are alternate and variously colored and shaped, and narrow terminal racemes of inconspicuous flowers that nearly lack petals.

Codiaeum variegatum, variegated croton, sometimes simply called croton, is native to Malaysia or Melanesia but is widely cultivated for its colorful and variable foliage. SHRUB to 4 m high (13 ft). LEAVES simple, alternate, blade variously shaped, usually 8–25 cm long (3½–10 in), sometimes lobed, divided to the midrib, or twisted, variously mottled with red, purple, and yellow. FLOWERS anytime during the year but the flowers are inconspicuous, borne in terminal racemes of separate male

Codiaeum variegatum, showing a range of color and leaf shape

Codiaeum variegatum, showing more variation

and female flowers, the male flowers many, on thin stalks and bearing many white stamens, the female ones sessile. Corolla of five minute, free petals, but the petal-like calyx white, five-lobed, 3–5 mm long (about ⅛–¼ in). FRUIT a subglobose, shallowly three-lobed capsule, infrequently formed in cultivation. PROPAGATE by cuttings, which is easily done. Fertile soils in sunny or partially shaded places are preferred. It is often grown as a hedge plant or foundation plant in the tropics, and as a greenhouse or indoor plant in temperate areas. Its colorful and variously shaped leaves, ease of growing, and hardy nature make it one of the most popular potted plants. This species probably has more named cultivars than any other tropical ornamental plant. Cultivars include 'Aucubifolium', with elliptic leaves, green spotted with yellow; 'Taeniosum', with the blade interrupted or cut to the midrib; 'Cornutum', with the blade bearing a horn-like projection near the tip; and 'Crispum', with the narrow blade twisted or wavy, among many others.

Colvillea FABACEAE

Colvillea, named after Charles Colville, 1770–1843, English governor of Mauritius, is a genus with a single tree species.

Colvillea racemosa Bojer

DISTINGUISHABLE by the feathery, bipinnately compound leaves and orange flowers in dense, hanging, ovoid racemes that appear in fall. Its leaves and seasonal flowering habit are similar to those of another tree endemic to Madagascar, *Delonix regia,* but the flowers of *Colvillea racemosa* are smaller, orange rather than red, and arranged in conical rather than loose inflorescences.

Colvillea racemosa, Colville's glory, is endemic to the island of Madagascar. The tree is widely if not commonly cultivated elsewhere in the tropics and subtropics for its elegant form, feathery leaves, and orange flowers. It is spectacular when flowering, with long, cone-shaped racemes of orange and orange-red flowers that bloom from the bottom upward, but the display lasts only a month or two, and most of the year the tree is inconspicuous. TREE to 15 m high (50 ft) or more with the lower trunk typically free of branches. LEAVES bipinnately compound, alternate, to 80 cm long (32 in), pinnae in 12 to 25 opposite pairs, each pinna with leaflets in 15 to 33 opposite pairs, blades oblong, 5–10 mm long (¼–⅜ in), rounded at both ends. FLOWERS seasonally, in fall, September to November in the northern hemisphere; flowers many, about 200, in dense, hanging, stalked, ovoid heads 21–30 cm long (8–12 in). Corolla of five free, orange, unequal, round to spoon-shaped petals 2–3 cm long (¾–1¼ in),

Colvillea racemosa

enclosed within the orange, cup-shaped calyx 2–2.7 cm long (¾–1⅛ in) with ten free, protruding, yellow stamens. FRUIT a several-seeded, flattened, narrowly oblong, woody pod 18–30 cm long (7–12 in). PROPAGATE by seeds or cuttings. Moist but well-drained soils in sunny places are preferred. It is often planted as a specimen or street tree but not as a shade tree since it is deciduous in winter.

Congea VERBENACEAE

Congea is a genus of seven to ten shrub or liana species found from Southeast Asia to Sumatra, some of which are cultivated for their attractive inflorescences.

Congea griffithiana Munir

Sometimes misidentified as *Congea velutina* Wight. DISTINGUISHABLE by the opposite leaves, velvety lower leaf surface, pink, petal-like bracts, and white flowers purple in the center. A related species, *C. pedicillata* Munir, differs in usually having three bracts and leaves velvety on both surfaces.

Congea griffithiana with petal-like bracts below the flowers

Congea griffithiana, pink congea, sometimes called shower of orchids, is native from Myanmar (Burma) to Malaysia but is widely if not commonly cultivated in the tropics for the pink bracts that surround the flowers. VINE-LIKE SHRUB, somewhat climbing or spreading, to 3 m high (10 ft). LEAVES simple, opposite, blade elliptic, 5–12 cm long (2–5 in), scabrous on the upper surface, velvety on the lower. FLOWERS continuously through the year but the plant is most attractive when in fruit; flowers four to eight, borne in heads surrounded by four or five elliptic to oblanceolate, woolly, pink bracts 2–3 cm long (¾–1¼ in). Corolla with fused petals, two-lipped, 6–9 mm long (¼–⅜ in), white with purple in the center, with four protruding stamens. FRUIT a dry, one-seeded, obovoid drupe. PROPAGATE by seeds or air layering. Moist but well-drained soils in sunny places are preferred. It is grown as a free-standing, vine-like shrub or liana on a trellis. Some pruning is needed to keep it in shape, but too much cutting inhibits flowering since the flowers form at the stem tips.

Cordia BORAGINACEAE

Cordia is a genus of 250 to 300 tree species found throughout the tropics, especially tropical America. Some are important for timber, medicine, and edible fruits, and some are grown as ornamentals because of their attractive flowers.

Cordia sebestena Linnaeus

DISTINGUISHABLE by the tree habit, alternate leaves, rough upper leaf surface, orange, funnel-shaped, crape flowers, and white drupe. Another species native to seashores found throughout the tropics, *Cordia subcordata* Lamarck, is also sometimes cultivated as an ornamental and differs most obviously in having a larger corolla and brown fruit.

Cordia sebestena

Cordia sebestena, geiger tree, is native to the West Indies and possibly to other Caribbean shores but is widely cultivated for its crape-like, red-orange flowers. The fruit is edible but not commonly eaten. **TREE** to 7 m high (23 ft). **LEAVES** simple, alternate, blade ovate to elliptic, 10–18 cm long (4–7 in), rough-hairy on the upper surface. **FLOWERS** continuously through the year; flowers many, borne in terminal panicles. Corolla of fused petals, funnel-shaped, 3–4 cm long (1¼–1⅝ in), limb shallowly five-lobed, 2.5–4 cm in diameter (1–1⅝ in), crape-like in texture, red-orange. **FRUIT** a white ovoid drupe 1–2.5 cm long (⅜–1 in). **PROPAGATE** by seeds, cuttings, or air layering. Moist but well-drained soils in sunny to partially shaded places are preferred, but it is adaptable to dry, even somewhat saline soils. Often planted as a street or specimen tree, it is also suitable for pruning to shape. It is ideal for seashore locations since it is resistant to salt spray.

Cordyline AGAVACEAE

Cordyline is a genus of about 15 tree-like species found mostly throughout the Old World tropics and warm temperate regions. Some are important for fibers, food from their tuberous roots, and as ornamentals.

Cordyline fruticosa (Linnaeus) Chevallier

Synonyms, *Cordyline terminalis* (Linnaeus) Kunth and *Taetsia fruticosa* (Linnaeus) Merrill. DISTINGUISHABLE by the sparsely branching, shrub-like habit, slender, ringed stems, often colorful, ginger-like leaves, and terminal panicles of pink flowers.

Cordyline fruticosa, ti, sometimes called ti plant, is native from the Himalayas to the islands of the Pacific Ocean and was an ancient introduction eastward across the tropical Pacific to Hawaii. In the Pacific, the sugar-laden, tuberous roots were formerly eaten after baking in underground ovens. In Hawaii, a brandy-like drink called okolehau was once fermented from the mashed roots. The leaves have long been used for fibers, clothing, food wrappers, and folk medicines, and currently are braided into leis in Hawaii, where the plant is considered sacred by many Hawaiians. SHRUB, sparsely branching, to 5 m high (16½ ft) but

Cordyline fruticosa with green leaves like those of wild plants

Cordyline fruticosa, a plant with curled leaves

usually much less, with a conspicuously ringed stem arising from a tuberous root. LEAVES simple, alternate, spirally arranged at the ends of the stems, blade lanceolate to oblong, 20–70 cm long (8–28 in), sometimes red, sometimes curved and shorter. FLOWERS at intervals throughout the year; flowers many, borne in axillary panicles of spikes. Corolla with fused tepals, tubular, 8–14 mm long (¼–⅝ in), divided about halfway into six segments, pink, purple, or white. FRUIT a red globose berry 6–8 mm in diameter (about ¼ in) but not forming in many cultivars. PROPAGATE by stem cuttings, suckers, or seeds when seeds are produced, but these do not often breed true. Fertile, well-drained soils in sunny or partially shaded places are preferred, but full sun is needed to bring out the color in the cultivars. The major present use is as an ornamental, alone or planted in hedges. A bewildering number of cultivars have been named, with variously colored, often red, and differently shaped leaves. Packaged stem cuttings are sold in the tourist trade in Hawaii and elsewhere, and the plant is favored as an indoor or outdoor potted plant.

Coreopsis ASTERACEAE

Coreopsis is a genus of 80 to perhaps more than 110 herb and shrub species found in North and South America and Africa. Some are used medicinally, and many as ornamentals.

Coreopsis tinctoria Nuttall

DISTINGUISHABLE by the bipinnately compound leaves, linear leaflets, and yellow flower heads with the ray florets red-brown to purple at the base. Another ornamental species, *Coreopsis lanceolata* Linnaeus, differs in having sparsely hairy, narrowly spoon-shaped, mostly basal leaves and yellow florets in heads to 6 cm in diameter (2½ in).

   Coreopsis tinctoria, which lacks a widely recognized common name, is a temperate species native to central North America but is widely cultivated in gardens in temperate as well as tropical areas for its yellow flower heads that, unlike those of most other members of the compos-

Coreopsis tinctoria with ray florets with red-brown to purple bases

Coreopsis lanceolata with yellow florets

ite family Asteraceae that resemble sunflowers *(Helianthus)*, have ray florets with dark bases. **HERB** to 1 m high (3¼ ft). **LEAVES** bipinnately compound, opposite, leaflets linear, 3–12 cm long (1¼–5 in). **FLOWERS** anytime during the year after maturity in the tropics; flowers borne in several long-stalked heads in panicles, each head surrounded by two dissimilar series of bracts. Ray florets about eight, obovate, 1–1.8 cm long (⅜–¾ in), lobed at the tip, yellow with a red-brown or purple base or sometimes all red-brown. Disk florets many, purplish with yellow stamens. **FRUIT** an elliptic-oblong achene 1.5–3 mm long (about ¹⁄₁₆–⅛ in). **PROPAGATE** by achenes. Well-drained soils in sunny places are preferred. It is often grown in beds or planters and is somewhat drought resistant.

Cosmos ASTERACEAE

Cosmos comprises about 26 annual or perennial herb or shrub species found in subtropical North America, especially Mexico, some cultivated for their flower heads. Two common ornamental species are included here.

Cosmos bipinnatus Cavanilles

Synonym, *Bidens formosa* (Bonato) Schultz Bipontinus. DISTINGUISH-ABLE by the opposite, deeply dissected leaves, filamentous leaflets, yellow disk florets, and seven or eight white to purple ray florets. A similar cultivated garden ornamental, *Cosmos caudatus* Kunth, differs in having pinnate rather than bipinnate leaves.

    Cosmos bipinnatus, garden cosmos, is native to Mexico but is widely cultivated in gardens in the tropics and subtropics for its red, pink, purple, or white flower heads, which are sometimes used commercially as cut flowers. HERB, annual, to 1 m high (3¼ ft) or more. LEAVES deeply bipinnately dissected, opposite, blades deeply divided into long, linear lobes. FLOWERS continuously through the year after maturity; flowers borne in one to several terminal, long-stalked heads surrounded by two dissimilar series of bracts. Ray florets usually seven or eight, obovate, 2.5–5 cm long (1–2 in), toothed at the tip, pink, red, purple, or white. Disk florets numerous, yellow. FRUIT a narrow achene with a pair of spreading barbs at the tip. PROPAGATE by achenes. The plant is drought resistant and well-drained

Cosmos bipinnatus, plants with variously colored ray florets

soils in sunny places are preferred. It is often planted in borders and beside other plants for support because of its weak stems. Several cultivars have been named.

Cosmos sulphureus Cavanilles

Synonym, *Bidens sulphurea* (Cavanilles) Schultz Bipontinus. DISTINGUISHABLE by the opposite, pinnately or bipinnately divided leaves, and heads of yellow ray and disk florets. The similar *Tagetes erecta* has more distinctly toothed leaf margins, usually many more ray florets, and an inflated flowering stalk.

    Cosmos sulphureus, yellow cosmos, is native to Mexico but is widely cultivated in gardens in the tropics and subtropics for its orange to yellow-orange heads and sometimes becomes adventive or fully naturalized. HERB, annual, to 1 m high (3¼ ft) or more. LEAVES simple, opposite, blade ovate in general outline and pinnately or bipinnately divided, usually 6–22 cm long (2½–9 in).

FLOWERS continuously through the year after maturity in the tropics but during the warm months in cooler climates; flowers in solitary, terminal, long-stalked heads surrounded by two series of lanceolate bracts. Ray florets usually five to eight, or many in double-flowered cultivars, obovate, toothed at the tip, 1.8–3.5 cm long (¾–1⅜ in), bright orange to yellow-orange. Disk florets numerous, yellow. FRUIT a narrow achene with two to four barbs at the tip. PROPAGATE by achenes. The plant is drought resistant and prefers well-drained soils in sunny places. It is often grown as a border plant. Several cultivars have been named.

Cosmos sulphureus

Costus ZINGIBERACEAE

Costus comprises 80 to 90 rhizomatous herb species native mostly to tropical America, with a few occurring from Africa to Melanesia. Some authors remove *Costus, Tapeinochilos,* and other genera from the ginger family Zingiberaceae to a separate family, Costaceae. Many *Costus* species, called spiral flags or spiral gingers, are cultivated for their flowers, including three of the most common ones treated here.

Costus malortianus H. Wendland

DISTINGUISHABLE by the tightly spiraled, ginger-like leaves and exquisite yellow, brown, and white flowers arising from an ovoid spike covered with green, closely overlapping bracts.

    Costus malortianus, stepladder plant, is native to Costa Rica but is widely cultivated for its colorful flowers and inflorescences and foliage. **HERB**, perennial, coarse, erect, unbranched, to 1.8 m high (6 ft), arising from a rhizome. **LEAVES** simple, alternate, spirally arranged, blade obovate, usually 10–30 × 7–18 cm (4–12 × 3–7 in), often variegated with darker oblique bands, waxy white beneath. **FLOWERS** anytime during the year; flowers many, borne singly among green overlapping bracts in a dense ovoid spike 6–8 cm long (2½–3½ in). Corolla of three fused petals 3.5–6 cm long (1⅜–2½ in), the labellum funnel-shaped, larger than the petals, bilobed, the larger lobe three-lobed at top, the lateral ones maroon with yellowish veins, the middle one bright yellow, enclosed within the corolla. **FRUIT** a many-seeded capsule. **PROPA-**

Costus malortianus

GATE by division; sometimes can be propagated by seeds. Fertile, moist, but well-drained soils in shaded or partially shaded places are preferred. It is often grown as a border plant in the tropics and in the greenhouse in temperate climates. One cultivar, 'Variegatus', has variegated foliage.

Costus speciosus (König) Smith

DISTINGUISHABLE by the shrub-like habit, spirally arranged leaves, red calyx, and large, white flowers marked with yellow in the center.

Costus speciosus, crape ginger, sometimes called Malay ginger, is native from the Himalayas to New Guinea and Australia but is widely cultivated for its white, crape-like flowers. What appears to be a corolla is actually a highly modified sterile stamen. Though the flowers are very attractive, they are not used commercially because they bruise easily. The plant sometimes escapes from cultivation and becomes naturalized but does not readily spread. HERB, perennial, erect, robust, unbranched, to 2 m high (6½ ft) or more, arising from a rhizome. LEAVES simple, alternate, spirally arranged, attached atop a sheath, blade oblanceolate to elliptic, 8–25 × 3–7 cm (3½–10 × 1¼–3 in), the lower surface silky pubescent. FLOWERS continuously through the year; flowers many, borne among purple bracts in a dense, ovoid to globose, terminal head 3–10 cm long (1¼–4 in). Corolla of three fused subequal petals 4–6 cm long (1⅝–2½ in) and a larger, cup-shaped labellum 5–9 cm long (2–3½ in) and to 10 cm wide (4 in), crape-like, white, with a yellow anther. FRUIT an ellipsoidal many-seeded capsule. PROPAGATE by division. Fertile, moist soils in shaded

Costus speciosus with an enlarged, petal-like stamen, the labellum

places are preferred. It is usually planted as a specimen or border plant. One cultivar, 'Variegatus', has attractive, variegated leaves.

Costus woodsonii Maas

Sometimes misidentified as *Costus spicatus* (Jacquin) Swartz or *C. spiralis* (Jacquin) Roscoe. **DISTINGUISHABLE** by the spirally arranged, ginger-like leaves, ovoid spikes covered with densely overlapping bracts, and orange, scarcely opening flowers.

Costus woodsonii, scarlet spiral flag, is native from Nicaragua to Colombia but is widely cultivated in the tropics for its yellow to orange flowers, produced one a time, an attractive contrast to the bright red, overlapping bracts that cover the spike. **HERB**, perennial, stout, erect, unbranched, to 2 m high (6½ ft) or more, arising from a rhizome. **LEAVES** simple, alternate, spirally arranged, subsessile atop a sheath, blade elliptic to obovate, usually 8–28 × 4–8 cm (3½–11 × 1⅝–3½ in), glossy green or sometimes variegated with irregular yellow stripes. **FLOWERS** continuously through the year; flowers many, borne one at time among tightly overlapping, glossy red bracts in a dense, ovoid to cylindrical spike usually 3–13 cm long (1¼–5 in) atop a leafy stem. Corolla of three fused yellow petals 0.6–1.5 cm long (¼–⅝ in), divided less than halfway to the base, with an oblong yellow to orange labellum 1.8–3 cm long (¾–1¼ in). **FRUIT** a many-seeded capsule. **PROPAGATE** by division, plantlets, or stem cuttings. Fertile, moist, but well-drained soils in sunny or partially shaded places are preferred. It is usually grown as a specimen or border plant.

Costus woodsonii

Couroupita LECYTHIDACEAE

Couroupita is a genus of 3 or 4 tropical American tree species, or as many as 20 according to some authors, some of which have good timber, and one of which is cultivated as an ornamental.

Couroupita guianensis Aublet

DISTINGUISHABLE by the tree habit, tangled woody inflorescences on the trunk, distinctive red flowers with many white stamens on a curved disk, and cannonball-like fruit.

Couroupita guianensis, cannonball tree, is native from Trinidad to Peru but is widely if not commonly cultivated in the tropics as a novelty because of its large, unusual, red flowers and its cannonball-like fruits, occurring with the flowers in tangled masses on the trunk. This combination of characteristics makes the plant easily recognizable. TREE to 20 m high (66 ft) or more, deciduous in some climates. LEAVES simple, alternate, blade oblanceolate, 10–25 cm long (4–10 in), leaves clustered at branch tips. FLOWERS most of the year; flowers many, in drooping, elongate, tangled racemes or panicles densely packed on the trunk. Corolla of five free petals 5.5–7 cm long (2 ¼–3 in), red, pink, or orange, with numerous white stamens in the center on a curved disk. FRUIT woody, globose, not splitting, to 20 cm in diameter (8 in), filled with yellow-green to purple, unpleasant smelling pulp and numerous small seeds. PROPAGATE by cuttings or seeds. Fertile, moist, but well-drained soils in sunny places are preferred. It is usually grown as a specimen tree and is not suitable for small yards because of its large size.

Couroupita guianensis

Crescentia BIGNONIACEAE

Crescentia is a genus of about six tropical American tree species, several of which are cultivated as novelties, and some with gourd-like fruits used in various ways.

Crescentia cujete Linnaeus

DISTINGUISHABLE by the tree habit, simple leaves in tight clusters, attractive, lightly colored, solitary, bell-shaped flowers on the branches, and large, round, gourd-like fruit. Another tree also grown as a novelty, *Crescentia alata* Kunth, Mexican calabash tree, differs in having trifoliate leaves and much smaller fruit.

Crescentia cujete, calabash tree, sometimes called gourd tree, is native to tropical America but is widely grown for its attractive form as a shade or specimen tree, as a novelty, and for the unusual fruits that form on

Crescentia cujete with simple leaves   *Crescentia alata* with trifoliate leaves

the branches. During their growth the fruits can be constricted with string to make various shapes and are fashioned into rattles, bowls, and cups in lieu of those made from the calabash vine, *Lagenaria siceraria,* normally used for the purpose. The wood of *C. cujete* is sometimes used in construction. The flowers are adapted to bat pollination and the pulp of the fruit is poisonous. TREE to 10 m high (33 ft). LEAVES simple, in tight clusters formed at the nodes, blade oblanceolate, usually 6–20 cm long (2½–8 in). FLOWERS anytime during the year; flowers solitary or borne in clusters of two or three growing from large branches. Corolla of fused petals, irregularly bell-shaped, two-lipped, folded on one side, 4–7.5 cm long (1⅝–3 in), greenish, yellow, or cream with pink or purple lines. FRUIT a subglobose, hard-shelled gourd 15–30 cm long (6–12 in), yellow turning black at maturity, filled with a many-seeded pulp. PROPAGATE by seeds, air layering, or cuttings. Fertile, moist soils in sunny places are preferred.

Crinum AMARYLLIDACEAE

Crinum comprises about 120 species widespread in the tropics and subtropics, especially in coastal areas. Many of these as well as some interspecific hybrids, all called crinum lilies, are cultivated for their large flowers, and one, *C. xanthophyllum,* for its yellow foliage. Four of the more common ornamental species are included here.

Crinum asiaticum Linnaeus

DISTINGUISHABLE by the large, basal, strap-shaped, green leaves, umbels of white, long-tubed flowers with long, linear tepal segments, long and protruding stamens free at the base, and subglobose, fleshy, green fruits. It differs from the similar spider lilies *(Hymenocallis),* which have a cup-shaped structure connecting the bases of the stamens.

　　Crinum asiaticum, the most commonly cultivated species of the genus, is native to tropical Asia but is widely cultivated for its umbels of large white flowers that make it one of the most easily recognized tropical ornamentals. The bulb is used as an emetic, the roots for poulticing wounds, and the leaves are applied to sprains, but the bulb is reportedly poisonous and the sap may cause irritation to the skin. The plant is sometimes called poison bulb. **HERB**, perennial, coarse, to 1.5 m high (5 ft) with a thick stem to 50 cm high (20 in), arising from a bulb. **LEAVES** simple, in a dense rosette atop the stem, blade sessile, linear-lanceolate, usually 60–130 × 10–15 cm (24–51 × 4–6 in), thick and somewhat fleshy, parallel veined, light green. **FLOWERS** more or less continuously through the year; flowers 20 to 30 or more, fragrant, borne in an umbel atop a long, thick stalk and enclosed within two large bracts. Corolla with

Crinum asiaticum

fused tepals, funnel-shaped, the tube above the ovary 8–12 cm long (3½–5 in), 4–7 mm in diameter (about ¼ in), greenish, the limb of six spreading segments 6–12 × 0.7–1.5 cm (2½–5 × ¼–⅝ in), usually white, with six long, protruding stamens with red filaments. **FRUIT** a subglobose, fleshy, one- to three-seeded capsule. **PROPAGATE** by offsets or seeds. Fertile, moist soils in sunny or partially shaded places are preferred. It is often planted to form boundaries, particularly in seaside locations since it is by nature a coastal species, and for the large white flowers favored in personal decoration.

Crinum augustum Roxburgh

Synonym, *Crinum amabile* var. *augustum* (Roxburgh) Herbert, which is possibly not distinct from *C. amabile* Donn and *C. pedunculatum* R. Brown. **DISTINGUISHABLE** by the basal, strap-shaped leaves often tinted red or purple, umbels of large pink flowers with six long, linear tepal

Crinum augustum

segments, long and protruding stamens free at the base, and large, fleshy, green, subglobose fruits.

Crinum augustum is native to the Seychelles and Mauritius, and perhaps elsewhere in the region, but is widely cultivated in the tropics for its wine red flowers. It is utilized in ways very similar to those of the more common *C. asiaticum* but adds more color since the leaves and flowers are reddish to pink. **HERB**, perennial, coarse, to 1.5 m high (5 ft) or more, with a thick stem arising from a bulb. **LEAVES** simple, in a dense rosette atop the stem, blade sessile, lanceolate, usually 80–130×8–15 cm (32–51 × 3½–6 in), thick, parallel veined, often tinted purple, not glossy. **FLOWERS** anytime during the year; flowers 20 to 30, borne in an umbel enclosed in two large ovate bracts on a stalk to 1 m high (3¼ ft). Corolla with fused tepals, funnel-shaped, the tube usually 7–11 cm long (3–4½ in), 3–5 mm in diameter (about ⅛–¼ in), dark pink, the limb of six spreading segments mostly 7–10 × 0.5–0.7 cm (3–4 × about ¼ in), white to wine red, with six long, protruding stamens in the center. **FRUIT** a subglobose, fleshy, one- to three-seeded capsule. **PROPAGATE** by bulb offsets or clump division. Fertile, moist soils in partially shaded places are preferred.

Crinum xanthophyllum Hannibal

Sometimes misidentified as *Crinum asiaticum* or *C. pedunculatum* R. Brown. **DISTINGUISHABLE** by the basal, strap-shaped, yellow leaves, umbels of large white flowers with six long, narrow tepal lobes, and long, protruding stamens free at the base. It is superficially similar to *C. asi-*

aticum but has much smaller, yellow leaves.

Crinum xanthophyllum, golden-leaf crinum, is possibly native to Melanesia but is cultivated elsewhere in the Pacific region for it foliage as well as its flowers. **HERB**, perennial, coarse, to 1 m high (3 ¼ ft) with a thick stem to 25 cm high (10 in) arising from an underground bulb. **LEAVES** simple, in a rosette atop the stem, blade sessile, lanceolate, 50–100 × 6–10 cm (20–40 × 2½–4 in), parallel veined, recurving and becoming yellow at maturity. **FLOWERS** anytime during the year; flowers 20 to 25, borne in an umbel atop a leafless stalk usually 15–25 cm high (6–10 in). Corolla with fused tepals, funnel-shaped, usually 16–23 cm long (6–9 in), divided halfway into six spreading linear segments 6–10 mm wide (¼–⅜ in), white, with six protruding stamens on red filaments. **FRUIT** a subglobose, fleshy, one- to three-seeded capsule. **PROPAGATE** by offsets. Well-drained soils in sunny places are preferred. Its colorful foliage makes it a favorite as a border plant and it can survive in relatively poor, sandy or even coralline soil.

Crinum xanthophyllum

Crinum zeylanicum Linnaeus

Synonyms, *Crinum latifolium* var. *zeylanicum* (Linnaeus) J. D. Hooker ex Trimen and *C. scabrum* Herbert. **DISTINGUISHABLE** by the basal, strap-shaped leaves, several nodding flowers, funnel-shaped corolla with elliptic tepal segments, white with a red medial stripe, and protruding stamens. It differs from the other species of *Crinum* included here in having fewer, drooping flowers with broader tepals.

Crinum zeylanicum

Crinum zeylanicum, milk-and-wine lily, is native from southern Africa to tropical Asia but is widely cultivated in the tropics for its drooping, rose-colored or white flowers. **HERB** to 90 cm high (36 in), arising from a large bulb. **LEAVES** simple, in a basal rosette, blade sessile, linear-lanceolate, 50–100 × 3–7 cm (20–40 × 1¼–3 in), green, rough edged, parallel veined. **FLOWERS** anytime during the year; flowers mostly 5 to 13, nodding, fragrant, borne in a terminal umbel atop the leafless stalk 40–60 cm long (16–24 in). Corolla with fused tepals, funnel-shaped, the tube narrow, 10–14 cm long (4–6 in), the segments elliptic, 8.5–13.5 cm long (3½–5 in), white with a pink or red stripe in the center, with six protruding stamens on white, often pink-tipped filaments in the center. **FRUIT** a subglobose, fleshy, one- to three-seeded capsule. **PROPAGATE** by offsets or seeds. Fertile, moist, but well-drained soils in sunny places are preferred. Though smaller than the other crinums, it is often planted as a low border or a specimen plant.

Crocosmia IRIDACEAE

Crocosmia comprises about seven perennial herbaceous, southern African species. One is a source of a yellow dye, and several are cultivated for their flowers. The name *Crocosmia* is from the Greek words meaning saffron smell—the leaves smell like saffron when immersed in water.

Crocosmia ×crocosmiiflora (P. L. V. Lemoine) N. E. Brown

Synonyms, *Montbretia crocosmiiflora* P. L. V. Lemoine, and *Tritonia cro-*

cosmiiflora (P. L. V. Lemoine) G. Nicholson. DISTINGUISHABLE by the *Iris*-like
leaves, zigzag spikes of orange flowers
marked with red at the base, and unequal
tepal segments.

Crocosmia ×crocosmiiflora, montbretia,
is a hybrid resulting from a cross between
C. aurea (Pappe ex J. D. Hooker) Planchon
and *C. pottsii* (J. MacNab ex J. G. Baker)
N. E. Brown and is widely grown, often as
a border plant, for its orange, long-lasting
flowers that are commonly used commercially as cut flowers. It is a temperate species that is more commonly grown in
cooler climates than in the tropics but it is
often found at higher elevations in the
tropics and sometimes escapes to form
large patches, as in Hawaii. HERB, peren-

Crocosmia ×crocosmiiflora

nial, to 1.2 m high (4 ft) or more, arising from a tuber. LEAVES simple,
basal, equitant, blade linear-lanceolate, the lower leaves 30–80 × 0.6–3
cm (12–32 × ¼–1¼ in), parallel veined. FLOWERS anytime during the
year; flowers many, in one-sided, zigzag spikes borne in an open, arching panicle to 60 cm high (24 in) atop a leafless stalk. Corolla with fused
tepals, deeply divided into six oblong, unequal segments 3–5 cm long
(1¼–2 in), orange with red markings at the base. FRUIT an ellipsoidal
capsule 5–7 mm long (about ¼ in). PROPAGATE by division. Well-drained
soils in sunny places are preferred.

Crossandra ACANTHACEAE

Crossandra is a genus of about 50 species, ranging from tropical Africa to
Asia, many grown for their brilliantly colored flowers or attractive foliage.

Crossandra infundibuliformis (Linnaeus) Nees

DISTINGUISHABLE by the subshrub habit, opposite or whorled leaves, and terminal racemes of orange to red or pink, one-lipped flowers with the five lobes all on one side.

    Crossandra infundibuliformis, firecracker flower, is native to India and Sri Lanka (Ceylon) but is widely cultivated for its pink to orange or red flowers with the corolla lobes all on one side, and its attractive, shiny, dark green leaves. SUBSHRUB to 1 m high (3¼ ft). LEAVES simple, opposite or in whorls of three or four, blade elliptic to oblong, 6–13 cm long (2½–5 in). FLOWERS continuously through the year; flowers several, borne in terminal racemes among overlapping, hairy, green bracts. Corolla of fused petals, narrowly salverform, tube curved, 1.8–2.8 cm long (¾–1⅛ in), split along the top to form the spreading, one-lipped, five-lobed limb 2.5–3.5 cm across (1–1⅜ in), red, orange, or salmon pink. FRUIT an oblong capsule, infrequently formed in cultivation. PROPAGATE by cuttings. Light, fertile soils in sunny places are preferred. In the tropics it is often planted in borders, and in temperate climates in the greenhouse as a potted plant.

Crossandra infundibuliformis

Cryptostegia ASCLEPIADACEAE

Cryptostegia is a genus of two vine-like shrub species endemic to Madagascar. Both have a milky latex similar to that of rubber *(Hevea brasiliensis).*

Cryptostegia grandiflora Roxburgh ex R. Brown

DISTINGUISHABLE by the vine-like, shrubby habit, milky sap, glossy green, opposite leaves, lavender, bell-shaped flowers, and paired follicles containing tufted seeds. *Cryptostegia madagascariensis* Roxburgh ex Decaisne differs in having a smaller corolla 3.5–4.5 cm long (1⅜–1¾ in) and shorter pods 6–9 cm long (2½–3½ in).

Cryptostegia grandiflora

Cryptostegia grandiflora, India rubber vine, is from Madagascar, not India. It is sometimes called Palay rubber vine. It is widely if not commonly cultivated in the tropics for its large lavender flowers, but because of its plumed, wind-borne seeds it occasionally escapes and becomes naturalized. In its native range it is grown for its stem fibers and for the poisonous latex that can be used to make a kind of rubber. **VINE-LIKE SHRUB** with milky sap. **LEAVES** simple, opposite, blade oblong, 4–11 cm long (1⅝–4½ in), dark green, leathery. **FLOWERS** anytime during the year; flowers 6 to 12, borne in terminal cymes. Corolla of fused petals, bell-shaped, 5–7 cm long (2–3 in) with five overlapping lobes, lavender with darker lavender inside, becoming lighter as the day progresses. **FRUIT** a pair of ovoid follicles usually 8–12 cm long (3½–5 in), containing numerous tufted seeds. **PROPAGATE** by seeds, cuttings, or air layering. Moist but well-drained soils in sunny places are preferred. It is often pruned into a shrub as a specimen or hedge plant, or is trained as a covering for fences, trellises, or buildings.

Cuphea LYTHRACEAE

Cuphea comprises more than 250 tropical and subtropical North and South American herb and small shrub species. Many are cultivated as ornamentals because of their flowers, and two of the most common of these are included here, and two others are mentioned.

Cuphea hyssopifolia Kunth

DISTINGUISHABLE by the low shrubby habit, opposite leaves, and flowers that are longitudinally grooved, small, purple or, rarely, white, and appear to lack a calyx.

Cuphea hyssopifolia, false heather, but not a member of the heather family Ericaceae, is native to Central America and Mexico but is commonly cultivated because of its attractively compact, heather-like habit and purple, sometimes white, flowers. It is sometimes called elfin plant or elfin herb. **SHRUB** to 70 cm high (28 in). **LEAVES** simple, opposite, blade linear to lanceolate or elliptic, 7–40 mm long (¼–1⅝ in), subsessile, arranged in one plane. **FLOWERS** continuously through the year; flowers solitary in the leaf axils. Corolla of six free obovate petals 4–7 mm long (about ¼ in), purple or sometimes white, arising at the top of a tubular, longitudinally grooved hypanthium, the calyx, 5–8 mm long (about ¼ in). **FRUIT** a small capsule enclosed within the hypanthium. **PROPAGATE** by cuttings, the technique most used, or by seeds. Fertile, well-drained soils in sunny or partially shaded places are preferred. It is often grown as a low border plant along pathways in the garden and as potted plant indoors or outdoors. A number of cultivars have been named, based mostly on differences of height and color.

Cuphea hyssopifolia

in). **FLOWERS** anytime during the year; flowers many, arranged on a short leafless stem in a dense conical panicle in clusters of two to five borne among curved, oblanceolate to oblong bracts to 6 cm long (2½ in), the upper bracts red to rose-colored, the lower ones green. Corolla funnel-shaped, of three equal, pale yellow petals fused at the base, 8–12 mm long (¼–½ in) and with three petal-like staminodes, a lateral equal pair and a longer one, the labellum. **FRUIT** an ellipsoidal, thin-walled capsule. **PROPAGATE** by division. Well-drained soils in shaded places are preferred.

Cycas CYCADACEAE

Cycas comprises about 20 to 40 palm-like conifer species. It is one of a number of genera of cycads, descendants of plants that flourished long before flowering plants. Many are cultivated for their unusual form, and some contain starch in their trunks that is eaten.

Cycas circinalis Linnaeus

Synonym, *Cycas rumphii* Miquel, a name used by some authors. **DISTIN-GUISHABLE** by the thick trunks, palm-like leaves, cylindrical male cones, and seeds forming on notched, spoon-shaped fertile leaves. Another, smaller, cultivated cycad native to Japan and southern China, *C. revolu-ta* Thunberg, differs most notably in having obovate, deeply lobed fertile leaves with smaller seeds, to 4 cm in diameter (1⅝ in).

Cycas circinalis is native from India to Polynesia though some authors refer most of the Pacific populations to a different species, *C. rumphii*. The roots contain symbiotic blue-green algae that fix nitrogen, allowing it to grow in soils low in nutrients. The leaves are sometimes used in decoration, and the starchy pith of the trunk is edible, though there is now reason to believe that eating it over long periods may cause an ailment similar to Parkinson's disease. Sometimes called sago palm, that name is a misnomer. It is not at all related to the true sago palms (*Metroxylon*) since it is not a palm. **PALM-LIKE TREE** to 5 m high (16½ ft) or more, dioecious, unbranched but sometimes with multiple stems

posite, blade oblong to lanceolate or ovate, usually 1.5–4 cm long
(⅝–1⅝ in). FLOWERS continuously through the year; flowers solitary in
the leaf axils. Corolla absent but the tubular hypanthium, the calyx,
2–3 cm long (¾–1¼ in), bright red with violet and white at the tip, with
a rounded, sac-like protuberance at the base. FRUIT a small ellipsoidal
capsule enclosed within the hypanthium. PROPAGATE by seeds or cuttings. Fertile, well-drained soils in sunny places are preferred.

Curcuma ZINGIBERACEAE

Curcuma is a genus of ten rhizomatous herbs found in tropical Asia,
some cultivated for their inflorescences. The grated rhizome of *C. longa*,
turmeric, is used as a yellow dye, a medicine, and as an important ingredient in preparing curry. Several of the species are cultivated for
their attractive flowers.

Curcuma zedoaria (Christmann) Roscoe

DISTINGUISHABLE by the ginger-like leaves and small yellow flowers
borne on leafless spikes among overlapping bracts, the upper ones

Curcuma zedoaria

pink. Several other similar species of
Curcuma with pink bracts are known,
making identification somewhat difficult.

Curcuma zedoaria, zedoary, is native
to India but is grown for its pink inflorescences, the upper bracts, because
the flowers are rather small and in-
significant. HERB, perennial, to 75 cm
high (30 in) or more, arising from an
aromatic underground rhizome, white
to yellow inside. LEAVES alternate, four
to six present at a time, simple, blade
oblong to lanceolate with a distinct
midrib, usually 25–45 cm long (10–18

Cuphea ignea A. L. P. P. de Candolle

DISTINGUISHABLE by the low shrubby habit, opposite leaves, and flowers that are longitudinally grooved, bright red with violet and white at the tip, and appear to lack a calyx. *Cuphea micropetala* Kunth differs in having six tiny petals and a yellowish to red hypanthium. *Cuphea llavea* Lexarza differs most conspicuously in having two bright red petals.

Cuphea ignea, cigar flower, sometimes called firecracker plant, is native to Mexico and perhaps the West Indies but is widely cultivated for its attractive flowers and shrubby habit. In the tropics it is often grown in gardens in low borders, on embankments and slopes, or as a tub plant indoors or outdoors, occasionally becoming naturalized; in temperate areas it is utilized as a greenhouse plant. The flowers are sometimes made into leis. SUBSHRUB to 1 m high (3¼ ft). LEAVES simple, op-

Cuphea llavea, flowers with two red petals at the top of the hypanthium

Cuphea ignea, flowers with a red hypanthium

after injuries, trunk covered with old frond bases. LEAVES pinnately compound, spirally arranged to form a conspicuous crown, blades narrowly oblong, mostly 1–2.5 m long (3¼–8¼ ft), leaflets leathery, mostly 13–25 cm long (5–10 in), dark green, changing to spines toward the base. CONES produced by male plants, seeds being formed on fertile leaves of females, which can occur almost anytime during the year. Male cone brown, cylindrical, 30–45 cm long (12–18 in), composed of numerous woody scales. SEEDS elliptic, 4–8 cm long (1⅝–3½ in), borne by females, four to ten on notch-edged, spoon-shaped fertile leaves 15–30 cm long (6–12 in). PROPAGATE by seeds or suckers. Poor soils in sunny or partially shaded places are preferred. This slow-growing relic of the age of dinosaurs is commonly cultivated because its palm-like form gives an attractive tropical look to gardens. It is often grown in rock gardens, as a specimen plant, or in tubs, or in the greenhouse in temperate climates.

Cyperus CYPERACEAE

Cyperus comprises about 600 herbaceous sedge species found throughout the world from the tropics to high-latitude temperate areas. Many are important as pasture plants, and many more as harmful weeds. A few are grown as ornamentals, two of the most common of which are included here.

Cyperus involucratus Rottbøll

Sometimes misidentified as *Cyperus alternifolius* Linnaeus, a similar species from tropical Africa. DISTINGUISHABLE by the leafless triangular stems, 8 to 25 spreading, terminal, tightly spiraled, leaf-like bracts, and dense inflorescences of brown spikelets.

Cyperus involucratus, umbrella sedge, sometimes called umbrella plant, is native to Madagascar but is widely cultivated for its umbrella-like foliage and often becomes weedy. SEDGE, perennial, erect, tuft forming, to 2 m high (6½ ft) or more, stems triangular in cross section, arising from woody rhizomes. LEAVES reduced to brown, bladeless

Cyperus involucratus

sheaths but the inflorescence has a tight, flat spiral of 8 to 25 leaf-like involucral rays 25–60 × 0.8–1.8 cm (10–24 × ¼–¾ in). FLOWERS anytime during the year. Spikelets 6- to 30-flowered, flattened, lanceolate to elliptic, green, 3–9 mm long (about ⅛–⅜ in), arranged in large, branching cormybs 10–30 cm across (4–12 in). PROPAGATE by division or seeds. Moist and even swampy soils in partially shaded places are preferred. It forms dense clumps and is often planted around ponds and along the edges of aquatic gardens but may need containment since it rapidly spreads by means of rhizomes.

Cyperus papyrus Linnaeus

DISTINGUISHABLE by the large habit and numerous brown spikelets borne on filamentous stalks in large terminal inflorescences.

Cyperus papyrus, papyrus, sometimes called Egyptian paper reed, is native to tropical East Africa and Madagascar but is widely cultivated elsewhere in the tropics and warm temperate regions in water gardens and has become naturalized in some places. In ancient Egypt, where this was the bulrush of the Bible, the fibrous pith of the stems was utilized to make a kind of paper.

Cyperus papyrus

SEDGE, perennial, creeping, clump forming, aquatic, to 5 m high (16½ ft) or more, arising from a short, thick, woody rhizome, stems triangular in cross section. **LEAVES** simple, reduced to brown, bladeless sheaths. **FLOWERS** anytime during the year. Spikelets linear, 6–10 mm long (¼–⅜ in) with six to ten flowers, the spikelets borne in cylindrical spikes 1–2.5 cm long (⅜–1 in), arranged in a large compound corymb atop spreading rays 10–30 cm long (4–12 in). **PROPAGATE** by offsets or division. Fertile, wet soils in sunny places are preferred, typically in standing water. It is often grown in dense clumps beside pools or ponds but may need attention since it rapidly spreads by means of rhizomes.

Dahlia ASTERACEAE

Dahlia is a genus of about 28 herb and shrub species found from Mexico to Colombia, many cultivated for their flowers and used locally for their edible tubers. Numerous hybrids and cultivars (more than 20,000 registered cultivars) have been developed, many in Europe in the nineteenth century when their cultivation was a passion, leading to the formation of the British National Dahlia Society in 1881.

Dahlia ×hortensis Guillaumin

Often misidentified as *Dahlia pinnata* Cavanilles. **DISTINGUISHABLE** by the hollow stems, opposite, pinnately compound or further divided leaves, two dissimilar series of bracts, and numerous, often red ray florets in typically nodding heads.

Dahlia ×hortensis is thought to have arisen in Europe from hybridization between *D. pinnata* Cavanilles or *D. variabilis* (Willdenow) Desfontaines and *D. coccinea* Cavanilles, resulting in a great variety of colors, shapes, and sizes in

Dahlia ×hortensis, one of many cultivars

thousands of named cultivars. **HERB**, perennial, hollow stemmed, to 2 m high (6½ ft). **LEAVES** pinnately compound or further divided, opposite, leaflets ovate, mostly 3–8 cm long (1¼–3½ in) with toothed margins. **FLOWERS** anytime during the year in the tropics; flowers in large, long-stalked, terminal, often nodding heads surrounded by two dissimilar series of bracts. Ray florets five or commonly many, mostly 2–6 cm long (¾–2½ in), variously colored but often red. Disk florets many, yellow. **FRUIT** a linear achene but infrequently formed because plants are hybrids. **PROPAGATE** by tubers. Well-drained soils in sunny places are preferred. Plants are grown mostly in temperate to subtropical areas but sometimes in the tropics as well, in borders in gardens, and often being sold in nurseries as potted plants and cut flowers.

Datura SOLANACEAE

Datura is a genus of eight to ten species called thorn apples, found mostly in tropical America, some of which contain hallucinogenic drugs also used medicinally. Some are cultivated for their large, attractive flowers but all parts of the plant are toxic.

Datura metel Linnaeus

Synonym, *Datura fastuosa* Linnaeus. **DISTINGUISHABLE** by the alternate leaves, flowers that are large, solitary, axillary, funnel-shaped, purple, and often double-flowered, and a capsule covered with blunt spines. *Datura stramonium* Linnaeus, Jimson weed, is sometimes cultivated but is more often weedy. That species has larger leaves and a shorter, white to lavender corolla, 6–8.5 cm long (2½–3½ in).

Datura metel, downy thorn apple, is probably native to Asia rather than America but is widely cultivated as a specimen plant or for its large flowers. The seeds and other parts of the plant, like those of other species of *Datura*, contain atropine, scopolamine, and other drugs, and are poisonous. Ingesting them can cause serious hallucinations, delirium, even death. **SHRUB** to 1.5 m high (5 ft) or more. **LEAVES** simple, alternate, blade usually ovate, 7–25 cm long (3–10 in) with toothed margins.

FLOWERS anytime during the year; flowers solitary, axillary. Corolla with fused petals, funnel-shaped, shallowly five-lobed at the end, sometimes double-flowered as in 'Pleniflora', usually 13–20 cm long (5–8 in) and purple on the outside and pale lavender to white inside, rarely white, blue, red, or yellow. FRUIT a green subglobose capsule 3–4 cm long (1¼–1⅝ in), covered with short, blunt spines. PROPAGATE by seeds or cuttings. Well-drained soils in partially shaded places are preferred. In temperate areas it is often grown indoors; in tropical climates it sometimes becomes naturalized in waste areas. The most attractive ornamental plants are double-flowered.

Datura metel, double-flowered

Delonix FABACEAE

Delonix is a genus of about ten species native from Africa to India, one of which is cultivated as an ornamental.

Delonix regia (Bojer ex W. J. Hooker) Rafinesque

DISTINGUISHABLE by the spreading form, deciduous, bipinnately compound leaves, red flowers with the upper petal marked with yellow and white, and long, hanging pods persisting during the period when the tree is leafless.

Delonix regia, royal poinciana, sometimes called just poinciana, is endemic to Madagascar but is no longer found in the wild. It is, however, one of the most popular and spectacular flowering trees in the world and is often planted as a street tree, sometimes heavily pruned to make an arch with other trees across the street, or is grown by itself as a speci-

Delonix regia

men tree because of its broad, spreading, umbrella shape and the masses of red flowers that cover the tree during its seasonal flowering. It is also called flamboyant, flame tree, or flame of the forest. The tree is deciduous in areas with a significant dry season and is often bare in winter before flowering begins. The seeds are sometimes used in seed leis in Hawaii. **TREE,** broad crowned, deciduous, to 15 m high (50 ft). **LEAVES** bipinnately compound, alternate, with 11 to 20 pairs of pinnae, each pinna with 15 to 35 pairs of leaflets, blades oblong to elliptic, 6–12 mm long (¼–½ in). **FLOWERS** seasonally in late winter to summer but particularly in midsummer; flowers many, borne in axillary and subterminal racemes. Corolla of five spreading, free, spoon-shaped petals 3.5–7 cm long (1⅜–3 in), red with the upper one marked with yellow and white, with a faintly fringed margin, and ten red stamens in the center. **FRUIT** a large, narrowly oblong, flattened, hanging, woody, black pod 16–60 cm long (6–24 in). **PROPAGATE** by seeds or cuttings. Well-drained soils in sunny places are preferred. In temperate areas it is grown in the greenhouse as a foliage plant but rarely flowers when potted.

Dichorisandra COMMELINACEAE

Dichorisandra is a tropical American genus of 25 to 35 herbaceous species, some of which are cultivated as house or garden plants.

Dichorisandra thrysiflora Mikan
DISTINGUISHABLE by the tightly spiraled, parallel-veined leaves, dense

terminal panicles, deep violet, three-parted flowers, white inside, and yellow anthers.

Dichorisandra thrysiflora, blue ginger, a misnomer since the plant is not a member of the ginger family Zingiberaceae nor is it really blue, is native to Brazil but is widely grown for its dense, deep violet (a rare color in tropical gardens) inflorescences that form at the top of the plant. **HERB**, erect, to 2 m high (6½ ft) with ringed stems. **LEAVES** simple, alternate, spirally arranged, blade elliptic to lanceolate, 18–36 × 4–11 cm (7–14 × 1⅝–4½ in) on a short petiole. **FLOWERS** seasonally, mostly late spring to fall; flowers

Dichorisandra thrysiflora

many, borne in a terminal, stalked, raceme-like panicle 9–20 cm long (3½–8 in), bearing green, narrowly lanceolate bracts. Corolla of three free, fleshy, ovate to obovate tepals 1⅜–1.8 cm long (⅝–¾ in), the side ones often wider than long, deep violet with white at the base, with yellow anthers. **FRUIT** an obovate capsule. **PROPAGATE** by cuttings, division, or seeds. Fertile, moist, but well-drained soils in shaded places are preferred, and plants do better in cool places. It is often grown as a border or understory plant in the tropics, and in the greenhouse or as a houseplant in temperate climates.

Dieffenbachia ARACEAE

Dieffenbachia is a genus of about 25 stout herbaceous tropical American species, some cultivated as house and shade plants for their colorful foliage.

Dieffenbachia maculata (Loddiges) D. Don

Synonym, *Dieffenbachia picta* (Loddiges) Schott. There is much debate on the taxonomy of dieffenbachias and some authors include *D. maculata* and *D. picta* in *D. seguine* (Jacquin) Schott, a species with dark green leaves. DISTINGUISHABLE by the erect habit and oblong to narrowly lanceolate leaves often flecked with white spots.

Dieffenbachia maculata, spotted dumbcane, is native to Brazil but is widely and commonly cultivated for its variegated leaves. The name dumbcane is derived from the effects of the calcium oxalate crystals in the plant's irritating sap, which when ingested causes paralysis and swelling of the tongue, silencing the person, and even causing death in children and animals. HERB, perennial, erect, to 2 m high (6½ ft) or more with a conspicuously ringed stem. LEAVES simple, alternate, blade oblong to narrowly lanceolate, 15–40 cm long (6–16 in) on a shorter petiole, green with white spots and flecks or white with green spots and

Dieffenbachia maculata

flecks. FLOWERS infrequently during the year; flowers many, borne tightly packed in a cylindrical spadix usually 14–17 cm long (6–7 in) with an oblong-lanceolate, persistent, greenish or white spathe 15–25 cm long (6–10 in). FRUIT a globose red-orange berry, infrequently formed in cultivation. PROPAGATE by stem cuttings or basal suckers. Fertile, moist, but well-drained soils in shaded places are preferred but full sun is required to develop its best color. It is one of the most common potted houseplants but is also grown outdoors for its tropical look. Most of the named variegated cultivars are derived from a natural mutant discovered in the United States in 1936.

Dietes IRIDACEAE

Dietes is a genus of six rhizomatous herbaceous species, five native to southeastern Africa and the other to Lord Howe Island in the Pacific Ocean east of Australia, some of which are cultivated as ornamentals because of their attractive flowers.

Dietes bicolor (Steudel) Sweet ex Klatt

Synonym, *Moraea bicolor* (Steudel) Spae. **DISTINGUISHABLE** by the equitant linear leaves typical of irises, tall, erect, panicles, three obovate, pale yellow tepal segments with a dark brown spot at the base, and three inner, similarly colored, petal-like staminodes lacking the brown spot.

    Dietes bicolor, sometimes called African iris, is native to tropical southeastern Africa but is widely grown in warm regions for its conspicuous, pale yellow and brown, short-lived flowers. **HERB**, perennial, erect, to 1 m high (3¼ ft) or more, arising from a creeping rhizome. **LEAVES** simple, basal, equitant, blade linear, grass-like, 60–120 × 0.4–1 cm (24–48 × ¼–⅜ in). **FLOWERS** continuously through the year; flowers many, in clusters of two to four in sheaths borne in a loose, branched panicle to 1 m long (3¼ ft) or more on an erect stalk with lanceolate bracts. Corolla with fused tepals, deeply split into three obovate to nearly round segments 2–4 cm long (¾–1⅝ in), pale yellow, rarely white, with a dark brown spot at the base, staminodes petal-like, pale yellow. **FRUIT** an obovoid many-seeded capsule. **PROPAGATE** by division or seeds. Moist soils in sunny

Dietes bicolor

places are preferred. It is often grown in borders, beside pools, in oriental gardens, or in mass plantings in the tropics, and as a potted plant in the greenhouse in temperate climates. The stems that have finished flowering should be cut back and the young seed pods removed for best results.

Dissotis MELASTOMATACEAE

Dissotis is a genus of 100 to 150 species of tropical and subtropical Africa, several of which are cultivated as ornamentals for their flowers. Like other members of the melastome family, they can become invasive weeds.

Dissotis rotundifolia (Smith) Triana

Synonym, *Dissotis plumosa* D. Don. **DISTINGUISHABLE** by the low, spreading habit, opposite leaves, bristly calyx projections, obovate pink petals, and yellow stamens with a conspicuous bend in the filament.

Dissotis rotundifolia

Dissotis rotundifolia, which lacks a well-known common name though it is sometimes called trailing dissotis, is native to tropical Africa but is widespread in cultivation for its deep pink flowers. **HERB**, perennial, low growing with creeping branches. **LEAVES** simple, opposite, blade ovate, 1.2–4 cm long (½–1⅝ in), surface hairy, with three or five parallel veins. **FLOWERS** continuously through the year; flowers one to three, borne at the stem tips, the calyx covered with bristles bearing terminal, star-shaped projections. Corolla of five free, obovate, deep pink petals 1.5–2.5 cm long (⅝–1 in) with ten yellow stamens having a conspicuous bend in their filaments. FRUIT a capsule, infrequently formed in cultivation. PROPAGATE by cuttings or seeds. Moist soils in sunny or partially shaded places are preferred. It is often grown in hanging baskets or planters, or as a ground cover, often for erosion control, but unfortunately it is so good at this that it has in some countries it becomes an aggressive weed in pastures and other sunny places. It should not be introduced to tropical areas where it is not already found.

Dracaena AGAVACEAE

Dracaena comprises 40 to 60 species of the Old World tropics from the Canary Islands eastward to Hawaii. Many authors separate most *Dracaena* species into another genus, *Pleomele*, which has led to some confusion in naming. Many are cultivated as ornamentals, including the interesting dragon tree, *Dracaena draco* (Linnaeus) Linnaeus, of the Canary Islands. Three widely cultivated species are described here, and another is mentioned in comparison.

Dracaena angustifolia
Roxburgh

Synonym, *Pleomele angustifolia* (Roxburgh) N. E. Brown. DISTINGUISHABLE by the leathery, linear, parallel-veined leaves with white margins, terminal panicles of yellowish white flowers in clusters of one to four, and orange globose berries.

Dracaena angustifolia, which lacks a widely recognized common name, is native from India to Australia and Melanesia but is widely cultivated in the tropics and subtropics for its attractive variegated foliage. SHRUB to 5 m high (16½ ft) or more, branched at the base.

Dracaena angustifolia

Leaves simple, spirally arranged, blade linear-lanceolate, 10–60 × 1–3 cm (4–24 × ⅜–1¼ in), leathery, drooping, with ivory-colored margins. **Flowers** intermittently during the year; flowers many, borne in clusters of one to four in a terminal panicle 8–75 cm long (3½–30 in), excluding the peduncle. Corolla with fused tepals, divided to near the base into six linear segments 2–3 cm long (¾–1¼ in), yellowish white. **Fruit** an orange globose berry 1.7–2.5 cm in diameter (¾–1 in). **Propagate** by cuttings. Moist but well-drained soils in sunny places are preferred. It is usually grown as a specimen plant or in rows against buildings.

Dracaena fragrans (Linnaeus) Ker-Gawler

Synonym, *Pleomele fragrans* (Linnaeus) Salisbury. **Distinguishable** by the sessile, parallel veined, green or variegated leaves, panicles of many-flowered heads of white flowers, and red to orange berries. Its leaves are not leathery and are narrower than those of *D. angustifolia*. A similar species, *D. deremensis* Engler, has leaves marked with several longitudinal white stripes and is intermediate in width between those of *D. fragrans* and *D. angustifolia*.

Dracaena fragrans, fragrant dracaena, is native to tropical West Africa but is widely cultivated for its attractive form. **Shrub** to 5 m high (16½ ft) or more with ringed stems to 10 cm in diameter (4 in). **Leaves** simple, spirally arranged, blade lanceolate, usually 30–100 × 3–10 cm (12–40 × 1¼–4 in), crowded at the stem tips, green or with longitudinal, yellowish stripes. **Flowers** usually once a year, mostly but not always in winter and spring; flowers many, fragrant, borne in globose heads in large terminal panicles. Corolla with fused tepals, tubular, divided about halfway into six oblanceolate segments 1.5–2 cm long (⅝–¾ in), white. **Fruit** a red to orange globose berry 1.2–2 cm in diameter (½–¾ in). **Propagate** by cuttings. Fertile, moist soils in shaded places are preferred. It is grown by itself as a specimen plant or in rows along buildings and makes an excellent potted houseplant since it is tolerant of neglect. Many cultivars have been named, some with attractive varie-

Dracaena fragrans   *Dracaena deremensis*

gated foliage, including the common one with a central yellow stripe, 'Massangeana'.

Dracaena marginata Lamarck

Synonym, *Pleomele marginata* (Lamarck) N. E. Brown and sometimes confused or equated with *Dracaena concinna* Kunth. DISTINGUISHABLE by the tree-like habit, distinct petioles, sword-shaped leaves usually having red margins, and seasonal panicles of fragrant white flowers.

Dracaena marginata, Madagascar dragon tree, is in fact native to Madagascar but is widely cultivated in the tropics for its attractive form. It is commonly called money tree in Hawaii, perhaps because it was first noted growing next to a bank. TREE or shrub to 6 m high (20 ft), forming many vertical trunks at the base, stems covered with conspicuous, diamond-shaped leaf scars. LEAVES simple, spirally arranged, sessile,

Dracaena marginata

Dracaena marginata 'Tricolor' with variegated leaves

blade sword-shaped, usually 15–45 × 0.7–3 cm (6–18 × ¼–1¼ in), sharp pointed, stiff, usually with red margins. **FLOWERS** mostly in spring; flowers many, borne in widely branching terminal panicles with a lanceolate bract at the base of each branch. Corolla with fused tepals, tubular, 1.3–1.8 cm long (½–¾ in), divided about two-thirds of the way into six narrow segments, white, fragrant. **FRUIT** a yellow-orange globose berry. **PROPAGATE** by stem cuttings, or by seeds, if available. Fertile, moist soils in sunny places are preferred. It is often planted as a border plant or by itself as a specimen tree since it forms attractive clumps, and it makes a good tub plant that can add a tropical look to an area. A colorful, variegated from, 'Tricolor', rainbow tree, is particularly attractive.

Duranta VERBENACEAE

Duranta is a genus of about 17 to perhaps as many as 30 tree and shrub species found from Florida to Brazil, some of which are cultivated for their attractive flowers or fruits.

Duranta erecta Linnaeus

Synonym, *Duranta repens* Linnaeus. DISTINGUISHABLE by the drooping branches, opposite or whorled leaves, hanging racemes of light blue to violet or all white flowers, and golden drupes.

Duranta erecta, golden dewdrop, is native to tropical America but is widely cultivated for its blue or white flowers and yellow-orange fruits, looking like golden dewdrops, that often cover the stems. The fruits are reported to be poisonous since they contain hydrocyanic acid. In small quantities this is used to treat people infected with intestinal worms.

The plant sometimes escapes from cultivation and becomes naturalized. SHRUB, spreading, or tree to 6 m high (20 ft) with drooping branches, sometimes spiny. LEAVES simple, opposite or in whorls, blade elliptic to ovate or obovate, 1.5–8 cm long (5⁄8–3½ in), margins toothed. FLOWERS continuously through the year and the fruits almost always present; flowers many, borne in hanging, upper axillary and terminal racemes mostly 5–30 cm long (2–12 in). Corolla with fused petals, salverform, 9–16 mm long (3⁄8–5⁄8 in) with a spreading limb of five rounded lobes, usually light blue to violet but sometimes white. FRUIT a globose drupe 6–12 mm in diameter (¼–½ in)

Duranta erecta

enclosed in the yellow-orange calyx. **PROPAGATE** by seeds and cuttings. Fertile, moist, but well-drained soils in sunny to partially shaded places are preferred but full sun is required for best color. It is often grown as a hedge or border plant and can be trained to form a small tree. It is also grown in the greenhouse in temperate climates. Several cultivars have been named, including 'Alba', with white flowers.

Eichhornia PONTEDERIACEAE

Eichhornia is a genus of five to seven aquatic herbaceous species from the southeastern United States to Argentina, several of which are cultivated as ornamentals used in pools in tropical to temperate climates.

Eichhornia crassipes (Martius) Solms-Laubach

DISTINGUISHABLE by the floating aquatic habit, inflated petioles, and erect spikes of attractive blue to blue-violet flowers with a patch of yellow in the center.

Eichhornia crassipes

Eichhornia crassipes, water hyacinth, is a free-floating aquatic plant native to Brazil and introduced throughout the warm regions of the world for its lavender and yellow flowers and its attractiveness in pools and ponds. It reproduces and grows so fast that in many places it has clogged lakes and rivers, however, causing much ecological and economic damage. **HERB**, perennial, aquatic, free-floating or rooting, to 40 cm high (16 in), bearing copious fibrous roots. **LEAVES** simple, in a basal rosette, blade leathery, ovate to kidney-shaped, usually 4–18 cm long (1⅝–7 in) on a longer inflated petiole. **FLOWERS** anytime during the year;

flowers many, borne in a spike 10–35 cm long (4–14 in) on a stalk with one or two conspicuous sheathing bracts near the middle. Corolla with fused tepals, two-lipped, deeply divided into six obovate to elliptic segments 3–4 cm long (1¼–1⅝ in), blue to blue-violet, the upper tepal with a yellow patch in the center. FRUIT a many-seeded capsule. PROPAGATE by division or buds. Standing or slowly moving waters in sunny areas are preferred. Because it is one of the world's worst aquatic weeds, it is banned from interstate commerce in the United States. Care should be taken when it is transplanted to new ponds but it is easy to control in confined areas.

Elaeocarpus ELAEOCARPACEAE

Elaeocarpus is a genus of about 250 tree species ranging from Madagascar to Hawaii. Some are utilized for edible fruits, beads from the seeds, and dyes, and some are cultivated as ornamentals.

Elaeocarpus grandis
F. von Mueller

Synonym, *Elaeocarpus angustifolius* Blume, a name used by some authors. DISTINGUISHABLE by the alternate leaves, toothed leaf margins, white flowers with petals fringed at the tip, and distinctive blue, globose drupes containing a single ornamented seed.

Elaeocarpus grandis, blue-marble tree, sometimes called quandong, is native to Queensland, Australia, but is cultivated as a timber tree and as an ornamental or novelty because of its blue, marble-like fruit and attractive scattering of red leaves. TREE to 20 m high (66 ft) or more. LEAVES simple, alter-

Elaeocarpus grandis with aging leaves turning red

nate, blade lanceolate to oblong, 8–20 cm long (3½–8 in), turning red before falling, margins crenate. **FLOWERS** intermittently during the year; flowers many, in axillary racemes borne on leafless branchlets. Corolla of five free petals 1.5–1.9 cm long (⅝–¾ in), fringed at the tip, white. **FRUIT** a blue globose drupe 1.5–3 cm in diameter (⅝–1¼ in), containing a single bony, irregularly ornamented seed. **PROPAGATE** by seeds or cuttings. Moist but well-drained soils in sunny places are preferred. It is often planted as a park, shade, or specimen tree but in some places it becomes invasive in native forests, apparently being spread by pigeons. The seeds can be made into necklaces, as is done in Hawaii.

Enterolobium FABACEAE

Enterolobium is a genus of five to ten tropical American tree species, some of which are used for timber or grazing for livestock, and at least two of which are cultivated as ornamentals.

Enterolobium cyclocarpum with ear-shaped pod

Enterolobium cyclocarpum
(Jacquin) Grisebach

DISTINGUISHABLE by the huge, spreading form, bipinnately compound leaves, small white flowers with protruding white stamens, and dark, ear-shaped pod.

Enterolobium cyclocarpum, ear-pod tree, sometimes called just ear tree or elephant's ear, is native from Central America to northern South America but is widely cultivated in the tropics as a fast-growing shade or park tree with a spreading crown, and as a novelty because of its unusual pods. These pods are used as food for cattle and horses in its native range, and the timber is of good quality. **Tree**, massive, to 30 m high (100 ft) or more with gray bark and spreading canopy. **Leaves** bipinnately compound, alternate, pinnae of 4 to 8 opposite pairs, each pinna with leaflets in 12 to 28 pairs, blades oblong, 8–18 mm long (¼–¾ in), unequally sided. **Flowers** seasonally in spring; flowers many, borne in one to several stalked axillary heads. Corolla funnel-shaped with five partly fused greenish white petals 5–7 mm long (about ¼ in) and many protruding white stamens. **Fruit** a pod twisted into a nearly circular shape, dark brown, 7–16 cm in diameter (3–6 in). **Propagate** by scarified seeds. Moist but well-drained soils in sunny places are preferred. Because of its huge size and thick, spreading roots, it is not recommended for use on small lots, and the falling branches can damage structures. The tree is usually deciduous for part of the year.

Epidendrum ORCHIDACEAE

Epidendrum is a huge genus with 500 to 1000 orchid species, many cultivated for their flowers. The name *Epidendrum* is from the Greek words meaning "upon trees," referring to the epiphytic habit of the plants.

Epidendrum ×*obrienianum*
Rolfe

Distinguishable by the sessile, leathery, two-ranked leaves and red, orange, or mauve flowers with a fringed, typically yellowish labellum.

Epidendrum ×*obrienianum,* scarlet orchid, sometimes called butterfly orchid or baby orchid, is a hybrid from a cross of two South American species, *E. evectum* J. D. Hooker × *E. radicans*

Epidendrum ×*obrienianum*

Pavón ex Lindley, and is widely cultivated in the tropics as a fairly hardy outdoor orchid, occasionally becoming naturalized, in Hawaii, for example. HERB, epiphytic or terrestrial, erect, 30–130 cm high (12–51 in) with gray-white roots forming at the lower nodes. LEAVES simple, alternate, two-ranked, blade sessile, ovate to oblong, 4–13 cm long (1⅝–5 in), leathery. FLOWERS continuously through the year; flowers many, borne in terminal racemes 15–50 cm long (6–20 in). Corolla of five unequal tepals 1.1–1.4 cm (⅜–⅝ in) long and a typically yellow, fringed labellum of similar length, scarlet, orange, or mauve. FRUIT an ellipsoidal capsule 3–5 cm long (1¼–2 in), infrequently formed. PROPAGATE by division or by plantlets that form along older stems. Well-drained soils in sunny or partially shaded places are preferred. It is often grown in pots in compost or rock material, or as an epiphyte on posts.

Epipremnum ARACEAE

Epipremnum is a genus of about eight climbing species ranging from Southeast Asia to Polynesia but the taxonomy of the genus has been confusing. Several are cultivated as ornamentals for their leaves. The name *Epipremnum* is from the Greek words meaning "upon tree trunks," referring to the method of growth of the plants.

Epipremnum pinnatum (Linnaeus) Engler

Synonyms, *Epipremnum aureum* (Linden & André) Bunting, a named used by some authors, *Pothos aureus* Linden & André, *Raphidophora aurea* (Linden & André) Birdsey & André, *R. pinnata* (Linnaeus) Schott, and *Scindapsus aureus* (Linden & André) Engler. DISTINGUISHABLE by the climbing habit, adventitious roots that cling to tree trunks, ovate to elliptic leaves often marked with yellow, and deeply incised margins on large leaves.

Epipremnum pinnatum, pothos, is native over the same range as the genus, Southeast Asia to Polynesia, but is widely cultivated as an ornamental with an attractive tropical look. All parts of the plant may cause stomach problems if ingested, belying the common name sometimes applied, taro vine. LIANA, high climbing, clinging to tree trunks by means of adventitious roots. LEAVES simple, alternate, blade ovate to elliptic, usually 40–80 cm long (16–32 in) when climbing, often with deep incisions on the margins when large, and with perforations along the midrib, green or streaked and variegated with yellow. FLOWERS continuously through the year but the cultivars rarely flower; flowers many, unisexual, tightly packed in a cylindrical spadix usually 10–15 cm long (4–6 in) with a longer, deciduous, cream-colored spathe attached at the base. FRUIT a small ellipsoidal berry, rarely formed in cultivation.

Epipremnum pinnatum, growing on the ground

PROPAGATE by stem cuttings. Fertile, moist soils in shaded places are preferred. When growing on the ground it has small, entire leaves and makes an excellent ground cover that excludes most weeds. When it climbs into trees (it is often planted as decoration for tall palm trunks) by means of its adventitious roots, the leaves are larger and often have split margins. It is also extremely easy to grow and requires little attention as a potted plant, in temperate as well as tropical climates. The most commonly cultivated 'Aureum', golden pothos, has variegated leaves.

Episcia GESNERIACEAE

Episcia is a genus of six to ten tropical American herb species as well as a hundred or more cultivars, several of which are cultivated for their colorful leaves or attractive flowers.

Episcia cupreata

Episcia cupreata
(W. J. Hooker) Hanstein

DISTINGUISHABLE by the low habit, leaves that are opposite, variously colored, and have a puckered surface, and two to four flowers with a spreading red limb.

Episcia cupreata, flame violet, a misnomer since it is not related to the violet family Violaceae, is native to Colombia and perhaps northward to Nicaragua but is widely cultivated in the tropics for its red flowers and attractive leaves. HERB, prostrate, somewhat succulent, stems hairy, rooting at the nodes. LEAVES simple, opposite, blade elliptic, 4–12 cm long (1⅝–5 in), margins scalloped, surface variegated with pale green, copper, reddish green, or all three colors, pubescent, puckered. FLOWERS continuously through the year; flowers two to four, borne in a fascicle atop a long, hairy peduncle. Corolla with fused petals, salverform and two-lipped, tube 2–3 cm long (¾–1¼ in), limb of five spreading, nearly round lobes 7–10 mm long (¼–⅜ in), red with a yellow throat, margins toothed and ciliate. FRUIT a two-valved capsule, infrequently formed in cultivation. PROPAGATE by cuttings, divisions, or offsets. Fertile, moist, but well-drained soils in shaded places are preferred. It is often grown in pots and hanging baskets, and sometimes indoors.

Erythrina FABACEAE

Erythrina comprises about 110 tree species found throughout the tropics and subtropics, many cultivated for their often bright red flowers. Two commonly cultivated ornamental species are included here. The name *Erythrina* is from the Greek word for red, referring to the typical flower color.

Erythrina crista-galli Linnaeus

DISTINGUISHABLE by the spreading tree habit, trifoliate leaves, and racemes of long-lasting, red, butterfly-like flowers produced throughout the year.

Erythrina crista-galli, cockspur coral tree, sometimes called cockscomb coral tree or coral tree, is native to Brazil but is widely cultivated for its long-lasting red flowers. These differ from those of most other erythrinas in bearing flowers throughout the year. In its native habitat, the flowers are pollinated by birds, which is typical of red-flowered plants. Unlike those of many other species of the genus, the attractive, dark green leaves are not deciduous. **TREE**, spreading, to 10 m high (33 ft) with furrowed bark. **LEAVES** trifoliate, alternate, leaflet blades ovate to elliptic, 5–12 cm long (2–5 in), of-

ten with spines on the petiole. **FLOWERS** most of the year, the flowers long lasting; flowers many, borne in leafy racemes or in a terminal raceme and axillary fascicles. Corolla papilionaceous, 3.5–6 cm long (1⅜–2½ in), bright red, with four unequal petals, the largest one, the banner, oval, reflexed, and with the fused stamens surrounded by the curved keel. **FRUIT** a linear-oblong pod 10–30 cm long (4–12 in), containing bean-like seeds. **PROPAGATE** by seeds, cuttings, or air layering. Well-drained soils in sunny places are preferred. The tree is usually planted by itself as a specimen for its colorful flowers rather than as a street tree.

Erythrina crista-galli

Erythrina variegata Linnaeus

DISTINGUISHABLE by the tree habit, trifoliate leaves, seasonal racemes of bright red, butterfly-like flowers, and dark, curved, linear-oblong pods that hang on the tree during its deciduous time of the year.

Erythrina variegata is a coral tree, sometimes called Indian coral tree or tiger's claw, native from the island of Zanzibar off the East African coast to the Marquesas Islands in the Pacific Ocean but is widely cultivated elsewhere for its seasonal red flowers, pollinated by birds. *Erythrina sandwicensis* O. Degener, related and endemic to Hawaii where it is called wiliwili, is locally popular as a park or specimen tree for its attractive orange to white, seasonal flowers. The seeds of both species are used for making seed leis. **TREE** to 20 m high (66 ft), often with a spiny trunk and branches. **LEAVES** trifoliate, alternate, leaflet blades ovate to nearly round, 4–25 cm long (1⅝–10 in), sometimes with white or yel-

Erythrina variegata var. *variegata*   *Erythrina sandwicensis*

low variegated veins or center area. FLOWERS seasonally, mostly winter and spring, with pods maturing in spring and summer; flowers many, borne in terminal or axillary racemes. Corolla papilionaceous, 4–6 cm long (1⅝–2½ in), red-orange, of four unequal petals with ten fused stamens. FRUIT a dark, curved, linear-oblong pod 12–30 cm long (5–12 in), containing kidney-shaped, bean-like seeds. PROPAGATE by seeds, cuttings, or air layering. Fertile, moist, but well-drained soils in sunny places are preferred. The most attractive variety *variegata* is grown for its variegated leaves, and another with ascending branches, sometimes called 'Tropic Coral', is popular for living fence posts but the spiny stems can be a drawback. The tree is deciduous and barren during winter, which is followed by the flowering season.

Etlingera ZINGIBERACEAE

Etlingera is a genus of about 57 rhizomatous perennial ginger species found from China to Polynesia.

Etlingera elatior (Jack) R. M. Smith

Synonyms, *Alpinia nutans* Roscoe, *Nicolaia elatior* (Jack) Horaninow, *N. speciosa* (Blume) Horaninow, and *Phaeomeria speciosa* (Blume) Koorders. DISTINGUISHABLE by the large ginger habit, two-ranked, ginger-like leaves, and large red or pink inflorescences on tall, leafless stalks.

Etlingera elatior, torch ginger, is native to Malaysia where it is no longer known in the wild. It is widely cultivated for its attractive form and red or pink inflorescences. With its huge, brightly colored inflorescences it is one the best known exotic plants. Its taxonomy has been confusing, with several seemingly unrelated names used in the literature. HERB, perennial, robust, erect, clump forming, to 6 m high (20 ft), arising from a rhizome, stems often red to purple. LEAVES simple, alternate, two-ranked, petiole 1–4 cm long (⅜–1⅝ in) attached atop a sheath, blade narrowly elliptic, usually 50–85 × 6–22 cm (20–34 × 2½–9 in). FLOWERS continuously through the year; flowers many, borne among large, densely packed, bright red to rose-pink bracts, the

Etlingera elatior

Eucalyptus deglupta

outer ones to 12 cm long (5 in), in an ovoid head atop a scaly stalk to 2.5 m high (8¼ ft). Corolla with fused tepals 3.5–4 cm long (1⅜–1⅝ in), lobed about halfway into three subequal segments, the labellum red with white or yellow margin. FRUIT a fuzzy, many-seeded, green to red, ovoid capsule. PROPAGATE by rhizome division. Fertile, moist, but well-drained soils in sunny or partially shaded places are preferred. It is often grown in clumps as a large border plant in the tropics and in the greenhouse in temperate climates.

Eucalyptus MYRTACEAE

Eucalyptus is a genus of more than 600 mostly Australian tree and shrub species, many cultivated for their timber, oil, tannins or as ornamentals. More than 200 species are cultivated worldwide.

Eucalyptus deglupta Blume
DISTINGUISHABLE by the tree habit, colorful, flaky bark, opposite, ovate to broadly elliptic leaves, and panicles of small white flowers bearing many white stamens.

Eucalyptus deglupta is the Mindanao gum, sometimes called bagras. Most of the ornamentals of the genus are temperate species but this one is native from the southern Philippines to New Guinea. It is widely planted elsewhere as a tropical timber tree but is prone to hurricane and fire damage. It is also widely cultivated as an ornamental species, mostly because of its colorful, flaky bark, and is usually grown as a specimen or street tree. TREE to 20 m high (66 ft) or more, fast growing. LEAVES simple, opposite, blade ovate to broadly elliptic, 8–18 cm long (3½–7 in). FLOWERS anytime during the year; flowers many, borne in terminal and axillary panicles. Corolla absent but flowers with numerous white stamens 5–10 mm long (¼–⅜ in) borne on the cup-shaped hypanthium 3–5 mm across (about ⅛–¼ in). FRUIT a woody, cup-shaped capsule about 5 mm across (¼ in). PROPAGATE by seeds. Deep, sandy soils in sunny places are preferred.

Eucharis AMARYLLIDACEAE

Eucharis is a genus of 17 to 20 herbaceous perennial, tropical American species, some of which are cultivated for their attractive flowers. The name *Eucharis* is from the Greek words meaning good looking, in reference to the flowers.

Eucharis amazonica Linden ex Planchon

Sometimes misidentified as *Eucharis grandiflora* Planchon & Lindley, also cultivated. DISTINGUISHABLE by the scapose herb habit, basal, elliptic leaves with parallel veins and a distinct midrib, and six-lobed white flowers with the six stamens united into a cup. The somewhat similar *Proiphys amboinensis* differs most noticeably in having mostly heart-shaped leaves and more flowers.

Eucharis amazonica, Amazon lily, sometimes called Eucharist lily or Madonna lily, is native to Ecuador but is widely cultivated for its fragrant white flowers, resembling large white daffodils. It is reportedly used to brew an emetic tea in its native range. HERB, erect, scapose, to 80 cm high (32 in), arising from underground, clump-forming bulbs. LEAVES simple, basal, blade usually elliptic, 25–40 cm long (10–16 in) on a petiole of similar length. FLOWERS anytime during the year; flowers

Eucharis amazonica

three to seven, fragrant, somewhat nodding, borne in a terminal umbel atop a leafless stalk 30–60 cm long (12–24 in). Corolla with fused tepals, funnel-shaped, with a narrow tube 3–4 cm long (1¼–1⅝ in) and six spreading ovate segments 3–5 cm long (1¼–2 in), white, with the six stamens united into a cup. FRUIT a deeply three-lobed capsule. PROPAGATE by offsets. Fertile soils in partially shaded places are preferred. It is typically grown as a border plant in the garden in tropical climates, and in greenhouses or conservatories in temperate climates.

Eugenia MYRTACEAE

Eugenia is a genus of 550 tropical and subtropical American tree and shrub species, or as many as 1000 according to some authors. Many species formerly put into this genus are now included in the genus *Syzygium*. Many are cultivated for edible fruits, and a few are grown as ornamentals.

Eugenia uniflora Linnaeus

DISTINGUISHABLE by the shrubby habit, opposite, dark green leaves, axillary, one- to three-flowered clusters of small flowers bearing many white stamens, and longitudinally eight-grooved, red fruit.

Eugenia uniflora, Surinam cherry, is native to South America from Guyana to Argentina but is widely cultivated for its sour but edible fruit and as an ornamental because of its dark, glossy green leaves. The slightly bitter fruits, a good source of vitamin C, are eaten raw or, more commonly, are made into jellies and preserves. SHRUB to 4 m high (13 ft). **LEAVES** simple, opposite, blade ovate, 2.5–7 cm long (1–3 in), glossy dark green on upper surface, lighter below. **FLOWERS** anytime during the year; flowers one to three, borne in axillary clusters, pedicel 1–1.8 cm long (⅜–¾ in). Corolla of four nearly round, white, deciduous petals 7–10 mm long (¼–⅜ in), with many white stamens. **FRUIT** a red, subglobose, one-seeded berry 1.5–3 cm long (⅝–1¼ in) with eight longitudinal grooves. **PROPAGATE** by seeds. Fertile, moist soils in sunny to partially shaded places are preferred but full sun is required for best shape. It is usually grown as a hedge, screen, or tub plant.

Eugenia uniflora

Euphorbia EUPHORBIACEAE

Euphorbia, the genus of spurges, comprises 1500 to 2000 herb, shrub, and tree species found throughout the world, especially in tropical and subtropical areas. The genus includes many weedy species, and many others have been put in a separate genus, *Chamaesyce,* by some authors. *Euphorbia* is characterized by a highly modified inflorescence called a cyathium (plural, cyathia) in which several male flowers consisting of a single stamen each are fused into a cup-like involucre around a single female flower. The spiny succulent species are often mistaken as cacti, members of the family Cactaceae, but the milky sap in spurges is a dead giveaway. Many species are cultivated for their foliage or flowers, eight of the most common of which are included here.

Euphorbia cotinifolia Linnaeus
DISTINGUISHABLE by the milky sap, red to purple, long-stalked ovate

Euphorbia cotinifolia

leaves, solitary terminal cyathia with six yellow glands and a scalloped margin, and three-lobed schizocarp.

Euphorbia cotinifolia, hierba mala, sometimes called red spurge, is native to tropical America and was originally named from Venezuela but is cultivated for its attractive purplish green leaves. The name hierba mala means bad herb in Spanish, probably because of its poisonous sap, which causes vomiting and can be fatal if ingested. The sap is also caustic to the skin, producing rashes and blisters. In its native range the plant is used as a fish and arrow poison. SHRUB to 2 m high (6½ ft) or more, sap milky. LEAVES simple, opposite or in 3s or 4s, blade ovate, 2–10 cm long (¾–4 in), glabrous, dark red to purplish green, on a long, thin petiole. FLOWERS anytime during the year but the flowers are inconspicuous in solitary terminal cyathia. Corolla absent but the involucre bears six yellow glands with a white, scalloped margin. FRUIT a three-lobed, subglobose schizocarp usually 4–6 mm long (about ¼ in). PROPAGATE by cuttings. Moist soils in hot, sunny or partially shaded places are preferred. It is often grown as a screen or specimen plant.

Euphorbia cyathophora Murray

Synonyms, *Euphorbia heterophylla* var. *cyathophora* (Murray) Boissier and *Poinsettia cyathophora* (Murray) Klotzsch & Garcke. DISTINGUISHABLE by the milky sap, alternate upper leaves marked with red at the base, typically notched leaf margins, terminal cyathia of inconspicuous flowers, and three-lobed schizocarp.

Euphorbia cyathophora, Mexican fire plant, sometimes called wild poinsettia or painted leaf, is native to the West Indies but is widely cultivated for the prominent red bases of the upper leaves. **HERB**, annual or perennial, to 1 m high (3¼ ft) with milky sap. **LEAVES** simple, alternate, blade usually oblong, fiddle-shaped, or elliptic, 3–9 cm long (1¼–3½ in), often with a notch on either side. **FLOWERS** continuously through the year after maturity; flowers borne in terminal cyathia above the upper leaves that are bright red, rarely pink, at the base. Corolla absent. **FRUIT** a flattened-globose, three-lobed schizocarp 3–6 mm long (about ⅛–¼ in). **PROPAGATE** by seeds. Well-drained soils in sunny places are preferred. It is often grown as a border plant in gardens or in cemeteries, particularly in areas of poor soil where few other ornamental species can survive. It is perhaps more commonly found as a weed.

Euphorbia cyathophora

Euphorbia lactea Haworth

DISTINGUISHABLE by the succulent shrubby habit, the milky sap, four-angled stems with the angles bearing paired thorns arising from small black caps, and white stripes between the angles. The very similar *Euphorbia antiquorum* Linnaeus, Malayan spurge tree, differs most obviously in lacking the white markings on the stems.

Euphorbia lactea, mottled candlestick, sometimes called mottled spurge or milkstripe euphorbia, is native to India but is widely cultivated as a novelty because of its similarity to cacti. Like most euphorbias it has a poisonous sap that can be harmful if it comes into contact with sores, eyes, mouth, or mucous membranes. This characteristic, as well as its thorny stems, can be a drawback, particularly in areas with foot traffic. **SHRUB** or small tree to 4 m high (13 ft) or more with succulent, green, four-angled stems bearing paired black thorns 2–4 mm long

Euphorbia lactea

Euphorbia leucocephala

(about ¹⁄₁₆–¹⁄₄ in), arising from cap-like structures spaced on the stem ridges, sap milky and sticky. LEAVES tiny, ovate, deciduous and absent most of the time. FLOWERS rarely; flowers in paired cyathia borne near the tips of the stems. Corolla absent but a yellowish gland is present on the cyathium. FRUIT a flattened-globose, deeply three-lobed schizocarp. PROPAGATE by cuttings. Well-drained soils in sunny places are preferred. It is a hardy plant that is tolerant of dry soil and saline conditions and is often grown as a specimen or sometimes in hedges. A cultivar crested at the tips of the branches, 'Cristata', looks particularly unusual.

Euphorbia leucocephala Lotsy

DISTINGUISHABLE by the milky sap, whorled, long-stalked leaves, seasonal terminal panicles of cyathia bearing white, petal-like bracts, and three-lobed schizocarp. It is very similar to a temperate U.S. prairie plant called snow on the mountain, *Euphorbia marginata* Pursh, which has white margins on the upper leaves.

Euphorbia leucocephala, white-lace euphorbia, which has several other names, including pascuita, and young (or little) Christ's (or boy's, or child's) flower, probably because it flowers around Christmastime in the northern hemisphere, is native to Central America but is widely cultivated for the white bracts that seasonally cover the bush. Like other euphorbias, the sap is poisonous. **SHRUB** to 2 m high (6½ ft) or more with milky sap. **LEAVES** simple, in whorls of 4 to 12, blade elliptic to broadly lanceolate, 3–8 cm long (1¼–3½ in) on a long petiole. **FLOWERS** seasonally, mostly in winter and spring; flowers in terminal panicles of cyathia. Corolla absent but the cyathium has five white, awl-shaped, petal-like bracts about 3 mm long (about ⅛ in), and the panicle bears many white to pink, oblanceolate to narrowly oblong bracts 6–18 mm long (¼–¾ in). **FRUIT** a green, subglobose, shallowly three-lobed schizocarp. **PROPAGATE** by cuttings. Moist but well-drained soils in sunny places are preferred. It is grown in hedges, screens, or alone as a specimen plant.

Euphorbia milii Desmoulins

Synonym, *Euphorbia splendens* Bojer ex W. J. Hooker. **DISTINGUISHABLE** by the succulent, thorny stems, milky sap, cyathia with the involucre having two bright red, petal-like bracts, and three-lobed schizocarp.

Euphorbia milii, crown of thorns, is native to Madagascar but is widely cultivated as a novelty because of its thorny stems and conspicuous red bracts. Like other euphorbias, it is poisonous. **SHRUB**, freely branching, thick stemmed, to 1.2 m high (4 ft) with milky sap and spines 4–20 mm long (¼–¾ in). **LEAVES** simple, alternate, blade obovate to oblanceolate, 1–12 cm long (⅜–5 in), appearing only on new growth. **FLOWERS** anytime during the year; flowers in cyathia, solitary or

Euphorbia milii

paired, or arranged in axillary panicles. Corolla absent but the involucre has two nearly round, bright red bracts 3–7 mm long (about ⅛–¼ in). **Fruit** a three-lobed schizocarp, infrequently formed in cultivation. **Propagate** by cuttings. Fertile, moist, but well-drained soils in partially shaded places are preferred but full sun is needed for optimal flower color and form. It is usually grown in rock gardens, in pots, or as a ground cover and can be trained on trellises. Several variations are distinguished, the most common of which is variety *splendens* (Bojer ex W. J. Hooker) Ursch & Leandri, considered by some authors to be a separate species.

Euphorbia neriifolia Linnaeus

Distinguishable by the shrubby habit, the milky sap, succulent, five-angled stems with thorns on the angles, and succulent leaves borne on the angles of the new, young stems. It differs from *Euphorbia lactea* and *E. antiquorum* Linnaeus, Malayan spurge tree, by the presence of the large, persistent leaves.

Euphorbia neriifolia

Euphorbia neriifolia, Indian spurge tree, sometimes called hedge euphorbia, is native to India but is widely cultivated as a novelty because of its striking resemblance to a cactus. Its sap, like that of other members of the genus, is poisonous and caustic to the skin. **Shrub** to 4 m high (13 ft) with milky sap and hard, succulent, five-angled stems bearing paired black spines. **Leaves** simple, borne in vertical rows on the stems, blade obovate, 8–15 cm long (3½–6 in), somewhat succulent and persistent on the younger parts of the plant. **Flowers** intermittently during the year; flowers in cyathia borne in short cymes. Corolla absent. FRUIT a three-lobed schizocarp. PROPAGATE by cuttings. Well-drained soils in sunny places are preferred. It is often planted as a novelty or specimen plant. The sharp spines can be a drawback when the species is planted near foot traffic. One cultivar, 'Cristata', has unusual, crested branches.

Euphorbia pulcherrima   Willdenow ex Klotzsch

DISTINGUISHABLE by the shrubby habit, milky sap, upper leaves bright red or, less commonly, other colors at flowering time, and cyathia with a conspicuous yellow gland. The similar *Euphorbia cyathophora* differs in being a somewhat weedy herb that flowers throughout the year.

Euphorbia pulcherrima, poinsettia, is native to western Mexico but is widely cultivated from the tropics to warm temperate regions for its large red bracts that appear with the flowers in winter and spring. Because of its winter flowering and red bracts it has become a symbol of Christmas in many areas, sometimes being called Christmas flower, and is commonly sold then as a potted plant. It has reported medicinal uses in Mexico but the sap is poisonous. SHRUB to 3 m high (10 ft) with milky sap. LEAVES simple, alternate, blade elliptic, ovate, or oblanceolate, 6–25 cm long (2½–10 in), often with one or two lobes on the margins. FLOWERS seasonally in winter; flowers borne in clusters of cup-shaped cyathia forming opposite an upper leaf, above the leaf-like bracts that are red or occasionally yellow, white, or pink, and in some forms double-flowered. Corolla absent, but the involucre bears a conspicuous yellow gland. FRUIT a subglobose, deeply three-lobed schizocarp

Euphorbia pulcherrima

1.3–2 cm long (½–¾ in). **PROPAGATE** by cuttings. Fertile soils in sunny places are preferred. It is grown as a seasonally colorful border or foundation plant outdoors in the tropics but in pots in the greenhouse in temperate climates. Hybridization and selection have produced some cultivars with white to pink bracts and shorter stems.

Euphorbia tirucalli Linnaeus

DISTINGUISHABLE by the shrubby habit, milky sap, pencil-like stems, and tiny, linear, deciduous leaves.

Euphorbia tirucalli, pencil tree, sometimes called milk bush or bone bush, is native to tropical Africa but has long been cultivated from India to Malaysia and is now widely grown as a novelty because of its leafless, narrowly cylindrical stems. In its native range, it has been used as a fish poison because of its poisonous, caustic sap. **SHRUB**, much-branched, nearly leafless, to 4 m high (13 ft) or more, with green, narrowly cylindrical stems with milky sap. **LEAVES** simple, alternate, blade linear to narrowly oblanceolate, usually 1–3 cm long (⅜–1¼ in), present only on the young stems and soon deciduous. **FLOWERS** intermittently during the year; flowers inconspicuous, borne in terminal and axillary cyathia. Corolla absent. **FRUIT** a three-lobed schizocarp, infrequently formed in cultivation. **PROPAGATE** by cuttings. Fertile, light soils in sunny places are preferred. It is usually planted by itself as a novelty or specimen plant but can be used for hedges or as a potted plant and is tolerant of adverse conditions. It is difficult to prune because of the poisonous sap that can irritate skin and inflame eyes, and that can be fatal if ingested.

Euphorbia tirucalli

Evolvulus CONVOLVULACEAE

Evolvulus is a genus of about 100 species, all but two of which are found in subtropical and tropical America, several cultivated as ornamentals for their flowers. The name *Evolvulus* is from the Greek word meaning untwist, referring to the nonclimbing habit of these plants, unlike most other members of the morning glory family Convolvulaceae.

Evolvulus glomeratus Nees & Martius

Called *Evolvulus pilosus* Nuttall by some authors, a species from the midwestern United States. DISTINGUISHABLE by the subshrub habit, pubescent, alternate leaves, and rotate flowers that are blue with a white center.

Evolvulus glomeratus, blue daze, is native to tropical America and was originally named from Brazil and Paraguay but is widely cultivated as a ground cover or grown in mass plantings because of its dense, low-growing foliage and attractive blue flowers. SUBSHRUB to 30 cm high (12 in) or more. LEAVES simple, alternate, blade elliptic to oblanceolate, 8–40 mm long (¼–1⅝ in), finely hairy on both surfaces. FLOWERS continuously through the year; flowers solitary and borne in the upper leaf axils. Corolla of fused petals, rotate, 1.5–2 cm long (⅝–¾ in), limb spreading, 1.8–2.5 cm in diameter (¾–1 in), blue with white in the center. FRUIT a four-seeded globose capsule, infrequently formed in cultivation. PROPAGATE by seeds or cuttings. Well-drained soils in sunny places are preferred. Most often cultivated is 'Blue Daze', a cultivar of subspecies *grandiflorus* (Parodi) Ooststroom.

Evolvulus glomeratus

Fagraea LOGANIACEAE

Fagraea is a genus of 35 to 50 species found from Sri Lanka to the Marquesas Islands. Some are used locally for timber and medicines, and some are planted as ornamentals because of their large, attractive flowers.

Fagraea berteroana A. Gray ex Bentham

DISTINGUISHABLE by the tree or shrub habit, opposite leaves with a basal, two-lobed swelling, terminal cymes of long, tubular, five-lobed white flowers fading to orange, and large, many-seeded, orange berry.

Fagraea berteroana, pua, is native from New Guinea to the Marquesas Islands but is also often cultivated in its native range and in Hawaii, where it is called pua kenikeni, for its white to yellow or pale orange, fragrant flowers, which are commonly used in leis and for scenting coconut oil. The fine quality wood is also used for carving and other purposes. In its native habitat it can often be found growing high up in other trees as an epiphyte, with long roots that eventually extend down to the ground and form a typical tree. TREE or shrub to 15 m high (50 ft), often beginning as an epiphyte or strangler, with distinct swelling in the leaf axil. LEAVES simple, opposite, blade obovate to elliptic, 10–20 cm long (4–8 in), somewhat succulent. FLOWERS continuously through the year; flowers several, borne in terminal cymes. Corolla with fused petals, salverform to funnel-shaped, tube 3–10 cm long (1¼–4 in) with a spreading limb of five obovate lobes 1.4–2.5 cm long (⅝–1 in), white but fading to yellow or pale orange. FRUIT an orange to red, ellipsoidal, many-seeded berry 3–5 cm

Fagraea berteroana

long (1¼–2 in). **PROPAGATE** by cuttings, air layering, or seeds, the latter slower than the other two methods. Well-drained soils in sunny or partially shaded places are preferred.

Ficus MORACEAE

Ficus includes about 800 to 1000 tree and shrub species native throughout the tropics and subtropics, but none native to Hawaii. Many begin life as an epiphyte and eventually surround their host plant and strangle it, hence a name for the banyans, strangler fig. One species, *F. carica* Linnaeus, is widely cultivated for its edible fruit, the fig, and others are grown as shade trees or novelties. *Ficus* species can be differentiated from each other by their habit, whether they are banyans or not, by leaf shape, and by fruits, but not readily by their flowers, which are all tiny and completely enclosed within the inflorescence receptacle, the syconium, that forms the fruit. All of them have milky sap and a terminal cap enclosing the growing bud. Because they lack the correct tiny wasp needed for pollination, most ornamental species do not form seeds outside their native range. Six ornamental species are included here.

Ficus benghalensis Linnaeus
DISTINGUISHABLE by the large banyan habit, milky sap, conical cap enclosing the growing point of the stem, leaves that are large, leathery, and dark green, and fruits that are paired, red, axillary, and berry-like.

Ficus benghalensis, Indian banyan, is native to India but is widely cultivated as a shade tree. It can become a

Ficus benghalensis

Ficus benghalensis, planted as street trees, forming a tree tunnel

Ficus benghalensis allowed to grow in its banyan habit, with hanging roots that form new trunks

huge banyan by sending down aerial roots that develop into trunks, making it a popular specimen tree. It is obviously not suitable for small yards if the tree is going to be allowed to become a banyan. One famous tree in India has spread to nearly 300 m in diameter (1000 ft). **BANYAN TREE** to 25 m high (82 ft) or more, spreading, with the fused, conical stipules enclosing the stem tip, sap milky. **LEAVES** simple, alternate, blade ovate to broadly elliptic, 10–25 long, dark green, leathery, coarsely veined, with a blunt to abruptly pointed tip. **FRUITS** can be found on the trees most of the year. Fruit a red subglobose syconium 1.4–2.0 cm long (⅝–¾ in), paired in the leaf axils. **PROPAGATE** by cuttings or air layering. Fertile, moist soils in sunny places are preferred. The trees are sacred to Hindus, who believe that Brahma was transformed into one. The sap yields an inferior rubber that is of little current use since it was replaced by the more valuable South American rubber tree, *Hevea brasiliensis* (Willdenow ex A. H. L. Jussieu) Müller Argoviensis.

Ficus benjamina Linnaeus

DISTINGUISHABLE by the tree habit, milky sap, drooping branches, conical cap enclosing the growing point of the stem, drooping branches, light green leaves, and fruits that are paired, axillary, and berry-like.

Ficus benjamina

Ficus benjamina, weeping fig, sometimes called Benjamin's fig, is native from India to northern Australia but is widely cultivated in the tropics and subtropics as an ornamental or street tree because of its graceful form with drooping branches (hence the name weeping fig) and dense foliage. Heavy fruit fall can be a problem on sidewalks. It forms aerial roots on the main trunk but not usually on the branches, so it is not a true banyan. TREE to 15 m high (50 ft) with the fused conical stipules enclosing the stem tip, sap milky. LEAVES simple, alternate, blade ovate to elliptic, 4–12 cm long (1⅝–5 in), typically light green, finely veined, with a sharp or attenuate tip. FRUITS can be found on the tree throughout the year. Fruit an orange, red, pink, or purple, subglobose syconium 7–12 mm long (¼–½ in), paired in the leaf axils. PROPAGATE by cuttings or air layering. Fertile, moist soils in sunny places are preferred. It is often grown as a specimen plant or in tubs. Its extensive underground root system can undermine structures, making the tree unsuitable for planting next to houses.

Ficus elastica Roxburgh ex Hornemann

DISTINGUISHABLE by the large banyan habit, milky sap, colorful stipules forming a cap over the growing point of the stem, leaves that are large, dark green, leathery, small, and with a colored midvein, and fruits that are paired, small, greenish yellow, axillary, and berry-like.

Ficus elastica, Indian rubber tree or rubber plant, also called Indian rubber fig, is native from India to Malaysia but is widely cultivated as a shade, park, or specimen tree and for its large, attractive leaves and colorful stipules. If allowed to grow outdoors on its own in the tropics, it can become a huge banyan tree with typical columnar, trunk-forming aerial roots. It needs frequent pruning to keep it under control. A commercial rubber was made from the sap early in the twentieth century but was thereafter replaced by the rubber from *Hevea*. BANYAN TREE to 25 m high (82 ft) or more with long, pink to purple stipules, sap milky.

Ficus elastica

LEAVES simple, alternate, blade elliptic, 8–35 cm long (3½–14 in), dark green and leathery, sometimes with a red midvein or tinted purple. FRUITS are infrequently found on the tree outside its native range. Fruit a greenish yellow subglobose syconium 6–12 mm long (¼–½ in), paired in the leaf axils. PROPAGATE by cuttings or air layering. Fertile, moist soils in sunny places are preferred. It is also a popular potted houseplant needing little attention and doing well even in temperate regions and in air-conditioned houses in the tropics. Several cultivars have been named, differing mostly in leaf color.

Ficus lyrata Warburg

DISTINGUISHABLE by the tree habit, milky sap, stipules forming a conical cap over the growing point of the stem, leaves that are large, leathery, and lyre-shaped, and large, berry-like fruits.

Ficus lyrata, fiddle-leaf fig, sometimes called banjo fig, is native to tropical Africa but is occasionally cultivated as a shade tree. When properly trimmed of its lower branches, the tree forms a high, dense canopy and attractive shape. Its large fleshy figs can be a minor nuisance when they fall and hit someone or litter the ground. TREE to 10 m high (33 ft), spreading, with persistent, dried stipules at the nodes, sap milky. LEAVES simple, alternate, blade oblong, obovate, or lyrate, fiddle-shaped, 20–40 cm long (8–16 in), leathery, dark green, heart-shaped at the base, strongly veined beneath. FRUITS can be found on the tree periodically throughout the year. Fruit a white-dotted globose syconium 3–5 cm in diameter (1¼–2 in), paired in the leaf

Ficus lyrata

axils with persistent stipules 3–5 cm long (1¼–2 in) below them. **PROP-AGATE** by air layering or cuttings. Fertile, moist soils in sunny places are preferred. In temperate climates it is sometimes grown indoors as a potted plant, at least when it is small.

Ficus microcarpa Linnaeus fil.

Sometimes misidentified as *Ficus retusa* Linnaeus, not commonly cultivated. **DISTINGUISHABLE** by the large size, banyan or spreading crown habit, milky sap, stipules forming a conical cap over the growing point of the stem, leaves that are small and oblong to obovate, and fruits that are paired, small, axillary, pink to purple, and berry-like.

Ficus microcarpa, Chinese banyan, is native from Sri Lanka to Micronesia but is widely cultivated as a shade or park tree. The hanging roots may or may not produce a banyan form but more often in cultivation it is grown as a large tree with an attractive, dense, spreading canopy. It is naturalized in Hawaii and elsewhere, establishing itself as an epiphyte on rocks and buildings, eventually becoming a large tree. The wasp needed for its fertilization is consequently present in those areas where it does become naturalized. **BANYAN TREE**, an epiphytic shrub when young that forms hanging aerial roots and eventually becomes huge, with stipules forming a sheath over the stem tip, sap milky. **LEAVES** simple, alternate, blade oblong to obovate, 2.5–8 cm long (1–3½ in), leathery, dark green. **FRUITS** can be found on the trees throughout the year. Fruit a pink to purple subglobose syconium 6–13 mm long (¼–½ in), paired in the leaf

Ficus microcarpa

axils. **PROPAGATE** by cuttings, air layering, or seeds. Fertile, moist soils in sunny or partially places are preferred. When young, it makes an attractive tub plant.

Ficus pumila Linnaeus

DISTINGUISHABLE by the prostrate woody habit, milky sap, small leaves with an unequally sided, heart-shaped base, and large, pear-shaped fruits that form on upright branches.

    Ficus pumila, climbing fig, sometimes called creeping fig, is native to China and Japan but is widely cultivated in tropical to warm temperate regions as an ornamental. It is often grown on stone or concrete walls, which it may entirely cover, and is popular for covering rock outcroppings. **SHRUB**, prostrate, clinging to rocks, trees, and other surfaces but the plant forming a shrub if left to itself, with fuzzy stipules forming a conical cap over the stem tip, sap milky. **LEAVES** simple, alternate, blade ovate and usually 1–3 cm long (⅜–1¼ in) when young, elliptic to oblong and 4–10 cm long (1⅝–4 in) when mature, leathery, rounded to unequally heart-shaped at the base. **FRUITS** can be found on the plant irregularly throughout the year. Fruit a purple, pear-shaped syconium 5–8 cm long (2–3½ in) but infrequently setting fertile seed. **PROPAGATE** by cuttings. Moist soils or rock surfaces in sunny places are preferred. Pruning is frequently needed to prevent the plant from becoming a shrub, which it tends to do when it reaches the top of a wall. Roots grow vigorously in pots and in some cases containing their growth in a bottomless container is recommended.

Ficus pumila

Filicium SAPINDACEAE

Filicium is a genus of three tree species found in Africa and, possibly, southern India. One is cultivated for its fern-like leaves. The name *Filicium* is from the Greek word for fern.

Filicium decipiens (Wight & Arnott) Thwaites

DISTINGUISHABLE by the tree habit, leaves that are alternate, pinnately compound, and fern-like, and axillary panicles of inconspicuous fruits and flowers.

   Filicium decipiens, fern tree, sometimes called fernleaf tree, is probably native to southeastern Africa but was long ago introduced to India, where it is widely cultivated. It is also grown elsewhere in the tropics as a shade or street tree. The flowers are seasonal, small, and inconspicuous, but the feathery, dark green foliage is attractive. **TREE** to 12 m high (40 ft). **LEAVES** even- or odd-pinnately compound, alternate, leaflets 6 to 16, blades 4–15 cm long (1⅝–6 in), opposite, oblanceolate, notched at the tip, dark glossy green, rachis narrowly winged. **FLOWERS** seasonally, mostly in winter; flowers many, borne in axillary panicles. Corolla of five free, tiny, white, inconspicuous petals 1–2 mm long (about ⅟₃₂–⅟₁₆ in). **FRUIT** a shiny purple ovoid drupe 9–12 mm long (⅜–½ in). **PROPAGATE** by seeds, the technique most used. Moist, well-drained soils in sunny places are preferred. The reddish brown wood is used for house building in Asia.

Filicium decipiens

Gaillardia ASTERACEAE

Gaillardia is a genus of 30 herbaceous species found mostly in temperate North America, some of which are cultivated for their colorful flower heads.

Gaillardia pulchella Fougeroux

DISTINGUISHABLE by the annual habit, sessile leaves, and long-stalked heads, each bearing 10 to 20 red and yellow ray florets notched at the tip.

    Gaillardia pulchella, Indian blanket or blanket flower, is a temperate species native to the western United States but is now widely cultivated in temperate to tropical climates for its colorful flower heads, sometimes escaping and becoming somewhat naturalized. Its common name apparently comes from the colorful pattern of the petal-like ray florets, reminiscent of a woven wool Indian blanket. **HERB**, annual, to 50 cm high (20 in). **LEAVES** simple, alternate, sessile, blade narrowly lanceolate, 2–7.5 cm long (¾–3 in). **FLOWERS** anytime during the year after maturity in the tropics; flowers in solitary, long-stalked heads borne at the tips of the stems and surrounded by two or three series of unequal lanceolate bracts. Ray florets 10 to 20, obovate, 1.5–3 cm long (⅝–1¼ in), three-toothed at the tip, reddish at the base and yellow toward the tip. Disk florets many, purplish. **FRUIT** a narrow, curved, club-shaped achene with some scales at the tip. **PROPAGATE** by achenes. Well-drained soils in sunny places are preferred. It is often grown in gardens or as a border plant. Several cultivars have been named.

Gaillardia pulchella

Galphimia MALPIGHIACEAE

Galphimia is a genus of 10 to 12 tropical and subtropical American shrub species, at least one of which is cultivated as an ornamental for its attractive flowers. The name *Galphimia* is an anagram of *Malpighia,* a related genus.

Galphimia gracilis Bartling

Often misidentified as *Thryallis glauca* (Cavanilles) Kuntze. DISTINGUISHABLE by the shrubby habit, alternate leaves with two small glands at the base, and yellow flowers bearing five clawed or stalked petals and ten red stamens. It is very similar to *Tristelleteia australasiae* but is a shrub rather than a vine and has smooth rather than winged fruits.

Galphimia gracilis, shower of gold, sometimes called spray of gold, is native to Mexico and Central America but is widely cultivated for its inflorescences of yellow flowers. SHRUB to 2 m high (6½ ft) or more. LEAVES simple, opposite, blade elliptic to ovate, 1.5–6 cm long (⅝–2½ in) with two small glands on the margins at the base. FLOWERS continuously through the year; flowers many, borne in terminal racemes. Corolla of five free, ovate to elliptic, clawed petals 7–12 mm long (¼–½ in), bright yellow, surrounding the ten red-stalked stamens. FRUIT a subglobose capsule but not usually formed in cultivation. PROPAGATE by seeds or cuttings. Fertile, moist, but well-drained soils in sunny or partially shaded places are preferred but full sun is necessary for optimal flower color and habit. It is planted by itself, in borders, or in low hedges, and periodic trimming is needed to prevent it from becoming scraggly.

Galphimia gracilis

Gardenia RUBIACEAE

Gardenia comprises about 200 tree and shrub species found throughout warm to warm temperate regions. Many are cultivated in the tropics and temperate climates for their fragrant white flowers, two of the most common and beautiful of which are included here.

Gardenia augusta (Linnaeus) Merrill

Synonym, *Gardenia jasminoides* Ellis. DISTINGUISHABLE by the opposite, glossy green leaves, interpetiolar stipules, and flowers that are large, solitary, terminal, white, and fragrant, with six to many spreading lobes.

Gardenia augusta, the gardenia, sometimes called cape jasmine, a misnomer since it is neither native to a cape area nor related to *Jasminum*, is native to China and Japan but is widely cultivated for its fragrant white flowers. The fruits were once used to make a commercial yellow dye. SHRUB to 2 m high (6½ ft) or more with interpetiolar stipules. LEAVES simple, opposite, blade elliptic to obovate or oblanceolate, usually 3–12 cm long (1¼–5 in), glossy green. FLOWERS in spring in cooler climates but anytime during the year or continuously in areas where the nighttime temperature is always warmer than 16 to 17°C (60–62°F); flowers solitary, terminal. Corolla with fused petals, salverform, tube 2–3.5 cm long (¾–1⅜ in), limb six-lobed or, more commonly, many-petaled in the double-flowered cultivars, spreading, 6–9 cm across (2½–3½ in), fragrant. FRUIT a narrowly obovate drupe usually with six linear persistent calyx lobes. PROPAGATE by cut-

Gardenia augusta, double-flowered

tings or, when fertile, seeds; sometimes grafted to the rootstocks of other *Gardenia* species. Moist but well-drained soils in partially shaded or sunny places are preferred. It is usually planted by itself as a specimen plant, or in hedges or as a screen, or as a houseplant in temperate climates. Periodic pruning is needed if it is to be kept from getting too tall. The flowers are usually used singly in commercial corsages rather than placed in flower arrangements since they age quickly. Several cultivars have been named and most of the common ones, including the popular 'Fortuniana', which looks like a *Magnolia* flower, are double-flowered. Another has variegated foliage.

Gardenia taitensis A. P. de Candolle

DISTINGUISHABLE by the shrubby habit, leaves that are large, glossy, and dark green, winged calyx, and large corolla with six to eight lobes.

Gardenia taitensis, Tahitian gardenia, sometimes called tiare, is native to Melanesia and perhaps eastward to Fiji and western Polynesia but was an ancient introduction farther east of the Marquesas Islands and is now widely cultivated elsewhere. The flowers are a favorite for making leis, are put singly over the ear, Polynesian style, and are used for scenting coconut oil. It is the national flower of Tahiti, where wearing flowers is an everyday occurrence. **SHRUB** or small tree to 4 m high (13 ft) or more with interpetiolar stipules. **LEAVES** simple, opposite, blade obovate, usually 5–16 cm long (2–6 in), glossy green, leathery. **FLOWERS** continuously through the year; flowers solitary at the tips of the stems. Corolla with fused petals,

Gardenia taitensis

salverform, tube 2–4.5 cm long (¾–1¾ in), limb of six to eight spreading, elliptic lobes 2–4.5 cm long (¾–1¾ in), white. FRUIT an obovoid or ellipsoidal drupe to 4 cm long (1⅝ in) with three to five longitudinal wings and persistent lanceolate calyx lobes but infrequently formed in cultivation. PROPAGATE by cuttings. Moist, well-drained soils in sunny places are preferred. It forms beautiful hedges with its dark green foliage and large, exquisite, white flowers but can be trained to be a small tree that is attractive as a colorful specimen plant.

Gerbera ASTERACEAE

Gerbera is a genus of about 30 herbaceous species found from South Africa to Bali, some cultivated, along with many hybrids, for their large, colorful flower heads.

Gerbera jamesonii Bolus ex J. D. Hooker

DISTINGUISHABLE by the basal rosette of deeply pinnately lobed leaves and long-stalked heads of numerous, variously colored, linear ray and disk florets.

Gerbera jamesonii

Gerbera jamesonii, Transvaal daisy, sometimes called Barberton daisy, is native to South Africa but is widely cultivated in the tropics and subtropics for its flower heads. HERB, perennial, stemless, clump forming. LEAVES simple, arranged in a basal rosette, blade oblanceolate with deeply pinnately lobed margins, 7–30 cm long (3–12 in), hairy on the lower surface, with a long petiole. FLOWERS anytime during the year in the tropics; flowers in a head on a long stalk arising from the leaf rosette and surrounded by two or three series of bracts. Ray florets in one or two series, or double-flowered, linear, 2–5 cm long (¾–2 in), light pink to orange or red, rarely white. Disk florets numerous, similar in color and shape to the ray florets. **Fruit** an achene with bristles on top. **Propagate** by root division, cuttings, seeds, or tissue culture. Sandy, well-drained soils in sunny places are preferred. It is usually planted in gardens along borders and in colorful mass plantings. Its large, long-stalked heads are among the best for cut flowers. Many cultivars have been named, differing in the color and size of the ray florets.

Gliricidia FABACEAE

Gliricidia is a genus of four to nine South American species, one of which is cultivated as an ornamental.

Gliricidia sepium (Jacquin) Kunth ex Walpers

Distinguishable by the tree habit, pinnately compound leaves, 7 to 23 elliptic to oblong leaflets, and short axillary racemes of pink and white, butterfly-like flowers.

Gliricidia sepium, madre de cacao, is native from Mexico to northern South America but is widely cultivated in the tropics as a shade tree, as a living fence post, and often as a cover plant in *Theobroma cacao* plantations, hence the name "mother of cocoa," for shade and to nitrify the soil. The seeds and bark reportedly are poisonous to rats and mice, and possibly also to horses and dogs. **Tree** or shrub to 12 m high (40 ft) or more. **Leaves** odd-pinnately compound, leaflets 7 to 23, blades elliptic to oblong, 3–7 cm long (1¼–3 in). **Flowers** seasonally, mostly in winter and spring; flowers many, borne in

Gliricidia sepium

short axillary racemes. Corolla papilionaceous, 1.6–2.3 cm long (⅝–⅞ in) with four free, unequal petals, rose-pink and white with some yellow, and ten fused stamens. FRUIT a flattened, linear-oblanceolate pod 10–16 cm long (4–6 in). PROPAGATE by scarified seeds or large cuttings. Fertile, moist, but well-drained soils in sunny places are preferred. The flowers may cover the tree, particularly in areas with a pronounced dry season, which causes the tree to be deciduous when the flowers form.

Gloriosa LILIACEAE

Gloriosa is a genus of one variable species or, according to some authors, five or six species. *Gloriosa* is cultivated as an ornamental for its attractive flowers.

Gloriosa superba Linnaeus

Synonym, *Gloriosa rothschildiana* O'Brien, a variation with wavy leaf

Gloriosa superba

margins, among other names. DISTINGUISHABLE by the scrambling habit, sessile leaves with a tendril at the tip, and orange flowers with six reflexed petals and six long, spreading stamens.

Gloriosa superba, climbing lily, sometimes called glory lily or gloriosa lily, is native from tropical Africa and Asia, or just Southeast Asia to Malaysia if the other species are recognized. The plant is poisonous and contains large amounts of a chemical called colchicine that is used in small amounts to treat gout. Contact with the tubers can cause skin irritation. HERB, perennial, scrambling, arising from a tuber and climbing to 1.5 m high (5 ft) by means of tendrils. LEAVES simple, alternate to nearly opposite, sessile, blade lanceolate to ovate, 8–15 cm long (3½–6 in), veins parallel, leaf tip extended into a coiling tendril. **FLOWERS** most of the year; flowers solitary on a long stalk borne at the leaf axil. Corolla of six free lanceolate tepals 4–9 cm long (1⅝–3½ in) with wavy margins, red with the basal portion yellow, reflexed back until they nearly touch, with six long-stalked stamens spreading horizontally. **FRUIT** an obovoid capsule. **PROPAGATE** by division. Fertile, well-drained soils in sunny places are preferred. It is widely cultivated for its flowers and is often planted to scramble through other plants, or is grown as a potted plant in the greenhouse in temperate climates. In areas with a dry season, the plant may temporarily die back.

Gloxinia GESNERIACEAE

Gloxinia is a genus of 8 to 15 tropical American species, some of which, along with hybrids, are cultivated as ornamentals for their large, attractive flowers.

Gloxinia perennis
(Linnaeus) Fritsch

DISTINGUISHABLE by the herbaceous habit, opposite, heart-shaped leaves, scalloped leaf margins, reddish lower leaf surface, and solitary, lavender to purple, bell-shaped flowers.

Gloxinia perennis, Canterbury bells, is native from Colombia to Brazil and Peru but is widely if not commonly cultivated as an ornamental for its pale purple flowers and attractive leaves. **HERB**, erect, to 1 m high (3¼ ft) or more, with red-mottled stems arising from a rhizome. **LEAVES** simple, opposite, blade heart-shaped, usually 8–18

Gloxinia perennis

cm long (3½–7 in), somewhat fleshy, lower surface often reddish, upper surface sparsely bristly, margins scalloped. **FLOWERS** continuously through the year; flowers solitary in the upper leaf axils. Corolla with fused petals, bell-shaped, pouched on the lower side, 2.5–4 cm long (1–1⅝ in), lavender to purple, hairy on the outside. **FRUIT** a capsule. **PROPAGATE** by seeds or rhizome cuttings. Fertile, moist, but well-drained soils in partially shaded places are preferred. It is often grown as a border plant in the tropics, or as a potted plant in the greenhouse in temperate climates.

Gomphrena AMARANTHACEAE

Gomphrena is a widespread tropical genus of about 100 annual and perennial herb species. Many are cultivated as bedding plants and as everlastings for cut flowers because of their attactive, papery bracts.

Gomphrena globosa Linnaeus
DISTINGUISHABLE by the herbaceous habit, opposite leaves, and globose, terminal heads of flowers borne among pink (rarely white or yellow), papery bracts.

Gomphrena globosa

Gomphrena globosa, globe amaranth, sometimes called bachelor's buttons, is native to tropical America but is widely cultivated in the tropics and temperate regions as a garden herb or is grown in planters for its attractive globose, dark pink or sometimes white or yellow inflorescences. The papery flowers, actually inflorescences with conspicuous bracts, are often used in leis and flower arrangements and, when dry, as everlastings in flower bouquets since they retain their color. **HERB**, annual, to 80 cm high (32 in), often with reddish stems. LEAVES simple, opposite, blade oblong or elliptic to obovate, usu-ally 2–8 cm long (¾–3½ in) with a clasping petiole base. FLOWERS any-time during the year after maturity; flowers many, borne in a solitary, terminal, deep pink, less commonly white or yellow, subglobose to ob-long head 1.5–4 cm in diameter (⅝–1⅝ in). Corolla of five free, tiny tepals surrounded by the usually deep pink bracts. FRUIT a tiny, dry, one-seeded utricle. PROPAGATE by seeds. Fertile, well-drained soils in sunny places are preferred.

Gossypium MALVACEAE

Gossypium is a genus of 20 to as many as 70 species native throughout the tropics and subtropics. The genus is important as the source of cot-ton, made from the fibers covering the seeds of some of the species. Be-cause of hybridization in the genus, there is much difference of opinion on the correct names for the species and their number.

Gossypium barbadense Linnaeus

Synonym, *Gossypium brasiliense* Macfadyen. DISTINGUISHABLE by the shrubby habit, palmately lobed leaves, yellow flowers often purple at the base, borne between a pair of fringed bracts, and capsules containing cotton-covered seeds. The similar *G. hirsutum* Linnaeus differs in having less deeply lobed leaves and smaller, lighter yellow flowers that mostly lack the purple at the base.

Gossypium barbadense, sea island cot-ton, is native to tropical America but is widely cultivated in tropical to warm temperate regions, including the south-ern United States, for commercial cot-ton. It is occasionally grown ornamen-tally, by itself as a specimen plant for its

Gossypium barbadense

yellow flowers or as a novelty because of the cotton bolls produced. **Shrub** to 3 m high (10 ft), gland-dotted throughout. **Leaves** simple, alternate, blade generally round to broadly ovate in outline, 8–20 cm long (3½–8 in), deeply three- to seven-lobed. **Flowers** intermittently during the year; flowers solitary, axillary. Corolla of five free obovate petals 4.5–7 cm long (1¾–3 in), pale yellow, sometimes purple at the base. **Fruit** an oval capsule filled with long-hairy (cotton) seeds and surrounded by leaf-like, linear-lobed bracts, the epicalyx. **Propagate** by seeds. Fertile, moist soils in sunny places are preferred.

Graptophyllum ACANTHACEAE

Graptophyllum is a genus of 10 to 15 shrub species found mostly in Australia and Melanesia, some cultivated as ornamentals for their colored or spotted leaves. The name *Graptophyllum* is from the Greek words meaning write and leaf, referring to the "caricature" on the leaves of the best-known species.

Graptophyllum pictum (Linnaeus) Griffith

Distinguishable by the shrubby habit, leaves that are opposite, brightly colored, and variegated, and terminal panicles of red-purple, two-lipped flowers. When sterile it looks somewhat like *Codiaeum variegatum* but is easily distinguished by its opposite rather than alternate leaves.

Graptophyllum pictum, caricature plant, is native from Southeast Asia to Malaysia but is widely cultivated for its red-purple flowers and, especially, attractive variegated leaves. No two leaves on the plant have exactly the same pattern but several cultivars have been named, based on the general form of the pattern, the caricature. **Shrub** to 3 m high (10 ft) or more. **Leaves** simple, opposite, blade oblong to lanceolate, 6–22 cm long (2½–9 in), green, red, or purple, typically with an irregular yellow, pink, or whitish blotch in the center. **Flowers** continuously through the year; flowers many, opening several at a time, borne in a narrow, terminal panicle bearing inconspicuous bracts. Corolla of fused petals, funnel-shaped, strongly two-lipped, 3–4 cm long (1¼–1⅝ in), divided about one-third of its length into five lobes, red-purple, with two slightly protruding stamens. FRUIT a woody, club-shaped capsule, infrequently formed in cultivation. PROPAGATE by cuttings. Fertile, moist, but well-drained soils in sunny or partially shaded places are preferred. It is often grown in colorful hedges or screens and sometimes as an indoor plant in cooler climates. It must be periodically pruned to retain its shape. An attractive cultivar with yellow leaves is called 'El Dorado', not to be confused with el dorado, *Pseuderanthemum carruthersii*.

Graptophyllum pictum

Grevillea PROTEACEAE

Grevillea a genus of about 250 shrub and tree species found from Australia to Melanesia, many useful for their timber and a few as ornamentals. The genus is named after Charles Greville, 1749–1809, founder of the Royal Horticultural Society.

Grevillea robusta A. Cunningham ex R. Brown

DISTINGUISHABLE by the tree habit, leaves that are opposite, nearly bipinnately compound, fern-like, and white-woolly on the lower surface, one-sided racemes of orange flowers with the curved corolla tube splitting along one side, and boat-shaped follicle.

Grevillea robusta, silk oak, sometimes called silky oak, a misnomer since it is not at all related to the oak family Fagaceae, is native to Australia but is widely cultivated in the tropics as a timber tree or windbreak and, with its orange flowers, as an ornamental street tree or

Grevillea robusta

screen. Leaf litter is a small drawback. It is naturalized in some places, such as Hawaii, where it has been extensively planted in reforestation projects. TREE, fast growing, to 25 m high (82 ft) or more. LEAVES pinnately compound and nearly bipinnate, alternate, leaflets in five to ten pairs 4–12 cm long (1⅝–5 in), deeply pinnately lobed into lanceolate segments or lobes, woolly white on the lower surface. FLOWERS anytime during the year; flowers many, borne in one-sided subterminal racemes or panicles of racemes. Corolla absent but the calyx petal-like, yellow-orange, salverform, tube curved, 6–9 mm long (¼–⅜ in), splitting along one side. FRUIT a boat-shaped follicle 1.5–2 cm long (⅝–¾ in). PROPAGATE by seeds or cuttings. Well-drained soils in sunny or partially shaded places are preferred, and the plant is drought resistant. In cooler climates it is often grown as a potted plant for its attractive foliage.

Grewia TILIACEAE

Grewia is a genus of about 150 tree and shrub species ranging from Australia to Africa, some of which are utilized for timber, edible fruits, or medicines, and some cultivated as ornamentals.

Grewia occidentalis Linnaeus

DISTINGUISHABLE by the shrubby habit, alternate leaves, toothed leaf margins, short mauve petals and longer, petal-like sepals, and many yellow-tipped stamens.

Grewia occidentalis, which lacks a well-known common name, is native from South Africa northward to Zimbabwe but is widely cultivated in the tropics and warm regions for its purple flowers. The bark is used in its native range by Zulus for dressing wounds, and several other medicinal uses have been reported. **SHRUB** or spreading small tree to 3 m high (10 ft) or more with the stem tips covered with stellate pubescence when young, and the branches marked by distinct lenticels. **LEAVES** alternate, simple, blade obovate to elliptic, 2–6 cm long (¾–2½ in), three-veined from the base, margins toothed. **FLOWERS** continuously through the year; flowers one to six in short-stalked axillary cymes. Corolla of five free, oblanceolate mauve petals 1–1.5 cm long (⅜–⅝ in) surrounded by five larger, narrowly lanceolate, similarly colored sepals to 2.5 cm long (1 in), with many yellow-tipped stamens in the center. **FRUIT** a square, usually four-lobed drupe to 1.5 cm in diameter (⅝ in) or more. **PROPAGATE** by seeds or layering. It is very adaptable to most soil and lighting conditions and is a spreading shrub or small tree that is sometimes planted for a hedge or shrubby border.

Grewia occidentalis

Guaiacum ZYGOPHYLLACEAE

Guaiacum is a genus of six tree species of warm regions of America, noted for their wood, which is the hardest of commercial timbers. They are also utilized for medicines, and two species are cultivated as ornamentals.

Guaiacum officinale

Guaiacum officinale Linnaeus

DISTINGUISHABLE by the opposite, pinnately compound leaves, four to six leaflets, axillary clusters of flowers with five blue petals, and yellow capsule.

Guaiacum officinale, lignum vitae, meaning wood of life in Latin, is native to the Caribbean Islands but is widely if not commonly cultivated in the tropics for the blue flowers and yellow-orange fruits that often cover the plant. The wood is one of the heaviest of commercial timbers—it sinks in water—and has been used in places where a very hard timber is needed, for bowling balls, for example. The sap and an extract of the wood have been used in herbal medicines. TREE, spreading, to 10 m high (33 ft). LEAVES pinnately compound, opposite, rachis 3–8 cm long (1¼–3½ in), leaflets four or six, blades obovate to elliptic, 2–6 cm long (¾–2½ in). FLOWERS mostly in late spring to early fall with the attractive fruits on the plant later in the year; flowers several, borne in axillary clusters, each flower on a stalk 1–3 cm long (⅜–1¼ in). Corolla of five free obovate petals 1–1.5 cm long (⅜–⅝ in), blue. FRUIT a flattened, yellow, obcordate capsule. PROPAGATE by seeds. Fertile, moist soils in sunny places are preferred. It is often planted as a small street tree or in gardens.

Hamelia RUBIACEAE

Hamelia is a genus of 16 tropical American species, or as many as 40 according to some authors. At least two are cultivated as ornamentals for their colorful flowers.

Hamelia patens Jacquin

Distinguishable by the shrubby habit, opposite leaves, interpetiolar stipules, and loose, forking cymes of tubular orange flowers with five minute lobes at the tip. It differs from Ixora spp. most obviously in having five rather than four corolla lobes.

Hamelia patens, scarletbush, sometimes called firebush, is native to tropical America and was originally named from Hispaniola but is widely cultivated for its orange flowers. **Shrub** to 4 m high (13 ft) or more, spreading, with finely pubescent stems and interpetiolar stipules. **Leaves** simple, opposite, blade elliptic to obovate, usually 3–11

Hamelia patens

cm long (1¼–4½ in). **Flowers** anytime during the year; flowers many, four to nine per branch, borne in forking terminal cymes. Corolla of fused petals, tubular, 1.8–2.8 cm long (¾–1⅛ in), minutely five-lobed at the tip, red-orange, with the stamens slightly protruding. **Fruit** a purplish black ovoid berry 8–12 mm long (¼–½ in). **Propagate** by seeds, cuttings, or air layering. Moist, well-drained soils in sunny places are preferred. It is planted by itself or in borders, occasionally as a hedge, but pruning inhibits flowering because the flowers are formed on the tips of branches.

Harpullia SAPINDACEAE

Harpullia is a genus of 26 tree species found from India to Polynesia, some used for timber and as ornamentals.

Harpullia pendula Planchon

Distinguishable by the alternate, pinnately compound leaves, axillary

Harpullia pendula

panicles of small white flowers, and red to yellow, two-lobed capsules that split open to expose the two large, shiny black seeds.

Harpullia pendula, Australian tulipwood, sometimes called just tulipwood, is native to Australia but is cultivated as a shade or street tree mostly because of its dark green foliage. The flowers are rather inconspicuous but the red to yellow, two-lobed fruits containing large, shiny black seeds are attractive. The yellow- and black-marked wood is used for making cabinets. TREE to 10 m high (33 ft) or more. LEAVES even- or odd-pinnately compound, alternate, leaflets four to ten, blades elliptic, mostly 6–15 cm long (2½–6 in). FLOWERS anytime during the year; flowers many, borne in axillary panicles mostly 6–16 cm long (2½–6 in). Corolla of five free, oblong to nearly round, white petals 3–5 mm long (about ⅛–¼ in). FRUIT a capsule 3–4 cm across (1¼–1⅝ in) composed of two spherical yellow to red lobes, each splitting open to release the large, shiny black seed. PROPAGATE by seeds. Moist but well-drained soils in sunny places are preferred.

Hedychium ZINGIBERACEAE

Hedychium comprises 40 to 50 robust rhizomatous herb species native from Malaysia to India and possibly Madagascar. Many are cultivated for their conspicuous, often aromatic flowers, and some for their rhizomes, which are used to make perfume. Three of the most common ornamental species are included here.

Hedychium coronarium König

DISTINGUISHABLE by the ginger-like leaves, conspicuous white, fragrant flowers, notched labellum, and single long white stamen.

Hedychium coronarium, white ginger, sometimes misleadingly called white ginger lily, is native to the Himalayas but is widely cultivated in the tropics and subtropics for its fragrant white flowers. These are sold as cut flowers and are worn in leis or singly in the hair in the Pacific islands for their beauty as well as their lovely fragrance. **HERB**, perennial, erect, unbranched, to 2 m high (6½ ft), growing from a rhizome. **LEAVES** simple, alternate, two-ranked, sessile at the top of the leaf sheath, blade elliptic to lanceolate, 20–60 × 3–10 cm (8–24 × 1¼–4 in), pubescent on lower surface. **FLOWERS** continuously through the year; flowers many, in groups of one to six, borne among large, green, overlapping bracts in an ellipsoidal spike 7–20 cm long (3–8 in) atop a leafy stem, fragrant. Corolla with fused tepals, white, the tube narrow, 6–9 cm long (2½– 3½ in), the segments linear, 3–5 cm long (1¼–2 in) with two petal-like oblanceolate staminodes 3.5–5.5 cm long (1⅜–2¼ in) and a petal-like,

subround, apically notched labellum slightly longer with a yellowish green or dull white patch in the center. **FRUIT** an oblong many-seeded capsule, infrequently formed in cultivation. **PROPAGATE** by rhizome division or seeds. Fertile, moist soils in sunny or partially shaded places are preferred. Plants are usually grown in mixed herbaceous borders or next to ponds in the tropics, and in pots in the greenhouse in temperate climates. Left to itself it may form dense thickets that spread by means of rhizomes and can be hard to eliminate when other uses for the land are contemplated.

Hedychium coronarium

Hedychium flavescens N. Carey ex Roscoe

Often misidentified as *Hedychium flavum* Roxburgh. **Distinguishable** by the ginger-like leaves, pale yellow, fragrant flowers, notched labellum, and single long, pale yellow stamen. A similar ornamental ginger, *H. coccineum* F. Buchanan, differs in having pinkish flowers and producing orange-lined fruits with red seeds.

Hedychium flavescens, yellow ginger, is native to India and the Himalayas but is widely cultivated in the tropics and subtropics for its fragrant, pale yellow flowers. The plant is seminaturalized in some places, such as Hawaii, spreading by vigorous rhizome growth, but since fruits do not form it cannot spread to other places without the rhizomes being transported. It is grown commercially for cut flowers, is favored in making leis, or is worn singly in the hair in the Pacific islands. **Herb**, perennial, erect, unbranched, to 2 m high (6½ ft) or more, growing

Hedychium flavescens with pale yellow flowers   *Hedychium coccineum* with pinkish flowers

from a rhizome. **LEAVES** simple, alternate, two-ranked, attached atop a sheath, blade narrowly lanceolate, usually 30–60 × 4–12 cm (12–24 × 1⅝–5 in), pubescent on lower surface. **FLOWERS** anytime during the year; flowers many, in groups of as many as four, borne among large, green, overlapping bracts in an ovoid spike 12–20 cm long (5–8 in) atop a leafy stem, fragrant. Corolla with fused tepals, the tube narrow, 6–9 cm long (2½–3½ in), the segments linear, 4–5 cm long (1⅝–2 in) with two petal-like oblanceolate staminodes 4–6 cm long (1⅝–2½ in) and a petal-like obcordate labellum as long, all parts pale yellow, the labellum with a darker patch in the center. **FRUIT** not known. **PROPAGATE** by rhizome division. Fertile, moist, but well-drained soils in partially shaded places are preferred. It, along with the similar *H. coronarium,* is one of the best known tropical plants and is grown in mixed herbaceous borders, in clumps as a specimen plant, or next to ponds, where it adds a tropical look.

Hedychium gardnerianum
Ker-Gawler

DISTINGUISHABLE by the ginger-like yellow flowers, notched labellum, single long red stamen, and fertile seed capsules.

Hedychium gardnerianum, Himalayan ginger, is native to the Himalayas and adjacent areas but is widely cultivated in tropical to warm temperate climates for its fragrant yellow and red flowers. Because it produces fruits and seeds attractive to birds it can become a pest in native forest areas, as it has done in Hawaii. Another common name, kahili ginger, is based on the similarity of the shape of its inflorescence to that of the

Hedychium gardnerianum

ancient Hawaiian feather standard, the kahili. **HERB**, perennial, erect, unbranched, to 2 m high (6½ ft), growing from a rhizome. **LEAVES** simple, alternate, two-ranked, attached atop a sheath, blade lanceolate, usually 25–45 × 8–15 cm (10–18 × 3½–6 in), appressed hairs beneath. **FLOWERS** mostly in winter; flowers many, borne among large, green, overlapping lanceolate bracts in a cylindrical spike usually 15–30 cm long (6–12 in) atop a leafy stem. Corolla with fused tepals, the tube narrow, 5–5.5 cm long (2–2¼ in), the segments linear, 3.5–5 cm long (1⅜–2 in) with two petal-like staminodes 2.5–3 cm long (1–1¼ in) and a petal-like obcordate labellum of similar length, all parts yellow, with a single red stamen 6–7 cm long (2½–3 in). **FRUIT** an orange, fleshy, three-parted, oblong capsule 1.5–2.5 cm long (⅝–1 in), containing many red seeds. **PROPAGATE** by rhizome division or seeds. Fertile, moist, but well-drained soils in partially shaded places are preferred. It is the most cold tolerant of the commonly cultivated gingers and in the tropics does best at higher elevations.

Helianthus ASTERACEAE

Helianthus comprises about 67 coarse annual and perennial herb species found in North and South America. Most are wildflowers of open places in temperate regions, but some are weedy and a few are cultivated as ornamentals for their yellow sunflower heads. Two ornamental species are included here.

Helianthus annuus Linnaeus

DISTINGUISHABLE by the often large size, leaves that are ovate and alternate, hispid leaf surface, many yellow ray florets, and black-tipped disk florets.

The well-known sunflower, *Helianthus annuus,* is native to temperate North America but it is widely cultivated in warm to temperate regions for its seeds, which are eaten or used to produce a cooking oil. **HERB**, annual, coarse, fast-growing, to 2 m high (6½ ft) or more. **LEAVES** simple, alternate, blade ovate, usually 10–40 cm long (4–16 in) on a petiole

Helianthus annuus

Helianthus annuus, a cultivar with yellow ray florets with a red-brown base

nearly as long, surface hispid. **FLOWERS** anytime during the year in warm climates; flowers in large, terminal and axillary, stalked heads surrounded by several series of ovate, long-tipped bracts. Ray florets many, narrowly oblong to lanceolate, 2.5–9 cm long (1–3½ in), yellow or sometimes with darker orange markings. Disk florets numerous, yellow with a black tip. **FRUIT** a flattened obovoid achene with two deciduous scales on top. **PROPAGATE** by achenes. The plant is drought resistant and prefers fertile, well-drained soils in sunny places. They are often grown in gardens, planters, or borders. The commercially grown plant has a very large flower head. Many cultivars have been named, most of them small compared to the commercial seed-producing one.

Helianthus argophyllus Torrey & A. Gray

DISTINGUISHABLE by the alternate, ovate leaves, woolly leaf surface, and large heads of many yellow ray florets and purple disk florets.

Helianthus argophyllus

Helianthus argophyllus, which lacks a distinctive common name, is native to temperate North America and was originally named from Texas but is widely if not commonly cultivated in the tropics and warm temperate regions for its large, colorful flower heads. **HERB**, annual, coarse, to 2 m high (6½ ft). **LEAVES** simple, opposite, or alternate on the upper stems, blade ovate to lanceolate, 10–25 cm long (4–10 in), surfaces white-hairy. **FLOWERS** anytime during the year in warm climates; flowers many, borne in large terminal heads surrounded by several series of bracts. Ray florets 15 or more, oblanceolate, 2.5–3.5 cm long (1–1⅜ in), yellow to orange-yellow. Disk florets numerous, purple. **FRUIT** an obovate achene 4–6 mm long (about ¼ in). **PROPAGATE** by achenes. Well-drained soils in sunny places are preferred. It is often planted in gardens, as a small specimen plant, or in borders. The leaves, which are covered with a white pubescence, are sometimes used in dried flower arrangements.

Heliconia HELICONIACEAE

Heliconia comprises about 100 large perennial herbaceous species, or as many as 250 according to some authors, found mostly in tropical America, with a few on islands in the southwestern Pacific Ocean region. Most are forest understory plants, and many are cultivated for their inflorescences, which are typically red, yellow, or orange to attract hummingbird pollinators. *Heliconia* hybridization and cultivation is a fast-growing part of the commercial horticulture industry, with a special society devoted to the plants. So many cultivars and hybrids, only a few of which are natural, are grown by *Heliconia* fanciers that only an expert can identify them all. A few are grown for their foliage as well. Six species of *Heliconia,* sometimes called lobster's claw, are included here.

Heliconia bihai (Linnaeus) Linnaeus

Synonym, *Heliconia humilis* (Aublet) Jacquin. **DISTINGUISHABLE** by the erect, long-stalked, banana-leaf-like foliage, erect inflorescences arranged in one plane, and 5 to 12 folded, red-orange, ovate bracts with green margins.

Heliconia bihai, a lobster's claw sometimes called firebird, is native to northern South America and some Caribbean islands but is widely cultivated for its attractive, erect, red-orange inflorescences. **HERB** to 6 m high (20 ft), coarse, clump forming, arising from branched rhizomes. **LEAVES** simple, opposite, two-ranked, blade banana-leaf-like, usually 60–180 cm long (24–71 in) on a petiole about half as long. **FLOWERS** continuously through the year in some cultivars, more restricted in others; flowers 7–30, borne within 5 to 12 or more thick, folded, ovate bracts mostly 10–25 cm long (4–10 in) and all red-orange or with green margins, arranged in one plane on the erect, axillary rachis 25–65 cm long (10–26 in). Corolla of six fused tepals mostly 5–7 cm long (2–3 in), white and green. **FRUIT** an ovoid drupe 9–11 mm long (about ⅜ in). **PROPAGATE** by division, the technique most used. Fertile, moist, but well-

Heliconia bihai 'Balisier' with red bracts with green margins

drained soils in sunny or partially shaded places are preferred. Plants are grown by themselves or in borders in the tropics, and in the greenhouse in temperate climates. The species is extremely variable, with numerous cultivars having been named.

Heliconia caribaea Lamarck

Distinguishable by the banana-leaf-like foliage, waxy white lower leaf surface, and 6 to 15 orange to dark red, sometimes lime green, closely overlapping bracts arranged in one plane.

Heliconia caribaea is native to the West Indies but is widely cultivated for its orange to red or purple, or sometimes lime green, bracts. Plants may be called purple heliconia or gold heliconia. **Herb** to 5 m high (16½ ft), coarse, often waxy white, arising from a rhizome. **Leaves** simple, alternate, two-ranked, blade banana-leaf-like, usually 60–130 cm long (24–51 in) on a petiole half or more as long, lower surface usually

Heliconia caribaea 'Cream'

waxy white. **Flowers** most of the year; flowers 9 to 22, borne within 6 to 15 or as many as 40 thick, folded, overlapping, ovate, orange to dark red, rarely green, bracts 8–25 cm long (3½–10 in), arranged in one plane on an erect inflorescence 20–40 cm long (8–16 in). Corolla of six fused tepals mostly 4.8–6 cm long (1⅞–2½ in), whitish with green tips. **Fruit** a one- to three-seeded drupe 9–11 mm long (about ⅜ in). **Propagate** by division, the technique most used. Fertile, moist, but well-drained soils in sunny or partially shaded places are preferred. Plants are grown by themselves or as border plants, and in the greenhouse in temperate climates. The species is quite variable, with a number of cultivars having been named and hybrids made.

Heliconia collinsiana Griggs

DISTINGUISHABLE by the large size, long-stalked, banana-leaf-like foliage, hanging inflorescences, and folded, loosely and spirally arranged red bracts. A similar ornamental species, *Heliconia pendula* Wawra, differs in having bracts that are distichous, in opposite pairs at right angles to each other, and that are glabrous rather than spirally arranged and waxy white.

    Heliconia collinsiana, sometimes called hanging red heliconia, is native to Guatemala but is widely cultivated for its red bracts and inflorescences. HERB to 5 m high (16½ ft), clump forming, arising from a rhizome, with shoots and some other parts often waxy white. LEAVES simple, alternate, two-ranked, blade banana-leaf-like, usually 1–2 m long (3¼–6½ ft) on a petiole nearly half as long. FLOWERS continuously through the year; flowers several, borne within 6 to 18 thick, folded, ovate, spirally arranged, red bracts 8–40 cm long (3½–16 in), pendulous on a red rachis, the lower one sometimes with a green keel and tip. Corolla of six fused tepals 4.5–6 cm long (1 ¾–2½ in), orange or yellow to green. FRUIT a one- to three-seeded drupe 1.2–1.5 cm long (½–⅝ in). PROPAGATE by division, the technique most used. Fertile, moist, but well-drained soils in sunny or partially shaded places are preferred. It belongs to the *Heliconia* group with hanging rather than erect inflorescences and is often grown by itself in tropical

Heliconia collinsiana

gardens or in groups as border plants. Like other heliconias, its foliage and flowers add a decidedly tropical look to areas where it is planted.

Heliconia latispatha Bentham

DISTINGUISHABLE by the banana-leaf-like foliage, erect inflorescences, and 7 to 17 folded, red, lanceolate, spirally and loosely arranged bracts yellow at the base.

Heliconia latispatha, golden lobster's claw, is native to tropical America from Mexico to northern South America but is widely cultivated in the tropics for its bracts, which are less spectacular, however, than those of many of the other species. The fibers from the petioles are sometimes used locally for various purposes. HERB to 4 m high (13 ft), arising from an underground rhizome. LEAVES simple, opposite and distichous, blade

banana-leaf-like, usually 40–120 cm long (16–48 in) on a shorter petiole. FLOWERS continuously through the year; flowers several, borne within 7 to 17 thick, folded, lanceolate bracts 10–15 cm long (4–6 in) that are red with yellow at the base and arranged spirally on the erect rachis 2–10 cm long (¾–4 in), the lower bract typically bearing a terminal leaf blade. Corolla of six fused tepals, usually 3.5–4.5 cm long (1⅜–1¾ in), green. FRUIT a schizocarp, infrequently formed in cultivation. PROPAGATE by division, the technique most used. Fertile, moist, but well-drained soils in sunny places are preferred. It is often grown in clumps or as a border plant. A number of cultivars have been named.

Heliconia latispatha 'Red-Yellow'

Heliconia psittacorum Linnaeus fil.

DISTINGUISHABLE by the small size, erect, long-stalked inflorescences, two to seven red, pink, yellow, or orange, waxy white bracts, and yellow-green to red flowers with a dark patch toward the tip.

Heliconia psittacorum, parakeet flower, sometimes called parrot flower, is native to northern South America but is widely cultivated for its erect, relatively short but prominent, mostly yellow-orange to red inflorescences. HERB to 1.5 m high (5 ft) or more, arising from an underground rhizome. LEAVES simple, alternate, blade lanceolate, usually 15–50 cm long (6–20 in), light green, on a short or long petiole. FLOWERS continuously through the year in some cultivars, more restricted in others; flowers several, borne in clusters above two to seven soft, waxy white, slightly folded, red, pink, yellow, or orange, lanceolate bracts

Heliconia psittacorum 'Andromeda'   *Heliconia* 'Golden Torch'

mostly 4–13 cm long (1⅝–5 in) in an erect, long-stalked, terminal inflorescence 7–18 cm long (3–7 in). Corolla of six narrow, fused tepals 3.5–4.5 cm long (1⅜–1¾ in), three-angled, yellow-green to yellow-orange or red, with a dark patch toward the tip. FRUIT a yellow subglobose drupe 5–10 mm long (¼–⅜ in). PROPAGATE by division, the technique most used. Fertile, moist, but well-drained soils in sunny or partially shaded places are preferred. It is often grown as a ground cover, border plant, or in mass plantings in the tropics since it is shorter than most of the other common heliconias, and indoors in the greenhouse in temperate climates. It spreads rapidly, and a barrier may be needed to keep it from infringing on other plantings. Numerous hybrids and cultivars are recognized, including a popular one formed by a cross with *H. spathocircinata* Aristeguieta, *Heliconia* 'Golden Torch'.

Heliconia rostrata Ruiz & Pavón

DISTINGUISHABLE by the banana-leaf-like foliage, hanging inflorescences, and overlapping, red, fuzzy bracts with a yellow tip and margins.

Heliconia rostrata

Heliconia rostrata, sometimes called hanging lobster's claw, is native to the Andes of Peru and Ecuador but is widely cultivated for its inflorescences. HERB, erect, to 5 m high (16½ ft), clump forming. LEAVES simple, alternate, distichous, blade banana-leaf-like, usually 60–120 cm long (24–48 in) on a petiole about half as long. FLOWERS continuously through the year; flowers several, borne within 10 to 35, sometimes as few as 4, thick, folded, ovate, distichous, fuzzy red bracts 6–15 cm long (2½–6 in) with broad yellow and green margins and tip, on a pendulous inflorescence 30–60 cm long (12–24 in) on a shorter rachis. Corolla of six fused, unequal tepals mostly 4–5 cm long (1⅝–2 in), yellow. Fʀᴜɪᴛ a one- to three-seeded drupe, infrequently formed in cultivation. Pʀᴏᴘᴀ-ɢᴀᴛᴇ by division. Fertile, moist, but well-drained soils in sunny or partially shaded places are preferred. It is often grown as a high border or hedge plant. It is one of the more commonly cultivated of the large heliconias and has pendulous rather than erect inflorescences.

Heliotropium BORAGINACEAE

Heliotropium is a genus of about 250 herb and low shrub species found throughout the world, many grown as garden ornamentals and some, widespread seashore plants. The name *Heliotropium* is from the Greek words meaning "turning toward the sun."

Heliotropium amplexicaule Vahl

Dɪsᴛɪɴɢᴜɪsʜᴀʙʟᴇ by the herbaceous habit, alternate leaves, wavy leaf margins, coiled cymes of tiny blue-violet flowers, and small, dry, four-parted fruit.

Heliotropium amplexicaule, blue heliotrope, is native to South America but is widely if not commonly cultivated in the tropics and subtropics as a ground cover and for its blue-violet flowers. In some places, such as Queensland, Australia, it is suspected of being poisonous to sheep. Hᴇʀʙ, perennial, spreading, to 30 cm high (12 in). Lᴇᴀᴠᴇs simple, alternate, subsessile, blade narrowly elliptic to oblanceolate, 3–8 cm long (1¼–3½ in)

Heliotropium amplexicaule

with wavy margins and hairy surface. **FLOWERS** continuously through the year in the tropics; flowers many, borne in scorpeoid, that is, coiled, cymes. Corolla of fused petals, trumpet-shaped, 6–8 mm long (about ¼ in), tube yellow, limb with five rounded lobes, blue-violet. **FRUIT** a dry subglobose drupe 2.5–4 mm long (about ⅛–¼ in), breaking at maturity into four brown nutlets. **PROPAGATE** by seeds. Rich, moist but well-drained soils in sunny places are preferred.

Hemerocallis LILIACEAE

Hemerocallis is a genus of 15 clump-forming perennial herbaceous species found from central Europe to Japan. Thousands of cultivars have been named in the genus. The name *Hemerocallis* is from the Greek words for day and beauty, referring to the 1-day life of the flowers.

Hemerocallis lilio-asphodelus Linnaeus

Synonym, *Hemerocallis flava* Linnaeus. **DISTINGUISHABLE** by the basal linear leaves, tall terminal panicles, and large, funnel-shaped, yellow flowers with six tepal segments 8–13 cm long (3½–5 in).

Hemerocallis lilio-asphodelus

Hemerocallis lilio-asphodelus, lemon daylily, sometimes called yellow daylily, is native from eastern Siberia to Japan but is widely cultivated in temperate and, to a lesser extent, tropical areas, mostly in cooler areas at higher elevations, for its yellow flowers. **HERB**, perennial, to 1 m high (3¼ ft), arising from a short rhizome. **LEAVES** nearly distichous and mostly basal, simple, linear, to 80 × 4 cm (32 × 1⅝ in), parallel veined. **FLOWERS** anytime during the year in the tropics; flowers several, borne in a loose, terminal panicle atop a stalk longer than the leaves, fragrant. Corolla with fused tepals, funnel-shaped, the tube 2–4 cm long (¾–1⅝ in), the six segments 8–13 cm long (3½–5 in), bright yellow. FRUIT a several-seeded capsule. PROPAGATE by division; sometimes can be propagated by seeds. Fertile, moist, but well-drained soils in sunny or partially shaded places are preferred. The flowers, popular commercially, live for only a day, opening in the morning and closing in the evening. The plant is often grown in mixed borders, mass plantings, or clumps.

Hemigraphis ACANTHACEAE

Hemigraphis is a genus of 70 to 90 herbaceous species found from Southeast Asia to New Caledonia, some of which are cultivated as ground covers.

Hemigraphis alternata (N. L. Burman) T. Anderson

Synonym, *Hemigraphis colorata* (Blume) Haller fil. DISTINGUISHABLE by the prostrate habit, opposite leaves, scalloped leaf margins, purple to metallic green leaf surface, and spikes of small, white, bell-shaped flowers.

Hemigraphis alternata, metal leaf, and known as red ivy, a misnomer since it is not related to the ivy family Araliaceae, is native to Malaysia but is widely cultivated as a ground cover and grown in hanging baskets for its attractive foliage. HERB, prostrate, rooting at the nodes, with vegetative parts purple. LEAVES simple, opposite, blade ovate to oblong, usually 4–10 cm long (1⅝–4 in), purple on the underside, bluish to metallic green on the upper, margins scalloped. FLOWERS continuously through the year; flowers many,

Hemigraphis alternata

several open at a time, borne in erect terminal and axillary spikes, each flower with a green ovate bract at its base. Corolla of fused petals, bell-shaped, 1.4–2.3 cm long (⅝–⅞ in), divided into five rounded lobes, white. FRUIT a spindle-shaped capsule, infrequently formed in cultivation. PROPAGATE by cuttings. Fertile, moist soils in partially shaded places are preferred. In full sun the leaves lose their metallic cast. It has become naturalized in lawns and along trailsides in many places since it does well in shade and the low habit allows it to survive frequent mowing. One cultivar, 'Exotica', sometimes called waffle plant, has unusual puckered leaves with the margins turned down.

Hibiscus MALVACEAE

Hibiscus comprises 200 to 300 tree and shrub species found throughout the tropics and subtropics, some occurring in temperate areas. The plants are very important as tropical ornamentals because of their large, colorful flowers, and a number of species are endemic to Hawaii and have been used in hybridization, leading to a profusion of variously colored cultivars. Six of the most common ornamental species are included here.

Hibiscus mutabilis Linnaeus

DISTINGUISHABLE by the alternate, lobed leaves, downy leaf surface, large white to pink flowers, and hairy capsule. It is similar to the many cultivars of *Hibiscus rosa-sinensis,* which, however, have mostly glabrous leaves and do not produce fruit.

   Hibiscus mutabilis, confederate rose, sometimes called cotton rose, misnomers since it is neither rose nor cotton, is native to southern China but is widely cultivated for its colorful flowers. The bark yields a useful fiber. SHRUB to 3 m high (10 ft) or more. LEAVES simple, alternate, blade generally round, 10–25 cm long (4–10 in), mostly three- to seven-lobed, surfaces, especially the lower one, covered with downy, star-shaped hairs. FLOWERS anytime during the year; flowers solitary, axillary, or several borne in terminal racemes, each with a series of eight to ten linear bracts at the base. Corolla of five free obovate petals 4–7 cm long (1⅝–3 in), white but aging to red or pink, sometimes double-flowered. FRUIT a hairy subglobose capsule 2–3 cm in diameter (¾–1¼ in). PROPAGATE by seeds or cuttings. Fertile, well-drained soils in sunny places are preferred. It is usually grown as a specimen plant because of its unusual flowers. One kind is a double-flowered white, another a double-flowered pink, and a third, very common, a double-flowered type that changes from white to pink, called changeable rose mallow though it is not a true mallow.

Hibiscus mutabilis with white flowers aging to pink

Hibiscus rosa-sinensis Linnaeus

DISTINGUISHABLE by the alternate, glabrous leaves, toothed leaf margins, flowers with numerous stamens fused into a staminal tube, and the absence of fruit.

Hibiscus rosa-sinensis, Chinese hibiscus, also called red hibiscus, Chinese rose, or rose of China, is neither a rose nor a native of China but rather is native to tropical East Africa though unknown in the wild. Also called shoeblack plant, the red petals are used to make shoe blacking and food coloring. SHRUB to 3 m high (10 ft). LEAVES simple, alternate, blade ovate, 4–12 cm long (1⅝–5 in), surface glabrous, margins toothed. FLOWERS continuously through the year; flowers solitary, axillary, with a whorl of five or more ovate to lanceolate bracts, the epicalyx, below the calyx. Corolla of five free obovate petals or sometimes double-flowered with many petals, usually 5–10 cm long (2–4 in), bright red or variously colored in the hybrids. FRUIT a capsule, infrequently formed in cultivation in the wet tropics. PROPAGATE by cuttings or grafting. Well-drained soils in sunny and partially shaded places are pre-

Hibiscus rosa-sinensis

ferred. It is now widely and commonly cultivated as an ornamental and is one of the most popular tropical hedge plants because of the large flowers always to be found on the plant. The flowers typically last a single day and close up at night after their brief blaze of glory. Numerous hybrids of various flower colors and shapes have been made, often by crossing with *H. schizopetalus,* and many of these are grown in the greenhouse in temperate areas. One hybrid, *H. ×flores-rosa,* has small, dark red, tightly rolled flowers that do not

Hibiscus, a hybrid involving *H. rosa-sinensis* with petals on the end of the staminal column

Hibiscus, a hybrid involving *H. rosa-sinensis* with yellow flowers

open; another common one, *H.* ×*archeri* W. Watson, has red petals with toothed tips; and a third one, *Hibiscus* 'Snow Queen', has leaves variegated with white.

Hibiscus sabdariffa Linnaeus

DISTINGUISHABLE by the alternate, deeply lobed leaves, solitary flowers with a pale yellow corolla purple at the base, numerous stamens fused into a staminal column, and fruit enclosed within a fleshy red calyx.

Hibiscus sabdariffa, roselle, sometimes called red sorrel or Jamaica sorrel, is probably native to West Africa but long ago spread elsewhere and is widely if not commonly cultivated in the tropics as an ornamental for its flowers. It is also grown as a minor food crop because of its edible calyx, which is used to flavor drinks, to make jams and jellies, and as a red dye. The leaves, seeds, and shoots are also edible. The plant is also grown in some places such as Indonesia and the West Indies for its

jute-like fiber. **SHRUB** to 2 m high (6½ ft) with red stems. **LEAVES** simple, alternate, blade ovate to round in outline, 4–15 cm long (1⅝–6 in), typically deeply three-lobed with toothed margins but sometimes unlobed. **FLOWERS** anytime during the year; flowers solitary, axillary, with a calyx that becomes red and fleshy at maturity, below which is a whorl of ten narrow bracts, the epicalyx. Corolla of five free obovate petals 4–5 cm long (1⅝–2 in), pale yellow with a purple base, surrounding the staminal column that encloses the five-lobed style. **FRUIT** an ovoid capsule 2–3 cm long (¾–1¼ in). **PROPAGATE** by seeds or cuttings. Well-drained soils in sunny places are preferred.

Hibiscus sabdariffa

Hibiscus schizopetalus (Masters) J. D. Hooker

DISTINGUISHABLE by the alternate leaves, toothed leaf margins, hanging flowers with reflexed red petals deeply bipinnately lobed, and numerous stamens fused into a staminal column.

Hibiscus schizopetalus, coral hibiscus, sometimes called fringed hibiscus, is native to East Africa but is widely cultivated for its red flowers with deeply lobed petals. **SHRUB** to 3 m high (10 ft). **LEAVES** simple, alternate, blade elliptic to ovate, 3–10 cm long (1¼–4 in) with toothed

margins. **FLOWERS** continuously through the year; flowers solitary, axillary. Corolla of five free, obovate, deeply bipinnately lobed, reflexed petals 5–7 cm long (2–3 in), red, sometimes with white or yellow margins, surrounding the long, hanging staminal column that encloses the five-lobed style. **FRUIT** a capsule, infrequently formed in cultivation. **PROPAGATE** by cuttings or seeds, but the cultivars do not breed true from seeds. Fertile, moist, but well-drained soils in sunny or partially shaded places are preferred. It is often grown by itself as a specimen plant, as a shrubby border, or as a foundation plant, and in temperate areas is raised in the greenhouse. It readily hybridizes with *H. rosa-sinensis* to form many cultivated hybrids.

Hibiscus schizopetalus

Hibiscus syriacus Linnaeus

DISTINGUISHABLE by shrubby habit, leaves with the lower half wedge-shaped, and often purplish flowers with the stamens fused into a staminal column.

Hibiscus syriacus, rose of Sharon, is native to warm temperate China but is widely cultivated elsewhere in tropical and warm temperate areas, including the Mediterranean, where it was introduced in the sixteenth century. **SHRUB** to 4 m high (13 ft). **LEAVES** simple, alternate, blade ovate, usually 5–8 cm long (2–3½ in) with the basal half wedge-shaped, the margins of the upper half shallowly lobed or toothed, surface glabrous. **FLOWERS** anytime during the year in the tropics; flowers solitary, axillary, or several borne in axillary and terminal racemes. Corolla of five free obovate petals or sometimes double-flowered, 3–6 cm long (1¼–2½ in), rose-colored, bluish, purple, red, pink, or white, surrounding the white staminal column that encloses the five-lobed style. **FRUIT** an oblong capsule. **PROPAGATE** by cuttings. Fertile, well-drained soils in sunny places are preferred. It makes an attractive ornamental because of its purple to white flowers and is usually planted in gardens and borders but it is less common in the tropics that the other *Hibiscus* species featured here.

Hibiscus syriacus

Hibiscus tiliaceus Linnaeus

DISTINGUISHABLE by the tree habit, alternate, heart-shaped leaves, velvety gray lower leaf surface, large yellow flowers purple at the base, and stamens fused into a staminal column.

Hibiscus tiliaceus, beach hibiscus, sometimes called yellow hibiscus or mahoe, is found throughout the tropics, where it is a common tree on beaches and in disturbed places, sometimes forming nearly impenetrable thickets, especially along streams. It is also cultivated for its yellow flowers. The flowers and sap of the plant are widely employed in a

Hibiscus tiliaceus, a plant in flower together with a leaf from a variegated cultivar

variety of medicines, the wood is useful for light construction, and the bark fibers are fashioned into cordage. **TREE** or scrambling shrub to 10 m high (33 ft). **LEAVES** simple, alternate, blade heart-shaped to round, 8–30 cm long (3½–12 in), lower surface velvety gray pubescent. **FLOWERS** continuously through the year; flowers solitary or several borne in cymes, terminal, on a long stalk. Corolla of five free obovate petals 4–7 cm long (1⅝–3 in), yellow, crape-like, purple at the base, with the stamens fused into a staminal column around the five-lobed style. **FRUIT** an oblong to ovoid capsule 1.3–2.8 cm long (½–1⅛ in). **PROPAGATE** by cuttings or seeds. Moist soils in sunny places are preferred. It is ideally suited to coastal locations and is often grown as a tree but can be grown on trellises for shade or trimmed into a dense hedge. One ornamental form has lobed, unusually sculptured leaves.

Hippeastrum AMARYLLIDACEAE

Hippeastrum is a genus of about 75 to 80 bulb-forming perennial herb species, all except one found in tropical and subtropical America, with many species and hybrids grown for their large flowers.

Hippeastrum reticulatum (L'Héritier) Herbert

DISTINGUISHABLE by the basal linear leaves, few-flowered umbels, and large, drooping, white, funnel-shaped flowers marked with red lines and margins. The related, commonly grown *Hippeastrum puniceum* (Lamarck) Urban, Barbados lily or red lily, differs most obviously in having red to salmon-colored flowers. There has been much hybridization in the genus, however, leading to confusion in the identification of species.

Hippeastrum reticulatum, which lacks a widely recognized common name, is native to southern Brazil but is widely cultivated for its white flowers. **HERB**, perennial, scapose, to 40 cm high (16 in), clump forming, arising from an underground bulb. **LEAVES** simple, basal, blade sessile, linear-lanceolate, 25–35 × 3.5–4 cm (10–14 × 1⅜–1⅝ in). **FLOWERS** mostly in winter and spring when the leaves appear; flowers three to five, slightly nodding, borne in an umbel on a waxy white peduncle 25–35 cm long (10–14 in). Corolla with fused tepals, funnel-shaped, drooping, 9–11 cm long (3½–4½ in), divided most of the way into six oblanceolate segments, white with red linear or reticulate markings, yellow-green at the base. **FRUIT** a three-lobed capsule, infrequently formed in cultivation. **PROPAGATE** by offsets or seeds. Fertile, moist soils

Hippeastrum reticulatum

Hippeastrum puniceum

in sunny places are preferred. It is often grown as a border or potted plant in the tropics, and in greenhouses and conservatories in temperate climates.

Hippobroma CAMPANULACEAE

Hippobroma is a genus with a single species, sometimes considered to be a part of the genus *Laurentia,* with 17 species.

Hippobroma longiflora (Linnaeus) G. Don

Synonyms, *Isotoma longiflora* (Linnaeus) Presl and *Laurentia longiflora* (Linnaeus) Petermann. DISTINGUISHABLE by the milky sap, narrow alternate leaves with coarsely toothed margins, solitary axillary flowers, and long, tubular corollas with five spreading lobes.

Hippobroma longiflora, star of Bethlehem, is native to the West Indies. It is widely cultivated in the tropics for its long, white flowers. The milky latex is reported to be poisonous and caustic to the skin. HERB, somewhat succulent, to 50 cm high (20 in) or more with milky sap. LEAVES simple, alternate, subsessile, blade linear-oblanceolate, usually 10–24 cm long (4–9 in) with coarsely toothed margins. FLOWERS anytime during the year after maturity; flowers solitary, axillary. Corolla of fused petals, tubular, 8–14 cm long (3½–6 in), divided about a quarter of its length into five spreading lobes, white. FRUIT a cylindrical capsule 1–2 cm long (⅜–¾ in) with persistent linear calyx lobes on top. PROPAGATE by seeds. Moist soils in sunny places are preferred. It may be grown in gardens, planters, or borders but

Hippobroma longiflora

often becomes naturalized in disturbed places such as along roadsides and on rock walls.

Hiptage MALPIGHIACEAE

Hiptage is a genus of 20 to 30 tree, liana, or vine-like shrub species found from Sri Lanka (Ceylon) to Fiji, some of which have a three-winged fruit. Some are used medicinally, and some are cultivated for their attractive or fragrant flowers.

Hiptage benghalensis (Linnaeus) Kurz

Synonym, *Hiptage madablota* Gaertner. DISTINGUISHABLE by the spreading shrubby habit, opposite leaves, compact axillary racemes of white and yellow flowers with fringed petals, and three-winged fruit.

Hiptage benghalensis, which lacks a widely recognized common name, is native from India to the Philippines but is widely if not commonly cultivated in the tropics for its attractive, fragrant flowers. VINE-LIKE SHRUB or liana with scandent branches to 5 m high (16½ ft) or more. LEAVES simple, opposite, blade usually elliptic and 6–18 cm long (2½–7 in) with an attenuate tip. FLOWERS intermittently during the year; flowers many, fragrant, borne in compact axillary racemes. Corolla of five free, elliptic to round, reflexed petals 1–1.7 cm long (⅜–¾ in), white with one petal yellow in the center, margins fringed. FRUIT a samara with three spreading, papery, oblanceolate to elliptic wings 2–5 cm long (¾–2 in). PROPAGATE by cuttings or seeds. Moist but well-drained soils in sunny places are preferred. It is of-

Hiptage benghalensis

ten grown by itself as a specimen plant, is trimmed at the base to form a small tree, or is trained as a liana. When grown as a shrub it must be periodically pruned to keep its shape.

Holmskioldia VERBENACEAE

Holmskioldia is a genus of 10 or 11 tree, shrub, and liana and scandent shrub species found from Africa to India, at least two of which are cultivated as ornamentals.

Holmskioldia sanguinea Retzius

DISTINGUISHABLE by the shrubby habit, opposite leaves with toothed margins, and red or yellow, two-lipped corolla above the similarly colored, spreading, saucer-shaped calyx. *Holmskioldia tettensis* (Klotzsch) Vatke, also cultivated as an ornamental, differs in having a pink to purplish calyx and a purple to blue corolla.

Holmskioldia sanguinea

Holmskioldia sanguinea, Chinese-hat plant, sometimes called mandarin's hat, cup-and-saucer plant, or parasol flower, is native to the montane region of Pakistan and India but is widely cultivated for its red flowers; *H. sanguinea* f. *citrina* Moldenke has yellow flowers. The common names come from the appearance of the flower, which resembles a saucer, the calyx, under a cup, the corolla. SHRUB or small tree to 3 m high (10 ft) or more. LEAVES simple, opposite, blade ovate, 3–10 cm long (1¼–4 in) with toothed margins. FLOWERS continuously through the year and most conspicuously in areas with a dry season; flowers several, borne in short terminal and upper ax-

illary cymes. Corolla with fused petals, funnel-shaped, 1.7–2.7 cm long
(¾–1⅛ in), two-lipped, unequally five-lobed, red or yellow, with a shallowly cup-shaped, red or yellow calyx below. **FRUIT** a brown subglobose
drupe. **PROPAGATE** by cuttings, air layering, or seeds. Fertile, well-
drained soils in sunny to partially shaded places are preferred. It is usually grown by itself as a specimen, screen, or border plant, and sometimes in large tubs, but it can also be trained as a vine. In temperate climates it is used as a potted plant in the greenhouse.

Homalocladium POLYGONACEAE

The name *Homalocladium* is from the Greek words meaning flat and
branch, aptly describing the one species.

Homalocladium platycladum (F. von Mueller) L. H. Bailey

Synonym, *Muehlenbeckia platyclados* (F. von Mueller) Meissner. **DISTIN-
GUISHABLE** by the shrubby, mostly leafless habit, stems that are flat,
jointed, and striated, and clusters of tiny white flowers borne at the
joints.

Homalocladium platycladum, ribbon
bush, sometimes called centipede
plant or tapeworm plant, is native to
New Guinea and the Solomon Islands.
With an appearance only its mother
could love, it is widely if not commonly cultivated as a novelty, by itself or as
part of a hedge or shrub border, because of its ribbon-like stems. **SHRUB**
to 4 m high (13 ft) with flat, finely striated stems having joints every 1–2.5
cm (⅜–1 in). **LEAVES** alternate, linear
to narrowly elliptic, mostly 1–4 cm
long (⅜–1⅝ in) but soon falling and
the plant appearing leafless most of

Homalocladium platycladum

the time. **FLOWERS** anytime during the year; flowers several, borne in sessile axillary clusters. Corolla absent, the calyx of five tiny free sepals about 2 mm long (about ¹⁄₁₆ in), white to greenish or pink. **FRUIT** berry-like, ovoid, red to purple, 3–4.5 mm long (about ⅛–¼ in). **PROPAGATE** by cuttings. Fertile, moist, but well-drained soils in sunny places are preferred. In temperate areas it is grown in the greenhouse but rarely flowers or fruits when planted in a container, no loss ornamentally since the flowers and fruits are small and unattractive.

Hoya ASCLEPIADACEAE

Hoya is a genus of 90 to 100 vine species, or as many as 230 according to some authors, found from Southeast Asia to Polynesia, many grown for their attractive umbels of waxy flowers. Many large and beautiful species are grown by *Hoya* fanciers, who have their own society dedicated to the growing of plants of this genus, often called wax flowers.

Hoya australis

Hoya australis R. Brown

DISTINGUISHABLE by the viny habit, milky sap, succulent opposite leaves, umbels of waxy white flowers red in the center, and pods containing silky-tufted seeds.

Hoya australis is a wax flower or wax plant native from Australia to Samoa but cultivated, often in pots, for its succulent leaves and waxy white flowers. The plant is used medicinally in western Polynesia. **VINE**, perennial, with milky sap. **LEAVES** simple, opposite, blade elliptic to nearly round, usually 5–12 cm long (2–5 in), glabrous, succulent. **FLOWERS** anytime during the year; flowers many, fragrant, borne in umbels from old flower spurs situated between the petiole pairs. Corolla of fused petals, rotate, 1.3–2 cm across (½–¾ in), deeply cut into five lobes, waxy white with red at the base, the stamens fused to the stigma to form a corona. FRUIT a cylindrical follicle filled with silky-tufted seeds. PROPAGATE by cuttings or seeds. Heavy, moist soils in sunny or partially shaded places are preferred.

Hydrangea HYDRANGEACEAE

Hydrangea is a genus of about 23 shrub species, or as many as 80 according to some authors, found from the Himalayas to the Philippines. Many are cultivated for their attractive inflorescences, and some are used medicinally. The genus is sometimes put into the family Saxifragaceae.

Hydrangea macrophylla (Thunberg) Seringe
DISTINGUISHABLE by the opposite leaves, toothed leaf margins, and large, dense heads of blue to pink flowers having two types of flowers—some with a corolla and calyx and some with a corolla-like calyx.

Hydrangea macrophylla, sometimes called florist's hydrangea, is native to eastern Asia but is widely cultivated in temperate areas and occasionally in the tropics for its pink to blue flowers. Many cultivars have been developed, their flower color often affected by soil pH. Acid soils generally produce blue to mauve flowers, and basic soils, red to pink. The color can be reversed with the addition of acids or bases to the soil. HERB or shrub to 1.5 m high (5 ft) or more. LEAVES simple, opposite, blade ovate, 8–20 cm long (3½–8 in) with

Hydrangea macrophylla

toothed margins. **FLOWERS** continuously through the year in the tropics; flowers many, of two types, a sterile one having an enlarged calyx and a fertile one having a small corolla and calyx, borne in dense terminal heads. Corolla not usually forming in the common cultivars but the calyx consisting of four or five nearly round, pink to blue sepals 7–16 mm long (¼–⅝ in). **FRUIT** not forming. **PROPAGATE** by cuttings. Rich, moist soils in partially shaded areas are preferred. Plants are often used in Christmas decorations in the southern hemisphere.

Hylocereus CACTACEAE

Hylocereus is a genus of 6 to 8 succulent tropical American cactus species, or as many as 20 according to some authors. Some have edible fruits, and some are cultivated as ornamentals.

Hylocereus undatus (Haworth) Britton & Rose

DISTINGUISHABLE by the vine-like, succulent, three-winged, thorny stems and large white flowers, forming for a short time, mostly in summer.

Hylocereus undatus

Hylocereus undatus, night-blooming cereus, sometimes called queen of the night, is native to Central America but is widely cultivated for its large, attractive, fragrant flowers that open in the evening and wilt in the morning sun. The plant is naturalized in some places such as tropical America, and the fruits are eaten in its native range. The production of fruit requires two genetically different individuals but most of the plants in an area have been propagated vegetatively and thus belong to the same clone, precluding fertilization, fruit development, and seed

Hylocereus undatus on a rock wall

set. **SHRUB**, succulent, scrambling, clinging to rocks and trees by means of adventitious roots. Stems jointed, three-winged, 3–6 cm wide (1¼–2½ in) with scalloped margins having cushions, areoles, bearing one to four spines 1–3 mm long (about ⅟₃₂–⅛ in). **LEAVES** absent. **FLOWERS** mostly in summer, each flower open a single night; flowers solitary, borne at an areole, with many ovate, leaf-like bracts at the base. Corolla funnel-shaped, 25–30 cm long (10–12 in) with many oblanceolate white petals 10–20 cm long (4–8 in) surrounded by many yellowish green linear sepals, with numerous stamens in the center. **FRUIT** a red oblong berry 6–12 cm long (2½–5 in), infrequently formed in cultivation. **PROPAGATE** by stem cuttings. Well-drained soils in sunny places are preferred. It is often planted on walls and fences, upon which it spreads extensively, and sometimes climbs into trees. The thorns can be a drawback if planted around houses.

Hymenocallis AMARYLLIDACEAE

Hymenocallis, the genus of spider lilies, comprises 30 to 40 herbaceous, bulb-forming perennial herb species of tropical to warm temperate America. Some are cultivated as ornamentals, and some are used medicinally.

Hymenocallis pedalis Herbert

Often misidentified as *Hymenocallis littoralis* (Jacquin) Salisbury (synonym, *Pancratium littorale* Jacquin). DISTINGUISHABLE by the basal linear leaves, umbels of large, white, long-tubed flowers, recurved linear tepal lobes, and long, protruding stamens united at the base by a staminal cup that is free of the corolla. It differs from *Hymenocallis latifolia* (Miller) M. J. Roemer most obviously in having two or three ovules in the ovary rather than four to eight, and from the better known *H. littoralis,* which is very similar, in having a staminal cup adhering to the tepals rather than free of them. The similar crinum lilies, *Crinum* spp., sometimes inaccurately called spider lilies, differ in not having the staminal cup.

Hymenocallis pedalis

Hymenocallis pedalis is a spider lily native to northern South America but is widely cultivated in the tropics for its fragrant white flowers. It sometimes becomes naturalized in coastal areas. HERB, perennial, scapose, to 1.2 m high (4 ft), arising from an underground bulb and forming dense clumps. LEAVES simple, basal, blade linear, usually 30–90 × 3–6 cm (12–36 × 1⅜–2½ in). FLOWERS anytime during the year; flowers usually 7 to 13, sessile, in umbels atop a flattened, leafless stalk to 1 m long (3¼ ft). Corolla with fused white tepals, salverform, tube narrow, 13–23 cm long (5–9 in), tepal segments six, spreading, linear, 9–13 cm long (3½–5 in), with the six long, protruding stamens united at the base to form a white, spreading disk a short distance above the fused tepals. FRUIT a fleshy capsule containing four to eight ovules, only one maturing to form a seed. PROPAGATE by offsets or seeds. Light, fertile, moist, but well-drained soils in sunny to partially shaded places are preferred but full sun is required for optimal flowering. One cultivar has leaves variegated with longitudinal white bands.

Impatiens BALSAMINACEAE

Impatiens comprises about 450 to 850 annual or perennial herb species found mostly in the Old World tropics from Africa to Asia but is absent from Australia. Many species are cultivated as houseplants or garden ornamentals for their colorful flowers or leaves or both. Two of the most common ornamental species are included here.

Impatiens balsamina Linnaeus

DISTINGUISHABLE by the alternate leaves with attenuate leaf base, toothed leaf margins, axillary flower clusters forming along the length of the stem, and colorful, spurred, two-lipped corolla.

Impatiens balsamina, garden balsam, sometimes called rose balsam or just balsam, is native to Southeast Asia but is widely cultivated for its colorful flowers, each bearing a spur and hood. The unusual fruits open explosively to eject the seeds. HERB, perennial or annual, to 60 cm high (24 in) with weak, succulent stems. LEAVES simple, alternate, blade narrowly elliptic to ovate or lanceolate, 6–15 cm

Impatiens balsamina

long (2½–6 in) with toothed margins and an attenuate base. **FLOWERS** continuously through the year; flowers one to three, borne in sessile axillary clusters, each flower with a narrow, curved, nectar-filled spur 1.5–2.5 cm long (⅝–1 in). Corolla two-lipped, with five unequal, free, white, pink, red, or purple, obcordate petals, the lower two the largest, 2.5–3.5 cm long (1–1⅜ in). **FRUIT** a fuzzy ovoid capsule 1.5–2 cm long (⅝–¾ in), opening explosively to eject the seeds. **PROPAGATE** by seeds. Moist, well-drained soils in partially shaded places are preferred. In the tropics it is grown outdoors in gardens and borders, and in temperate areas as an indoor potted plant or summer bedding plant. Several variously colored cultivars have been named.

Impatiens wallerana J. D. Hooker

Synonym, *Impatiens sultani* J. D. Hooker. **DISTINGUISHABLE** by the alternate leaves with attenuate leaf base bearing stalked glands, clusters of flowers mostly toward the tip of the plant, and colorful, spurred, two-lipped corolla with a spreading limb.

Impatiens wallerana, sultan's flower, sometimes called busy lizzie (or lizzy), is native to tropical Africa but is widely cultivated in the tropics and subtropics as a garden ornamental for its colorful flowers. The plant is a favorite in biology classes because the colorful pollen is applied to a slide in a sugar solution and viewed under a microscope to demonstrate pollen germination. Also of interest is the fruit, which opens explosively to eject the seeds. **HERB**, perennial or annual, to 90 cm high (36 in) with weak, succulent stems. **LEAVES** simple, alternate, blade elliptic to ovate, 4–12 cm long (1⅝–5 in) with toothed margins and a long petiole bearing stalked glands. **FLOWERS** continuously through the year; flowers one to three, borne in short-stalked, axillary clusters, each flower with a curved, nectar-filled spur 3–5 cm long (1¼–2 in). Corolla rotate, two-sided, with five free obovate petals mostly 1.8–3 cm long (¾–1¼ in), often notched at the tip, white, pink, red, or purple, with the purple stamens united to form a hood over the ovary. **FRUIT** a glabrous ovoid capsule 1.5–2.5 cm long (⅝–1 in), open-

Impatiens wallerana

Impatiens, a dark-leaved cultivar, the result of hybridization of *I. wallerana* with other species from New Guinea

ing explosively to eject the seeds. PROPAGATE by cuttings, division, or seeds, but seeds of cultivars often do not breed true. Fertile, moist soils in shaded places are preferred. It is often grown as a potted plant, bedding plant, or border plant but the weak stems are easily broken. Plants become scraggly with age and must periodically be replanted. Cultivars in a bewildering variety of colors have been named, many having been formed by hybridization with species from New Guinea, and some of these cultivars have dark leaves.

Ipomoea CONVOLVULACEAE

Ipomoea comprises about 500 herbaceous and woody vine species, rarely shrubs, found throughout the tropics and subtropics. Two are cultivated for food—the sweet potato, *I. batatas,* for its edible tuber, and swamp cabbage or ung-choi, *I. aquatica,* for its edible leaves. Many others are common weeds in open places, and still others are cultivated for their flowers. Four ornamental species are included here.

Ipomoea cairica (Linnaeus) Sweet

DISTINGUISHABLE by the viny habit, slightly milky sap, alternate, deeply palmately lobed leaves, and funnel-shaped mauve flowers darker in the center.

Ipomoea cairica is a morning glory that lacks a well-known common name but might be called ivy-leaved morning glory. It is probably native to tropical Africa but is widely cultivated for its attractive mauve flowers. In some places the vine becomes naturalized and weedy, as it has in Hawaii. VINE, perennial, twining, with slightly milky sap. LEAVES simple, alternate, blade ovate to round, 3–10 cm long (1¼–4 in), deeply palmately divided into five to seven lobes. FLOWERS continuously through the year; flowers one to several, borne in long-stalked, axillary cymes. Corolla of fused petals, funnel-shaped, 5–7 cm long (2–3 in), limb spreading, 5–9 cm long (2–3½ in) and in diameter, shallowly five-lobed, mauve with a darker center. FRUIT a four-seeded subglobose capsule 1–1.2 cm long (⅜–½ in). PROPAGATE by seeds. Well-drained soils in sunny places are preferred. It is often grown on wire fences and trellises, which it can easily cover.

Ipomoea cairica

Ipomoea fistulosa Martius ex Choisy

Synonyms, *Ipomoea carnea* subsp. *fistulosa* (Martius ex Choisy) D. Austin, a name used by some authors, and *I. crassicaulis* (Bentham) Robinson. **DISTINGUISHABLE** by the shrubby habit, milky sap, alternate leaves, and bell-shaped, rich pink corolla darker in the center.

Ipomoea fistulosa, bush morning glory, is native to tropical America and was originally named from Brazil but is widely cultivated in the tropics for its large, attractive, pink flowers. **SHRUB,** erect, scarcely branching, to 3 m high (10 ft) or more, with milky sap. **LEAVES** simple, alternate, blade nearly heart-shaped to lanceolate, 10–22 cm long (4–9 in) on a long petiole. **FLOWERS** continuously through the year; flowers many, borne in upper axillary clusters. Corolla of fused petals, bell-shaped, 6–9 cm long (2½–3½ in), 7–

Ipomoea fistulosa

11 cm in diameter (3–4½ in) when open, rich pink shading to purple at the base. **FRUIT** a subglobose four-seeded capsule, infrequently formed in cultivation. **PROPAGATE** by cuttings. Moist, well-drained soils in sunny places are preferred. Unlike most members of the family and genus, it is a shrub rather than a vine and is often planted in rows or hedges.

Ipomoea horsfalliae J. D. Hooker

DISTINGUISHABLE by the viny habit, clear sap, alternate, deeply palmately lobed leaves, and crimson, rarely pink, funnel-shaped flowers.

Ipomoea horsfalliae, prince's vine, is native to the West Indies but is widely if not commonly cultivated in the tropics for its crimson or, rarely, pink flowers. **VINE,** widely branching, climbing to 10 m high (33 ft), with clear sap. **LEAVES** simple, alternate, blade ovate or more commonly deeply palmately three- to five-lobed, round in outline, 6–18 cm long (2½–7 in). **FLOWERS** continuously through the year; flowers

Ipomoea horsfalliae

Ipomoea quamoclit

many, borne in long-stalked axillary clusters. Corolla of fused petals, salverform, 4–6 cm long (1⅝–2½ in), limb spreading, shallowly five-lobed, to 5 cm in diameter (2 in), crimson or rarely pink. FRUIT a subglobose capsule, infrequently formed in cultivation. PROPAGATE by cuttings, air layering, or scarified seeds. Fertile, moist, but well-drained soils in sunny to partially shaded places are preferred. It is often grown on fences or trellises, which are soon covered with masses of continuously produced flowers, or to cover embankments.

Ipomoea quamoclit Linnaeus

Synonym, *Quamoclit pennata* (Desroussaux) Bojer. DISTINGUISHABLE by the thin-stemmed, viny habit, feathery, pinnately lobed leaves, and five-lobed scarlet flowers.

Ipomoea quamoclit, cypress vine, is native to tropical America but is widely cultivated for its relatively small but prominent scarlet flowers and pinnately dissected, fern-like leaves, which are unusual for *Ipomoea* or for the family Convolvulaceae. VINE, herbaceous, thin stemmed, twining or sprawling, with clear sap. LEAVES simple but appearing feather-like and pinnately compound, alternate, blade ovate to elliptic, 4–10 cm long (1⅝–4 in), deeply divided into 9 to 19 pairs of linear lobes. **Flowers** continuously through the year after maturity; flowers one to three, borne in long-stalked axillary clusters. Corolla of fused petals, salverform, 2–3.5 cm long (¾–1⅜ in), limb shallowly five-lobed, 1.5–2 cm in diameter (⅝–¾ in), scarlet, rarely white. **Fruit** a small, brown, four-seeded, ovoid capsule. **Propagate** by seeds. Well-drained soils in sunny places are preferred. It is often grown in gardens, sometimes as a low climber. In some places it escapes to become adventive but does not spread far or readily.

Iresine AMARANTHACEAE

Iresine is a genus of about 80 herb or shrub species found in tropical and temperate areas, particularly in South America and Australia. Some are used medicinally, and some are cultivated as ornamentals because of their leaves.

Iresine herbstii W. J. Hooker

Distinguishable by the large, herbaceous habit, opposite dark, variegated leaves, notched leaf tip, and lower leaf surface with tiny yellow hairs.

Iresine herbstii, blood leaf, sometimes called beefsteak plant or chicken gizzards, is native to Brazil but is widely cultivated for its colorful foliage. **Herb** to 2 m high (6½ ft), dioecious, with red stems. **Leaves** simple, opposite, blade ovate to subround, 2–10 cm long (¾–4 in), deep red or less commonly variegated with green, white, yellow, or all three colors, notched at the tip, usually with tiny

Iresine herbstii

yellow hairs on the lower surface. FLOWERS infrequently in cultivation; flowers many, densely crowded in terminal and subterminal, widely branching panicles of spikes on separate male and female plants. Corolla of five free, white, lanceolate to oblong tepals 1–1.5 mm long (about ⅟₃₂–⅟₁₆ in). FRUIT a tiny utricle containing a single shiny black seed but infrequently formed in cultivation. PROPAGATE by cuttings, the technique most used. Moist but well-drained soils in sunny places are preferred and bright sunlight is required to bring out optimal leaf color. It is often grown as a border plant, as a low hedge where color is needed, as a bedding plant, or as an outdoor potted plant, or indoors in cooler climates. Several cultivars have been named.

Ixora RUBIACEAE

Ixora, a name derived from that of an Indian deity, comprises 300 to 400 shrub and small tree species native throughout the tropics, especially in Southeast Asia and the islands of Malaysia. Most of the species are restricted to original forests but many are cultivated for their inflorescences of colorful, often red flowers. There is much confusion and disagreement on the names of the species because of variation and hybridization. Three of the most common ornamental species are included here.

Ixora casei Hance

Synonyms, *Ixora carolinensis* Hosokawa, *I. longifolia* Smith, and sometimes misidentified as *I. macrothrysa* Teijsmann & Binnendijk. DISTINGUISHABLE by the shrubby habit, relatively large, opposite leaves, interpetiolar stipules, and large clusters of long, red, four-lobed flowers.

Ixora casei, giant red ixora, is perhaps native to Micronesia but is widely cultivated in the tropics for its large inflorescence of bright red to orange flowers, among the largest of the ornamental ixoras. SHRUB to 3 m high (10 ft) or more with interpetiolar stipules. LEAVES simple, opposite, blade elliptic to oblanceolate, leathery, 10–20 cm long (4–8 in) with an acute base. **FLOWERS** continuously through the year; flowers numerous, 50 to 100 or more, borne in dense clusters in terminal, panicle-like inflorescences. Corolla with fused petals, salverform, tube slender, 2.5–4 cm long (1–1⅝ in), divided into four spreading ovate lobes 7–15 mm long (¼–⅝ in), red or sometimes light orange. **FRUIT** a purplish subglobose drupe 6–14 mm in diameter (¼–⅝ in). **PROPAGATE** by cuttings, seeds, or air layering. Moist but well-drained soils in sunny to partially shaded places are preferred. It is planted alone as a specimen plant or in borders where red or orange colors are desired. Some pruning is needed to keep it in shape.

Ixora casei, a plant with red flowers and the less commonly grown one with light orange flowers

Ixora coccinea Linnaeus

Synonyms, *Ixora coccinea* var. *lutea* (Hutchinson) Corner and *I. lutea* Hutchinson. **DISTINGUISHABLE** by the opposite leaves, interpetiolar stipules, rounded to heart-shaped leaf bases, and dense clusters of red, sometimes pink or orange, tubular flowers with four spreading, acute lobes between which are found the anthers. *Ixora chinensis* Lamarck, Chinese ixora, a very similar cultivated shrub with red flowers, differs mainly in having mostly rounded corolla lobes. *Ixora siamensis* Wallich ex G. Don, sometimes considered to be just a variety of *I. coccinea,* differs mainly in having pink flowers.

Ixora coccinea, a red ixora sometimes called flame of the woods, is native to Southeast Asia but is widely cultivated as a hedge plant and for its red flowers. Some authors recognize several varieties of the species;

Ixora coccinea with red flowers

others recognize some of these as separate species. **SHRUB** to 2 m high (6½ ft) with interpetiolar stipules. **LEAVES** simple, opposite, blade usually elliptic to oblanceolate, 3–10 cm long (1¼–4 in), rounded to heart-shaped at the base, leathery, dark green, subsessile. **FLOWERS** continuously through the year; flowers mostly 15–50, in several clusters in short, terminal, panicle-like inflorescences, with a pair of leaf-like bracts below. Corolla with fused petals, salverform, tube 3–4 cm long (1¼–1⅝ in) with four spreading, acute, elliptic lobes 9–14 mm long (⅜–½ in), red or sometimes orange, yellow, or pink, with four stamens attached between the lobes.

Ixora coccinea with yellow flowers, sometimes considered to be *I. coccinea* var. *lutea*

Ixora coccinea, dwarf cultivars, one with red flowers and one with pale yellow flowers

Ixora siamensis with pink flowers

Ixora chinensis with rounded corolla lobes

FRUIT a black subglobose drupe. **PROPAGATE** cuttings or seeds. Fertile, moist, but well-drained soils in partially shaded places are preferred. In temperate areas it is grown indoors in greenhouses or houses as a potted plant. It is grown in hedges, planters, tubs, or in borders and can withstand severe pruning. Several cultivars are recognized, including the popular dwarf ixora, a low shrub with dense inflorescences and small leaves.

Ixora finlaysoniana Wallich ex G. Don

DISTINGUISHABLE by the opposite leaves, interpetiolar stipules, purple petioles, large, dense clusters of long-tubed white flowers with four spreading lobes between which are found the anthers, and relatively large ovate calyx lobes with white margins.

Ixora finlaysoniana is a white ixora native to Thailand or the surrounding area but is widely if not commonly cultivated for its fragrant white flowers. Less common than most other *Ixora* ornamentals, perhaps because it has white rather than red flowers, it lacks a widely rec-

Ixora finlaysoniana

ognized common name and might be called Siamese white ixora. **Shrub** to 3 m high (10 ft) or more with interpetiolar stipules. **Leaves** simple, opposite, blade narrowly elliptic to oblong or oblanceolate, 6–16 cm long (2½–6 in) on a purple petiole about 1 cm long (⅜ in). **Flowers** continuously through the year; flowers numerous, more than 75, borne in several dense clusters in a terminal, panicle-like inflorescence. Corolla with fused petals, salverform with a slender tube 2–4 cm long (¾– 1⅝ in), divided into four spreading ovate lobes 5–7 mm long (about ¼ in), white. **Fruit** a subglobose drupe, infrequently formed in cultivation. **Propagate** by cuttings. Moist, well-drained soils in partially shaded places are preferred. It is often grown as a specimen plant rather than as part of a hedge.

Jacaranda BIGNONIACEAE

Jacaranda is a genus of about 30 tropical American tree and shrub species, some utilized for timber, pulp, and medicines, and some cultivated for their conspicuous, seasonal flowers.

Jacaranda mimosifolia D. Don

Synonym, *Jacaranda acutifolia* of some authors, not Humboldt & Bonpland. **Distinguishable** by the tree habit, leaves that are opposite, feathery, and bipinnately compound, tiny leaflets, and narrowly bell-shaped lavender flowers that cover the tree in late spring and summer.

Jacaranda mimosifolia is native to northwestern Argentina but is widely grown in tropical and subtropical regions for its flowers and fern-like leaves. The attractive wood, called green ebony, is sometimes used in carpentry. TREE to 15 m high (50 ft), deciduous. LEAVES bipinnately compound, fern-like, opposite, pinnae in 8 to 20 pairs, leaflets numerous, blades elliptic to lanceolate, mostly 8–16 mm long (¼–⅝ in). FLOWERS seasonally, mostly in late spring and summer; flowers many, borne in dense terminal panicles. Corolla of fused petals, narrowly bell-shaped, 4–5.5 cm long (1⅝–2¼ in), two-lipped with five lobes, lavender blue to pale purple. FRUIT a flat, nearly round capsule 4.5–7 cm across (1¾–3 in), containing many winged seeds. PROPAGATE by seeds or cuttings.

Jacaranda mimosifolia

Fertile, well-drained soils in sunny places are preferred. It is often grown as a shade, street, or garden tree, and thousands line the streets of Pretoria, South Africa. The tree is spectacular during its flowering season when pale purple blossoms cover the tree, afterward carpeting the ground with a lavender layer. Optimal flowering occurs in areas with a distinct dry season, which also causes the tree to be dry-season deciduous.

Jasminum OLEACEAE

Jasminum includes 200 to 450 shrub and vine species native throughout the tropics and subtropics, a few extending into temperate regions. Many are cultivated for their fragrant flowers, some for use in commercial perfumes. Jasmines can be distinguished from similar white-flowered members of the dogbane family Apocynaceae by their lack of milky sap and the presence of only two stamens rather than five. Four of the most commonly cultivated species are included here.

Jasminum grandiflorum Linnaeus

Synonyms, *Jasminum officinale* f. *grandiflorum* (Linnaeus) Kobuski and *J. officinale* var. *grandiflorum* (Linnaeus) Stokes, names used by some authors. DISTINGUISHABLE by the viny habit, clear sap, leaves that are opposite and odd-pinnately compound, white corolla with four or five spreading lobes, and two stamens in the corolla tube.

Jasminum grandiflorum, Spanish jasmine, sometimes called poet's jasmine, is in fact native to the Arabian Peninsula but is cultivated throughout tropical to warm temperate regions for its fragrant flowers. VINE, slender, woody. LEAVES odd-pinnately compound, opposite, leaflet blades usually seven, ranging from three to nine, elliptic to ovate, the lateral ones 1–3 cm long (⅜–1¼ in), the terminal one larger. FLOWERS continuously through the year; flowers several, borne in upper axillary and terminal clusters. Corolla with fused petals, salverform, tube 1.4–2.4 cm long (⅝–⅞ in), reddish, limb of five, rarely four, spreading, oblanceolate lobes 1.2–2 cm long (½–¾ in), pure white or tinged with red. FRUIT a two-lobed berry, infrequently formed in cultivation. PROPAGATE by cuttings. Fertile, well-drained soils in sunny places are preferred. As an ornamental it is often grown by itself or trained on a trellis. *Jasminum grandiflorum* subsp. *floribundum* (R. Brown ex Fresenius) P. S. Green, known only in cultivation, is used by the French perfume industry to make the commercial jasmine oil.

Jasminum grandiflorum

Jasminum laurifolium Roxburgh

Synonym, *Jasminum nitidum* Skan. DISTINGUISHABLE by the shrubby habit, clear sap, leaves that are opposite, simple, and have an attenuate tip, white corolla with 9 to 11 spreading lobes, and two stamens in the reddish corolla tube.

Jasminum laurifolium, angel-wing jasmine, is native to Melanesia but is cultivated for its fragrant flowers, though probably less frequently than the other jasmines included here. **SHRUB**, spreading, to 2 m high (6½ ft). **LEAVES** simple, opposite, blade ovate to lanceolate, 5–12 cm long (2–5 in) with an attenuate tip. **FLOWERS** continuously through the year; flowers five to ten, borne in loose terminal clusters, each flower with five to seven linear calyx lobes. Corolla with fused petals, salverform, tube 1.5–2.3 cm long (⅝–⅞ in), reddish purple, limb deeply cut into 9 to 11 spreading, narrowly oblong, acute

Jasminum laurifolium

lobes 1.3–2.2 cm long (½–⅞ in), white on the inside and often tinted red-purple on the outside. **FRUIT** a globose two-lobed berry, infrequently formed in cultivation. **PROPAGATE** by cuttings. Well-drained soils in sunny places are preferred. It is often planted in pots, in garden borders, or grown standing by itself as a colorful specimen plant. The commonly grown plant is *J. laurifolium* f. *nitidum.*

Jasminum multiflorum (N. L. Burman) Andrews

Synonym, *Jasminum pubescens* (Retzius) Willdenow. **DISTINGUISHABLE** by the shrubby habit, fuzzy stems, clear sap, leaves that are opposite, simple, and pubescent, a corolla that is white, fragrant, six- to nine-lobed, and two stamens in the corolla tube.

Jasminum multiflorum, downy jasmine, sometimes called star jasmine, is native to India but is widely cultivated in the tropics and subtropics for its white flowers, fragrant especially at night. The dried flow-

Jasminum multiflorum

ers are used to flavor tea in China. **Shrub**, spreading or sometimes climbing, to 2 m high (6½ ft) with fuzzy stems. **Leaves** simple, opposite, blade ovate, 3–7 cm long (1¼–3 in), usually finely pubescent on both surfaces. **Flowers** continuously through the year; flowers several, borne in short, compact, axillary and terminal clusters. Corolla with fused petals, salverform, tube 1.2–2.2 cm long (½–⅞ in), limb deeply cut into six to nine narrow, acute, spreading lobes 1.2–2 cm long (½–¾ in), white, fragrant. **Fruit** a two-lobed berry, infrequently formed in cultivation. **Propagate** by cuttings. Fertile, well-drained soils in sunny to partially shaded places are preferred. It is often grown as a colorful hedge or foundation plant, sometimes in large planters or tubs, and can be trained as a vine on a trellis.

Jasminum sambac (Linnaeus) Aiton

Distinguishable by the shrubby habit, clear sap, leaves that are opposite, simple, and bluntly tipped, few-flowered inflorescences of white flowers bearing four to nine corolla lobes or double-flowered, and two stamens in the corolla tube. It looks like a miniature *Gardenia* but is distinguished by its two stamens rather than four or five.

Jasminum sambac, Arabian jasmine, is native to India but is widely cultivated in the tropics and subtropics. In India it is one of the most commonly grown ornamental plants, in China it is used to scent jasmine tea, in Hawaii it is popular for making leis, and in the Philippines it is the national flower. Another name for it, pikake, comes from the Hawaiian word for peacock, because nineteenth century Hawaiian

Princess Kaiulani loved both peacocks and jasmines. **Shrub** to 1.5 m high (5 ft) with downy stems. **Leaves** simple, opposite, blade elliptic to ovate, 3–9 cm long (1¼–3½ in) on a short petiole. **Flowers** anytime during the year; flowers several, borne in terminal and axillary clusters. Corolla with fused petals, salverform, tube 1–2 cm long (⅜–¾ in), limb deeply cut into four to nine (or double-flowered) spreading, blunt, usually elliptic lobes 1.1–1.5 cm long (⅜–⅝ in), white, fragrant. **Fruit** a two-lobed berry, infrequently formed in cultivation. **Propagate** by cuttings. Fertile, moist, but well-drained soils in sunny to partially shaded places are preferred. It is often grown as a foundation or border plant, or in mass plantings. A popular double-flowered cultivar, 'Grand Duke of Tuscany', looks like a miniature gardenia.

Jasminum sambac

Jatropha EUPHORBIACEAE

Jatropha comprises 125 to 175 mostly tree and shrub and some herb species native to tropical and subtropical America, Africa, and eastward to India. Some are used for medicines, often as a purge since most are somewhat poisonous, for oils, and as ornamentals. Four of the most commonly cultivated ornamental species are included here.

Jatropha curcas Linnaeus

Distinguishable by the shrubby habit, alternate, shallowly lobed leaves, small greenish flowers, and green, walnut-sized fruit containing three large seeds.

Jatropha curcas

Jatropha curcas, physic nut, is native to tropical America from Mexico to Brazil and the West Indies but is widely cultivated as an ornamental. The seed contains an oil used in making paint and soap, and the oil is also strongly purgative and poisonous. The seeds and the leaves, also somewhat purgative, are sometimes used in herbal medicines. **SHRUB** to 4 m high (13 ft). **LEAVES** simple, alternate, blade broadly ovate, 4–20 cm long (1⅝–8 in), shallowly three- to seven-lobed. **FLOWERS** intermittently during the year; flowers many, borne in terminal and upper axillary cymes. Corolla of five free yellow-green petals 5–8 mm long (about ¼ in). **FRUIT** an ellipsoidal capsule 2.5–3.5 cm long (1–1⅜ in), containing three oily seeds. **PROPAGATE** by cuttings or seeds. Moist but well-drained soils in sunny places are preferred. It is planted mostly as a hedge, a support plant for *Vanilla* vines (a nonornamental use), or as a living fence post since both its flowers and leaves are uninteresting.

Jatropha integerrima Jacquin

Synonym, *Jatropha hastata* Jacquin. **DISTINGUISHABLE** by the alternate leaves with a tiny pair of glands at the base, long-stalked axillary cymes bearing unisexual flowers, each with five red petals, and three-seeded capsule.

    Jatropha integerrima, peregrina, sometimes called rose-flowered jatropha, is native to the West Indies and was originally named from Cuba but is widely cultivated for its red flowers. Like other euphorbs it is poisonous and if consumed acts as a drastic purge. **TREE** or shrub to 4 m high (13 ft). **LEAVES** simple, alternate, blade ovate, 4–14 cm long (1⅝–6 in), often with one or more shallow marginal lobes and a pair of tiny glands on the margins near the base. FLOW-ERS continuously through the year; flowers unisexual, many, borne in long-stalked axillary cymes with both male and female flowers. Corolla of five free, obovate, red petals 1.5–2.2 cm long (⅝–⅞ in), with yellow stamens. FRUIT a subglobose capsule 1–1.4 cm long (⅜–½ in), splitting at maturity into three sections. PROPAGATE by cuttings. Fertile, moist, but well-drained soils in sunny to partially shaded places are preferred. It is often planted in rows as a screen or by itself as a specimen plant, and it needs periodic pruning to keep its shape.

Jatropha integerrima

Jatropha multifida Linnaeus

DISTINGUISHABLE by the alternate, deeply palmately lobed leaves with pinnately lobed margins, flat-topped, many-flowered inflorescences, and red unisexual flowers.

Jatropha multifida, coral plant, is native to tropical America from Texas to Brazil but is widely cultivated as a novelty because of its unusual form and attractive, lobed leaves. The seeds and sap are poisonous but are, with the leaves, sometimes used in local medicines. SHRUB, branching at the base, to 3 m high (10 ft). LEAVES simple, alternate, blade round, palmately divided to near the base into 7 to 11 entire or pinnately lobed segments mostly 7–20 cm long (3–8 in), on a long petiole with a branching filiform stipule at the base. FLOWERS continuously through the year; flowers many, borne in red, flat-topped, long-stalked axillary cymes, the outer flower male, the inner one or more

Jatropha multifida

Jatropha podagrica

female. Corolla of five free, obovate, bright red petals 4–5 mm long (about ¼ in). **FRUIT** a shallowly three-lobed, ovoid capsule 2–3 cm long (¾–1¼ in). **PROPAGATE** by seeds or cuttings. Relatively dry soils in sunny places are preferred. It is often grown by itself as a specimen plant.

Jatropha podagrica W. J. Hooker

DISTINGUISHABLE by the succulent stem swollen at the base, alternate leaves with the petiole attached within the blade margin, and flat-topped cymes of attractive red unisexual flowers.

Jatropha podagrica, gout stalk, sometimes called gout plant or Guatemala rhubarb, is native from Central America to northern South America but is widely cultivated as a novelty because of its swollen stem and base as well as for its red inflorescences. Like other members of the genus, it is poisonous. **SHRUB** to 2 m high (6½ ft) with a succulent stem and a thick swollen base. **LEAVES** simple, alternate, blade broadly ovate, the larger ones 20–40 cm long (8–16 in), peltate, margin entire to shallowly three- to five-lobed. **FLOWERS** continuously through the year; flowers borne in red, flat-topped, terminal cymes, the few female flowers surrounded by the many males. Corolla of five free, obovate, bright red petals 3–8 mm long (about ⅛–¼ in). **Fruit** a shallowly three-lobed, ovoid capsule 1.3–1.8 cm long (½–¾ in). **Propagate** by seeds. Relatively dry soils in sunny places are preferred. It is usually grown by itself as a specimen plant rather than in clusters or as a hedge.

Justicia ACANTHACEAE

Justicia comprises about 420 herb, shrub, or rarely, small tree species, or as many as 600 according to some authors, found throughout the tropics and subtropics. Many are cultivated for their colorful flowers or bracts or both, and some are widespread weeds naturalized in disturbed places. Three of the best known ornamental species are included here.

Justicia betonica Linnaeus

Synonym, *Nicoteba betonica* (Linnaeus) Lindau. **Distinguishable** by the opposite leaves, erect spikes covered by overlapping white bracts with green veins, and small, white to violet, two-lipped flowers with purple markings.

Justicia betonica, white shrimp plant, is native from India to tropical East Africa but is widely cultivated for its purplish flowers and overlapping white bracts. Though it sometimes becomes naturalized or adventive, it does not readily spread. **Shrub** to 2 m high (6½ ft) or more. **Leaves** simple, opposite, blade ovate to lanceolate, 6–20 cm long (2½–8 in). **Flowers** continuously through the year; flowers many, borne in an erect terminal spike sometimes branched at the base with an

Justicia betonica

overlapping white, green veined, ovate bract below each flower. Corolla of fused petals, funnel-shaped, two-lipped, 1.2–1.8 cm long (½–¾ in), white at the base and violet to rose-colored with purple markings on the upper portion. **FRUIT** a club-shaped capsule 1.5–1.8 cm long (⅝–¾ in). **PROPAGATE** by cuttings or seeds. Fertile, moist, but well-drained soils in sunny or partially shaded places are preferred. It is usually grown in mass plantings or as a hedge in front of taller shrubs. Cultivars with green or yellow bracts have been named.

Justicia brandegeeana Wasshausen & L. B. Smith

Synonym, *Beloperone guttata* Brandegee, and sometimes misspelled *J. brandegeana*. **DISTINGUISHABLE** by the alternate leaves, spikes covered with overlapping red ovate bracts, and white, two-lipped flowers.

   Justicia brandegeeana, shrimp plant, is native to Mexico but is widely cultivated for its white flowers and overlapping red bracts. **SHRUB** to 1.5 m high (5 ft) with pubescent young stems. **LEAVES** simple, opposite, blade ovate to elliptic, usually 3–6 cm long (1¼–2½ in), pubescent. **FLOWERS** continuously through the year; flowers many, borne in a curving terminal spike sometimes branching at the base with an overlapping, brick red to pink, sometimes green to yellowish, ovate bract below each flower. Corolla of fused petals, two-lipped, 2.5–3.2 cm long (1–1¼ in), white with pink, red, or purple spots, usually one or two maturing at a time in the spike. **FRUIT** a capsule usually 1–1.5 cm long (⅜–⅝ in). **PROPAGATE** by cuttings or divisions of old clumps, the usual methods. Light, well-drained soils in sunny to partially shaded places are

Justicia brandegeeana

preferred but bright sun may fade the color of the bracts. The contrasting white bracts and red flowers make it particularly appealing. It is often grown in hedges, borders, or in front of taller shrubs but can also be grown as a tub or potted plant, outdoors in the tropics and as a houseplant in colder climates.

Justicia carnea Lindley

Synonyms, *Cyrtanthera carnea* (Lindley) Bremekamp, *Jacobinia carnea* (Lindley) Nicholson, and *J. magnifica* (Nees) Lindau. DISTINGUISHABLE by the opposite leaves, inconspicuous linear-lanceolate bracts, and dense terminal panicles of pink to rose-red, two-lipped flowers. The similar *Pachystachys spicata* differs in having bright red rather than rose-colored to pink flowers.

Justicia carnea, flamingo plant, sometimes called jacobinia, is native to northern Brazil but is widely cultivated for its dense inflorescence of attractive pink flowers. Unlike many ornamental justicias, it has notable flowers but inconspicuous bracts. SHRUB or robust herb to 2 m high (6½ ft) with four-angled stems. LEAVES simple, opposite, blade lanceolate to ovate or oblong, 6–25 cm long (2½–10 in), surfaces gray-green, the lower often reddish. FLOWERS continuously through the year; flowers many, borne among inconspicuous linear-lanceolate bracts in a dense terminal panicle usually 6–15 cm long (2½–6 in). Corolla of fused petals, two-lipped, 5–7 cm long (2–3 in), divided about halfway into an upper two-lobed lip and a lower three-lobed lip, sticky on the outside, pink to rose-colored, rarely white. FRUIT a capsule, infrequently formed in culti-

Justicia carnea

vation. **PROPAGATE** by cuttings. Moist, well-drained soils in sunny or partially shaded places are preferred. It is often grown as a specimen plant, outdoors in the tropics and in the greenhouse in cooler climates.

Kalanchoe CRASSULACEAE

Kalanchoe comprises about 125 succulent shrub and herb species found in the Old World tropics, especially Africa and Madagascar. Many of the hardy, drought-resistant species are cultivated for their succulent habit or prominent flowers or both, and three of the most common ornamental species are included here.

Kalanchoe blossfeldiana Poellnitz

DISTINGUISHABLE by the subshrub habit, leaves that are succulent and alternate, crenate red leaf margins, and spreading panicles of red or yellow four-lobed flowers.

Kalanchoe blossfeldiana

Kalanchoe blossfeldiana, flaming Katie, is native to Madagascar but is widely cultivated for its attractive succulent habit and red or yellow flowers. There is apparently much hybridization in this "species," which may account for its variability and the number of cultivars. **SUBSHRUB**, perennial, to 40 cm high (16 in) or more. **LEAVES** simple, alternate, succulent, blade elliptic to ovate, oblanceolate on upper stems, 2–10 cm long (¾–4 in), margins red, crenate. **FLOWERS** anytime during the year; flowers many, in spreading, terminal panicles. Corolla of fused petals, red or sometimes yellow, salverform, tube 8–11 mm long (¼–½ in), lobes four, spreading, about half as long as the tube. **FRUIT** of four follicles from separate ovaries. **PROPAGATE** by seeds or cuttings. Well-drained soils in sunny or partially shaded places are preferred. It is often grown as a low border plant, especially where color is needed, in rock gardens, and as a potted plant or window-box plant in temperate and tropical areas.

Kalanchoe pinnata (Lamarck) Persoon

Synonyms, *Bryophyllum calycinum* Salisbury and *B. pinnatum* (Lamarck) Kurz, a name used by some authors. **DISTINGUISHABLE** by the succulent habit, leaves that are alternate and simple or pinnately compound with scalloped purple margins, and tall panicles of hanging, tubular, red, four-lobed flowers.

Kalanchoe pinnata, air plant, sometimes called life plant, is native to tropical Africa or Madagascar but is widely cultivated in the tropics and subtropics. **HERB**, succulent, to 1.5 m high (5 ft) with pith-filled stems somewhat woody at the base. **LEAVES** simple or pinnately compound, opposite, blade of simple leaves ovate to elliptic, usually 7–25 cm long (3–10 in), margins purple, crenate. **FLOWERS** anytime during the year; flowers many, pendulous, in terminal panicles to 120 cm long (48 in). Corolla of fused petals, red, tubular, 4–5.5 cm long (1⅝–2¼ in), four-lobed about one-third of its length. **FRUIT** of four narrowly ovoid follicles 1–1.5 cm long (⅜–⅝ in) from separate ovaries. **PROPAGATE** by the plantlets that form on the edges of the leaves. Fertile, well-drained soils in sunny to partly shaded places are preferred. It is often grown in planters or pots and in rock gardens, and sometimes becomes natu-

Kalanchoe pinnata

ralized as a weed of dry places. It is also grown as a novelty because of its ability to form new plants from leaves fallen on the ground, hence the common names.

Kalanchoe tubiflora (Harvey) R. Hamet

Synonym, *Bryophyllum tubiflorum* Harvey, *Kalanchoe delagonensis* Ecklon & Zeyher, both names used by some authors. **DISTINGUISHABLE** by leaves that are succulent, mottled, and nearly cylindrical, plantlets forming near the leaf tips, and terminal cymes of drooping, orange to red, four-lobed flowers.

Kalanchoe tubiflora, chandelier plant, is native to Madagascar but is widely cultivated as an ornamental. **HERB** to 1 m high (3¼ ft) or more with a distinct stem. **LEAVES** simple, alternate, blade subcylindrical, succulent, 3–15 cm long (1¼–6 in), mottled gray-green and reddish brown or black, with three to nine tiny teeth at the apex, between which plantlets are produced. **FLOWERS** seasonally, mostly in late fall to spring or the wet season; flowers many, pendulous, borne in terminal cymes 10–20 cm wide (4–8 in). Corolla of fused petals, orange to scarlet, tubular, 2.5–4.2 cm long (1–1¾ in), four-lobed about one-quarter of its length, lobes obovate. **FRUIT** of four separate follicles, infrequently formed in cultivation. **PROPAGATE** by plantlets produced on the tips of the leaves, leaf or stem cuttings, or seeds. Well-drained soils in sunny to partially shaded places are preferred. It is often grown in planters, in pots outdoors or as a houseplant, and in water-conserving gardens, often escaping from cultivation to grow in relatively dry places.

Kalanchoe tubiflora

Kigelia BIGNONIACEAE

Kigelia is a genus with a single species, which is cultivated as an ornamental oddity.

Kigelia africana (Lamarck) Bentham

Synonym, *Kigelia pinnata* (Jacquin) A. P. de Candolle. DISTINGUISHABLE by the spreading tree habit, opposite, pinnately compound leaves, long, hanging racemes of large purple flowers, and persistent sausage-like fruit.

Kigelia africana, sausage tree, is native to tropical West Africa. The fruit is not, as the name would imply, edible but it is used in some places in Africa as a scouring pad and to flavor beer. The timber is sometimes used for canoes and other things. The attractive dark red flowers, which are unpleasant smelling, open at night when they can be pollinated by bats and last only a day. TREE, spreading, to 10 m high (33 ft). LEAVES odd-pinnately compound, opposite, leaflets 7 to 13, blades ovate to oblong, 4–18 cm long (1⅝–7 in). FLOWERS mostly in spring and summer; flowers several, borne in narrow, hanging, axillary panicles to 2 m long (6½ ft). Corolla of fused petals, irregularly bell-shaped, 9–13 cm long (3½–5 in), two-lipped, yellowish on the outside, purple inside. FRUIT oblong, hard, 30–50 cm long (12–20 in), not splitting, hanging on the stalk for several months. PROPAGATE by seeds. Fertile, well-drained soils in sunny places are preferred. It is widely cultivated in the tropics as a shade tree, as a novelty, and as a specimen plant for its large, sausage-shaped fruits, hanging on long

Kigelia africana

stalks from the branches for many months. Because of its size the tree is not suitable for small yards. It is also grown in the greenhouse in temperate areas for its foliage.

Lagerstroemia LYTHRACEAE

Lagerstroemia comprises 53 tree and shrub species native from India to Australia, many valuable for timber or as ornamentals. Two ornamental species commonly cultivated in tropical and warm temperate climates are included here.

Lagerstroemia indica Linnaeus

DISTINGUISHABLE by the tree habit, opposite leaves, and seasonal flowers with purple to white, stalked, crape-like petals.

   Lagerstroemia indica, crape myrtle, is native to eastern Asia, from China or the Himalayas, but is widely cultivated in the tropics and subtropics for the pink, white, or purple flowers that seasonally cover the tree. TREE to 4 m high (13 ft). LEAVES simple, opposite, often somewhat offset, blade ovate to obovate, 3–10 cm long (1¼–4 in), subsessile. FLOWERS seasonally, mostly in late spring and summer; flowers many, unscented, borne in terminal, sometimes leafy panicles. Corolla of five free, nearly round petals 1.8–2.5 cm long (¾–1 in), pink, purple, or white, with a narrow base, the claw, half as long. FRUIT a globose capsule usually 8–10 mm long (¼–⅜ in). PROPAGATE by cuttings or air layering; sometimes can be propagated by seeds but the seeds may not breed true for the cultivars. Fertile, well-drained soils in sunny places are preferred, and optimal flowering occurs in areas with

Lagerstroemia indica

a hot dry season. The leaves are deciduous in cooler climates, and a tree will not flower for a while after pruning. Plants are often grown by themselves or used as hedges or screen plants. More than 150 cultivars have been named, some formed from hybridization with other species.

Lagerstroemia speciosa (Linnaeus) Persoon

Synonym, *Lagerstroemia flos-reginae* Retzius. **DISTINGUISHABLE** by the shrubby habit, opposite leaves, and seasonal flowers with pink to white, stalked, crape-like petals.

Lagerstroemia speciosa, queen's crape myrtle, sometimes called pride of India or rose of India, is probably native from Southeast Asia to the Philippines but not India. The durable wood has been used commercially for a number of purposes, including railroad ties, and various parts of the plant are used medicinally. **TREE** to 15 m high (50 ft) or more. **LEAVES** simple, opposite, blade usually elliptic, 8–30 cm long (3½–12 in) on a short petiole. **FLOWERS** seasonally, mostly in spring to early fall; flowers many, unscented, borne in large terminal panicles, the lower part with flowers in threes and the upper part with flowers solitary. Corolla of five free, nearly round petals 2–3 cm long (¾–1¼ in) on short stalks, pink to nearly white, surrounding the numerous yellow stamens. **FRUIT** an ovoid to subglobose capsule 2–2.5 cm long (¾–1 in), enclosed within the 6-lobed, 12-grooved calyx. **PROPAGATE** by cuttings and root shoots, the technique most used since seeds do not breed true. Fertile, well-drained soils in sunny places are preferred. It is

Lagerstroemia speciosa

widely cultivated as an ornamental tree, often along avenues, because of the flowers that cover the tree seasonally. The slow-growing trees are sometimes grown in temperate areas in pots that are put into greenhouses during winter. The leaves are deciduous in areas with a dry season. The dried fruits are used in dry flower arrangements.

Lantana VERBENACEAE

Lantana comprises 150 to 160 shrub and herb species found mostly in tropical America, with a few in southern Africa. Many are cultivated for their clusters of flowers, and some are thorny and weedy. Two of the most commonly cultivated ornamental species are included here.

Lantana camara Linnaeus

DISTINGUISHABLE by the shrubby habit, opposite leaves, toothed leaf margins, and multicolored hemispheric heads of tiny two-lipped flowers.

Lantana camara

Lantana camara, lantana or shrub verbena, is native to the West Indies but is widely cultivated for its multicolored flowers. The wild plant, variety *aculeata* (Linnaeus) Moldenke, is one of the worst weeds in the tropics because of its thorny stems and leaves that are unpalatable to grazing animals. The fruits and foliage are somewhat poisonous and the foliage may irritate the skin. **SHRUB** to 2 m high (6½ ft) or more with prickly (var. *aculeata*) or smooth (var. *camara*) stems. **LEAVES** simple, opposite, blade ovate, 3–13 cm long (1¼–5 in) with toothed margins and scabrous surface. **FLOWERS** continuously through the year; flowers many, borne in dense, terminal, hemispheric heads 2.5–4 cm in diameter (1–1⅝ in). Corolla with fused petals, salverform, two-lipped, tube 6–10 mm long (¼–⅜ in), limb 6–10 mm wide (¼–⅜ in) with five spreading, rounded lobes, variously colored, yellow or orange turning pink or red, or in the common cultivated plant, orange turning red in the same cluster. FRUIT a fleshy, shiny black, subglobose drupe 3–5 mm in diameter (about ⅛–¼ in). PROPAGATE by seeds; sometimes can be propagated by cuttings or air layering for preferred cultivars. Fertile, moist, but well-drained soils in sunny places are preferred. Many cultivars have been named, often grown as border plants or in mass plantings in the tropics and as potted plants in temperate climates. The flowers change color as they mature, from light to dark. The pungent smell of the leaves is objectionable to some people.

Lantana montevidensis (Sprengel) Briquet

Synonym, *Lantana sellowiana* Link & Otto. DISTINGUISHABLE by the low shrubby habit, opposite leaves, toothed leaf margins, and hemispheric heads of pink, two-lipped flowers.

Lantana montevidensis, trailing lantana, is native to southern Brazil and Argentina but is widely cultivated in tropical to warm temperate regions for its pink flowers. SHRUB, low, with long-trailing stems lacking prickles. LEAVES simple, opposite, blade ovate to round, 1–4 cm long (⅜–1⅝ in) with toothed margins and scabrous surface. FLOWERS continuously through the year; flowers many, borne in dense, terminal and axillary, hemispheric heads. Corolla with fused petals, salverform, two-lipped, tube 7–12 mm long (¼–½ in), limb spreading, 6–12 mm wide (¼–½ in), with five rounded, spreading lobes, pink with a yellow and white throat.

Lantana montevidensis

FRUIT a fleshy, dark purple, subglobose drupe 3.5–5 mm in diameter (⅛–¼ in), infrequently formed in cultivation. **PROPAGATE** by cuttings, by layering when the stems touch the ground, and seeds. Fertile, moist, but well-drained soils in sunny to partially shaded places are preferred but bright sun is needed for optimal flowering. It is too short to be used as a hedge and is usually planted as a ground cover, in hanging baskets, or in planters.

Lawsonia LYTHRACEAE

Lawsonia is a genus with a single species and is named after a Scottish physician, Isaac Lawson, d. 1747, who helped pay for one of Linnaeus's early publications.

Lawsonia inermis Linnaeus

DISTINGUISHABLE by the shrubby habit, opposite leaves, flowers with four wrinkled, kidney-shaped petals, and eight longer stamens.

Lawsonia inermis

Lawsonia inermis, henna, is probably native from eastern Asia westward to India. It is now occasionally cultivated in the tropics and subtropics as an ornamental plant, often in hedges, and is grown in the greenhouse in temperate areas. Since ancient times the crushed leaves have been used to prepare a reddish or yellowish hair dye and cosmetic in India, China, Egypt, and elsewhere, and the bark is often used in herbal medicines. **SHRUB** or tree to 6 m high (20 ft) with or without spiny branches. **LEAVES** simple, opposite, blade ovate to elliptic, 1.5–4 cm long (⅝–1⅝ in). **FLOWERS** anytime during the year; flowers many, fragrant, borne in leafy terminal panicles. Corolla of four free, cream-colored (var. *alba*) or red (var. *rubra*), wrinkled, kidney-shaped petals 2–4 mm long (about ¹⁄₁₆–¼ in), usually with eight longer white stamens. **FRUIT** a reddish subglobose capsule 5–8 mm in diameter (about ¼ in). **PROPAGATE** by seeds or cuttings. Well-drained or dry soils in sunny places are preferred.

Leea LEEACEAE

Leea is a genus of about 35 to 70 Old World tree and shrub species, some of which are used locally in medicines, and some cultivated as ornamentals.

Leea guineensis G. Don

Synonym, *Leea manillensis* Walpers. **DISTINGUISHABLE** by the opposite leaves divided three times, often purple, attenuate leaflet tips, and flat-topped inflorescences of small flowers. *Leea indica* Linnaeus differs in having pinnate leaves and yellow flowers, and *L. aculeata* Blume ex Sprengel differs in having a spiny trunk and white flowers.

Leea guineensis is native to tropical Africa but is widely cultivated for its attractive glossy green or sometimes purplish foliage and large clusters of red or purplish flowers. **SHRUB** to 5 m high (16½ ft). **LEAVES** tripinnately compound, alternate, the leaflets in threes, elliptic, 3–12 cm long (1¼–5 in), tip long-attenuate, surfaces green or, in a popular cultivar, purplish, especially the lower surface. **FLOWERS** at any time during the year; flowers numerous, borne in dense, large, flat-topped, terminal cymes produced at

Leea guineensis

the base of the highest leaf. Corolla of five free, ovate, reflexed petals 4–6 mm long (about ¼ in), red or purple, surrounding a staminal tube of five fused stamens. **Fruit** a dark red subglobose berry 1–1.5 cm in diameter (⅜–⅝ in). **Propagate** by cuttings or seeds. Fertile soils in shaded places are preferred. It is often grown as a hedge plant in the tropics, but in temperate areas is raised in greenhouses as a foliage plant.

Leucophyllum SCROPHULARIACEAE

Leucophyllum is a genus of 12 species found in Mexico and the southwestern United States, at least two of which are cultivated as ornamentals. The name *Leucophyllum* is from the Greek words meaning white leaf, referring to the gray leaves of some species.

Leucophyllum frutescens (Berlandier) I. M. Johnston
Distinguishable by the shrubby habit, opposite, gray or silvery leaves, and solitary, lavender, bell-shaped flowers.

Leucophyllum frutescens

Leucophyllum frutescens, ash plant, sometimes called Texas ranger, is a drought-resistant, warm temperate plant native to Texas and Mexico, but is also cultivated in the tropics and subtropics. **Shrub** to 2 m high (6½ ft) or more with gray, scaly foliage and stems. **Leaves** simple, alternate, blade oblanceolate to obovate, 1.5–3 cm long (⅝–1¼ in). **Flowers** most of the year; flowers solitary in the leaf axils. Corolla with fused petals, bell-shaped, slightly two-lipped, 1.8–3 cm long (¾–1¼ in) with five rounded lobes, lavender, throat white with darker spots, pubescent on the inside. **Fruit** a small capsule. **Propagate** by cuttings. Well-drained soils in sunny places are preferred. It is often grown by itself as a specimen plant or in hedges or borders for its gray foliage and attractive lavender flowers. Several cultivars have been named, varying most obviously in the degree of leaf pubescence.

Ligustrum OLEACEAE

Ligustrum is a genus of 40 to 50 shrub and tree species found in warm areas from Europe to Asia, many cultivated in warm temperate and subtropical places, often as hedge plants and street trees. The name *Ligustrum* is the Latin word for privet.

Ligustrum japonicum Thunberg

DISTINGUISHABLE by the shrubby habit, dark green, opposite leaves, and panicles of small white flowers with two protruding stamens. The similar *Ligustrum sinense* Loureiro, Chinese privet, differs most obviously in having densely pubescent branchlets and narrower panicles; *L. lucidum* Aiton fil., glossy privet, differs in having generally larger, sharply tipped leaves; and *L. ovalifolium* Hasskarl, California privet, differs in having a denser, pyramidal inflorescence and stamens not protruding.

Ligustrum japonicum

Ligustrum japonicum, Japanese privet, is native to warm temperate areas of Japan, Korea, and China, and like other privets does not extend very far into the tropics because of its cooler habitat requirements. Thus it is a temperate plant sometimes grown in the tropics. SHRUB to 4 m high (13 ft) or more with glabrous stems. LEAVES simple, opposite, blade broadly elliptic to ovate, 2–6 cm long (¾–2½ in), leathery, dark glossy green on the upper surface, gland-dotted on the lower, tip rounded or blunt. FLOWERS intermittently during the year in the tropics; flowers many, borne in spreading, terminal and upper axillary panicles. Corolla with fused petals, bell-shaped, 6–11 mm long (¼–⅜ in), divided about halfway into four reflexed, elliptic lobes, white, fragrant, with two protruding stamens. FRUIT a black subglobose berry 7–10 mm long (¼–⅜ in). PROPAGATE by cuttings or seeds. Well-drained soils in sunny to partially shaded places are preferred. It is usually cultivated as a screen or hedge plant, or grown in mass plantings, especially in Florida, where it is one of the most common hedge plants. Sometimes it is trimmed to form a small tree. It is somewhat salt tolerant and does well in coastal plantings.

Livistona ARECACEAE

Livistona is a genus of 28 palm species found from India to Australia, and the Solomon Islands and the Philippines, several cultivated as ornamentals and the buds of some eaten locally.

Livistona chinensis (Jacquin) R. Brown ex Martius

DISTINGUISHABLE by the palm habit, fan-shaped leaves with long, drooping lobe tips, and ovoid to globose, blue-green fruits.

Livistona chinensis, Chinese fan palm, is native to the small island chains south of Japan but is widely cultivated throughout the tropics and subtropics as an ornamental palm, planted in clusters or by itself as a specimen plant. PALM to 10 m high (33 ft) or more, monoecious, with a furrowed solitary trunk to 30 cm in diameter (12 in). LEAVES simple, alternate, blade fan-shaped, to 1.6 m in diameter (5¼ ft), the margins divided more than halfway into drooping, lanceolate segments, each deeply cleft into two lobes, dull green, on a petiole about as long as the blade and with marginal spines near the base when young. FLOWERS intermittently during the year; flowers many, borne in axillary panicles to 1.7 m long (5¾ ft). Corolla of three small yellow petals 3–5 mm long (about ⅛–¼ in). FRUIT an ovoid to globose, blue-green drupe 1.5–2.5

Livistona chinensis

cm long (⅝–1 in). **PROPAGATE** by seed. Fertile, moist, but well-drained soils in sunny to partially shaded places are preferred. It is tolerant of cold temperatures and is sometimes grown indoors as a tub plant when young. Several varieties are recognized, based on fruit shape and size.

Lonicera CAPRIFOLIACEAE

Lonicera is a genus of 150 to 200 shrub and vine species found mostly in temperate regions. Many, generally called honeysuckles, are cultivated for their attractive or fragrant flowers.

Lonicera japonica Thunberg

DISTINGUISHABLE by the viny habit, fuzzy stems, opposite leaves, and usually paired, white, funnel-shaped flowers aging to yellow.

    Lonicera japonica, Japanese honeysuckle, is native to Japan but is widely cultivated in temperate to tropical areas for its fragrant flowers.

Lonicera japonica

The flowers produce a copious nectar attractive to pollinating insects, and to children. **VINE-LIKE SHRUB** with fuzzy, somewhat twining stems. **LEAVES** simple, opposite, blade elliptic to ovate, 3–8 cm long (1¼–3½ in). **FLOWERS** anytime during the year in the tropics; flowers in stalked, axillary pairs or several as in 'Halliana'. Corolla of fused petals, two-lipped, funnel-shaped, 3.5–5 cm long (1⅜–2 in), white, rarely purplish, aging to yellow, fuzzy on the outside, split about halfway into an upper four-lobed lip and an entire, narrow lower lip, with five long, protruding stamens in the center. **FRUIT** a black subglobose berry 5–8 mm long (about ¼ in), infrequently formed in cultivation. **PROPAGATE** by air layering or cuttings or seeds. Fertile, well-drained soils in sunny places are preferred. The vine is often planted over fences or by itself but can get out of hand if not regularly trimmed. Several cultivars have been named, including the vigorous and sometimes invasive 'Halliana', with pure white flowers.

Macfadyena BIGNONIACEAE

Macfadyena is a genus of three or four tropical American liana species, one cultivated as an ornamental.

Macfadyena unguis-cati (Linnaeus) A. H. Gentry

Synonym, *Doxantha unguis-cati* (Linnaeus) Rehder. **DISTINGUISHABLE** by the viny habit, opposite leaves with two terminal leaflets, three-branched tendrils on some of the leaf tips, and axillary clusters of funnel-shaped yellow flowers.

Macfadyena unguis-cati, cat's-claw vine, sometimes called yellow trumpet vine, is native to the West Indies and South America but is widely cultivated for its yellow flowers and dark green foliage. The name *unguis-cati* is from the Latin words meaning cat's claw, referring to the tendrils. **VINE**, perennial, climbing. **LEAVES** compound, opposite, leaflets two, blades ovate to elliptic, 3–7 cm long (1¼–3 in), glossy dark green, some terminating in a three-branched tendril. **FLOWERS** continuously through the year; flowers several, borne in short-stalked axillary clusters. Corolla of fused petals, funnel-shaped, 5.5–7 cm long (2¼–3 in), bright yellow, limb with five rounded lobes. **FRUIT** a cylindrical capsule 25–40 cm long (10–16 in),

Macfadyena unguis-cati

containing many flattened, winged seeds. **PROPAGATE** by cuttings, air layering, or seeds. Fertile, well-drained soils in sunny places are preferred. This vigorous vine is often grown in the tropics on fences or trellises to produce a hedge-like growth, whereas in temperate areas it is sometimes grown in the greenhouse.

Malpighia MALPIGHIACEAE

Malpighia is a genus of 25 to 40 shrub and tree species found from the southwestern United States to Peru, some cultivated for their edible fruits (acerola, *M. glabra* Linnaeus, for example) and some as ornamentals.

Malpighia coccigera Linnaeus

DISTINGUISHABLE by the shrubby habit, fascicles of small, holly-like leaves with spine-tipped margins, and flowers with five stalked, white to pale pink petals with a fringed margin.

Malpighia coccigera

Malpighia coccigera, Singapore holly, a misnomer since is not related to the holly family Aquifoliaceae, is native to the West Indies, not Singapore, but is widely cultivated in the tropics and in temperate climates. **SHRUB** to 2 m high (6½ ft). **LEAVES** simple, opposite and sometimes clustered in fascicles, blade ovate, 0.5–4 cm long (¼–1⅝ in), the larger ones with a spine-tipped margin. **FLOWERS** anytime during the year; flowers one or two, axillary on a long, thin stalk. Corolla of five free, nearly triangular, clawed petals 8–12 mm long (¼–½ in), white to pale pink with a fringed margin. **FRUIT** a red drupe-like capsule, infrequently formed in cultivation. **PROPAGATE** by cuttings or seeds. Moist but well-drained soils in sunny to partially shaded places are preferred. It is often grown as a dwarf hedge plant, a foundation plant, or in planters in tropical areas and in the greenhouse in temperate areas. It has small, attractive, holly-like leaves, small but conspicuous flowers, and edible fruits that are occasionally eaten. The spiny leaf margins are a drawback.

Malvaviscus MALVACEAE

Malvaviscus is a genus of three or four tropical American tree or shrub species, at least two of which are cultivated as ornamentals. The name *Malvaviscus* is from the Latin words meaning glue and mallow, referring to the sticky seeds of some species.

Malvaviscus penduliflorus Moçiño & Sessé ex A. P. de Candolle

Synonym, *Malvaviscus arboreus* var. *penduliflorus* (Moçiño & Sessé ex A. P. de Candolle) Schery but the less common *M. arboreus* Cavanilles differs in having much broader leaves with a fuzzier surface, and flowers only half as large. **DISTINGUISHABLE** by the alternate leaves, flowers that are solitary, hanging, red, and that scarcely open, and stamens fused into a long stamen tube.

Malvaviscus penduliflorus, turk's cap, sometimes called wax mallow, is native from Mexico to Brazil but is not known to exist in the wild. It is widely cultivated in the tropics and in the greenhouse in temperate regions for its red flowers, attractive to butterflies and hummingbirds. Another common name, sleeping or sleepy hibiscus, refers to the corolla, which never opens, some people

Malvaviscus penduliflorus

mistakenly believing it has yet to open. **SHRUB** to 3 m high (10 ft). **LEAVES** simple, alternate, blade ovate to lanceolate, 3–16 cm long (1¼–6 in), sometimes shallowly three-lobed, nearly glabrous on both surfaces. **FLOWERS** continuously through the year; flowers solitary, axillary, pendulous, with a whorl of about seven narrow bracts, the epicalyx, below the calyx. Corolla of five free, obovate to oblong, bright red petals 4.5–7 cm long (1¾–3 in), not opening, surrounding the stamens, which are fused into a staminal column around the ten-lobed style. **FRUIT** unknown. **PROPAGATE** by cuttings. Moist but well-drained soils in sunny places are preferred. It is often grown by itself as a specimen plant or in hedges, and needs periodic pruning to keep it in shape. A pink-flowered cultivar has also been named.

Mandevilla APOCYNACEAE

Mandevilla is a tropical American genus of about 115 to 120 herb, subshrub, and liana species, several cultivated for their attractive flowers.

Mandevilla ×amabilis (of Backhouse's garden) Dress

DISTINGUISHABLE by the viny habit, milky sap, opposite, glossy green leaves, and long-stalked racemes of rose-colored to pink, funnel-shaped flowers yellow in the center.

Mandevilla ×amabilis

Mandevilla ×amabilis is apparently a hybrid involving *M. splendens* (J. D. Hooker) Woodson and another, unidentified species (previously thought to be two other species) that originated in England in 1868. The common cultivar is 'Alice du Pont', also sometimes known as 'Splendens Hybrid', grown for its flowers. The common name pink allamanda is misleading since it does not belong to the related genus *Allamanda*. **LIANA** with thin stems to 10 m long (33 ft), sap milky.

LEAVES simple, opposite, blade oblong to broadly elliptic, 7–20 cm long (3–8 in) on a short petiole. **FLOWERS** anytime during the year; flowers several, borne in long-stalked, axillary racemes. Corolla of fused petals, funnel-shaped, 7–10 cm long (3–4 in), limb 8–10 cm across (3½–4 in) with five spreading, rounded lobes, pink to rose-colored with yellow in the throat. **FRUIT** a slender capsule but rarely forming. **PROPAGATE** by cuttings. Fertile, well-drained soils in sunny or partially shaded places are preferred. It is often planted on trellises or fences.

Manihot EUPHORBIACEAE

Manihot is a genus of about 100 to 200 herb, shrub, and tree species found from the southwestern United States to Argentina, a few cultivated as ornamentals for their foliage, and some as a source of food.

Manihot esculenta Crantz

Synonym, *Manihot utilissima* Pohl. **DISTINGUISHABLE** by the shrubby habit, milky sap, leaves that are alternate, palmately three-lobed, and variegated with white, flowers that are small and greenish, and ovoid, six-winged capsule.

Manihot esculenta, cassava or tapioca, though native to tropical America, is no longer found in the wild state. The nonvariegated plant was a major food crop in pre-Columbian tropical America. It has been spread throughout the tropics as a root crop that is often planted where the soil has become depleted by other crops. The plant is protected from insects by high levels of cyanide, making the sap and uncooked tuber poisonous, but "sweet" cultivars with little poison are now common in cultivation. **SHRUB** to 3 m high (10 ft), branching only at the base, sap milky. **LEAVES** simple, alternate, divided to the base into three lanceolate lobes or rarely unlobed, lobes mostly 8–20 cm long (3½–8 in), variegated with white or pale yellow along the midrib, with a red petiole and midveins. **FLOWERS** anytime during the year; flowers several, borne in short terminal panicles. Corolla absent but the bell-shaped calyx petal-like and greenish white or marked with red, 7–10 mm long

Manihot esculenta 'Variegata'

(¼–⅜ in). **FRUIT** an ovoid six-winged capsule 1.2–1.8 cm long (½–¾ in). **PROPAGATE** by cuttings. Fertile, moist soils in partially shaded places are preferred. The variegated cassava used as an ornamental, sometimes called variegated tapioca, is 'Variegata'.

Mansoa BIGNONIACEAE

Mansoa is a genus of 15 tropical South American liana species, several cultivated as ornamentals for their colorful flowers.

Mansoa hymenaea (A. P. de Candolle) A. H. Gentry

Synonym, *Pseudocalymma alliaceum* (Lamarck) Sandwith. **DISTINGUISH-ABLE** by the viny habit, opposite, pinnately compound leaves with two leaflets and often a terminal tendril, garlic-like aroma of the foliage, and purple to mauve, funnel-shaped flowers.

    Mansoa hymenaea, garlic vine, is native to Guyana and Brazil but is cultivated elsewhere in the tropics for its mauve flowers and as a novelty because of the garlic-like odor of its leaves, which are not, however, used as a spice. LIANA, high-climbing. LEAVES compound, opposite, with or without an unbranched terminal tendril, leaflets two, elliptic to ovate, 4–15 cm long (1⅝–6 in), dark glossy green. FLOWERS intermittently during the year; flowers several, borne in stalked axillary clusters. Corolla of fused petals, funnel-shaped, 4.5–7 cm long (1¾–3 in), limb with five rounded lobes, purple fading to mauve. FRUIT a long, narrow, flattened capsule 12–25 cm long (5–10 in) filled with flattened, winged seeds. PROPAGATE by seeds or cuttings. Moist but well-drained soils in sunny places are preferred. It is often grown on trellises and fences, upon which it makes a dense, attractive cover.

Mansoa hymenaea

Maranta MARANTACEAE

Maranta is a genus of 20 rhizomatous, perennial, tropical American species. Some are grown as ornamentals, especially as houseplants, or as a source of food.

Maranta arundinacea Linnaeus

DISTINGUISHABLE by the basal rhizome, zigzag branches, ginger-like leaves that are often variegated with white.

Maranta arundinacea, arrowroot, sometimes called obedience plant, is native to northern South America and perhaps northward to Mexico but is widely cultivated in the tropics for its edible rhizomes, containing the starch called arrowroot. Other, unrelated species are sometimes called arrowroot, however. HERB to 1.2 m high (4 ft) or more with fork-

Maranta arundinacea 'Variegata'

ing, zigzag branches arising from starchy rhizomes. LEAVES simple, alternate, blade ovate to lanceolate, 12–21 cm long (5–8 in), often variegated if an ornamental, sessile from a long sheath that envelops the stem. FLOWERS infrequently during the year; flowers paired, borne among several lanceolate bracts on a forked panicle. Corolla with fused petals, 2–2.5 cm long (¾–1 in), white, lobed less than halfway into three lobes. FRUIT leathery, oblong, one-seeded. PROPAGATE by rhizome division or seeds. Fertile, moist, but well-drained soils in sunny to partially shaded places are preferred. The cultivar 'Variegata', with variegated leaves, is cultivated as an ornamental, outdoors as a border plant or indoors as a potted plant. The family Marantaceae also contains numerous other ornamentals with colorful leaves, particularly the genus *Calathea*.

Medinilla MELASTOMATACEAE

Medinilla is a genus of about 150 liana or vine-like shrub species, or as many as 400 according to some authors, found from tropical Africa to Polynesia. At least one is cultivated as an ornamental for its large, attractive inflorescences.

Medinilla magnifica Lindley

DISTINGUISHABLE by the shrubby habit, opposite subsessile leaves, hanging panicles bearing large pink bracts, and pink flowers with conspicuously curved, yellowish anthers.

Medinilla magnifica, magnificent medinilla, is native to the Philippines but is widely cultivated for its large, spectacular, pink flowers and inflorescences. **SHRUB** to 3 m high (10 ft). **LEAVES** simple, opposite, blade elliptic, usually 20–40 cm long (8–16 in), subsessile. **FLOWERS** anytime during the year; flowers many, borne in conical axillary panicles bearing whorls of large, pink, elliptic bracts to 10 cm long (4 in). Corolla of five free petals 8–15 mm long (¼–⅝ in), pink, borne atop the cup-like pink calyx, surrounding the ten yellowish, curved, linear anthers affixed to yellow, conspicuously bent filaments. **FRUIT** a cup-like purple-pink berry. **PROPAGATE** by cuttings or seeds. Fertile, moist soils in humid, partially shaded places are preferred. It is often grown by itself as a specimen plant, as a border plant, or is trained on arbors or arches, and it is grown in the greenhouse in temperate areas.

Medinilla magnifica

Melaleuca MYRTACEAE

Melaleuca is a genus of about 100 shrub and tree species found mostly in Australia, several useful for timber or medicinal oils, and some grown as ornamentals.

Melaleuca quinquenervia (Cavanilles) S. T. Blake

Synonym, *Melaleuca viridiflora* var. *rubriflora* Brongniart & Grisebach, and sometimes misidentified as *M. leucadendra* (Linnaeus) Linnaeus. **DISTINGUISHABLE** by the tree habit, paper-like, exfoliating bark, leaves that are opposite, narrow, and parallel veined, and spikes of flowers bearing many white stamens.

Melaleuca quinquenervia, paper bark tree, sometimes called cajeput tree, is native from Australia to New Caledonia but is widely cultivated

Melaleuca quinquenervia

in the tropics and subtropics, mostly because of its exfoliating, paper-like bark. The numerous seeds produced are readily dispersed, making the tree a harmful weed in wet places, especially in marshes in Florida and Hawaii, for example, and the species should not be introduced to new areas. The leaves yield cajeput oil, used in herbal medicines, and the wood is used in cabinetmaking and boatbuilding. TREE to 15 m high (50 ft) or more with conspicuous white bark coming off in paperlike layers. LEAVES simple, mostly alternate, elliptic to lanceolate, mostly 4–10 cm long (1⅝–4 in) with five to nine parallel veins. FLOWERS intermittently during the year; flowers many, sessile, borne in one to three terminal cylindrical spikes beyond which the axis becomes leafy. Corolla of five small, free, green to red petals that soon fall, with many bristle-like white stamens to 2 cm long (¾ in), looking like a bottlebrush. FRUIT a sessile woody capsule 4–6 mm in diameter (about ¼ in), densely packed on the stem. PROPAGATE by seeds. Moist soils in sunny places are preferred. It is usually planted as a street, specimen, or park tree but can also be pruned into an attractive hedge.

Melia MELIACEAE

Melia is a genus of 3 to 15 tree and shrub species found from Africa to Australia, some cultivated as ornamentals and some used medicinally. The name *Melia* is from the Greek word for ash tree *(Fraxinus),* to which these plants are not related.

Melia azedarach Linnaeus

DISTINGUISHABLE by the alternate, bipinnately compound leaves, margins of leaflets toothed, axillary panicles of purple to white flowers, stamens united into a staminal column, and yellow drupes that remain on the tree through much of the year.

Melia azedarach, chinaberry tree, sometimes called bead tree, pride of India, or Persian lilac though it is neither from Iran nor related to the lilac family Oleaceae, is native to somewhere in the Old World tropics but is widely cultivated for its lilac-colored flowers. Some parts of the plant are used in herbal remedies but the fruit is reported to be poisonous to humans. The tree also reportedly has insecticidal properties, which would not be surprising since it is related to the neem tree, *Azadirachta indica* A. H. L. Jussieu, used to make a natural insecticide. **TREE** to 12 m high (40 ft) or more, somewhat deciduous. **LEAVES** bipinnately compound, alternate, pinnae in three to five pairs, each pinna usually with three to five pairs of leaflets, blades ovate or lanceolate to elliptic, 2–9 cm long (¾–3½ in) with toothed margins and attenuate tip. **FLOWERS** anytime during the year with the old, wrinkled fruits present on the tree much of the year; flowers many, borne in axillary panicles. Corolla of five free, linear-oblong, reflexed, lavender to purple or white petals 8–11 mm long (¼–⅜ in) surrounding the ten stamens united into a tube. **FRUIT** a yellow subglobose drupe 1.3–2 cm long (½–¾ in) that remains on the tree for a long time. **PROPAGATE** by seeds or cuttings. Well-drained soils in sunny to partially shaded places are preferred. It is often

Melia azedarach

planted as a shade or street tree, or by itself as a specimen tree, but one drawback is excessive leaf litter.

Merremia CONVOLVULACEAE

Merremia is a genus of about 80 vine species found throughout the tropics, some being serious weeds in plantations. Some are grown for their flowers. The genus differs from the related *Ipomoea* by its smooth rather than spiny pollen grains.

Merremia tuberosa (Linnaeus) Rendle

Synonym, *Ipomoea tuberosa* Linnaeus. **DISTINGUISHABLE** by the viny habit, alternate, palmately veined leaves, yellow, funnel-shaped corolla, and large, papery calyx lobes surrounding the fruit.

Merremia tuberosa wood rose, sometimes called yellow morning glory, is native to tropical America. It is widely cultivated for its flowers

Merremia tuberosa, flowers and papery calyx

and the large papery calyx, the "wood rose," used in dry floral arrangements. **VINE**, somewhat woody, climbing, sap clear. **LEAVES** simple, alternate, blade round in outline, 6–25 cm long (2½–10 in), palmately divided into five to seven lobes. **FLOWERS** intermittently during the year; flowers several, borne in long-stalked axillary clusters. Corolla of fused petals, funnel-shaped, bright yellow, 4.5–7 cm long (1¾–3 in), limb 5–6 cm in diameter (2–2½ in). **FRUIT** a four-seeded subglobose capsule 3–3.5 cm long (1¼–1⅜ in) surrounded by the large, papery sepals. **PROPAGATE** by seeds, cuttings, or division. Fertile, well-drained soils in sunny places are preferred. It is often grown on trellises, fences, or trees but its rapid growth can soon cover them.

Mirabilis NYCTAGINACEAE

Mirabilis is a genus of 45 to 60 tropical American herb and subshrub species, some cultivated for their edible or medicinal tubers, and some as ornamentals. The name *Mirabilis* is from the Latin word meaning wonderful.

Mirabilis jalapa Linnaeus

DISTINGUISHABLE by the opposite leaves and tubular, purple or yellow, corolla-like calyx with a spreading limb that opens in the late afternoon.

Mirabilis jalapa, four-o'clock, sometimes called marvel of Peru, probably is native to Peru but is widely cultivated for its flowers, opening in the late afternoon, hence its common name, and wilting by morning. It is often grown as a border plant and in gardens. The plant is used medicinally, as a dye plant, and for making cosmetics in various parts of its range. **HERB** or subshrub to 1 m high (3¼ ft), arising from a tuber. **LEAVES** simple, opposite, blade heart-shaped to ovate, 2–12 cm long (¾–5 in). **FLOWERS** continuously through the year; flowers several, borne in short, dense, terminal and axillary cymes. Corolla absent but the calyx petal-like, salverform, purple, sometimes white or yellow, 3–6 cm long (1¼–2½ in) with a spreading limb and five protruding stamens. **FRUIT** dry, ovoid, one-seeded, called

Mirabilis jalapa

an anthocarp. **PROPAGATE** by seeds or division of the tuber. It is adaptable to most soils, and sunny places are preferred. It sometimes becomes naturalized but is not reported to be a troublesome weed.

Molineria AMARYLLIDACEAE

Molineria comprises seven herbaceous perennial species found from Malaysia to Australia. The genus is sometimes included, instead, in the family Hypoxidacae, and some authors consider it to be part of another genus, *Curculigo*.

Molineria capitulata (Loureiro) Herbert

Synonyms, *Curculigo capitata* (Loureiro) Kuntze, a name used by some authors, *C. recurvata* Dryander, and *Molineria recurvata* (Dryander) Herbert. **DISTINGUISHABLE** by the pleated, palm-like leaves that arise from the tuberous roots, and yellow flowers borne on a short leafless stalk.

Molineria capitulata, palm grass, neither grass nor palm, is native to the islands and mainland of Southeast Asia, an area that used to be

Molineria capitulata

called Indo-Malaya, and Australia, but it is widely cultivated. The leaves, which sway in breezes, are superficially very similar to those of palm seedlings, with which the plants are often confused. **HERB**, scapose, to 2 m high (6½ ft), arising from tuberous roots. **LEAVES** simple, basal, blade elliptic to lanceolate, to 100 × 12–20 cm (40 × 5–8 in), strongly pleated, on a petiole to nearly as long. **FLOWERS** anytime during the year; flowers several, sessile, borne among green, lanceolate, fuzzy-edged bracts in a dense umbel 3–11 cm long (1¼–4½ in) atop a leafless, brown-hairy stalk 3–12 cm long (1¼–

5 in). Corolla with fused tepals, the tube short, the tepal segments six, ovate, 9–12 mm long (⅜–½ in), yellow. **Fruit** a white berry 6–8 mm long (about ¼ in). **Propagate** by division, offsets, or seeds. Fertile soils in shaded places are preferred. It is usually grown closely packed as a tall ground cover, excluding most low-growing species by the dense shade it produces.

Monstera ARACEAE

Monstera is a genus of about 22 terrestrial and climbing tropical American herbaceous species, some cultivated for their attractive or unusual, usually perforated leaves. The name *Monstera* is from the Latin word meaning marvel or monster, referring to the odd-looking leaves.

Monstera deliciosa Liebmann

Distinguishable by the climbing habit, large heart-shaped leaves with perforations on the blade, and spathe-and-spadix inflorescence.

Monstera deliciosa, sometimes called splitleaf philodendron or Swiss-cheese plant, is native to high elevations in Central America but is widely grown for its large, perforated leaves, increasing in size as the plant ages and giving a distinctly tropical ambiance to where it is grown. The edible fruit, called ceriman, tastes like something between banana, *Musa* spp., and pineapple, *Ananas comosus.* It is eaten when ripe but can cause irritation to the throat when unripe. Other parts of the plant can cause minor stomach problems, and contact with the sap may irritate the skin. **Liana** or epiphyte when mature,

Monstera deliciosa

shrub-like when young, perennial, robust, with long adventitious roots forming at the nodes of the thick stems. LEAVES simple, alternate, two-ranked, blade heart-shaped, leathery, usually 50–120 cm long (20–48 in) on a petiole of similar length, and when mature with notches and large perforations called fenestrae, Latin for windows. FLOWERS intermittently during the year; flowers many, borne tightly packed in a cylindrical spadix 20–30 cm long (8–12 in) with a long, deciduous, elliptic, cream-colored spathe attached at the base. FRUIT a yellow to purplish subglobose and angular berry 8–12 mm long (¼–½ in), coming off together in plates, smelling like pineapple. PROPAGATE by stem cuttings with a leaf attached or by seeds. Fertile, moist, but well-drained soils in shaded places are preferred. It is often trained on arches or arbors, and with support from these, or a tree, it can become a high climber. In temperate climates it is grown in the greenhouse or as a houseplant.

Murraya RUTACEAE

Murraya is a genus of 4 to 11 tree and shrub species found from Sri Lanka (Ceylon) to Melanesia, including *M. koenigii* (Linnaeus) Sprengel, the leaves of which are used as a spice for curry. Most are grown as ornamental hedge or screen plants.

Murraya paniculata (Linnaeus) Jack

Synonym, *Murraya exotica* Linnaeus. DISTINGUISHABLE by the shrubby habit, leaves that are alternate and pinnately compound, and dense racemes of strongly aromatic flowers with five oblanceolate white petals.

Murraya paniculata, orange jessamine or jasmine, a misnomer because it is not a member of the jasmine family Oleaceae, and sometimes called mock orange or satin wood, is native from Southeast Asia to Australia but is widely and commonly cultivated in the tropics. The yellow wood is of commercial value in Asia, and the dark green leaves are used in flora arrangements. SHRUB to 2 m high (6½ ft), to 8 m (27 ft) when not pruned. LEAVES odd-pinnately compound, alternate, leaflets 5 to

11, blades elliptic to obovate, mostly 2–6 cm long (¾–2½ in), sometimes oblique at the base, glossy dark green. **FLOWERS** several times during the year, often with local populations in bloom at the same time; flowers many, borne in short, dense, terminal and upper axillary racemes. Corolla of five free, oblanceolate, white petals 1.2–2.2 cm long (½–⅞ in), strongly aromatic. **FRUIT** an orange ellipsoidal to ovoid berry 1–1.3 cm long (⅜–½ in). **PROPAGATE** by seeds or cuttings. Well-drained soils in full sun or partially shaded areas are preferred. It is often grown as a hedge plant for its dense, dark green foliage and extremely fragrant flowers but it can also be trimmed to form a tree, heavily pruned into animal shapes (topiary), or grown as a potted plant.

Murraya paniculata

Musa MUSACEAE

Musa is a genus of about 35 large herbaceous species ranging from Asia to Australia. The taxonomy of the genus is very complex, with many of the commercially grown bananas being triploid hybrids. Some others are used for fiber and others as ornamentals.

Musa uranoscopus Loureiro

Synonym, *Musa coccinea* Andrews, a name used by some authors. **DISTINGUISHABLE** by the large herbaceous habit, banana leaves, and terminal raceme of orange to yellow flowers borne among red bracts.

Musa uranoscopus, red banana, also known as scarlet banana, is native to Southeast Asia but is occasionally cultivated for its red and yellow-orange inflorescences. **HERB**, perennial, to 2 m high (6½ ft) or more

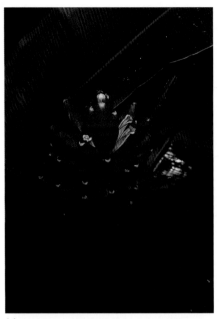

Musa uranoscopus

with thick, fleshy pseudostems formed by the leaf bases, arising from a rhizome. LEAVES simple, alternate, spirally arranged, blade banana-leaf-like, 45–120 × 15–33 cm (18–48 × 6–13 in). FLOWERS anytime during the year; flowers many, unisexual, borne among red or sometimes magenta, yellow- to orange-tipped bracts to 15 cm long (6 in) in an erect terminal raceme. Corolla with six fused tepals, five fused together and one free, 3.5–5 cm long (1⅜–2 in), orange to yellow, the free tepal with a leaf-like tip. FRUIT a fleshy orange berry 4–5 cm long (1⅝–2 in). PROPAGATE by division or seeds. Fertile, moist, but well-drained soils in partially shaded places are preferred. The leaves are shredded by strong winds, so some wind protection may be needed. It is grown by itself or mixed with other plants in gardens in the tropics, and is grown as a potted plant in the greenhouse in temperate climates, these often being used commercially as cut flowers.

Mussaenda RUBIACEAE

Mussaenda comprises about 100 erect or scrambling shrub species native to the Old World tropics, many cultivated for their flowers, the most attractive of which are produced in hybrids. Three mussaendas, one a hybrid involving the other two, are included here.

Mussaenda erythrophylla Schumacher

DISTINGUISHABLE by the opposite, pubescent leaves, interpetiolar stipules, pale yellow, five-lobed corolla red on the inside, and one enlarged, bright red sepal.

Mussaenda erythrophylla, Ashanti blood, sometimes called red mussaenda, is native to Ghana but is widely if not commonly cultivated for its white flowers and bright red, petal-like calyx lobes. SHRUB to 3 m high (10 ft) with interpetiolar stipules. LEAVES simple, opposite, blade broadly ovate to elliptic, 8–15 cm long (3½–6 in), surface pubescent. FLOWERS continuously through the year; flowers several, borne in branching terminal panicles, each flower with an enlarged, ovate, bright red sepal 5–13 cm long (2–5 in). Corolla with fused petals, salverform, tube 2–3 cm long (¾–1¼ in), divided into five spreading ovate lobes, usual-

Mussaenda erythrophylla

ly pale yellow with red in the center, red-hairy on the outside. FRUIT a club-shaped berry. PROPAGATE by cuttings. Fertile, moist soils in partially sunny or shaded places are preferred. It is often grown by itself or as a shrub border in the tropics, and as a potted greenhouse plant in temperate areas. Several cultivars have been named and the species is one of the parents of *Mussaenda* 'Queen Sirikit'.

Mussaenda philippica L. C. Richard

DISTINGUISHABLE by the opposite leaves, interpetiolar stipules, yellow, five-lobed corolla, and five white, leaf-like calyx lobes.

Mussaenda philippica is a white mussaenda native to the Philippines. SHRUB to 2.5 m high (8¼ ft) or more, with interpetiolar stipules. LEAVES simple, opposite, blade usually elliptic to ovate, 7–15 cm long (3–6 in). FLOWERS continuously through the year; flowers several, borne in terminal panicles, each flower with five (one in the wild plant) enlarged,

Mussaenda philippica 'Aurorae'

Mussaenda 'Queen Sirikit'

leaf-like, white, ovate to elliptic calyx lobes 3–7 cm long (1¼–3 in). Corolla with fused petals, salverform, usually 2–3 cm long (¾–1¼ in), limb spreading, 1–1.5 cm wide (⅜–⅝ in), bright yellow. FRUIT an ovoid berry, infrequently formed in cultivation. PROPAGATE by cuttings. Moist, well-drained soils in sunny places are preferred. The most spectacular and most commonly grown plant is the cultivar 'Aurorae', not found in the wild, called Doña Aurora and named for the wife of Manuel Luis Quezon y Molina, 1878–1944, president of the Philippines. It differs from the wild plant in having all five calyx lobes white and leaf-like, not just one, and is one of the parents of *Mussaenda* 'Queen Sirikit'. It is usually grown standing alone as a specimen plant rather than in hedges, and is trimmed to be a spreading shrub. Pruning promotes flowering.

Mussaenda 'Queen Sirikit'

DISTINGUISHABLE by the shrubby habit, opposite leaves, interpetiolar petioles, yellow corolla, and five large, pink, leaf-like calyx lobes.

Mussaenda 'Queen Sirikit' is a pink mussaenda believed to be a hybrid between *M. erythrophylla* and *M. philippica* 'Aurorae'. It is named after a queen of Burma (Myanmar). It has spread rapidly in cultivation because of its pink, bract-like calyx lobes. **SHRUB** to 4 m high (13 ft) or more with interpetiolar stipules and fuzzy stems. **LEAVES** simple, opposite, blade elliptic, usually 5–20 cm long (2–8 in). **FLOWERS** continuously through the year; flowers several, borne in dense terminal panicles, each flower with five large, pink, ovate calyx lobes 3–8 cm long (1¼–3½ in). Corolla with fused petals, salverform, usually 1.6–2.5 cm long (⅝–1 in) with a spreading five-lobed limb 1.2–2 cm wide (½–¾ in). **FRUIT** a fuzzy ovoid berry. **PROPAGATE** by cuttings or air layering. Moist but well-drained soils in partially shaded places are preferred but it needs full sun for optimal flowering. It is usually planted standing alone as a specimen plant rather than in hedges.

Nandina BERBERIDACEAE

Nandina is a genus with a single species. The name *Nandina* is from the Japanese appellation for the plant.

Nandina domestica Thunberg

DISTINGUISHABLE by the shrubby habit, leaves that are bi- or tripinnately compound, alternate, and red when developing and when aged, white flowers with six yellow stamens, and small orange berries.

Nandina domestica, heavenly bamboo, a misnomer since it is not a bamboo nor even a monocot, is a warm temperate rather than a true tropical species and is native from India to Japan but is widely cultivated in warm regions for its attractive foliage and

Nandina domestica

red fruit. The plant is popular in Japanese gardens and in the East is planted at the front entrance of houses, often as a tub or bonsai plant, for good luck. It is also popular in China, where the plant is considered sacred. SHRUB to 2.5 m high (8¼ ft) or more but usually much shorter. LEAVES bi- or tripinnately compound, alternate, pinnae opposite, leaflets odd-pinnate in groups of one to five per pinna, blades lanceolate, 2–6 cm long (¾–2½ in), red when young and when aged. FLOWERS most of the year in the tropics; flowers many, borne in terminal panicles. Corolla of three to six free, elliptic petals 6–8 mm long (about ¼ in), with six yellow stamens persisting after the petals fall. FRUIT a red globose berry 7–10 mm long (¼–⅜ in). PROPAGATE by seeds or cuttings. Moist but well-drained soils in sunny to partially shaded places are preferred. Many cultivars have been named.

Neomarica IRIDACEAE

Neomarica is a genus of 13 to 15 species found in tropical America and western Africa. Some, commonly called maricas, are cultivated for their attractive flowers.

Neomarica caerulea (Loddiges) Sprague

DISTINGUISHABLE by the creeping rhizomes, *Iris*-like leaves, loose panicles of flowers with three lavender to blue tepal segments that are brown and yellow at the base. *Neomarica gracilis* (W. J. Hooker) Sprague differs in having white tepals with yellow and brown markings at the base.

Neomarica caerulea, is a marica that is sometimes called twelve apostles. It is native to Brazil but is widely grown for its blue flowers. HERB, perennial, erect, to 1.5 m high (5 ft) or more, arising from a creeping rhizome. LEAVES simple, basal, equitant and fan-like, blade linear, to 150 × 5.5 cm (59 × 2¼ in). FLOWERS anytime during the year; flowers three to seven, borne in several lanceolate bracts to 18 cm long (7 in) in a panicle arising from a fold in an erect, leaf-like stalk. Corolla with fused tepals, deeply divided into three elliptic segments 4–6.5 cm long

Neomarica caerulea with lavender to blue flowers

Neomarica gracilis with white flowers

(1⅝–2⅝ in), lavender to blue with brown bars on yellow at the base. **FRUIT** a cylindrical many-seeded capsule. **PROPAGATE** by plantlets, rhizome division, or seeds. Fertile, moist soils in partially shaded places are preferred. It is often planted in a border, as a ground cover, or among shrubs in the tropics, and as a potted plant in the greenhouse in temperate climates.

Nerium APOCYNACEAE

Nerium is a genus of several shrub species ranging from the Mediterranean region to Japan. Some authors recognize only a single variable species. The name *Nerium* is from an ancient Greek word for the plant.

Nerium oleander Linnaeus

DISTINGUISHABLE by the shrubby habit, whorled, narrowly elliptic

Nerium oleander

leaves, and terminal clusters of purple to white, funnel-shaped flowers with a conspicuous row of filaments at the base of the five corolla lobes.

Nerium oleander, oleander, sometimes called rosebay, is native to the Mediterranean region but is widely cultivated in warm regions, particularly dry climates, for its pink, white, or purple flowers. All parts of the plant are poisonous and can be fatal if ingested. Deaths have occurred when the cut stems were used as barbecue skewers. Even the smoke from burning wood can be toxic. **SHRUB** to 5 m high (16½ ft) or more with clear sap. **LEAVES** simple, arranged in whorls of three, blade narrowly elliptic, usually 8–18 cm long (3½–7 in), surface finely veined. **FLOWERS** continuously through the year; flowers many, borne in dense terminal clusters. Corolla of fused petals, funnel-shaped, 3.5–5.5 cm long (1⅜–2¼ in), with a spreading limb 4–6 cm across (1⅝–2½ in), five-lobed, or double-flowered in 'Carneum Florepleno' or 'Mrs. Roeding', with a ring of filamentous appendages in the center, pink, purple, or white. **FRUIT** pod-like, cylindrical, usually 7–12 cm long (3–5 in), filled with hairy seeds. **PROPAGATE** by cuttings, air layering, or seeds. Well-drained soils in sunny places are preferred. It is often grown as hedges, screens, or in borders, especially in sunny places in saline or dry habitats since it is very hardy, salt tolerant, and drought resistant. Frequent pruning is needed to keep it in shape. In cooler climates it is often grown as a potted plant. Several cultivars have been named, differing in flower color, size, and number of petals, and some are double-flowered.

Nymphaea NYMPHAEACEAE

Nymphaea is a genus of 35 to 50 aquatic herbaceous species widely distributed in tropical to temperate regions. Many are cultivated as ornamentals, and some for their edible seeds. Extensive hybridization involving the cultivated species makes their taxonomy difficult.

Nymphaea capensis Thunberg

DISTINGUISHABLE by the aquatic habit, floating, heart-shaped to round leaves, flowers of numerous lanceolate, blue to red petals, and spongy, many-seeded berry.

Nymphaea capensis, blue waterlily, sometimes called Cape blue waterlily, is native to southern and eastern Africa and Madagascar but is widely cultivated elsewhere in tropical and subtropical ponds and pools because of its flowers, becoming naturalized in wet places such as ditches and ponds. The seeds and tubers are edible though not widely eaten. HERB, perennial, aquatic, rooting in the mud and forming tubers. LEAVES simple, alternate, leaf blade heart-shaped to nearly round, 16–25 cm across (6–10 in) on a long petiole, floating on the surface of the water. FLOWERS anytime during the year; flowers solitary on long stalks rising above the water. Corolla of numerous, free, lanceolate, blue, white, pink, or red petals 4–7 cm long (1⅝–3 in), surrounding the numerous yellow stamens and staminodes. FRUIT a many-seeded spongy berry, developing underwater after the passé flower becomes submerged. PROPAGATE by seeds

Nymphaea capensis var. *zanzibariensis* 'Rosea'

or division. Sunny places in shallow ponds are preferred, and full sun is needed for optimal flowering. It is sometimes grown in mud-filled jars set on pond bottoms. Two plants commonly grown are *N. capensis* var. *capensis,* with blue to white petals, and *N. capensis* var. *zanzibariensis* 'Rosea', with pink to reddish petals.

Ochna OCHNACEAE

Ochna is a genus of about 86 Old World tropical tree and shrub species, several grown as ornamentals.

Ochna thomasiana Engler & Gilg

Synonym, *Ochna kirkii* Oliver. **DISTINGUISHABLE** by the alternate leaves, bristle-toothed leaf margins, flowers with five yellow petals, and shiny black fruits borne on a fleshy red disk. A similar, widely cultivated species, *O. serrulata* (Hochstetter) Walpers, known by the same common names as *O. thomasiana,* differs in having narrower leaves with sharp teeth rather than bristle-bearing margins.

Ochna thomasiana

Ochna thomasiana, Mickey Mouse plant, sometimes called bird's-eye bush, is native to southeastern Africa but is widely cultivated for its yellow flowers and unusual fruit. The large drupelet fruits look vaguely like mouse ears. **SHRUB** to 2 m high (6½ ft) or more. **LEAVES** simple, alternate, blade elliptic, 3–12 cm long (1¼– 5 in), glabrous, with bristle-toothed margins. **FLOWERS** intermittently during the year; flowers several, borne in axillary and terminal clusters. Corolla of five free, obovate, yellow petals 1.8–2.5 cm long (¾–1 in), with many yellow stamens in the center. **FRUIT** composed of one to five black ovoid drupelets 7–10 mm long (¼–⅜ in) borne on a fleshy red disk around the long, red style, with a red, persistent calyx. **PROPAGATE** by seeds or cuttings. Light, well-drained soils in sunny places are preferred. It is usually planted by itself as a specimen plant rather than being grown in hedges.

Ocimum LAMIACEAE

Ocimum is a genus of 50 to 150 species native throughout the tropics and subtropics, especially in Africa. Many have fragrant foliage and some are used as spices, basil, *O. basilicum* Linnaeus, for example. The name *Ocimum* is based on an ancient Greek word for the plant.

Ocimum tenuiflorum Linnaeus

Synonym, *Ocimum sanctum* Linnaeus. **DISTINGUISHABLE** by the four-angled purple stems, opposite, strongly aromatic leaves, tiny white two-lipped flowers with protruding stamens, and papery two-lipped fruit. The similar sweet basil, *O. basilicum,* commonly grown as a spice, differs in having larger leaves, flowers, and fruits.

    Ocimum tenuiflorum, holy basil, a translation of a former scientific name, *O. sanctum,* or sometimes just called basil, is native to somewhere in tropical Asia. It is grown for its aromatic leaves, used for scenting coconut oil and for other purposes. It also escapes or becomes naturalized in some places but has not been reported as a serious weed. **SUBSHRUB**, annual or short-lived perennial, branching, to 1 m high (3¼ ft) with square, pubescent, often purple stems and strongly aromatic leaves.

Ocimum tenuiflorum

LEAVES simple, opposite, blade elliptic or oblong to ovate, 1.5–6 cm long (⅝–2½ in), margins entire to shallowly toothed, surface often pubescent, sometimes purple tinged. FLOWERS continuously through the year; flowers in whorls of four to six in terminal racemes. Corolla with fused petals, two-lipped, 3–5 mm long (about ⅛–¼ in), pink to pale lavender, with protruding stamens. FRUIT of four subglobose nutlets enclosed within the papery, strongly two-lipped, awn-tipped calyx 3–5 mm long (about ⅛–¼ in). PROPAGATE by seeds. Moist but well-drained soils in partial shade are preferred.

Odontonema ACANTHACEAE

Odontonema is a genus of about 26 to 40 herb and shrub species widespread in the New World tropics and subtropics, several cultivated as ornamentals for their attractive flowers.

Odontonema tubiforme (Bertoloni) Kuntze

Synonym, *Odontonema strictum* (Nees) Kuntze. There is confusion about the correct name for what is called *O. tubiforme* here. Some authors use the name *O. cuspidatum* (Nees) Kuntze for this, the red-flowered species, and *O. tubiforme* for a less common lavender-flowered species. Here the two are considered as one species. DISTINGUISHABLE by the opposite, attenuate leaves, dense terminal racemes bearing inconspicuous bracts, and red, tubular, five-lobed flowers. Its tubular flowers are very similar to those of *Russelia equisetiformis* but its broad rather than linear leaves easily distinguish it.

Odontonema tubiforme, fire spike, is native to Central America but is widely cultivated for its dense inflorescen-

Odontonema tubiforme

ces of red flowers. **SHRUB** to 2 m high (6½ ft). **LEAVES** simple, opposite, blade ovate to elliptic, 8–25 cm long (3½–10 in) with an attenuate tip. **FLOWERS** continuously through the year; flowers many, borne in narrow terminal racemes sometimes branched at the base, each flower with an inconspicuous bract below it. Corolla of fused petals, tubular with five short lobes at the tip, 2.2–3.5 cm long (⅞–1⅜ in), bright red. **FRUIT** a club-shaped capsule, infrequently formed in cultivation. **PROPAGATE** by cuttings or clump division. Fertile, moist soils in sunny or partially shaded places are preferred. Often grown as a hedge plant, little care is needed once it is established.

Ophiopogon LILIACEAE

Ophiopogon is a genus of about 20 rhizomatous or tufted perennial species found from the islands and mainland of southeastern Asia, an area that used to be called Indo-Malaya, to the Himalayas and Japan. Several are cultivated as evergreen turf-forming plants.

Ophiopogon japonicus
(Linnaeus fil.) Ker-Gawler

Synonym, *Mondo japonicum* (Linnaeus fil.) Farwell. **DISTINGUISHABLE** by the turf-like habit and clustered, linear leaves, drying at the tips. The small white to pale blue flowers rarely form in the tropics.

Ophiopogon japonicus, mondo grass (but not a member of the grass family Poaceae), sometimes and perhaps more accurately called dwarf lily turf, is native to Japan and Korea but is widely cultivated in warm places, though not often in the hot tropics, as a ground cover or border. **HERB** arising from

Ophiopogon japonicus

creeping underground stems. LEAVES grass-like, in clusters, sessile, linear, 15–35 cm × 2–6 mm (6–14 × about $\frac{1}{16}$–$\frac{1}{4}$ in), dark green, somewhat recurved, dying back at the tip. FLOWERS not formed in tropical lowlands; flowers several, borne in a loose raceme 5–10 cm long (2–4 in). Corolla with fused tepals, bell-shaped, 4–5 mm long (about $\frac{1}{4}$ in), divided into six segments, white to pale blue. FRUIT a blue globose capsule 5–10 mm long ($\frac{1}{4}$–$\frac{3}{8}$ in) but not formed in tropical lowlands. PROPAGATE by division. Fertile, moist, but well-drained soils in sunny to shaded places are preferred. Little care other than watering is needed after it becomes established. Though it is referred to as turf or grass, it will not stand foot traffic. Several cultivars have been named.

Opuntia CACTACEAE

Opuntia is a tropical and temperate American genus of about 300 species, mostly of arid areas. Some have edible fruit (prickly pear), some contain poisonous alkaloids (including the hallucinogenic mescaline), and many are cultivated as ornamentals, especially in dry areas.

Opuntia cochinellifera (Linnaeus) Miller

Synonym, *Nopalea cochinellifera* (Linnaeus) Salm-Dyck. DISTINGUISHABLE by the cactus habit, flattened, succulent, usually spineless stems, flowers forming at the tips of the stems, and many red tepals and stamens.

Opuntia cochinellifera, cochineal cactus, is probably native to Mexico but is widely cultivated as a novelty succulent plant, often in water-conserving gardens, and sometimes becomes naturalized. It has been grown as a source of food for cochineal insects, which are cactus mealybugs, that live on it. These insects are collected to make cochineal, an orange or red dye, depending on how the insects were dried. Though superseded by aniline dyes for dyeing cloth, cochineal has made something of a comeback with increased interest in natural dyes and may be used in cosmetics, foods, and medicines. SHRUB, succulent, to 4 m high (13 ft) with a distinct trunk. Stems, called joints, elliptic and flattened,

10–40 cm long (4–16 in) with spine-less areoles or rarely spiny. **LEAVES** tiny, present only briefly. **FLOWERS** continuously through the year; flowers solitary or several in a group on the tips of the stems. Corolla of many free outer tepals and longer inner tepals, 0.5–2 cm long (¼–¾ in), obovate, red, surrounding the many long, red, protruding stamens. **FRUIT** a fleshy, red, subglobose berry 2.5–4 cm long (1–1⅝ in). **PROPAGATE** by cuttings or seeds. Well-drained soils in sunny places are preferred. It is appealing as an ornamental cactus since it usually lacks spines.

Opuntia cochinellifera

Orthosiphon LAMIACEAE

Orthosiphon is a genus of 35 to 40 herb and subshrub species found from Africa to Australia, at least one of which is cultivated for its unusual flowers that bear long, protruding stamens.

Orthosiphon aristatus (Blume) Miquel

Synonyms, *Orthosiphon spiralis* (Loureiro) Merrill and *O. stramineus* Bentham, a name used by some authors. **DISTINGUISHABLE** by the four-angled purple stems, opposite leaves with toothed margins, and terminal racemes bearing whorls of white two-lipped flowers with long, protruding stamens.

Orthosiphon aristatus is native from India to Australia but is widely cultivated for its flowers with long stamens, giving rise to the common name cat's whiskers. The leaves are used in traditional Chinese medicine for treating diabetes. **HERB**, perennial, to 1.5 m high (5 ft), with square, purple, finely pubescent stems. **LEAVES** simple, opposite, blade

Orthosiphon aristatus

ovate to lanceolate, 2–9 cm long (¾–3½ in), margins toothed. **FLOWERS** continuously through the year; flowers in whorls of four to six in terminal racemes. Corolla with fused petals, two-lipped, the tube 1.5–2.5 cm long (⅝–1 in), the lips 8–12 mm long (¼–½ in), white or pale blue, with four long, protruding, white stamens purple at the tip. **FRUIT** of four small ovoid nutlets enclosed within the papery two-lipped calyx. **PROPAGATE** by seeds or cuttings. Well-drained soils in sunny places are preferred. It is usually planted by itself as a specimen plant, or with vigorous trimming it can be used as a ground cover, sometimes becoming naturalized.

Otacanthus SCROPHULARIACEAE

Otacanthus is a genus of four herbaceous Brazilian species, one of which is cultivated as an ornamental for its colorful flowers.

Otacanthus caeruleus Lindley

DISTINGUISHABLE by the opposite leaves, solitary axillary flowers, and mauve, two-lipped, snapdragon-like corolla white in the center.

    Otacanthus caeruleus, Amazon blue, native to Brazil, is cultivated elsewhere in the tropics for its mauve flowers, an uncommon color in tropical gardens. Though more commonly grown during the last century, it has come back into popularity more recently and hence is found in few books on ornamental flowers. **HERB**, somewhat woody, to 60 cm high (24 in) with four-angled stems and fragrant foliage and stems. **LEAVES** simple, opposite, blade ovate to elliptic, 5–9 cm long (2–3½ in), with finely toothed margins, and sessile on a winged petiole. **FLOWERS** continuously through the year; flowers solitary, axillary, but appearing like a short, leafy, terminal raceme. Corolla with fused petals, two-lipped, tube 2.5–3.5 cm long (1–1⅜ in), limb with one upper and one lower subround lip 2–3 cm in diameter (¾–1¼ in), mauve with white in the throat. **FRUIT** a capsule, infrequently formed in cultivation. **PROPAGATE** by cuttings. Moist but well-drained soils in sunny places are preferred. It is grown in flower beds or borders.

Oxalis OXALIDACEAE

Oxalis is a genus of 500 to 700 mostly herbaceous species found throughout the world, some of which are common and widespread weeds. Some have edible leaves or are used locally in medicines, and some are cultivated as ornamentals. The name *Oxalis* is from the Greek word meaning acid, referring to the typically bitter taste of these herbs.

Oxalis debilis Kunth

Synonyms, *Oxalis corymbosa* A. P. de Candolle, a name used by some authors, and *O. martiana* Zuccarini. **DISTINGUISHABLE** by the herbaceous stemless habit, long-stalked basal leaves with three terminal, heart-shaped leaflets, and umbels of pink flowers with ten stamens.

Otacanthus caeruleus

Oxalis debilis

Oxalis debilis, pink wood sorrel, is native to tropical South America but is widely cultivated in the tropics to subtropics for its pink flowers. **HERB**, perennial, stemless, to 30 cm high (12 in), arising from scaly bulbs. **LEAVES** trifoliate, basal, blade with three obcordate, subsessile leaflets 1.5–4 cm long (⅝–1⅝ in) borne atop a long, pubescent petiole. **FLOWERS** continuously through the year; flowers several, borne in umbels atop a long, pubescent stalk. Corolla of five free, pink, oblanceolate petals 1–1.8 cm long (⅜–¾ in). **FRUIT** a cylindrical capsule, forcefully ejecting the small black seeds but infrequently formed in cultivation. **PROPAGATE** by division. Rich, moist soils in sunny places are preferred. It often escapes from gardens and persists in disturbed areas, and may be hard to eradicate where not wanted because of its underground bulbs. The ornamental plant belongs to subspecies or variety *corymbosa.*

Pachystachys ACANTHACEAE

Pachystachys comprises 12 tropical American shrub species, several of which have prominent flowers and are widely cultivated as ornamentals outdoors in tropical climates and in the greenhouse in temperate climates. Two species are included here. The name *Pachystachys* is from the Greek words meaning thick spike, referring to the inflorescences.

Pachystachys lutea Nees

DISTINGUISHABLE by the opposite leaves and terminal ovoid spikes covered with overlapping, orange, ovate bracts among which are borne the small, white, strongly two-lipped flowers.

Pachystachys lutea, yellow shrimp plant, sometimes called golden candle, lollipops, or lollipop plant, is native to Peru but is widely cultivated for its white flowers borne among attractive light orange bracts. **SUBSHRUB** to 1.5 m high (5 ft). **LEAVES** simple, opposite, blade narrowly oblanceolate to elliptic, 6–17 cm long (2½–7 in). **FLOWERS** continuously through the year; flowers many, borne in a terminal ovoid spike with a pale orange, overlapping, ovate bract below each flower. Corolla of fused petals, tubular, curving, two-lipped, 3.5–5 cm long (1⅜–2 in), white, with two protruding stamens. FRUIT a capsule, infrequently formed in cultivation. PROPAGATE by cuttings, the usual method. Fertile, moist, but well-drained soils in partially shaded or sunny areas are preferred. It has become popular and has been introduced over most of its current range only more recently. It is often grown in pots, particularly in the greenhouse in temperate climates, and in borders with other shrubs but it is too short and weak stemmed to be of much use as a hedge plant.

Pachystachys lutea

Pachystachys spicata
(Ruiz & Pavón) Wasshausen

Often misidentified as *Pachystachys coccinea* (Aublet) Nees, also called cardinal's guard. DISTINGUISHABLE by the shrubby habit, opposite leaves, terminal ovoid spikes of overlapping, green, ovate bracts, and bright red, strongly two-lobed corolla.

Pachystachys spicata, cardinal's guard, is native to tropical South America but is widely cultivated for its red flowers rather than colorful bracts prominent in other members of the genus and family. SHRUB to 2 m high (6½ ft).

Pachystachys spicata

Leaves simple, opposite, blade elliptic to oblanceolate, 10–30 cm long (4–12 in). **Flowers** continuously through the year; flowers many, borne in a dense, terminal, ovoid spike with a green, overlapping, ovate bract below each flower. Corolla of fused petals, tubular, curved, two-lipped, 5–6 cm long (2–2½ in), bright red, with two protruding stamens. **Fruit** a capsule, infrequently formed in cultivation. **Propagate** by cuttings. Fertile, moist, but well-drained soils in partially shaded places are preferred. It is often planted by itself as a specimen plant, as a tub plant, or with other shrubs rather than as a hedge plant.

Pandanus PANDANACEAE

Pandanus is a genus of as many as 750 vine and tree-like species, many called screwpines, of the Old World tropics. The taxonomy of the genus is very confusing, with hundreds of species named on the basis of morphological characters that may be too variable to be useful in classification.

Pandanus tectorius with syncarp broken open

Pandanus tectorius Parkinson

Synonym, *Pandanus odoratissimus* of some authors, not Linnaeus fil., among numerous other names. **Distinguishable** by the palm-like habit, prop roots, long, spiny-edged leaves, and woody, pineapple-like fruit.

Pandanus tectorius is a screwpine of which many large-fruited varieties are cultivated on the Pacific islands, especially on atolls where few other trees can grow, but if reproduced from seed the plant goes back to the small-fruited wild type. It is one of the most useful Pacific island plants because the

Pandanus veitchii with variegated leaves

leaves are used to make mats, hats, clothing, and formerly, sails, and the fruit and seeds are edible. The plant is also popular as an ornamental because of its unusual, palm-like form. TREE with conspicuous prop roots and prickly stems. LEAVES spirally arranged at the branch tips, linear, to 2 m long (6½ ft), M-shaped in cross section, margins and midrib of lower surface prickly. FLOWERS intermittently during the year; flowers unisexual on separate male and female trees. Male flowers tiny, in dense panicles among large, white, lanceolate bracts. Female flowers in a round to ovoid head. FRUIT a subglobose, woody, fibrous syncarp to 30 cm long (12 in), comprising and breaking up into woody fruits called phlanges with several terminal stigmas. PROPAGATE by seeds or cuttings. Well-drained or moist soils in sunny places are preferred. Related species with variegated leaves, such as *P. sanderi* Masters and *P. veitchii* Masters & Moore, are also popular as ornamentals.

Papilionanthe ORCHIDACEAE

Papilionanthe is a genus of 11 epiphytic orchid species found from the Himalayas to Malaysia, many cultivated for their flowers or used in hybridization. Some authors combine the genus with *Vanda*.

Papilionanthe 'Agnes Joaquim'

Synonym, *Vanda* 'Miss Joaquim'. DISTINGUISHABLE by the epiphytic habit, long cylindrical leaves, and pink flowers with pink tepals and a darker pink labellum.

Papilionanthe 'Agnes Joaquim' is a vanda orchid that is a natural hybrid originally found in the garden of Miss Agnes Joaquim in Singapore in 1893 by Henry N. Ridley, director of the botanical garden there. The parental species are *P. hookeriana* (Reichenbach fil.) Schlechter and *P. teres* (Lindley) Schlechter, both formerly included in the genus *Vanda*. HERB, erect, epiphytic, with green stems to 2 m long (6½ ft), rooting at the nodes and base. LEAVES simple, alternate, blade sessile, cylindrical, usually 10–20 cm long (4–8 in). FLOWERS continuously through the year; flowers several, borne in erect terminal racemes 15–30 cm long

(6–12 in). Corolla of five subequal ovate tepals 2–5 cm long (¾–2 in), pink,
with a slightly longer, darker pink labellum with two basal lobes. FRUIT
not forming. PROPAGATE by division.
For an orchid, the plant is easy to grow.
Tree-fern trunks or coconut husks in
sunny or partially shaded places are
preferred. 'Agnes Joaquim' is one of several cultivars from the cross, commonly grown in the tropics for cut flowers
used in corsages, leis, and singly for
decoration, especially in Hawaii where
it is particularly popular, and it is the
national flower of Singapore. In areas
of high demand the flowers are sometimes sold by weight rather than by
number.

Papilionanthe 'Agnes Joaquim'

Parkinsonia FABACEAE

Parkinsonia is a genus of 19 species found in dry areas of the Americas
and Africa, at least two of which are cultivated for their unusual green,
leafless branches.

Parkinsonia aculeata Linnaeus

DISTINGUISHABLE by the tree habit, drooping branches, thorny stems,
bipinnately compound leaves, tiny deciduous leaflets, and axillary racemes of yellow flowers, each with four petals and ten stamens.

    Parkinsonia aculeata, Jerusalem thorn, sometimes called Mexican
palo verde, is native to the Caribbean, in the New World, not the Old. It
is widely if not commonly cultivated as a novelty because of its unusual, weeping form and for reforestation in dry areas. TREE to 10 m high
(33 ft) with green stems, branches, and trunk, and groups of three axil-

Parkinsonia aculeata

lary thorns to 2.5 cm long (1 in) or more. LEAVES bipinnately compound but appearing pinnate, alternate, leaflets drooping, with a narrow, flattened rachis to 60 cm long (24 in) or more bearing numerous, as many as 80 or more, elliptic, deciduous leaflets 4–10 mm long (about ¼–⅜ in). FLOWERS anytime during the year; flowers in axillary racemes to 15 cm long (6 in). Corolla of four oblanceolate petals 1.4–1.8 cm long (⅝–¾ in), yellow, with ten stamens. FRUIT a narrow, one- to several-seeded pod 5–20 cm long (2–8 in), constricted between the seeds. PROPAGATE by scarified seeds. Well-drained soils in sunny places are preferred. As an ornamental it is usually grown by itself as a specimen plant, as a hedge plant, or in water-conserving gardens, but its thorns can be a drawback when the tree is planted in accessible places.

Parmentiera BIGNONIACEAE

Parmentiera is a genus of nine tropical American tree species, some grown for timber, edible seeds, and ornamentals, mostly as oddities.

Parmentiera cereifera Seemann

DISTINGUISHABLE by the tree habit, leaves that are opposite and trifoliate, flowers that are large, bell-shaped, and often produced on the trunk, and long, hanging, waxy white, candle-like fruits.

    Parmentiera cereifera, candle tree, sometimes called Panama candle tree, is native to Panama but is widely if not commonly cultivated as a novelty because of its hanging, candle-like fruits. The fruits are eaten in the native range of the species. TREE or large shrub branching near the base, to 8 m high (26 ft). **LEAVES** trifoliate, opposite, rachis winged, leaflet blades obovate to elliptic, 1.5–9 cm long (⅝–3 ⅞ in), margins toothed to entire. **FLOWERS** intermittently during the year; flowers solitary on stem tips, or more commonly in fascicles of one to four, arising from the trunk. Corolla of fused petals, bell-shaped, 4–7 cm long (1⅝–3 in) with five rounded lobes, greenish white, surrounded by a boat-shaped calyx. **FRUIT** berry-like, hanging, narrowly cylindrical and candle-shaped, 40–60 cm long (16–24 in) or more, waxy white to yellow, many-seeded. **PROPAGATE** by seeds. Well-drained soils in sunny places are preferred. It is usually grown by itself as a specimen tree.

Parmentiera cereifera

Pedilanthus EUPHORBIACEAE

Pedilanthus is a genus of 14 succulent shrub species found in subtropical North America and Central America, some cultivated as ornamentals. The name *Pedilanthus* is from the Greek words meaning shoe and flower, aptly referring to the flowers of some of the species, slipper flowers.

Pedilanthus tithymaloides (Linnaeus) Poiteau

DISTINGUISHABLE by the subshrub habit, milky sap, zigzag, green and often white-striped stems, and inconspicuous flowers, each cyathium surrounded by a red bract with a sac-like base.

Pedilanthus tithymaloides, redbird cactus, a misnomer since the plant is not in the cactus family, sometimes called slipper flower, is native to the West Indies but is widely cultivated for its red cyathia and sometimes for its variegated foliage ('Variegatus'). The somewhat poisonous

Pedilanthus tithymaloides

sap can cause stomach upset if ingested, and is irritating to the skin and eyes. **SUBSHRUB**, somewhat fleshy, to 1 m high (3¼ ft) or more, with milky sap and often with zigzag stems. **LEAVES** simple, alternate, blade ovate, elliptic, or obovate, 4–10 cm long (1⅝–4 in), often variegated with white or yellow. **FLOWERS** continuously through the year; flowers several, in cyathia borne in terminal clusters, each cyathium conical, surrounded by a two-lipped red bract 8–12 mm long (¼–½ in) with a sac-like base. **FRUIT** a shallowly three-lobed ovoid capsule 5–8 mm long (about ¼ in). **PROPAGATE** by cuttings. Sandy, well-drained soils in sunny places are preferred. It is usually planted in garden borders, in mass plantings, or in pots, and in temperate climates it is cultivated as a potted plant in the greenhouse or as a houseplant. Little care is required and it is able to grow in poor, relatively dry, even coralline soil. Relatively unattractive individuals can be made bushier and more attractive by pruning. Several subspecies are recognized.

Pelargonium GERANIACEAE

Pelargonium is a genus of about 280 herb and shrub species found in temperate and tropical regions from Africa to New Zealand. Many are cultivated as "geraniums" with many hybrids and cultivars involving a number of different parental species. The name *Pelargonium* is from the Greek word meaning stork, referring to the narrow beak shape of the fruits.

Pelargonium ×hortorum L. H. Bailey

Distinguishable by the round to kidney-shaped leaves often with a colored band near the scalloped margin, and long-stalked umbels of five-parted flowers, red to white. Also cultivated in warm areas, *Pelargonium graveolens* L'Héritier, rose geranium, differs in having toothed, palmately lobed leaves and pink flowers.

Pelargonium ×hortorum, zonal geranium, also called bedding geranium, is not a true *Geranium* though it is a member of the family Geraniaceae. It is a hybrid between two southern African species, *P. inquinans* (Linnaeus) L'Héritier and *P. zonale* (Linnaeus) L'Héritier. Another name, fish geranium, comes from the fishy odor of the leaves. **Subshrub** to 1 m high (3¼ ft) with large ovate stipules. **Leaves** simple, alternate, blade nearly round to kidney-shaped, 3–11 cm in diameter (1¼–4½ in), sur-face pubescent, sometimes with a reddish or white band parallel to the scalloped margin. **Flowers** continuously through the year in the tropics; flowers many, borne in upper axillary, long-stalked umbels. Corolla of five obovate, equal or unequal petals 1.5–2.2 cm long (⅝–⅞ in), red, pink, or white. **Fruit** an ovoid capsule with a persistent style several times longer than the fruit. **Propagate** by cuttings. Well-drained soils in sunny places are preferred. It is widely cultivated in gardens and greenhouses in tropical to warm temperate areas, often as a garden, potted, or tub plant, indoors or outdoors, for its red, white, or pink flowers. Many cultivars have been named.

Pelargonium ×hortorum

Peltophorum FABACEAE

Peltophorum is a genus of seven to nine tree species found in the tropics and subtropics, several cultivated as ornamentals and others utilized for timber, medicines, and dyes.

Peltophorum pterocarpum (A. P. de Candolle) Backer ex K. Heyne

Synonym, *Peltophorum inerme* (Roxburgh) Llanos ex Blanco. DISTIN-GUISHABLE by the large tree habit, alternate, bipinnately compound leaves, terminal racemes of yellow flowers having five petals with frilly margins, and reddish brown pods.

　　Peltophorum pterocarpum, yellow poinciana, sometimes called yellow flamboyant or copperpod, is native from Southeast Asia to northern Australia but is widely grown in the tropics for its attractive leaves and form, and for its seasonal, conspicuous yellow flowers and reddish brown pods. The bark is used medicinally and for producing a dye used

Peltophorum pterocarpum

in coloring batik in Indonesia, and the flowers are sometimes used in arrangements. TREE, stately, broad crowned, to 15 m high (50 ft). LEAVES bipinnately compound, alternate, mostly with 7 to 10 pairs of pinnae, each pinna with 10 to 20 pairs of leaflets, blades oblong, mostly 1.3–3 cm long (½–1¼ in). FLOWERS most of the year in the tropics but seasonally in some climates, then mostly in late spring and summer, with the same tree sometimes flowering again later in the year; flowers many, borne in terminal racemes. Corolla of five free, ovate to nearly round, yellow petals 1–2.5 cm long (⅜–1 in) with frilly margins. FRUIT a narrowly oblong or lanceolate pod 5–15 cm long (2–6 in), reddish brown, persisting on the tree. **PROPAGATE** by scarified seeds and cuttings. Well-drained soils in sunny places are preferred. Though less spectacular than the related *Delonix regia,* it is commonly planted as a specimen, shade, or street tree. In temperate areas it is grown in the greenhouse as a foliage plant. In areas with a pronounced dry season it may lose its leaves for a short time during that period.

Pennisetum POACEAE

Pennisetum is a genus of 70 to 80 species found in warm areas throughout the world, many of which are pasture grasses and weeds, with a few used as grain crops.

Pennisetum macrostachyum (Brongniart) Trinius

Considered by some authors as a cultivar, 'Purpureum', of fountain grass, *Pennisetum setaceum* (Forsskål) Chiovenda, a weedy species. **DISTINGUISHABLE** by the grass habit, large size, purple foliage, and large, drooping, feathery panicles.

Pennisetum macrostachyum is a grass with no widely recognized common name, probably native to Indonesia but widely cultivated for its foliage. **GRASS**, clump forming, to 3 m high (10 ft) or more, growing from a rhizome. **LEAVES** simple, alternate, blade narrowly lanceolate, usually 30–60 × 1.5–3 cm (12–24 × ⅝–1¼ in), usually purple, with a long-attenuate tip. **FLOWERS** anytime during the year; flowers many, in spikelets borne in terminal,

Pennisetum macrostachyum var. *atropurpureum*

open, drooping, spike-like panicles 10–35 cm long (4–14 in). Spikelets one- to three-flowered, 4.5–6 mm long (about ¼ in) with a ring of basal, plumose bristles mostly 1–3 cm long (⅜–1¼ in). **PROPAGATE** by division. Well-drained soils in sunny places are preferred. It is often grown by itself to form large clumps or as a border plant. The commonly cultivated plant, variety *atropurpureum,* has purple foliage and inflorescences.

Pentas RUBIACEAE

Pentas is a genus of about 34 herb and shrub species found in the Arabian Peninsula, Africa, and Madagascar, some cultivated as ornamentals. The name *Pentas* is from the Greek word for five, referring to the number of flower parts though most dicots also have flower parts in multiples of five.

Pentas lanceolata (Forsskål) **Deflers**

Pentas lanceolata, a plant with pink flowers, above, and the less commonly grown, two-toned plant

DISTINGUISHABLE by the herbaceous habit, opposite leaves, interpetiolar stipules, and dense cymes of white, pink, red, or purple tubular flowers with five spreading lobes.

Pentas lanceolata, star cluster, sometimes called Egyptian star cluster, is native to Yemen and tropical East Africa but is widely cultivated for its variously colored flowers, sometimes escaping from cultivation to become naturalized. **HERB**, perennial, to 1 m high (3¼ ft) or more with interpetiolar stipules and fuzzy stems. **LEAVES** simple, opposite, blade lanceolate to elliptic, 3–16 cm long (1¼–6 in), surface pubescent, distinctly veined, with an attenuate base. FLOWERS continuously through the year; flowers many, borne in dense terminal cymes. Corolla with fused petals, salverform, tube 1.5–2.3 cm long (⅝–⅞ in), limb of five spreading, ovate lobes 4–7 mm long (about ¼ in), white, pink, red, or purple. FRUIT a top-shaped capsule 3–5 mm long (about ⅛–¼ in). PROPAGATE by seeds or cuttings. Fertile, moist, but well-drained soils in partially shaded places are preferred. It is often planted to add color to gardens and borders. In temperate areas it is grown in the greenhouse, and the cut flowers are sometimes sold commercially. Several subspecies are recognized by some authors but the taxonomy is complex and the subspecies difficult to distinguish from each other.

Peperomia PIPERACEAE

Peperomia is a genus of about 1000 herbaceous species native throughout the tropics but because of their tiny flowers, lacking petals and sepals, they are often very difficult to distinguish from each other. Many are grown as houseplants, some with colorful foliage.

Peperomia obtusifolia
(Linnaeus) A. Dietrich

DISTINGUISHABLE by the alternate, dark green, leathery leaves and thin spikes of inconspicuous green flowers.

Peperomia obtusifolia, pepper face, sometimes called baby rubber plant or jade plant, is native to tropical America but is widely cultivated for its attractive, dark green or sometimes variegated ('Variegata') leaves. HERB, succulent, to 40 cm high (16 in) with prostrate stems rooting at the nodes.

Peperomia obtusifolia

Leaves simple, alternate, blade fleshy, obovate to elliptic or nearly round, 3–10 cm long (1¼–4 in), dark green, glabrous. **Flowers** anytime during the year; flowers embedded in one or two long, thin subterminal spikes 5–20 cm long (2–8 in). Corolla and calyx both absent. **Fruit** a tiny drupe, infrequently formed in cultivation. **Propagate** by cuttings, the technique most used. Fertile, moist, but well-drained soils in shaded places are preferred. Like other peperomias, it does well in wet, shady places and is often grown in pots, rock gardens, or as a ground cover. In temperate areas it is commonly grown indoors as a houseplant or in the greenhouse.

Petraea VERBENACEAE

Petraea is a genus of about 30 tropical American vine, shrub, and small tree species, some cultivated for their attractive flowers.

Petraea volubilis Linnaeus

Petraea volubilis

Distinguishable by the shrubby habit, opposite, rough-surfaced leaves, and axillary racemes of flowers with a five-lobed mauve corolla surrounded by five longer, narrower, lavender to blue calyx lobes.

Petraea volubilis, sandpaper vine, sometimes called queen's wreath or purple wreath, is native from Panama to Mexico but is widely cultivated for its blue to purple flowers, unusual colors in tropical gardens. The two-toned color of the flowers makes them particularly attractive and distinctive. **Vine-like shrub,** woody, climbing to 12 m high (40 ft). **Leaves** simple, opposite, blade elliptic, usually 6–17 cm long (2½–7 in), rough on both surfaces. **Flowers** anytime during the year;

flowers many, borne in axillary, erect or hanging racemes. Corolla with fused petals, mauve, salverform, tube 6–9 mm long (¼–⅜ in), limb of five spreading, rounded lobes 5–9 mm long (¼–⅜ in), surrounded by the five larger, narrowly oblong, blue to lavender calyx lobes. FRUIT an obovoid drupe, infrequently formed in cultivation. PROPAGATE by cuttings. Moist, well-drained soils in shaded places are preferred. It is grown by itself as a specimen plant or is trained as a liana on a fence or trellis. Pruning should be done following flowering for best results.

Philodendron ARACEAE

Philodendron is a tropical American genus of about 500 herb, shrub, and climbing species, many cultivated for their attractive foliage though they often are poisonous to children and pets because of the presence of an irritating sap. The name *Philodendron* is from the Greek words meaning tree loving, referring to the epiphytic or viny habit of these plants.

Philodendron bipinnatifidum Schott

Synonym, *Philodendron selloum* C. Koch. DISTINGUISHABLE by the aerial roots, heart-shaped pinnately lobed leaves with the lobes also pinnately lobed, and spathe-and-spadix inflorescence. It is similar to *Monstera deliciosa,* which differs in having holes rather than marginal indentations and lobes on the leaves.

Philodendron bipinnatifidum, tree philodendron or lacy tree philodendron, is native to Brazil and Paraguay but is widely grown for its attractive form and doubly divided leaves. The leaves become larger and more deeply lobed as the plant ages. All parts of the plant may cause stomach problems if ingested, and the sap may be irritating to the skin. HERB, tree-like, unbranched, stems decumbent to erect, to 2 m high (6½ ft), marked by conspicuous leaf scars between which long aerial roots develop. LEAVES simple, spirally arranged, blade heart-shaped to 1.5 m long (5 ft), reflexed, deeply lobed with the lobes further pinnately divided, on a petiole of similar length. FLOWERS intermittently dur-

Philodendron bipinnatifidum

ing the year; flowers many, unisexual, borne in a spadix surrounded by and shorter than the spathe, which is 20–35 cm long (8–14 in) and green to dark red externally, cream-colored internally. FRUIT berries borne tightly packed on the spadix. PROPAGATE by cuttings, and by seeds resulting from hand pollination. Fertile, moist, but well-drained soils in shaded or partially shaded places are preferred. It is often planted by itself or in groups to give a tropical look, and in temperate climates it is grown in the greenhouse or used as a houseplant. Several cultivars have been named, one of which, 'Variegatum', is variegated.

Phoenix ARECACEAE

Phoenix is a genus of 17 palm species found from the Canary Islands eastward to Sumatra, some cultivated as ornamentals and some important as fruit (dates), sugar, and toddy. The name *Phoenix* is based on the Greek word for the date palm, *P. dactylifera*.

Phoenix dactylifera Linnaeus

DISTINGUISHABLE by the large palm habit, drooping, pinnately compound leaves in a terminal cluster, leaf scars higher than broad covering the stem, and large panicles of white flowers and date fruits. Another commonly cultivated ornamental palm, *Phoenix canariensis* Chabaud, Canary date palm, differs in having leaf scars broader than high and foliage deep green. A third species grown outdoors and indoors in pots, *P. roebelinii* O'Brien, pygmy date palm, differs most obviously by its much smaller size.

Phoenix dactylifera, date palm

Phoenix roebelinii, pygmy date palm

Phoenix dactylifera, date palm, is native to North Africa eastward to India and was originally cultivated for its edible, commercial fruit, the date, for its leaves used for thatch, mats, and hats, and for many other practical uses. It is widely grown elsewhere in the tropics and subtropics as an ornamental palm, particularly in southern California and Florida, and is tolerant of salty soil. PALM to 30 m high (100 ft), dioecious, clump forming if basal suckers are not removed, with the trunk covered with leaf scars that are higher than broad. LEAVES pinnately compound, alternate, blades to 3 m long (10 ft) or more with numerous linear, two-ranked leaflets 20–30 cm long (8–12 in), gray-green, the lower ones forming spines. FLOWERS intermittently during the year but usually not in cooler climates; flowers many, in panicles to 1.2 m long (4 ft) that hang when in fruit. Corolla of three white petals 4–4.5 mm long (about ¼ in). FRUIT a yellow-brown to red oblong drupe 4–7 cm long (1⅝–3 in) but not usually forming when grown as an ornamental, and usually only in hot, dry climates. PROPAGATE by seeds or basal suckers. Well-drained soils in hot, sunny places are preferred. The lower pinnae form spines, which can be a drawback if the palm is planted near foot traffic.

Phyla VERBENACEAE

Phyla is a genus of 15 species widely distributed in warm and warm temperate regions, some grown as ornamental ground covers.

Phyla nodiflora (Linnaeus) E. Greene

Synonyms, *Lippia nodiflora* (Linnaeus) Michaux and *L. repens* of gardens. DISTINGUISHABLE by the prostrate habit, opposite or whorled leaves, toothed leaf margins, and long-stalked ovoid heads of tiny white to pink, four-lobed flowers.

Phyla nodiflora, sometimes called mat grass or turkey tangle, is not a grass. It is native to warm temperate America and was originally described from the state of Virginia. HERB, prostrate, creeping, rooting at the nodes. LEAVES simple, opposite or in whorls, blade obovate to ob-

Phyla nodiflora

lanceolate, usually 1–4 cm long (⅜–1⅝ in) with the margins of the upper half toothed. **FLOWERS** anytime during the year; flowers many, borne in long-stalked, axillary, subglobose to ovoid heads 5–25 mm long (¼–1 in). Corolla with fused petals, salverform, tube about 2 mm long (about ¹⁄₁₆ in), limb about 2 mm across (about ¹⁄₁₆ in) with four spreading, rounded lobes, white to pink with a yellow or red throat. **FRUIT** a capsule 1.5–2 mm long (about ⅛ in), breaking into two segments. **PROPAGATE** by seeds. Well-drained soils in sunny places are preferred. Widely cultivated as a ground cover, it sometimes becomes naturalized in open, disturbed places, particularly along roadsides or in lawns where its low growth form allows it to survive frequent mowing.

Pilea URTICACEAE

Pilea includes 250 to 600 herb species found throughout the tropics, with some occurring in temperate areas. All have small, inconspicuous flowers but several are cultivated as ground covers or for their attractive foliage. Four cultivated species are included here.

Pilea cadierei Gagnepain & Guillaumin

DISTINGUISHABLE by the herbaceous habit, opposite leaves palmately three-veined from the base and with the upper surface marked with pale green to silvery blotches, and head-like inflorescences of tiny green flowers.

Pilea cadierei, aluminum (aluminium in areas where British English is spoken) plant, is native to Southeast Asia, perhaps Vietnam, but is widely cultivated for its attractive, colorful foliage with pale green blotches or silvery patches. **HERB**, perennial, coarse, to 40 cm high (16 in) with succulent stems. **LEAVES** simple, opposite, blade elliptic to obovate, 4–9 cm long (1⅝–3½ in), surface marked with pale green or silvery blotches and palmately three-veined from the base. **FLOWERS** anytime during the year; flowers many, borne in one to three or more small, long-stalked, head-like axillary cymes. Corolla absent, calyx tiny, four-parted, green. **FRUIT** a tiny green achene. **PROPAGATE** by cuttings or division. Moist but well-drained soils in partially shaded places are preferred. It is usually grown in pots or in shady places around houses, or indoors in temperate climates.

Pilea cadierei

Pilea depressa (Swartz) Blume

DISTINGUISHABLE by the prostrate, weak-stemmed habit, small, opposite leaves with toothed margins, and inconspicuous, tiny green flowers.

Pilea depressa, baby's tears, is native to the Caribbean but is widely cultivated in the tropics for its attractive form and small-leaved foliage. **HERB**, prostrate, creeping, rooting at the nodes. **LEAVES** simple, opposite, blade obovate to nearly round, usually 4–16 mm long (about ¼–⅝ in), margins toothed on the upper part, petiole nearly as long as the blade. **FLOWERS** anytime during the year but the flowers are inconspicuous, many, borne in small, upper axillary cymes. Corolla absent, calyx tiny, four-parted, green. **FRUIT** a tiny achene, infrequently formed in

Pilea depressa

Pilea nummularifolia

cultivation. **PROPAGATE** by cuttings. Fertile, moist, but well-drained soils in partially shaded places are preferred. It is usually grown in hanging baskets from which the weak stems with their small leaves (hence the name baby's tears) hang, or as a ground cover where the stems spread across the ground and root at the nodes.

Pilea nummularifolia
(Swartz) Weddell

DISTINGUISHABLE by the creeping habit, opposite leaves, deeply embossed, wrinkled, mint-like leaves, and tiny, inconspicuous, green flowers. Its leaves are larger than those of the similar, prostrate *Pilea depressa*.

Pilea nummularifolia, creeping Charlie, is native to the Caribbean area and was originally named from Jamaica but is widely cultivated for its attractive leaves and creeping habit. **HERB,** prostrate to ascending, creeping, with hairy stems rooting at the nodes. **LEAVES** simple, opposite, blade round to ovate, 2–6 cm long (¾–2½ in), surfaces sparsely hairy, wrinkled, margins crenate. **FLOWERS** anytime during the year but the flowers are inconspicuous, many, unisexual, borne in short, dense, upper axillary cymes. Corolla absent, calyx four-lobed, green, 0.4–2.3 mm long (about ¹⁄₆₄–¹⁄₈ in). **FRUIT** a tiny green ovoid achene. **PROPAGATE** by cuttings, the technique most used. Fertile, moist soils in partially shaded places are preferred. It is usually grown as a ground cover, often between stepping stones, in pots, or in hanging baskets in the tropics, and as a potted or hanging basket plant in greenhouses and houses in temperate climates.

Pilea serpyllacea (Kunth) Liebmann

Similar or identical to *Pilea serpyllifolia* (Poiret) Weddell and often misidentified as a variety of *P. microphylla* (Linnaeus) Liebmann. **DISTINGUISHABLE** by the erect, herbaceous habit, tiny leaves on branches arranged in one plane, and tiny inconspicuous, green flowers.

Pilea serpyllacea is native to northern South America but is widely cultivated in the tropics for its unusual, fern-like foliage. The pollen is expelled explosively, hence the common name artillery plant. **HERB**, erect, to 30 cm high (12 in) or more, somewhat succulent, glabrous. **LEAVES** simple, opposite in unequally sized pairs, blade usually obovate, 2–7 mm long (about ¹⁄₁₆–¹⁄₄ in), somewhat succulent. **FLOWERS** anytime during the year but the flowers are inconspicuous, unisexual, tiny, borne in short axillary cymes or sessile clusters. Corolla absent, calyx tiny, four-parted, green. **FRUIT** a tiny green achene. **PROPAGATE** by cuttings, the technique most used. Well-drained soils in sunny places are preferred. It is often grown in gardens as a border plant, ground cover, or potted plant and is very similar to, but

Pilea serpyllacea

larger than, the prostrate garden weed *P. microphylla,* with which it has been confused in the literature.

Pithecellobium FABACEAE

Pithecellobium is a genus of 20 tropical American spiny tree and shrub species, some used for food (the pulp in the pod), timber, and medicines, and some cultivated as ornamentals.

Pithecellobium dulce (Roxburgh) Bentham

DISTINGUISHABLE by the tree habit, spiny stems, bipinnately compound leaves with two leaflets per pinna, tiny white flowers with protruding stamens, and spirally twisted pods with black seeds embedded in a white matrix.

   Pithecellobium dulce, Manila tamarind, sometimes called Madras thorn, is in fact native from Mexico to Venezuela but is widely cultivated as a street tree, shade tree, or as a thorny hedge plant. The tree also has many uses other than as an ornamental: a drink is sometimes made from the pulp of the fruit, the wood is used for timber, fallen pods are used for cattle food, seeds are used in leis, a yellow dye and tannin are obtained from the bark, and various parts of the tree have been used in local remedies. TREE to 15 m high (50 ft) or more with stipular spines. LEAVES bipinnately compound, alternate, pinnae two, leaflets two per pinna, blades elliptic, unequally sided, 1–5.5 cm long (⅜–2¼ in). FLOWERS continuously through the year; flowers many, borne in axillary panicles or racemes of heads to 2 cm in diameter

Pithecellobium dulce

(¾ in), including the stamens. Corolla of fused petals, funnel-shaped, 2.5–4 mm long (about ⅛–¼ in), deeply four- to six-lobed, surrounding the numerous white stamens. **FRUIT** a spirally twisted cylindrical pod 10–15 cm long (4–6 in), containing three to eight glossy black seeds embedded in a red to white aril. **PROPAGATE** by seeds. Well-drained soils in sunny places are preferred. In some places such as Hawaii where it is called 'opiuma, the tree has become naturalized as a weed in dry places since it is a hardy plant that can endure drought and heat. There is a cultivar with variegated foliage.

Pittosporum PITTOSPORACEAE

Pittosporum is a genus of about 150 to 200 tree and shrub species native to tropical and temperate Africa, Asia, Australia, New Zealand, and eastward across the Pacific to Hawaii. Some are utilized locally for timber, and many are cultivated as ornamentals.

Pittosporum tobira (Thunberg) Aiton fil.

DISTINGUISHABLE by the shrubby habit, leathery, dark green leaves with a convex surface, and white, five-parted petals (but not usually forming in the tropics).

Pittosporum tobira, tobira, sometimes called Japanese pittosporum or mock orange, is native to Japan, Korea, and China but is widely cultivated in warm temperate and occasionally tropical places for its attractive, dark green or occasionally variegated ('Variegatum') foliage. **SHRUB** to 4 m high (13 ft) or more if not trimmed. **LEAVES** simple, alternate, blade obovate, 4–10 cm long (1⅝–4 in), often convex, sometimes variegated, blunt at the tip. **FLOWERS** seasonally, usually in spring but infrequently in the tropics; flowers many, fragrant, borne in terminal umbels. Corolla of five free, spoon-shaped petals 1–1.2 cm long (⅜–½ in), white. **FRUIT** a globose capsule that splits wide open at the tip to reveal the red seeds, or the capsule may be sterile. **PROPAGATE** by cuttings, or where seeds form, by seeds. Well-drained soils in sunny places are preferred. It is one of the most common hedge plants in warm temper-

Pittosporum tobira in flower

Pittosporum tobira in fruit

ate areas but in the tropics does best at cooler, higher elevations. It is often planted in borders, as screens, in oriental gardens, or is even trimmed into the shape of animals or other things, the art of topiary.

Plectranthus LAMIACEAE

Plectranthus comprises about 300 species found from southern Africa eastward to the Pacific Ocean islands. The genus includes most of the species formerly put into *Coleus,* except variegated coleus, *Solenostemon scutellarioides.* The name *Plectranthus* is from the Greek words meaning spur flower, referring to the floral spur of some members of the genus.

Plectranthus amboinicus (Loureiro) Sprengel

Synonyms, *Coleus amboinicus* Loureiro and *C. aromaticus* Bentham. DIS-TINGUISHABLE by the four-angled stems, leaves that are opposite, somewhat succulent, fragrant, and pubescent, and narrow racemes of tiny pale blue to pink, two-lipped flowers.

Plectranthus amboinicus is called Spanish thyme and Mexican oregano among many other common names involving mint, thyme, or oregano (*Mentha, Thymus,* and *Origanum* are other genera of the family Lamiaceae). The species is of uncertain origin but is perhaps native to tropical southern Africa and was long ago spread elsewhere in the tropics. It is cultivated for its attractive leaves and flowers, as a spice, and as a fragrance for scenting coconut oil and laundry. **HERB,** somewhat succulent, weak stemmed, aromatic, to 1 m high (3¼ ft) or more with square stems. **LEAVES** simple, opposite, blade triangular to heart-shaped, 4–15 cm long (1⅝–6 in), margins toothed, surface densely pubescent. **FLOWERS** anytime during the year; flowers in

Plectranthus amboinicus

whorls of 10 to 20 in terminal racemes. Corolla with fused petals, two-lipped, 8–12 mm long (¼–½ in), pale blue to mauve or pink. **FRUIT** of four small nutlets enclosed within the fuzzy calyx. **PROPAGATE** by cuttings, the technique most used. Fertile, well-drained soils in partially shaded places are preferred. It sometimes escapes or becomes naturalized in disturbed places.

Plumbago PLUMBAGINACEAE

Plumbago, the genus of leadworts, comprises 10 to 12 species widely distributed in the tropics and subtropics, with one, *P. zeylanica* Linnaeus, ranging from Africa to Hawaii. Some are used commonly for medicines, and some are cultivated for their attractive flowers. The name *Plumbago* is from the Greek word meaning lead, since the plants were thought to be a cure for lead poisoning.

Plumbago auriculata Lamarck

Synonym, *Plumbago capensis* Thunberg. **Distinguishable** by the weak-stemmed, shrubby habit, alternate or clustered leaves, long-tubed, pale blue to white flowers, and sticky calyx surrounding the fruit. A similar species with red flowers, *P. indica* Linnaeus, red leadwort, is also occasionally cultivated as an ornamental.

Plumbago auriculata, Cape plumbago, sometimes called Cape leadwort or blue plumbago, is native to South Africa but is widely cultivated in the tropics and subtropics, and in the greenhouse in temperate regions, for its pale blue flowers, white in one cultivar. The plant has some medicinal uses but is moderately poisonous if eaten. **Shrub**, weak stemmed, to 2 m high (6½ ft) or more. **Leaves** simple, alternate or in

Plumbago auriculata with pale blue flowers

Plumbago indica with red flowers

clusters of uneven sizes, blade elliptic to oblanceolate, usually 2–7 cm long (¾–3 in). **FLOWERS** continuously through the year; flowers many, borne in terminal, flat-topped spikes, each flower with a five-ribbed calyx 1–1.4 cm long (⅜–⅝ in) and covered with gland-tipped hairs. Corolla with fused petals, salverform, tube narrow, 2.5–4 cm long (1–1⅝ in), with a spreading limb of five obovate lobes 1–1.5 cm long (⅜–⅝ in), pale blue to white. **FRUIT** a small nut enclosed within the calyx. **PROPAGATE** by seeds or cuttings. Fertile, well-drained soils in sunny places are preferred and the plant is drought resistant after it is established. It is often planted to form low hedges or borders and is sometimes trained as a vine on arches or arbors. Periodic heavy pruning and bright sunlight induce prolific flowering.

Plumeria APOCYNACEAE

Plumeria comprises seven or eight tropical American tree species, four according to some authors, several cultivated as ornamentals because of their fragrant large flowers. The name *Plumeria,* albeit misspelled, commemorates Charles Plumier, 1646–1704, French botanist and traveler. The two most common species are included here.

Plumeria obtusa Linnaeus

DISTINGUISHABLE by the small tree habit, milky sap, succulent stems, dark, leathery green leaves notched at the tip and clustered at the stem tips, and white, five-lobed flowers yellow in the center. The easiest way to distinguish it from *Plumeria rubra* is by the shiny upper leaf surface of *P. obtusa,* the leaves rounded or notched at the tip, and white flowers, never yellow (except in the center) or red.

Plumeria obtusa, Singapore frangipani, sometimes called Singapore plumeria, is native to the Caribbean area, not Singapore, but is widely cultivated, though less commonly than *P. rubra,* as an ornamental tree and for its fragrant white flowers. The white latex is irritating to the skin of some people and can cause upset stomach if ingested. **TREE**, spreading, to 5 m high (16½ ft) or more with thick stems and copious milky

Plumeria obtusa

sap. **LEAVES** simple, spirally arranged and clustered at the stem tips, blade oblanceolate, usually 10–25 cm long (4–10 in), leathery, glossy green above, gray beneath, rounded or notched at the tip. **FLOWERS** continuously through the year; flowers many, borne in terminal clusters. Corolla of fused petals, funnel-shaped, usually 7–9 cm long (3–3½ in) to 9 cm in diameter (3½ in) with a limb of five rounded lobes white with yellow in the center. **FRUIT** a pair of cylindrical pods to 20 cm long (8 in). **PROPAGATE** by stem cuttings, which is easily done; these are sometimes sold in packages. The plant is adaptable to most soil conditions but well-drained soils in hot sunny places are preferred. It is planted as a specimen tree, small shade tree, or shrubby border, and around temples in Asia, hence another common name, temple tree. The flowers make attractive leis but age and turn brown more quickly than those of other plumerias. Several cultivars have been named and these are sometimes grafted onto one tree to make a novelty.

Plumeria rubra Linnaeus

Synonyms, *Plumeria acuminata* Aiton and *P. acutifolia* Poiret. **DISTIN-GUISHABLE** by the small tree habit, milky sap, succulent stems, dark, leathery green, acute leaves clustered at the stem tips, and white with yellow or red, five-lobed flowers.

    Plumeria rubra, frangipani, sometimes called pagoda tree and, like *P. obtusa*, temple tree, is native to dry, hot areas from Mexico to Panama but is one of the most common and best known ornamental trees

throughout the tropics. The attractive, colorful, fragrant flowers are favored for making leis, and a scented oil is made from their extract. The
name frangipani is apparently taken from the name of a Renaissance
Italian nobleman who made a perfume with a fragrance similar to that
of the flowers of this tree. TREE, spreading, deciduous, to 7 m high (23
ft) with thick, swollen stems and copious milky sap. LEAVES simple, spirally arranged and clustered at the stem tips, blade elliptic to oblanceolate, 20–40 cm long (8–16 in), leathery, tip acute, upper surface not
shiny. FLOWERS continuously through the year but is sometimes flow-
erless while leafless in winter; flowers several, borne in terminal clusters. Corolla of fused petals, funnel-shaped, 5–8 cm long (2–3½ in)
with a limb 6–11 cm wide (2½–4½ in), deeply cut into five rounded
lobes, white with a yellow center and reddish outside [f. *acutifolia*
(Poiret) Woodson], reddish with a yellow center [f. *rubra*], or mostly yel-

Plumeria rubra f. *rubra* with reddish flowers,
yellow at the center

Plumeria rubra f. *lutea* with yellow flowers

low [f. *lutea* (Ruiz & Pavón) Woodson]. **FRUIT** a pair of cylindrical, divergent pods to 20 cm long (8 in), infrequently formed in cultivation. **PROPAGATE** simply by planting stem cuttings; it is one of the easiest trees to grow. The plant is adaptable to most soils conditions but well-drained soils in sunny places are preferred. It is grown for its variously colored, fragrant flowers and is planted as a small shade tree, a specimen plant, or in shrubby borders, and sometimes in tubs. Many cultivars have been named.

Podranea BIGNONIACEAE

Podranea is a tropical African genus of two species. The name *Podranea* is an anagram of *Pandorea,* a genus to which the species were formerly assigned.

Podranea ricasoliana (Tanfani) Sprague

Podranea ricasoliana

DISTINGUISHABLE by the viny or vine-like shrub habit, opposite, pinnately compound leaves, toothed leaf margins, and many-flowered panicles of funnel-shaped pink flowers with red lines inside.

Podranea ricasoliana, pink trumpet vine, is native to southern Africa but is widely if not commonly cultivated in the tropics for its pink flowers. **LIANA** or vine-like shrub. **LEAVES** odd-pinnately compound, opposite, leaflets 7 to 11, blades ovate to lanceolate, 2–7 cm long (¾–3 in), margins toothed, tips acuminate. **FLOWERS** continuously through the year; flowers many, borne in terminal panicles. Corolla of fused petals, funnel-shaped, 5–7 cm long

(2–3 in) with five rounded lobes, pink with red veins inside. FRUIT a long, narrow capsule to 35 cm long (14 in). PROPAGATE by seeds, cuttings, or air layering. Fertile, well-drained soils in sunny places are preferred. It is often grown on fences or trellises, or hanging from trees, which it festoons with its attractive flowers. In temperate areas it is grown in the greenhouse.

Polianthes AGAVACEAE

Polianthes is a genus of two tuberous perennial Mexican herb species, both cultivated for their attractive flowers. The name *Polianthes* is from the Greek words meaning bright flower.

Polianthes tuberosa Linnaeus

DISTINGUISHABLE by the underground tubers, clustered sessile leaves, and long, terminal spike of fragrant, waxy white, funnel-shaped flowers with 6 or 12 tepal lobes.

Polianthes tuberosa, tuberose, has been cultivated for centuries in Mexico as an ornamental for its fragrant white flowers and as an additive to chocolate, but it is no longer known in the wild. HERB, erect, to 1 m high (3¼ ft) from a underground tuber. LEAVES simple, erect, clustered around the tubers, sessile, the lower ones to 60 × 1.5 cm (24 × ⅝ in), the upper ones gradually reduced to bracts, green, deeply grooved in the lower half. FLOWERS anytime during the year; flowers many, fragrant, borne in a lax terminal spike to 1 m long (3¼ ft). Corolla with fused petals, funnel-shaped, 3.5–5.5 cm long (1⅜–2¼ in), divided

Polianthes tuberosa

about halfway into 6 or 12 elliptic lobes, white or tinged with violet. FRUIT an oblong capsule, infrequently formed in cultivation. PROPA-GATE by division of the tubers or by offsets. Sandy, well-drained soils in sunny places are preferred, particularly at higher elevations in the trop-ics. It is widely cultivated as a garden ornamental in the tropics, and in-doors in temperate climates. It is also grown commercially for cut flow-ers, especially the double-flowered 'The Pearl'.

Polyscias ARALIACEAE

Polyscias comprises more than 100 shrub or small tree species native to the Old World tropics from Africa to Polynesia. Many are cultivated for their often variegated foliage, often as hedge plants. There is confusion on the naming of many of the cultivars, including assigning them to their correct species, because vegetatively at least, the cultivars of a spe-cies may appear more different from each other than the species usual-

Polyscias filicifolia

ly do. Four commonly cultivated spe-cies, some called aralia or panax though not to be confused with the related gen-era *Aralia* or *Panax*, are included here.

Polyscias filicifolia
(C. Moore) L. H. Bailey

Synonym, *Polyscias cumingiana* of some authors, not (Presl) Fernández-Villar. DISTINGUISHABLE by the shrubby ha-bit, sheathing petiole bases, leaves that are alternate, pinnately compound, yel-low-green, and have lobed or toothed margins, and terminal panicles of um-bels of tiny greenish flowers.

Polyscias filicifolia, fern-leaf aralia, sometimes called angelica, is probably native to somewhere in the area of the islands and mainland of south-eastern Asia, an area that used to be called Indo-Malaya, but is widely cultivated for its attractive, yellow-green, fern-like foliage. SHRUB to 4 m high (13 ft) or more with sheathing petiole bases. LEAVES odd-pinnately compound, alternate, leaflets 9 to 17, blades narrowly elliptic, mostly 9–25 cm long (3½–10 in) with lobed or toothed margins, yellow-green. FLOWERS anytime during the year; flowers many, borne in umbels arranged in terminal panicles. Corolla of five free, greenish petals about 3 mm long (about ⅛ in). FRUIT a subglobose drupe. PROPAGATE by cuttings. The plant is adaptable to most soils but well-drained ones in partially shaded places are preferred. It is often planted as a hedge where a yellow-green border is desired. Some authors consider the species to be only a cultivar of what is often called *P. cumingiana.*

Polyscias fruticosa (Linnaeus) Harms

Synonyms, *Nothopanax fruticosum* (Linnaeus) Miquel and *Panax fruticosum* Linnaeus. DISTINGUISHABLE by the shrubby habit, sheathing petioles, leaves that are alternate and pinnate to tripinnate, and terminal panicles of umbels of tiny greenish flowers.

Polyscias fruticosa, Ming aralia, sometimes called parsley panax, is probably native to somewhere in Malaysia but is widely cultivated for its foliage and as a hedge plant. SHRUB to 4 m high (13 ft) with sheathing petiole bases. LEAVES odd-pinnately compound to tripinnately compound, alternate, leaflets usually 9 to 13, blades of the smallest divisions usually lanceolate, 3–11 cm long (1¼–4½ in), sometimes mottled yellow. FLOWERS anytime during the year; flowers in umbels of 8 to 40, ar-

Polyscias fruticosa

ranged in terminal panicles. Corolla of five free, tiny, white, inconspicuous petals. FRUIT a subglobose drupe 4–5 mm long (about ¼ in).
PROPAGATE by cuttings. Moist to dry soils in partially shaded places are
preferred. Less commonly cultivated than some of the other *Polyscias*
species, it is grown outdoors in the tropics and in the greenhouse in
temperate areas.

Polyscias guilfoylei (Bull) L. H. Bailey

Synonyms, *Nothopanax guilfoylei* (Bull) Merrill and *Panax laciniatus* of
gardens. DISTINGUISHABLE by the shrubby habit, sheathing petioles,
leaves that are alternate, pinnately compound or further divided, and
have toothed and typically white leaf margins, and terminal panicles of
umbels of tiny white flowers.

    Polyscias guilfoylei, Guilfoyle panax, sometimes misleadingly called
wild coffee since it is not related to true coffee, *Coffea* in the family Ru-

Polyscias guilfoylei   *Polyscias guilfoylei* 'Filicifolia'

biaceae, is probably native to somewhere in Melanesia but is widely cultivated for its attractive foliage. **SHRUB** or small tree to 7 m high (23 ft) with sheathing petiole bases. **LEAVES** odd-pinnately compound or the leaflets further irregularly divided, alternate, leaflets five to nine, blades elliptic to oblong, 4–18 cm long (1⅝–7 in), margins often white and toothed to deeply lobed. **FLOWERS** infrequently during the year; flowers borne in umbels of 10 to 25, arranged in terminal panicles. Corolla of five or six free, tiny, white, inconspicuous petals. **FRUIT** a subglobose drupe. **PROPAGATE** by cuttings or air layering. Moist to dry soils in sunny or partially shaded places are preferred. It is often cultivated in the tropics as a hedge or screen plant, sometimes in pots, and as a potted plant in cooler climates. Two kinds of plants are mainly cultivated, the typical pinnate type and, less commonly, the more dissected types such as 'Filicifolia' and 'Laciniata'.

Polyscias scutellaria (N. L. Burman) Fosberg

Synonyms, *Polyscias balfouriana* (Sander ex André) L. H. Bailey and *P. pinnata* J. R. Forster & J. G. A. Forster. **DISTINGUISHABLE** by the shrubby habit, sheathing petioles, leaves that are pinnately compound and have entire to deeply lobed margins, and terminal panicles of umbels of tiny greenish flowers.

Polyscias scutellaria is a panax that lacks a well-known common name. It is probably native to the forests of the Solomon Islands and Vanuatu, the former New Hebrides, but cultivars derived from the wild plant are widely grown, often as hedge plants. **SHRUB** or small tree to 4 m high (13 ft), with sheathing petiole bases and spotted stems. **LEAVES** odd-pinnately compound, alternate, leaflets one to five, blades broadly elliptic to nearly round, mostly 3–20 cm long (1¼–8 in), the margins sometimes variously lobed and toothed ('Tricochleata') or entire and often white. **FLOWERS** infrequently during the year; flowers borne in umbels of 8 to 24, arranged mostly in terminal panicles. Corolla of five to seven free, tiny, greenish, inconspicuous petals 2–3 mm long (about ⅟₁₆–⅛ in). **FRUIT** a subglobose drupe. **PROPAGATE** by cuttings. The plant

Polyscias scutellaria

Polyscias scutellaria 'Tricochleata' with yellow-ish green leaflets with toothed margins

is adaptable to most soils, preferably in partially shaded or sunny places. Many cultivars have been named, including the most common-ly grown cultivar, 'Tricochleata' with yellowish green leaflets further di-vided and margins sharply toothed.

Portulaca PORTULACACEAE

Portulaca comprises about 40 annual herb species, or as many as 200 ac-cording to some authors, found throughout the tropics and subtropics, many of them weeds. Some species with conspicuous flowers are culti-vated as potted plants or garden ornamentals, two of the most com-mon purslanes are included here.

Portulaca grandiflora W. J. Hooker

DISTINGUISHABLE by the succulent stems, leaves that are linear, succulent, and alternate, and terminal, solitary flowers with five to many variously colored or striped petals.

Portulaca grandiflora, rose moss, neither a moss nor a rose, sometimes called garden purslane, is native to tropical America and was originally named from Argentina but is widely cultivated in the tropics to temperate regions as a garden plant for its flowers, which come in various colors. Each flower opens in the early morning and lasts only a day. **HERB**, prostrate to ascending, succulent, with stems to 30 cm long (12 in). **LEAVES** simple, alternate, blade linear to awl-shaped, 1–3 cm long (⅜–1¼ in), succulent, with long hairs in the axils.

Portulaca grandiflora, double-flowered

FLOWERS continuously through the year; flowers solitary, terminal. Corolla of five free obovate petals 1–3 cm long (⅜–1¼ in) or, more typically, double-flowered, pink, red, yellow, white, or striped, with many stamens in the center. **FRUIT** a small capsule opening when the top splits off. **PROPAGATE** by seeds or cuttings. The plant is adaptable to most soils, especially dry soils in sunny places, and is drought resistant. Full sun is needed for optimal flowering. It is often grown in planters, in beds as a ground cover, in hanging baskets, in rock gardens, or in herbaceous borders. Many cultivars have been named, some double-flowered.

Portulaca oleracea Linnaeus

DISTINGUISHABLE by the succulent stems, leaves that are oblanceolate to elliptic, succulent, and alternate or opposite, and five-parted, variously colored flowers ('Wildfire').

The ornamental known as 'Wildfire' is apparently a cultivar of *Portu-*

Portulaca oleracea 'Wildfire'

laca oleracea, purslane or pigweed, a cosmopolitan weed of tropical to temperate climates that in the wild form is mostly a prostrate succulent with small yellow flowers. The origin of the cultivar is unclear but it has become popular in cultivation only more recently and is thus not found in most references. **HERB**, erect to ascending, succulent, with stems to 40 cm long (16 in) or more arising from the base. **LEAVES** simple, alternate or opposite, blade oblanceolate to elliptic, 1–4 cm long (⅜–1⅝ in), subsessile. **FLOWERS** continuously through the year; flowers several, sessile, in terminal clusters. Corolla of five free obovate petals 1–2 cm long (⅜–¾ in), red, yellow, mauve, or white, with many yellow stamens in the center. **FRUIT** a small subglobose capsule opening when the top splits off to release the numerous tiny black seeds. **PROPAGATE** by seeds. It is adaptable to most soils in sunny places and is drought resistant. 'Wildfire' is often grown in planters or in large beds with the differently colored plants mixed together.

Portulacaria PORTULACACEAE

Portulacaria is a genus of three succulent shrub species, or according to some authors a single variable one, found in South Africa. The name *Portulacaria* is from the Greek name for purslane *(Portulaca),* to which the genus is related.

Portulacaria afra (Linnaeus) Jacquin

DISTINGUISHABLE by the shrubby habit, branches that are red, succu-

lent, and horizontal, and shiny green, succulent leaves.

Portulacaria afra, jade plant or jade tree,
sometimes called elephant bush and, in
Afrikaans, spekboom, is widely cultivated
in the tropics and subtropics for its attractive succulent leaves, reminiscent of pieces
of jade. In South Africa the plant covers
large, mountainous areas and is used as fodder for cattle. **SHRUB** to 3 m high (10 ft) with
red succulent stems and oppositely arranged, horizontal branches. **LEAVES** simple, opposite, blade obovate, 1–1.5 cm long
(⅜–⅝ in), succulent, shiny green. **FLOWERS**
rarely in cultivation, in spring in its native
habitat; flowers unisexual, many, borne in
terminal clusters. Corolla of five tiny, free,
red petals. **FRUIT** a small three-winged cap-

Portulacaria afra

sule, infrequently formed in cultivation. **PROPAGATE** by cuttings, the
technique most used. It is adaptable to most soils and is drought resistant but does best in moderately fertile, well-drained soils in sunny or
partially shaded places. Several cultivars have been named.

Pritchardia ARECACEAE

Pritchardia is a genus of 33 to 37 species ranging from Fiji to Hawaii, but
most are endemic to the latter archipelago. Some are cultivated as ornamentals because of their attractive fan-like leaves.

Pritchardia pacifica Seemann & H. Wendland

DISTINGUISHABLE by the palm habit, stiff, fan-shaped leaves, spineless
petioles, and large panicles producing dark brown drupes. A similar Fi-
jian species grown as an ornamental, *Pritchardia thurstonii* F. von
Mueller & Drude, Thurston fan palm, differs in having a single long-

Pritchardia pacifica with shorter inflorescences

Pritchardia thurstonii with an inflorescence extending beyond the leaves

stalked panicle longer than the leaves, and smaller dark red fruits 5–7 mm in diameter (about ¼ in).

Pritchardia pacifica, Fiji fan palm, is probably native only to Tonga in the southwestern Pacific Ocean but is widely cultivated as an ornamental palm because of its attractive, pleated, fan-shaped leaves. In Fiji and Tonga, the large leaves were used as fans for royalty. The small fruits are edible but are eaten mostly by children. **PALM** to 10 m high (33 ft) or more with a solitary trunk to 30 cm in diameter (12 in). **LEAVES** simple, alternate, blade round, to 1.5 m in diameter (5 ft), divided about one-third of the way into 75 to 90 linear lobes split at the apex, lower surface scaly, petiole without spines. **FLOWERS** anytime during the year; flowers many, borne in two or three axillary panicles shorter than the leaves. Corolla of three yellow-green petals 7–8 mm long (about ¼ in). **FRUIT** a dark brown globose drupe 1.1–1.5 cm in diameter (⅜–⅝ in). **PROPAGATE** by seeds. Fertile, well-drained soils in sunny to partially shaded places are preferred, and in its native habitat it lives on limestone soil. It is often grown by itself as a specimen plant or sometimes in tubs when young.

Proiphys AMARYLLIDACEAE

Proiphys comprises three species ranging from Malaysia to Australia, all of which are cultivated for their umbels of attractive white flowers.

Proiphys amboinensis (Linnaeus) Herbert

Synonym, *Eurycles amboinensis* (Linnaeus) Lindley. **DISTINGUISHABLE** by the scapose herb habit, heart-shaped to broadly ovate leaves on a long petiole, and many-flowered scapes with funnel-shaped flowers comprising six white tepals. It is similar to *Eucharis amazonica,* which differs most obviously in having narrower, elliptic leaves and fewer flowers, three to seven, per inflorescence.

Proiphys amboinensis, Brisbane lily, is native to Malaysia and, according to some authors, northern Australia, but is widely cultivated in the tropics for its white flowers. The leaves are used medicinally in its native range. **HERB**, scapose, to 60 cm high (24 in) or more from an underground bulb. **LEAVES** simple, basal, blade heart-shaped to broadly ovate, 15–30 cm long (6–12 in) with parallel veins, on a petiole usually slightly longer than the blade. **FLOWERS** anytime during the year; flowers 5 to 25, borne atop a scape to 60 cm long (24 in), not fragrant. Corolla with fused petals, funnel-shaped, tube 2.5–4 cm long (1–1⅝ in), with six oblanceolate tepals, creamy white, as long as the tube. **FRUIT** a globose capsule, usually one-seeded. **PROPAGATE** by division, offsets, or seeds. Fertile soils in shaded places are preferred. It is often grown as a border plant in gardens.

Proiphys amboinensis

Pseuderanthemum ACANTHACEAE

Pseuderanthemum comprises 60 to 80 herb, shrub, or rarely, climbing species found throughout the tropics but concentrated in Malaysia and Melanesia. Several are cultivated as ornamentals, mostly because of their colorful foliage. Two ornamental species are included here.

Pseuderanthemum bicolor (Schrank) Radlkofer

Synonym, *Eranthemum bicolor* Schrank. **DISTINGUISHABLE** by the leaves that are opposite, narrow, and dark, shallowly toothed margins, and axillary clusters of white five-lobed flowers mottled with pink or purple spots. The similar *Pseuderanthemum carruthersii* differs in having more flowers in terminal racemes.

Pseuderanthemum bicolor, with no well-known common name, is native to the Philippines but is widely cultivated for its small but conspicuous flowers and attractive purple leaves. **SHRUB** to 2 m high (6½ ft). **LEAVES** simple, opposite, blade lanceolate to elliptic, 5–14 cm long (2–6

Pseuderanthemum bicolor

in), reddish to dark purple. **FLOWERS** continuously through the year; flowers several, borne in axillary fascicles with inconspicuous bracts. Corolla of fused petals, salverform, tube 2–3 cm long (¾–1¼ in) with five spreading lobes 1–1.7 cm long (⅜–¾ in), white but often pale purple in the center and the lobes spotted or mottled pink to purple. **FRUIT** a club-shaped capsule, infrequently formed in cultivation. **PROPAGATE** by cuttings. Moist but well-drained soils in partially shaded places are preferred. It is often grown in hedges but is not nearly as commonly cultivated as the better known *P. carruthersii*.

Pseuderanthemum carruthersii (Seemann) Guillaumin

Synonyms, *Eranthemum atropurpureum* Bull and *Pseuderanthemum atropurpureum* (Bull) Radlkofer. Opinions differ on the correct names for the varieties. Purple pseuderanthemum is often called *P. carruthersii* var. *atropurpureum* and is very similar to *P. bicolor*, which, however, has fewer flowers in axillary fascicles. The plant with yellow, net-veined leaves, el dorado, formerly called *P. reticulatum* (J. D. Hooker) Radlkofer, is often called *P. carruthersii* var. *reticulatum*. **DISTINGUISHABLE** by the shrubby habit, opposite, leaves that are dark or yellow and net veined, and terminal panicles of rose-colored to white flowers with purple spots.

Pseuderanthemum carruthersii is apparently native to New Caledonia or Vanuatu (the former New Hebrides) or both. It is widely and commonly cultivated for the dark purple or yellow variegated leaves and the relatively small, attractive, white to purple flowers. **SHRUB** to 2 m

high (6½ ft) or more. **LEAVES** simple, opposite, blade elliptic to oblong
or ovate, 6–15 cm long (2½–6 in), dark green (var. *carruthersii*) to purple or variegated with purple (var. *atropurpureum*), pink, green, and
white, or with yellow venation (var. *reticulatum*). **FLOWERS** continuously through the year; flowers many, borne among inconspicuous bracts
in narrow terminal panicles. Corolla of fused petals, funnel-shaped,
2–2.5 cm long (¾–1 in), divided about halfway into five rounded lobes,
rose-purple, or white with purple spots. **FRUIT** a club-shaped capsule,
infrequently formed in cultivation. **PROPAGATE** by cuttings. Fertile,
moist, but well-drained soils in sunny to partially shaded places are preferred but full sun is necessary for optimal leaf color development. It is
usually grown as a colorful hedge, in mixed beds, or as a foundation
plant and must be pruned to keep its shape. The most popular plant is

Pseuderanthemum carruthersii var. *carruthersii*
with dark leaves

Pseuderanthemum carruthersii var. *reticulatum*
with yellow-veined leaves, a piece resting
atop a less commonly grown variegated form

probably the one called el dorado, variety *reticulatum,* which has green leaves that change to a yellow network.

Pterocarpus FABACEAE

Pterocarpus is a genus of 20 tree species found throughout the tropics, many used for their timber or for dyes, and some cultivated as ornamentals. The name *Pterocarpus* is from the Greek words meaning winged fruit, referring to that typical characteristic of the genus.

Pterocarpus indicus Willdenow

DISTINGUISHABLE by the large tree habit, pinnately compound leaves of 5 to 11 leaflets, seasonal panicles of yellow, butterfly-like flowers, and flattened one-seeded pod with a wing-like edge.

    Pterocarpus indicus, Burmese rosewood, sometimes called narra, is native from Southeast Asia eastward to the Caroline Islands and Vanuatu, the former New Hebrides, and is widely cultivated in the region as a timber tree as well as an ornamental. The fine timber, with its rose-like fragrance, is used extensively in Asia for making furniture, and the bark has been used for tanning. The tree has been planted in reforestation schemes in Hawaii, and it is the national tree of the Philippines. **TREE**, spreading, to 20 m high (66 ft) or more with flaky bark and often a buttressed trunk. **LEAVES** odd-pinnately compound, alternate, leaflets 5 to 11, alternate, blades elliptic to ovate or lanceolate, 5–16 cm long (2–6 in). **FLOWERS** typically seasonally, mostly in spring and early summer, with the dried pods persist-

Pterocarpus indicus with round, winged pods

ing most of the year; flowers many, borne in axillary panicles to 20 cm long (8 in) or more. Corolla papilionaceous with five unequal petals 1–1.6 cm long (⅜–⅝ in), yellow, surrounding the ten stamens. FRUIT a flattened pod 4–6 cm in diameter (1⅝–2½ in) with a wing-like edge, not splitting, one-seeded. One kind (f. *echinatus*) has the center part of the fruit covered with soft bristles. PROPAGATE by scarified seeds or cuttings. Fertile, moist, but well-drained soils in sunny to partially shaded places are preferred. It is often planted as a specimen, park, or shade tree but is too large for small gardens.

Punica PUNICACEAE

Punica is a genus of two species found from southeastern Europe to the Himalayas with one, *P. protopunica* I. B. Balfour, endemic to the island of Socotra off the southern coast of the Arabian Peninsula.

Punica granatum Linnaeus

DISTINGUISHABLE by the small tree habit, often spiny stems, oblanceolate to elliptic leaves clustered on short branches, corolla of five or many red petals, and large red edible fruit (not formed in the double-flowered cultivar).

Punica granatum, pomegranate, is probably native to the Middle East, perhaps Iran, but grows wild or naturalized from southern Europe to northern India. It is widely cultivated for its delicious edible fruit, which is eaten fresh, made into a fresh drink, or processed into a syrup known as grenadine, which is used as a beverage or cocktail flavoring. TREE to 6 m high (20 ft) or more, often with spiny stems. LEAVES simple, opposite, often on short

Punica granatum 'Flore Pleno', double-flowered

axillary branches, blade elliptic to oblanceolate, 2–8 cm long (¾–3½ in). **FLOWERS** anytime during the year; flowers solitary or a few borne in fascicles, terminal on short branches. Corolla of five to eight free, obovate to nearly round petals, or double-flowered in the common cultivar, 1.5–2.7 cm long (⅝–1⅛ in), red, sometimes white or yellow, with numerous stamens, or none in double-flowered plants. **FRUIT** a red globose berry 5–13 cm in diameter (2–5 in) with the many seeds embedded in a red jelly, but infrequently formed in ornamental cultivars. **PROPAGATE** by cuttings, air layering, or seeds. Fertile, well-drained soils in sunny places are preferred. The best quality fruits grow in dry climates. 'Flore Pleno', double-flowered and sterile so without fruit, is popular as an ornamental and is grown by itself as a specimen plant or in tubs, hedges, or borders. 'Nana' has small flowers and leaves.

Pyrostegia BIGNONIACEAE

Pyrostegia is a genus of three to five tropical American liana species, one of which is cultivated as an ornamental. The name *Pyrostegia* is from the Greek word for fire, referring to the flower color.

Pyrostegia venusta (Ker-Gawler) Miers

Synonym, *Pyrostegia ignea* (Vellozo) Presl. **DISTINGUISHABLE** by the viny habit, pinnately compound leaves of two or three leaflets, three-parted tendrils often replacing the terminal leaflet, the margins of the leaflet entire, and clusters of tubular orange flowers five-lobed at the tip. The somewhat similar *Tecomaria capensis* differs in having five to nine leaflets with toothed margins.

Pyrostegia venusta, flame vine, sometimes called flaming trumpet vine or orange trumpet vine, is native to Brazil but is widely cultivated for its profusion of orange flowers. **VINE**, woody, climbing. **LEAVES** compound, opposite, leaflets two or three, blades ovate, 4–11 cm long (1⅝–4½ in) with a three-parted tendril sometimes replacing the third leaflet. **FLOWERS** continuously through the year; flowers in clusters of two to eight borne in a leafy terminal panicle or on short lateral branches. Corolla of fused petals, tubular, 5–7 cm long (2–3 in) with five ovate lobes at the tip, bright orange. **FRUIT** a narrow cylindrical capsule 25–30 cm long (10–12 in), containing many winged seeds. **PROPAGATE** by cuttings or air layering. Fertile, moist, but well-drained soils in sunny places are preferred. Growth may be prolific, and the climbing stems may cover trellis, trees, or fences near which it is planted. It is often grown in the greenhouse in temperate areas.

Quassia SIMAROUBACEAE

Pyrostegia venusta

Quassia is a genus of 35 species found in tropical America, some cultivated as medicines (vermifuge seeds), timber, or for insecticidal properties, and a few as ornamentals.

Quassia amara Linnaeus

DISTINGUISHABLE by the alternate, pinnately compound leaves, five leaflets, winged rachis, and long racemes or panicles of racemes of closed, red, conical flowers with ten protruding stamens.

Quassia amara is native to South America and was originally named from Suriname but is widely if not commonly cultivated in the tropics for its red flowers. The leaves are used

Quassia amara

medicinally as bitterwood, sometimes called quassia wood. **SHRUB** or small tree to 5 m high (16½ ft) or more. **LEAVES** odd-pinnately compound, alternate, with one terminal and four opposite leaflets and a narrowly winged petiole, blades oblanceolate, mostly 5–15 cm long (2–6 in) with an attenuate tip, usually with red veins and midrib. **FLOWERS** continuously through the year; flowers many, borne in long, terminal racemes or panicles of racemes. Corolla conical and closed, of five free lanceolate petals 2.3–4 cm long (⅞–1⅝ in), red, with ten protruding stamens. **FRUIT** of five black ovoid berries 1–1.5 cm long (⅜–⅝ in) borne on the red receptacle. **PROPAGATE** by cuttings or seeds. Moist but well-drained soils in partially shaded places are preferred. It is usually grown as a specimen plant or in hedges or borders.

Quisqualis COMBRETACEAE

Quisqualis is a genus of about 17 species of vine-like shrubs found from tropical Asia to New Guinea. The name *Quisqualis* is from the Latin words meaning how and what, originally deriving from the Malay name for the plant, *udani,* punned through the Dutch *hoedanig*—How, what?

Quisqualis indica Linnaeus

DISTINGUISHABLE by the vine-like shrubby habit, opposite leaves, and flowers with a corolla-like, long-tubed, red to pink calyx. It might be mistaken for an *Ixora,* which has stipules between the paired leaf bases, however, and the four rather than five flower lobes. *Ixora* also is characterized by a tiny green calyx, lacking in *Quisqualis indica.*

Quisqualis indica, Rangoon creeper, is native from Myanmar (Burma) to New Guinea but is widely cultivated for its clusters of fragrant long flowers. The attractive flowers turn from white, to pink, then to red with age, and all three colors can be found in the same inflorescence. Various parts of the plant are used in herbal medicines in Asia, especially the seeds, as a vermifuge, but the plant can be poisonous. **VINE-LIKE SHRUB** growing into a liana to 8 m high (26 ft), sometimes with long spines. Leaves simple, opposite, mostly elliptic, blade 8–16 cm long (3½–6 in), glabrous. Flowers anytime during or continuously through the year; flowers many, borne in one or three terminal spikes at the ends of the main branches and single spikes on the lateral branches. Corolla of five free, oblong to oblanceolate petals 1–2.5 cm long (⅜–1 in) or double-flowered, white when opening but turning pink to red, atop a long, tubular calyx tube 3.5–7 cm long (1⅜–3 in). Fruit drupe-like, ellipsoidal, 2.5–3.5 cm long (1–1⅜ in) with five longitudinal wings. Propagate by cuttings, suckers, or seeds. Moist, well-drained soils in sunny

Quisqualis indica

places are preferred. It is often grown by itself as a shrubby specimen plant or is trained as a vine on trellises, but pruning is needed to control its vigorous growth. Several cultivars have been named, one double-flowered.

Ravenala STRELITZIACEAE

Ravenala is a genus with a single species cultivated as an ornamental. The name *Ravenala* is based on its native name in Madagascar.

Ravenala madagascariensis Sonnerat

Distinguishable by the palm-like habit, banana-leaf-like leaves arranged in a fan-like crown, and large white flowers borne in 7 to 12 folded, green, boat-shaped bracts. The similar *Strelitzia nicolai* differs in having the petioles much shorter than the blade and fewer boat-like bracts.

    Ravenala madagascariensis, traveler's palm, sometimes called traveler's tree, does not belong to the palm family and is more closely related to bananas. The common names come from the copious amount of

Ravenala madagascariensis

rainwater and liquid plant secretions that collect in the leaf bases and flower bracts, forming a reservoir for the thirsty traveler. Unlike popular belief, the plants do not align themselves so that compass direction can be determined. The seeds are edible. The plant is, as the scientific name *madagascariensis* suggests, native to Madagascar but is widely grown in the tropics and subtropics for its white flowers and palm-like form. In its native habitat the plants are pollinated by ruffled lemurs. **PALM-LIKE TREE**, clump forming, to 10 m high (33 ft) or more, developing a distinct trunk with age. **LEAVES** simple, alternate, 20 to 30, two-ranked, forming a fan-like crown, blade paddle-shaped, 1.5–3 × 0.6–1 m (5–10 × 2–3¼ ft) on a petiole as long or longer than the blade, surface gray-green with the margins often split and like that of the similar banana (*Musa* spp.) leaf. **FLOWERS** intermittently during the year; flowers several, borne within a single cluster of 7 to 12 large, green, folded, distichous, boat-shaped bracts to 50 cm long (20 in). Corolla of five free subequal tepals 15–24 cm long (6–9 in) and one shorter tepal, white to yellowish. **FRUIT** an oblong woody capsule to 8 cm long (3½ in), containing many seeds covered with blue arils. **PROPAGATE** by seeds or offshoots. Fertile, moist, but well-drained soils in sunny or partially shaded places are preferred but if it is not grown in a protected place, wind can shred the leaves. It is often grown by itself outdoors as a specimen plant in the tropics and in the greenhouse in temperate climates. Removal of the offshoots is necessary to keep the plant from forming clumps.

Rhaphiolepis ROSACEAE

Rhaphiolepis is a genus of 14 evergreen shrub species found in warm temperate areas of eastern Asia, some of which are cultivated in tropical to temperate areas.

Rhaphiolepis umbellata (Thunberg) Makino

DISTINGUISHABLE by the shrubby habit, leaves that are alternate, concave, and leathery, and panicles or racemes of five-parted white flowers with many stamens.

Rhaphiolepis umbellata

Rhaphiolepis umbellata, Yeddo hawthorn, is native to Japan but is widely cultivated in warm temperate to subtropical regions, sometimes the tropics, Hawaii, for example, for its attractive foliage and white, apple-blossom-like flowers. **SHRUB** to 4 m high (13 ft) or more. **LEAVES** simple, alternate, blade obovate to nearly round, or elliptic (f. *umbellata*), 3–9 cm long (1¼–3½ in), thick and leathery, margins usually revolute, sometimes toothed, lower surface pubescent. **FLOWERS** anytime during the year in the tropics; flowers many, borne in terminal and upper axillary panicles or racemes. Corolla of five free, obovate, white petals 7–10 mm long (¼–⅜ in), with many stamens. **FRUIT** a waxy, purple, subglobose berry 8–12 mm long (¼–½ in). **PROPAGATE** by cuttings or seeds. Fertile, moist, but well-drained soils in sunny to partially shaded places are preferred. It is often planted in borders, low hedges, or mass plantings and is popular in oriental gardens. In cold climates it is sometimes grown as a potted plant that is brought indoors in winter.

Rhapis ARECACEAE

Rhapis is a genus of 12 small, clump-forming palm species found from southern China to Malaysia, at least two of which are cultivated as ornamentals.

Rhapis excelsa (Thunberg) Henry ex Rehder
DISTINGUISHABLE by the clump forming, small palm habit, fan-shaped leaves with toothed or blunt tips, and stems covered by a fibrous mesh.

Rhapis excelsa, lady palm, sometimes called bamboo palm, is native to southern China and Japan but is widely cultivated elsewhere in the tropics and subtropics as an ornamental. Walking canes are sometimes made from the thin stems. **PALM** to 3 m high (10 ft) or more, dioecious, clump forming, with stems covered by a fibrous network of leaf sheaths. **LEAVES** simple, alternate, blade fan-shaped, usually 25–50 cm in diameter (10–20 in) with the margins cut to the base into 4 to 14 narrow pinnae blunt or toothed at the tips. **FLOWERS** intermittently and infrequently during the year but the flowers are inconspicuous, unisexual, many, borne on axillary panicles to 30 cm long (12 in). Corolla of three triangular yellow petals 4–6 mm long (about ¼ in). **FRUIT** a white subglobose drupe, infrequently formed in cultivation. **PROPAGATE** by suckers formed at the base. Fertile, moist soils in shaded or partially places are preferred. This hardy palm is one of the most commonly

Rhapis excelsa

grown tub plants indoors and out and is frequently planted to form hedges or screens. Many cultivars have been named, mostly from Japan, where growing them is practically a national horticultural pastime.

Rondeletia RUBIACEAE

Rondeletia is a tropical American genus of about 125 shrubs and tree species, several of which are cultivated as ornamentals for their colorful flowers.

Rondeletia odorata Jacquin

DISTINGUISHABLE by the opposite leaves, interpetiolar stipules, convex leaf surface, and compact panicles of five-lobed red flowers with orange in the center. It is similar to some red ixoras, which, however, mostly have a thinner tube, four petals, and lack orange in the center.

Rondeletia odorata, lacking a widely recognized common name, is native to Cuba but is widely if not commonly cultivated for its red and orange flowers. **SHRUB** to 3 m high (10 ft) or more with interpetiolar stipules. **LEAVES** simple, opposite, blade usually elliptic, 4–10 cm long (1⅝–4 in), leathery, scabrous on upper surface, margins revolute. **FLOWERS** continuously through the year; flowers many, borne in terminal panicles of cymes, not fragrant as the scientific name would imply. Corolla with fused petals, funnel-shaped, tube 1.2–2 cm long (½–¾ in), divided into five rounded, reflexed lobes 4–6 mm long (about ¼ in), red with orange in the center. **FRUIT** a globose capsule 3–4 mm long (about ⅛–¼ in). **PROPAGATE** by

Rondeletia odorata

cuttings. Fertile, moist, but well-drained soils in sunny places are pre-ferred. It is usually grown standing alone or in hedges but because it is difficult to grow it is not very frequent in cultivation. It is similar to but much less popular than species of *Ixora*, though equally as attractive.

Rosa ROSACEAE

Rosa is a genus of about 100 shrub species found mostly in northern temperate regions. Many are cultivated for their fragrant flowers, and some for making attar of roses and perfumes. Numerous cultivars have been selected and hybrids made, many with numerous petals instead of the normal five of wild roses. Roses, as a group, do not thrive in the tropics, but several kinds are occasionally cultivated.

Rosa ×*damascena* Miller

DISTINGUISHABLE by the shrubby ha-bit, thorny stems, pinnately com-pound leaves, leaflets with toothed margins, and small rose flowers with many petals.

Rosa ×*damascena*, damask rose, is one of the numerous roses that have resulted from hybridization, and it is widely cultivated in the tropics and subtropics. SHRUB to 1.5 m high (5 ft) with thorny stems. LEAVES odd-pin-nately compound, alternate, leaflets mostly five to nine, blades ovate to elliptic, 1–6 cm long (⅜–2½ in) with toothed margins. FLOWERS continu-ously through the year; flowers one to four, borne in terminal clusters. Co-rolla of many free obovate petals 1–2

Rosa ×*damascena*

cm long (⅜–¾ in), red or white. **FRUIT** not forming. **PROPAGATE** by cuttings and grafting. It is adaptable to most soils in sunny places and is often planted next to houses and as a border. It is also used for cut flowers.

Roystonea ARECACEAE

Roystonea is a genus of six to ten palm species found in areas bordering the Caribbean, several cultivated as ornamentals or for their edible palm hearts (terminal buds) or for both purposes. The genus was named after General Roy Stone, an American engineer in Puerto Rico.

Roystonea regia (Kunth) O. F. Cook

Synonym, *Oreodoxa regia* Kunth. **DISTINGUISHABLE** by the tall palm habit, the trunk bottle-shaped and swollen above the base, pinnately compound leaves, and a distinct green crownshaft. A similar palm, *Roystonea oleracea* (Jacquin) O. F. Cook, cabbage palm, is grown as an ornamental and for the edible palm hearts, and differs in having the trunk thickest at the base.

Roystonea regia, royal palm, sometimes called Cuba royal palm, is native to Cuba but is widely cultivated throughout the tropics and subtropics, especially as a stately street palm because of its tall, straight trunk and gracefully arching fronds. In its native range the leaves and trunks are used for building materials. **PALM** to 25 m high (82 ft), monoecious, usually thicker in the middle than at the top or bottom, with a distinct elongate crownshaft and plumose crown. **LEAVES** pinnately compound, alternate, blades narrowly oblong, to 4 m long (13 ft) with numerous leaflets borne in two ranks. **FLOWERS** anytime during the year; flowers many, in large panicles borne below the crownshaft, enclosed before maturity in a cylindrical spathe to 1 m long (3¼ ft). Corolla of three ovate petals 4–6 mm long (about ¼ in) united at the base. **FRUIT** a dull red to purple subglobose drupe 8–13 mm long (¼–½ in). **PROPAGATE** by seeds. Moist, well-drained soils in sunny places are preferred. It is one of the most popular palms but its large size precludes it from being grown for long in the greenhouse outside the tropics. It is

Roystonea regia

best viewed at a distance for full appreciation and is thus not suited to small yards.

Russelia SCROPHULARIACEAE

Russelia is a genus of 40 to 50 tropical American shrub and subshrub species, several cultivated as ornamentals.

Russelia equisetiformis Schlechter & Chamisso

DISTINGUISHABLE by the shrubby habit, drooping branches, tiny bract-like leaves in whorls at the axils, and red tubular flowers five-lobed at the tip. The flowers are very similar to those of *Odontonema tubiforme*, which is easily distinguished by its broad rather than scale-like leaves.

Russelia equisetiformis, coral plant, sometimes called fountain bush or firecracker plant, is native to Mexico but is widely cultivated as a novelty for its distinctive habit, with mostly leafless stems, and for its small, attractive, red flowers. **SHRUB**, spreading, to 1.5 m high (5 ft) with numerous green, drooping, angular stems. **LEAVES** simple, arranged in whorls of five to eight, blade usually reduced to linear scales but sometimes ovate to elliptic, 1–2.5 cm long (⅜–1 in). **FLOWERS** continuously through the year; flowers borne in whorls of one to four in loose, stalked cymes at the leaf axils. Corolla with fused petals, tubular, 1.5–2.5 cm long (⅝–1 in), shallowly five-lobed at the tip, bright red. **FRUIT** a subglobose capsule, infrequently formed in cultivation. **PROPAGATE** by air layering where the stems touch the ground or by cuttings. Fertile, sandy soils in sunny places are

Russelia equisetiformis

preferred. Because it is mostly leafless it is adapted to dry places and is often grown in shrub borders and rock gardens in the tropics, and in pots or hanging baskets in temperate areas. Periodic pruning is needed to keep it in shape.

Salix SALICACEAE

Salix is a genus of 300 to 500 tree and shrub species found mostly in sub-arctic and temperate regions, collectively known as willows. They are used for timber, pulp, and medicines. The bark of many contains salicin, a natural analgesic and the precursor of aspirin. Some are culti-vated as ornamentals, mostly in temperate climates.

Salix babylonica Linnaeus

DISTINGUISHABLE by the tree habit, branches that are long and droop-ing, and leaves that are narrow, curved, and alternate.

Salix babylonica, weeping willow, is native to somewhere in Asia but is widely cultivated in warm temperate to tropical regions because of its dis-tinctive drooping branches. Thus it is not a tropical plant but a warm tem-perate plant cultivated in the tropics. TREE to 8 m high (26 ft) or more with graceful drooping branches almost reaching the ground. LEAVES simple, alternate, blade curved-linear, 8–14 cm long (3½–6 in), margins toothed. FLOWERS anytime during the year but the flowers are inconspicuous, unisex-ual on separate male and female trees, in short, hanging catkins borne on short branches. Corolla and calyx ab-sent. FRUIT a capsule, infrequently

Salix babylonica

formed in cultivation. **Propagate** by cuttings. Moist but well-drained soils in sunny places are preferred but the plant is often grown in wet places, such as along the margins of streams or lakes. It is often grown by itself as a specimen plant, often near ponds where the branches can overhang the water for the most picturesque effect. Its proclivity to seek out and clog drain pipes is a problem.

Salvia LAMIACEAE

Salvia is a genus of 550 to 900 species found throughout the world, many grown for their aromatic leaves (also used for fragrance and in cooking), medicinal uses, and ornamental flowers. The name *Salvia* is from the Latin word meaning to save or heal, referring to the reputed healing properties of the plants.

Salvia splendens Sello ex J. A. Schultes

Distinguishable by the herbaceous habit, four-angled stems, heart-shaped leaves, terminal racemes bearing whorls of flowers, and usually red, sometimes purple or pink, two-lipped corolla with matching calyx. The similar *Salvia coccinea* B. Jussieu ex Murray, red sage, often found as a weed, differs in having a shorter corolla and a greenish calyx.

Salvia splendens with matching red calyx and corolla

Salvia splendens, scarlet sage, is native to southern Brazil but is widely cultivated in the tropics and warm temperate areas for its scarlet, purple, or pink flowers and sometimes escapes or becomes naturalized in disturbed areas. **Herb,** perennial, to 2 m high (6½ ft) or more, often much shorter, with aromatic foliage and square stems. **Leaves** simple, opposite, blade ovate,

Salvia splendens 'Atropurpurea' with purplish flowers

Salvia coccinea with green calyx and red corolla

4–12 cm long (1⅝–5 in), margins shallowly toothed. **FLOWERS** continuously through the year; flowers borne in whorls of two to six in terminal racemes. Corolla with fused petals, two-lipped, 3–5 cm long (1¼–2 in), scarlet or less commonly white, violet, or pink, with a similarly colored calyx. **FRUIT** of four small nutlets borne within the calyx. **PROPAGATE** by seeds. Fertile, well-drained soils in sunny places are preferred. It is often grown in gardens, along borders, or in mass plantings for its colorful flowers. The common red plant is sometimes called variety *splendens,* purple sage is 'Atropurpurea', and many other cultivars have been named.

Samanea FABACEAE

Samanea is a tropical American genus of about 18 tree species, some used for timber or as ornamentals. Some authors include the genus in *Albizia,* a much larger genus.

Samanea saman (Jacquin) Merrill

Synonyms, *Albizia saman* (Jacquin) F. von Mueller and *Pithecellobium saman* (Jacquin) Bentham. **DISTINGUISHABLE** by the huge, spreading tree habit, bipinnately compound leaves, flat-topped heads of flowers bearing conspicuous red stamens, and sausage-shaped pods persisting on the tree.

Samanea saman, monkeypod tree, sometimes called saman, is native from Mexico to Brazil but is widely cultivated as an ornamental. The leaves close up at night, also during rain, hence another common name, rain tree. The good quality wood is often used for carving, especially in making handicrafts, the pods are used as cattle food, and the seeds are used in seed leis. **TREE**, spreading, to 25 m high (82 ft) with rough, fissured bark. **LEAVES** bipinnately compound, alternate, with four to seven pinnae, each pinna bearing two to eight pairs of leaflets, blades ovate to obovate, 1.5–6 cm long (⅝–2½ in), dark green. **FLOW-**

Samanea saman

ERS seasonally, mostly in spring and summer; flowers many, borne in axillary, flat-topped heads. Corolla funnel-shaped, of five fused petals 7–12 mm long (¼–½ in), pink with greenish or yellow tips, and many red stamens 2–3.5 cm long (¾–1⅜ in). **FRUIT** a sausage-shaped pod 6–20 cm long (2½–8 in) with thickened seams. **PROPAGATE** by scarified seeds or cuttings. Fertile, moist, but well-drained soils in sunny places are preferred. It is particularly popular as a tropical street, park, and shade tree because of its large, spreading crown, attractive, dark green foliage, and red flowers. The tree is so large and has such an extensive surface root system that it is not recom-

Samanea saman, the spreading crown providing shade

mended for small lots. Leaves may fall in winter, leaving only the persistent pods on the tree.

Sambucus CAPRIFOLIACEAE

Sambucus is a genus of 20 to 25 shrub and small tree species found in temperate and subtropical America and Europe. Some are utilized for their edible fruits, including elderberry, *S. canadensis* Linnaeus, which are used for pies, jellies, and wines, and some are cultivated as ornamentals.

Sambucus mexicana Presl ex A. L. P. P. de Candolle

DISTINGUISHABLE by the shrubby habit, leaves that are opposite and pinnately compound, toothed leaflet margins, and large, flat-topped cymes of small, white, four- or five-lobed flowers.

Sambucus mexicana

Sambucus mexicana, Mexican elder, is native to Texas and Mexico but is widely cultivated in tropical to warm temperate regions for its large, dense inflorescences of tiny white flowers. TREE to 5 m high (16½ ft) or more. LEAVES odd-pinnately compound, opposite, leaflets five to nine, rarely three, blades elliptic to lanceolate or ovate, 4–11 cm long (1⅝–4½ in), subsessile, margins toothed. FLOWERS continuously through the year in the tropics; flowers numerous, borne in large, many-branched, flat-topped terminal cymes. Corolla of fused petals, rotate, 5–9 mm wide (¼–⅜ in), deeply divided into four or five spreading elliptic lobes, white. FRUIT a purplish black globose berry 5–8 mm long (about ¼ in). PROPAGATE by cuttings. Fertile, moist, but well-drained soils in sunny or partially shaded places are preferred. It is usually planted as a specimen plant or is grown in the garden border, and it is reported to be naturalized in some places, Hawaii, for example.

Sanchezia ACANTHACEAE

Sanchezia is a genus of 20 to 30 tropical American shrub species, at least one of which is cultivated as an ornamental.

Sanchezia speciosa Leonard

Synonym, *Sanchezia nobilis* J. D. Hooker. DISTINGUISHABLE by the shrubby habit, four-angled stems, opposite leaves with yellow veins, and spikes of tubular orange flowers borne among orange to red bracts.

Sanchezia speciosa, which lacks a widely recognized common name, is native to tropical South America but is widely cultivated as a colorful ornamental shrub for both its flowers and foliage. **SHRUB** to 3 m high (10 ft) with four-angled stems. **LEAVES** simple, opposite, blade oblong to elliptic, 10–40 cm long (4–16 in), green or with yellow veins. **FLOWERS** continuously through the year; flowers several, borne in clusters on an erect terminal spike sometimes divided at the base, with an ovate orange to red bract below each flower cluster. Corolla of fused petals, tubular, 4.5–5.5 cm long (1¾–2¼ in) with five short, rounded lobes, yellow to orange, bearing oblanceolate orange

Sanchezia speciosa

sepals half as long, two protruding stamens. **FRUIT** a narrowly cylindrical capsule, infrequently formed in cultivation. **PROPAGATE** by cuttings. Light, sandy, moist but well-drained soils in partially shaded, humid areas are preferred. The attractive inflorescences with contrasting red and orange and the dark green leaves with striking yellow veins make it popular as a hedge, screen, or border plant, and it is sometimes grown in tubs. Stalks that have finished flowering should be cut back to obtain a denser form and to keep the plant low.

Sansevieria AGAVACEAE

Sansevieria is a genus of 50 to 60 succulent herb species found from tropical Africa to southern Asia. Some are cultivated for their leaf fibers (African bowstring hemp), used to make rope, sails, and paper, and some as ornamentals for their attractive leaves.

Sansevieria trifasciata Prain

Synonym, *Sansevieria guineensis* (Jacquin) Willdenow. **DISTINGUISH-ABLE** by the creeping underground rhizome and leaves that are stiff, erect, basal, sword-shaped, and have mottled surfaces or white margins. Another species occasionally cultivated, *S. cylindrica* Bojer, has long, narrow, and cylindrical rather than flat leaves.

Sansevieria trifasciata, bowstring hemp, sometimes called mother-in-law's tongue, is native to tropical Africa but is widely cultivated in the tropics and subtropics for its erect, strap-shaped, variegated leaves. Fibers extracted from the leaves are used to make twine, mats, and as the common name implies, bowstrings. **HERB**, stemless, arising from a creeping underground rhizome. **LEAVES** simple, borne in fascicles of one to six, typically two or three, from the rhizome, erect, blade linear-lanceolate, sessile, usually 50–100 × 1.5–9 cm (20–40 × ⅝–3½ in), var-

Sansevieria trifasciata var. *trifasciata* without white leaf margins, growing with *S. trifasciata* 'Laurentii' with white margins

iegated, stiff and succulent with an acute tip. **FLOWERS** intermittently during the year; flowers many, fragrant, borne in clusters in basal racemes or narrow panicles 25–75 cm long (10–30 in), arising among the leaves. Corolla with fused tepals, tubular, 1.5–2.8 cm long (⅝–1⅛ in), divided more than halfway into six linear segments, greenish white, fragrant. **FRUIT** an orange one- to three-seeded globose berry 7–10 mm in diameter (¼–⅜ in). **PROPAGATE** by division. Well-drained soils in sunny or partially shaded places are preferred. Bright sunlight may lead to bleaching of the leaf colors. It is often planted as a ground cover, border plant, or hardy potted plant that requires little care, the latter especially in temperate climates where it is a popular greenhouse subject or house-plant. Many naturally occurring varieties or cultivars are recognized, the two most common of which are variety *trifasciata* with irregular, lighter colored, transverse bands, and 'Laurentii' with yellow margins.

Saraca FABACEAE

Saraca is a genus of 8 to 11 tree or shrub species found from India to Indonesia, several cultivated for their flowers. The asoka, *S. asoka* (Roxburgh) W. J. J. O. de Wilde, is traditionally believed to be the tree under which Buddha was born.

Saraca indica Linnaeus

DISTINGUISHABLE by the tree habit, alternate, pinnately compound leaves, short-stalked leaflets, and dense panicles of red flowers that lack a corolla but have a red stalk and four red calyx lobes surrounding the eight stamens. Another species occasionally cultivated, *Saraca declinata* Miquel, differs in having stalked leaves, and leaflet stalks at least 5 mm long (¼ in).

Saraca indica, sorrowless tree, is native to southern and Southeast Asia but is widely if not commonly cultivated in the tropics as a shade or small garden tree and for its red and orange flowers. TREE to 10 m high (33 ft). LEAVES even-pinnately compound, alternate, leaflets in three to five pairs with the lowest pair nearly at the base of the petiole, blades elliptic to narrowly so, 10–35 cm long (4–14 in), petiole less than 8 mm long (¼ in). FLOWERS anytime during the year; flowers many, in short, dense, terminal panicles or on short branches

Saraca indica

at the base of a leaf, each flower on a stalk 2–3 cm long (¾–1¼ in) that looks like a corolla tube and bears a small red or orange bract that looks like a calyx. Corolla absent but flowers with four petal-like, elliptic to obovate, orange or red sepals 7–12 mm long (¼–½ in), with eight long, equal stamens in the center. FRUIT a flattened, black, oblong to elliptic pod usually 5–13 cm long (2–5 in). PROPAGATE by air layering and scarified seeds, but the seeds do not always breed true. Fertile, moist, but well-drained soils in partially shaded places are preferred.

Scadoxus AMARYLLIDACEAE

Scadoxus is a genus of nine herbaceous African species, some cultivated for their attractive red flowers.

Scadoxus multiflorus (Martyn) Rafinesque

Synonym, *Haemanthus multiflorus* Martyn. DISTINGUISHABLE by the bulbs, leaves that are basal and spirally arranged, seasonal flowers borne in hemispheric umbels, and prominent red to pink stamens.

Scadoxus multiflorus

Scadoxus multiflorus, blood lily, is native to tropical Africa but is widely if not commonly cultivated for its red inflorescences that look like powder puffs, hence another common name, powder-puff lily. The flowers, which turn pink as they age and last about a week, are seasonal and appear on the plant just before the leaves come out. After the growing season the plant reverts to a leafless bulb until the next flowering season, so the plant is inconspicuous or unseen most of the year. It is often grown in garden borders and as a houseplant; it is poisonous to livestock. **Herb**, perennial, arising from a bulb. **Leaves** spirally arranged, blade elliptic to oblanceolate, usually 15–35 cm long (6–14 in), lacking a distinct midvein, glabrous, with a winged, clasping petiole. **Flowers** seasonally, mostly in summer; flowers many, borne in a dense, round to hemispheric umbel 12–20 cm in diameter (5–8 in) on a scape usually 30–75 cm long (12–30 in). Corolla of six red, fading to pink, linear tepals 3.5–5 cm long (1⅜–2 in), joined for their bottom third, with six long, protruding stamens with red filaments. **Fruit** a red one- to three-seeded berry. **Propagate** by bulbs and offsets. Well-drained soils in sunny places are preferred.

Schefflera ARALIACEAE

Schefflera comprises 125 to 450 tree, shrub, and epiphyte species, or according to some authors as many as 900 depending on how related genera are treated, found throughout tropical and subtropical regions. Some are cultivated as ornamentals for their leaves, including the two ornamental species included here.

Schefflera actinophylla (Endlicher) Harms
Synonym, *Brassaia actinophylla* Endlicher. **Distinguishable** by the tree habit, large, palmately compound leaves, sheathing petiole bases, and red flowers borne on 10 to 14 long, spreading inflorescence branches.

Schefflera actinophylla is native to Australia and New Guinea but is widely cultivated as an ornamental. It is often grown as a specimen plant, giving a tropical look to the area, and as a potted plant, indoors in cooler climates, because of its attractive, unusual, palmately lobed leaves and distinctive red, radiating inflorescence branches. The inflorescence branches lead to the common names, octopus tree or umbrella tree. **Tree** to 10 m high (33 ft), beginning as an epiphyte or strangler with sheathing leaf bases. **Leaves** alternate, palmately compound into 5 to 16 leaflets, blades elliptic to ovate, the largest ones 10–30 cm long (4–12 in). **Flowers** anytime during the year; flowers sessile, borne in heads of 10 to 14 arranged on many long, terminal, paniculate branch-

Schefflera actinophylla

es. Corolla of five free, small, ovate, red, deciduous petals 4–6 mm long (about ¼ in). **Fruit** a small black drupe fused to others to make a sub-globose multiple fruit 6–10 mm long (¼–⅜ in). **Propagate** by seeds, cuttings, or air layering. Fertile, moist, but well-drained soils in sunny to shaded places are preferred. Pruning is needed if the plant is to be kept small. Seeds are readily dispersed by birds and the tree can become naturalized in forests, as it has in Fiji and Hawaii, for example, and as a weed of disturbed areas.

Schefflera arboricola (Hayata) Hayata

Distinguishable by the shrubby habit, sheathing petiole bases, and alternate, palmately compound leaves with six to nine oblanceolate leaflets. It is similar to *Schefflera actinophylla* when not flowering but differs in being shrubby and having smaller leaflets.

Schefflera arboricola, dwarf umbrella tree, sometimes called dwarf schefflera, is native to Taiwan but is widely cultivated for its attractive foliage, similar to but smaller than that of *S. actinophylla*. **Shrub** to 4 m high (13 ft) with sheathing petiole bases. **Leaves** alternate, palmately compound into six to nine leaflets, blades oblanceolate, 3–11 cm long (1¼–4½ in), leathery, dark glossy green. **Flowers** intermittently during the year but infrequently in cultivation; flowers 5 to 12 in umbels borne on long, spreading branches of a terminal panicle to 35 cm long (14 in). Corolla of five small yellow petals 3–4 mm long (about ⅛–¼ in) that fall early, with five protruding white stamens. **Fruit** a small orange drupe, infrequently formed in cultivation. **Propagate** by cuttings.

Schefflera arboricola

Moist but well-drained soils in sunny to shaded places are preferred. It is often grown in pots or as a hedge plant, sometimes as a bonsai plant, and often indoors, especially in cooler climates. Pruning is needed to keep the vigorous growth under control. A variegated cultivar, 'Variegata', is sometimes grown.

Senna FABACEAE

Senna, considered by some authors to be part of *Cassia,* comprises about 260 tree, shrub, and herb species native throughout tropical to warm temperate regions. It differs from *Cassia* most obviously in having splitting fruits and all its stamens with straight filaments. Many are cultivated as ornamentals, two of the most common of which are included here.

Senna alata (Linnaeus) Roxburgh

Synonym, *Cassia alata* Linnaeus. **DISTINGUISHABLE** by the shrubby habit, alternate, pinnately compound leaves with 6 to 13 pairs of large leaflets, erect racemes covered by orange to yellow bracts, five-parted yellow flowers, and transversely winged black pods.

Senna alata

Senna alata, candlebush, sometimes called ringworm bush or acapulco, is native to tropical America but is widely cultivated in the tropics to warm temperate regions for its yellow and orange flowers. The leaves contain prussic acid and are widely used medicinally to treat ringworm and other fungal skin infections. **SHRUB** to 4 m high (13 ft). **LEAVES** even-pinnately compound, alternate, with 6 to 13 pairs of leaflets, blades mostly oblong,

7–21 cm long (3–8 in), slightly notched at the tip. FLOWERS continuously through the year; flowers many, borne in terminal racemes, each flower with a prominent orange or yellow ovate bract below it. Corolla of five free, obovate to nearly round petals 1.3–2 cm long (½–¾ in). FRUIT a narrowly oblong, black, papery pod 12–20 cm long (5–8 in) with four wings extending its entire length. PROPAGATE by seeds or cuttings. Moist but well-drained soils in sunny places are preferred. It is sometimes grown in mass plantings to provide winter color, or by itself as a specimen plant. The plant occasionally becomes naturalized but does not readily spread.

Senna surattensis

Senna surattensis (N. L. Burman) Irwin & Barneby

Synonym, *Cassia surattensis* N. L. Burman. DISTINGUISHABLE by the small tree habit, alternate, pinnately compound leaves, six to ten pairs of leaflets waxy white on the lower surface, five-parted yellow flowers with ten stamens, and strap-shaped pods. A similar ornamental species, *Senna siamea* (Lamarck) Irwin & Barnaby (synonym, *Cassia siamea* Lamarck), kassod tree, differs in having smaller flowers 9–16 mm long (⅜–⅝ in) and larger fruits 18–30 cm long (7–12 in).

Senna siamea with smaller flowers

Senna surattensis, scrambled-eggs bush, sometimes called glaucous cassia and, in Hawaii, kolomona, is native to Australia or Southeast Asia but is widely cultivated for its yellow flowers. TREE, spreading, to 6 m high (20 ft) or more. LEAVES odd-pinnately compound, alternate, with 6 to 10 pairs of leaflets, blades obovate to elliptic, 1.5–5 cm long (⅝–2 in), waxy white (glaucous) on lower surface. FLOWERS continuously through the year; flowers several, borne in axillary racemes. Corolla of five free, ovate to oblong, yellow petals 1.2–2.7 cm long (½–1⅛ in), with ten subequal stamens in the center. FRUIT a membranous, strap-shaped pod 5–12 cm long (2–5 in). PROPAGATE by scarified seeds. Fertile, well-drained soils in sunny places are preferred. It is often grown by itself as a specimen plant, unlike many other species of its genus or the related *Cassia,* since it is too short to be used as a street tree. It sometimes becomes naturalized but does not readily spread.

Sesbania FABACEAE

Sesbania is a genus of about 50 herb, shrub, and tree species found throughout the tropics and subtropics. Some are utilized for fibers from the bark, medicines, food (edible flowers, pods, and leaves), and fodder, and some are cultivated as ornamentals.

Sesbania grandiflora (Linnaeus) Poiret

DISTINGUISHABLE by the small tree habit, alternate, pinnately compound leaves, axillary racemes of large, white or red, butterfly-like flowers, and long, hanging, linear pods.

Sesbania grandiflora, sesban, sometimes called vegetable hummingbird or scarlet wisteria, is possibly native to the islands and mainland of southeastern Asia, an area that used to be called Indo-Malaya, but has been widely cultivated so long that this is not certain. The flowers, young pods, and leaves are edible, as salad ingredients or boiled, and are also used for cattle fodder. The bark and leaves have been used medicinally in some places. TREE, short-lived, to 10 m high (33 ft). LEAVES even-pinnately compound, alternate, leaflets mostly in 15 to 20 pairs, blades oblong, 1.5–4 cm long (⅝–1⅝ in). **FLOWERS** continuously through the year; flowers two to four, borne in axillary racemes. Corolla papilionaceous, 6–10 cm long (2½–4 in), white to red, with four unequal free petals and ten fused stamens. **FRUIT** a hanging linear pod usually 30–60 cm long (12–24 in). **PROPAGATE** by scarified seeds. Fertile, moist soils in sunny places are preferred. The short-lived tree is usually grown for its white or red [*S. grandiflora* var. *coccinea* (Poiret) Persoon] flowers and is often planted in borders.

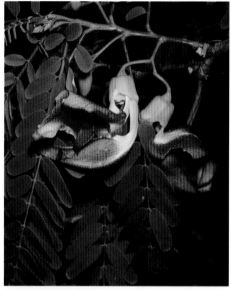

Sesbania grandiflora

Solandra SOLANACEAE

Solandra is a genus of eight to ten tropical American climbing shrub species, some used in Mexico as hallucinogens in sacred ceremonies, and some grown as ornamentals for their large, attractive flowers.

Solandra maxima (Sessé & Moçiño) P. S. Green

Synonyms, *Datura maxima* Sessé & Moçiño, *Solandra hartwegii* N. E. Brown, and sometimes misidentified as *S. nitida* Zuccarini. **DISTINGUISHABLE** by the viny habit, leaves that are large, alternate, and glossy green, and flowers that are large, funnel-shaped, and golden yellow with purple lines inside.

Solandra maxima, cup of gold, sometimes called chalice vine, is native to Mexico but is widely cultivated for its attractive, glossy foliage and large yellow flowers. The flowers, present for only part of the year, are poisonous to eat. **VINE-LIKE SHRUB** with stems reaching to 60 m long (200 ft) if not trimmed. **LEAVES** simple, alternate, blade usually broadly elliptic, 8–18 cm long (3½–7 in), glossy green. **FLOWERS** inter-

Solandra maxima

mittently during the year; flowers usually solitary, terminal on a thick stalk. Corolla with fused petals, funnel-shaped, 20–25 cm long (8–10 in) and 10–17 cm in diameter (4–7 in), shallowly five-lobed, golden yellow with five purple lines inside, fragrant. FRUIT a pulpy berry, infrequently formed in cultivation. PROPAGATE by cuttings. Fertile, moist, but well-drained soils in sunny places are preferred. It is often grown on walls, arches, or strong trellises in the tropics. In temperate areas it is grown in the greenhouse but pruning is needed to keep the vigorous growth under control.

Solanum SOLANACEAE

Solanum comprises about 1400 tree, shrub, vine, and herb species found throughout the world in tropical to temperate climates. The genus includes the potato, *S. tuberosum* Linnaeus, and eggplant, *S. melongena* Linnaeus, as well as many other food plants (edible roots, leaves, or fruits). Some are important weeds, and some are cultivated as ornamentals.

Solanum seaforthianum Andrews

DISTINGUISHABLE by the viny habit, alternate, pinnately lobed leaves, and drooping panicles of five-parted, blue to purple flowers with five sessile yellow stamens. A similar species, *Solanum wendlandii* J. D. Hooker, potato vine, differs mainly in having larger flowers and somewhat prickly stems, petioles, and midribs.

    Solanum seaforthianum, called star potato vine, Brazilian nightshade, or St. Vincent lilac, is native to the West Indies but is cultivated for its rather small but attractive purple flowers. Unripe fruits are poisonous to humans. VINE, climbing to 5 m high (16½ ft) or more, with glabrous stems. LEAVES pinnately divided, rarely simple, alternate, leaflets or lobes ovate to elliptic, 5–10 cm long (2–4 in), base unequal. FLOWERS anytime during the year; flowers many, borne in drooping, terminal and axillary panicles. Corolla with fused petals, star-shaped with five lobes 8–13 mm long (¼–½ in), blue or purple, with five yellow sessile stamens in the center. FRUIT a red globose berry 7–12 mm in diameter (¼–½ in). PROPAGATE by seeds and cuttings. Fertile, moist, but well-drained soils in partially shaded places are pre-

Solanum seaforthianum

ferred. Unlike most members of the genus, it is a vine and is often grown on trellises in the tropics and in the greenhouse in temperate climates. It is somewhat weedy and has become naturalized in some places.

Solenostemon LAMIACEAE

Solenostemon is a genus of 60 herb or subshrub species of the Old World tropics formerly included in *Coleus* or *Plectranthus*. Some are cultivated for their edible tubers, and some as ornamentals for their attractive leaves.

Solenostemon scutellarioides (Linnaeus) Codd

Synonyms, *Coleus blumei* Bentham, *C. scutellarioides* (Linnaeus) Bentham, *Plectranthus blumei* (Bentham) Launert, and *P. scutellarioides* (Linnaeus) R. Brown. DISTINGUISHABLE by the four-angled stems, opposite, often variously colored leaves, scalloped leaf margins, and small, blue to purple, two-lipped flowers in whorls in racemes or panicles.

Solenostemon scutellarioides

Solenostemon scutellarioides, coleus or variegated coleus, is native from India to China but is widely and commonly cultivated in gardens in the tropics and subtropics for its colorful foliage. Some green-leaved cultivars are used as spices in Southeast Asia. **Herb**, perennial, to 1.5 m high (5 ft) with square stems. **Leaves** simple, opposite, blade usually ovate, 3–15 cm long (1¼–6 in), margins scalloped, surface variously colored with green, purple, red, white, or all four colors. **Flowers** anytime during the year; flowers in whorls of 8 to 12 or more in terminal racemes or panicles of racemes. Corolla with fused petals, two-lipped, 8–13 mm long (¼–½ in), tube white, lips blue to purple. **Fruit** of small subglobose nutlets enclosed within the papery, strongly two-lipped calyx. **Propagate** by cuttings, which easily root in water, or seeds, often obtained in seed packets. Fertile, moist soils in sunny to partially shaded places are preferred but some shade leads to optimal leaf color. It is often grown as a border, potted, or hanging basket plant, and sometimes in mass plantings. In temperate areas it is a popular indoor potted plant. It is extremely variable in the size, shape, and color of the leaves, with more than 200 cultivars named, having foliage described as antlered, parsley-leaved, fringed, fingered, or fern-leaved.

Solidago ASTERACEAE

Solidago, the genus of goldenrods, includes more than 100 species found mostly in North America, many invasive and weedy but some medicinal, and some cultivated as ornamentals for their colorful inflorescences.

Solidago nemoralis Aiton

DISTINGUISHABLE by the large herbaceous habit, leaves that are narrow, alternate, and grayish green, and large axillary panicles of tiny yellow flower heads. A similar cultivated species, *Solidago canadensis* Linnaeus, has wider leaves, mostly more than 10 mm wide (⅜ in) versus 5–8 mm (about ¼ in), three-veined most of their length.

Solidago nemoralis is a goldenrod native to temperate North America but is widely cultivated in temperate and tropical regions for its large inflorescences of yellow flower heads. HERB, coarse, to 2 m high (6½ ft) or more. LEAVES simple, alternate, blade narrowly elliptic, 3–10 cm × 5–8 mm (1¼–4 × about ¼ in) but smaller in the flowering part of the plant, grayish green and short-pubescent on both surfaces, one-nerved and pinnately veined. FLOWERS anytime during the year after maturity in the tropics; flowers many, borne in small heads arranged in narrow axillary panicles and surrounded by several series of bracts. Ray florets several in one series, 2.5–4 mm long (about ⅛–¼ in), yellow. Disk florets several, yellow. FRUIT a narrowly ovoid achene with many bristles on top. PROPAGATE by achenes. The plant is fairly adaptable to various soils and light conditions. It is often planted in gardens and borders.

Solidago nemoralis

Spathiphyllum ARACEAE

Spathiphyllum is a genus of about 36 rhizomatous perennial herbaceous species found in tropical America and from Malaysia to the Solomon Islands, many cultivated for their *Anthurium*-like spathe-and-spadix inflorescences.

Spathiphyllum wallisii Regel

DISTINGUISHABLE by the stemless habit, elliptic basal leaves, and white leaf-like spathe below the white spadix.

Spathiphyllum wallisii is an aroid, sometimes called spathe flower but with no well-known common name other than that of the genus, native to Panama and Costa Rica. It is widely cultivated for its white spathes. All parts of the plant can cause stomach problems if ingested, and the sap may be irritating to the skin. **HERB**, erect, stemless, to 80 cm high (32 in) or more. **LEAVES** simple, alternate, basal, blade usually elliptic, 15–50 cm long (6–20 in) on a petiole of similar length. **FLOWERS** continuously through the year; flowers many, borne densely packed in a white cylindrical spadix 3–11 cm long (1¼–4½ in) with a concave, white, leaf-like, attenuate spathe attached at the base, 8–18 cm long (3½–7 in). **FRUIT** a white berry, infrequently formed in cultivation. **PROPAGATE** by division, seeds, or tissue culture. Fertile, moist soils in partially shaded places are preferred. It is often grown in borders, as a ground cover, or as a potted plant in the tropics, and is grown in greenhouses and conservatories in temperate climates. The most common cultivar, 'Clevelandii', is obscure in origin but is probably a hybrid resulting from a cross between two tropical American species.

Spathiphyllum 'Clevelandii', probably a hybrid involving *S. wallisii*

Spathodea BIGNONIACEAE

Spathodea is a genus of one tree species native to tropical Africa though some authors recognize *S. nilotica* as a separate species.

Spathodea campanulata Palisot de Beauvois

Synonym, *Spathodea nilotica* Seemann. **DISTINGUISHABLE** by the large tree habit, opposite, pinnately compound leaves, flowers that are large, orange, boat-shaped, and tulip-like, and woody capsules containing numerous winged seeds.

Spathodea campanulata, African tulip tree, sometimes called flame of the forest, is native to tropical Africa but is widely cultivated for its dense clusters of large, orange, bell-shaped flowers. In many places children squeeze the unopened buds to produce a stream of water like that from a squirt gun. A drawback to its cultivation is that it can escape from cultivation and become naturalized in native forests, in Hawaii, for example, spreading by means of windblown seeds. **TREE** to 15 m high (50 ft) or more. **LEAVES** odd-pinnately compound, opposite, leaflets 9 to 19, blades ovate to obovate, 7–13 cm long (3–5 in). **FLOWERS** continuously through the year; flowers many, borne in short, dense, terminal racemes, each flower with a curved, golden brown, boat-like calyx. Corolla of fused petals, irregularly bell-shaped, 10–14 cm long (4–6 in), bright orange, rarely yellow. **FRUIT** a narrow woody capsule 15–22 cm long (6–9 in), opening along two seams to re-lease the numerous winged seeds. **PROPAGATE** by seeds, but not breeding true for 'Kona

Spathodea campanulata

Gold', or stem or root cuttings. Fertile, well-drained soils in sunny places are preferred. It is often planted as a street, park, or shade tree and requires little attention once established. The trees often become hollow and hazardous with age, and planting them next to buildings is not recommended. 'Kona Gold' is a cultivar with yellow flowers.

Spathoglottis ORCHIDACEAE

Spathoglottis is a genus of about 40 to 60 terrestrial orchid species ranging from northern India to Polynesia, many cultivated as outdoor ornamentals for their attractive flowers.

Spathoglottis plicata Blume

Distinguishable by the large, basal, pleated leaves, terminal racemes of pink flowers with five similar tepals, and a yellow, nearly glabrous swelling, the callus, on the labellum. Another species frequent in cultivation, *Spathoglottis unguiculata* (Labillardière) Reichenbach fil., differs in being shorter and having the yellow callus strongly hairy.

Spathoglottis plicata

Spathoglottis plicata, Philippine ground orchid, is native from Southeast Asia to Polynesia but is widely cultivated in the tropics as a hardy outdoor ornamental. **Herb,** terrestrial, erect, to 1 m high (3¼ ft), arising from an ovoid rhizome. **Leaves** simple, basal, several, blade linear-lanceolate, usually 30–90 cm long (12–36 in), plicate. **Flowers** continuously through the year; flowers many, borne in a terminal raceme 30–100 cm long (12–40 in) on a leafless stalk. Corolla of five similar elliptic tepals 1.5–3 cm long (⅝–1¼ in), dark purple to pink, rarely white, with a narrowly spoon-shaped labellum of similar length with a yellow, sparsely hairy swelling, the callus, at the base. FRUIT a cylindrical capsule 3.5–4 cm long (1⅜–1⅝ in). PROPAGATE by division or seeds. Fertile, moist, but well-drained soils in shaded places are preferred. It often becomes naturalized, unusual for orchids, where it is introduced.

Stachytarpheta VERBENACEAE

Stachytarpheta is a genus of 60 to 100 species of tropical and subtropical America, many of them widespread weeds but some cultivated as ornamentals for their small, colorful flowers. The name *Stachytarpheta* is from the Greek words meaning thick spike, aptly describing the rat's tail inflorescence.

Stachytarpheta mutabilis (Jacquin) Vahl

DISTINGUISHABLE by the subshrub habit, opposite, pubescent leaves, toothed leaf margins, and narrow terminal spikes bearing small, pink, five-lobed flowers.

Stachytarpheta mutabilis, pink snake-weed, is native from Mexico to Brazil but is widely if not commonly cultivated in the tropics for its pink flowers. SUBSHRUB to 2 m high (6½ ft) or more. LEAVES simple, opposite, blade usually ovate, 5–20 cm long (2–8 in), margins toothed, surface densely pubescent, petiole winged. FLOWERS continuously through the year; flowers many, embedded in narrow, elongate, terminal spikes, each looking like a rat's tail, to 70 cm long (28 in) or more. Corolla with fused petals, curved, salverform tube 1.5–2.2 cm long (⅝–⅞ in) with the five rounded lobes forming the spreading limb 1–1.7 cm wide (⅜–¾ in),

Stachytarpheta mutabilis

usually pink but sometimes red or purple. **Fruit** a two-seeded schizo-carp embedded in the rachis. **Propagate** by seeds. Moist but well-drained soils in sunny places are preferred. It is often grown by itself as a specimen plant, or in borders, but is unsuitable for hedges since it a subshrub and tends to become scraggly. Although many other species of *Stachytarpheta* are aggressive weeds, that does not seem to be a problem with *S. mutabilis*.

Stapelia ASCLEPIADACEAE

Stapelia, the genus of carrion flowers, comprises 45 to 50 herbaceous, often succulent and leafless species widely distributed in the tropics. Many are cultivated for their showy but fetid flowers, attractive to pollinating flies whose maggots eat carrion.

Stapelia gigantea N. E. Brown

Stapelia gigantea

Synonym, *Stapelia nobilis* N. E. Brown. **Distinguishable** by the leafless habit, erect, purplish, four-ridged stems with soft spines at the angles, flowers that are large, solitary, star-shaped, and yellow with transverse crimson lines, and pods bearing numerous silky seeds.

Stapelia gigantea is a carrion flower native to South Africa but widely cultivated as a succulent and as a novelty for its large, unusual, foul-smelling flowers. Their odor and color, something like that of carrion, attract pollinating flies looking for a place to lay their eggs. When sterile, plants can confused with cacti, which are entirely unrelated and usually spiny. **Succulent** perennial herb branching at the base with purplish, finely pubescent, cylindrical, vertically four-ridged stems to 40 cm high (16 in), bearing soft spines on the margins, sap clear unlike most members of the milkweed family Asclepiadaceae. **Leaves** absent. **Flowers** anytime during the year; flowers solitary or paired, axillary. Corolla of fused petals, stellate, 16–40 cm in diameter (6–16 in), divided about halfway into five triangular, attenuate lobes, purple on the outside, yellow with crimson transverse lines and purple hairs, foul smelling. **Fruit** a pair of follicles 10–20 cm long (4–8 in), containing numerous silky-tufted seeds. **Propagate** by seeds. Dry soils in sunny places are preferred. Because of the silky-tufted seeds, the plant sometimes become weedy or naturalized in arid places, as in parts of Hawaii.

Stemmadenia APOCYNACEAE

Stemmadenia is a genus of 20 tropical American tree and shrub species, several cultivated for their attractive flowers.

Stemmadenia litoralis (Kunth) Allorge

Synonym, *Stemmadenia galeottiana* (A. Richard) Miers. **Distinguishable** by the small tree habit, milky sap, opposite leaves, and large funnel-shaped flowers. It is similar to *Tabernaemontana divaricata* but has much larger flowers that always have five lobes.

Stemmadenia litoralis, lecheso, is native to central America but is widely if not commonly cultivated for its relatively large, attractive, white, fragrant flowers. The sap is reported to be poisonous, characteristic of many other members of the family Apocynaceae, aptly named the dogbane family. **Tree**

Stemmadenia litoralis

to 8 m high (26 ft) with milky sap. LEAVES simple, opposite, blade elliptic, usually 10–24 cm long (4–9 in), glossy green. FLOWERS continuously through the year; flowers several, borne in short terminal clusters,
often appearing axillary, each flower with five rounded calyx lobes
1–1.8 cm long (⅜–¾ in), fragrant. Corolla of fused petals, funnel-
shaped, 7–9 cm long (3–3½ in), limb 5–10 cm wide (2–4 in) with five
rounded lobes, white with yellow inside. FRUIT a pair of spreading,
orange, ovoid, capsule-like segments 2.5–5 cm long (1–2 in). PROPA-
GATE by cuttings. Moist but well-drained soils in sunny places are preferred. It is often grown as a tall border plant but not usually as a hedge
since it is more a tree than a shrub.

Stephanotis ASCLEPIADACEAE

Stephanotis is a genus of 5 to 15 vine-like shrub species widespread in
the Old World tropics. The name *Stephanotis* is from the Greek words
meaning crown and ear, referring to the shape of the corona of stamens
of some species.

Stephanotis floribunda Brongniart

Synonym, *Marsdenia floribunda* (Brongniart) Schlechter, a name used
by some authors. DISTINGUISHABLE by the viny habit, clear sap, opposite leaves, and short-stalked clusters of three to eight fragrant, pure
white, funnel-shaped flowers.

  Stephanotis floribunda, Madagascar jasmine, a misnomer since the
plant is not related to *Jasminum,* is native to Madagascar but is widely
cultivated for its waxy white, fragrant flowers used in leis, wreaths, and
other decorations. The flowers, with a long-tubed corolla, are not typical of the milkweed family Asclepiadaceae. Some authors include the
species in *Marsdenia,* a genus of more than 100 species. VINE-LIKE
SHRUB, twining, with clear sap. LEAVES simple, opposite, blade oblong
to elliptic, usually 4–10 cm long (1⅝–4 in), glabrous. FLOWERS continuously through the year; flowers mostly three to eight in stalked clus-

ters arising between the petiole pairs. Corolla of fused petals, funnel-shaped, usually 4–5.5 cm long (1⅝–2¼ in) with five rounded, spreading lobes, waxy white or tinted pink. FRUIT an ovoid to elliptic follicle 8–15 cm long (3½–6 in) filled with silky-tufted seeds. PROPAGATE by cuttings, air layering, or seeds. Fertile, moist, but well-drained soils in sunny places are preferred. The plant is cultivated outdoors on trellises and fences in the tropics and in the greenhouse in cooler areas, but is not too easy to grow.

Stephanotis floribunda

Sterculia STERCULIACEAE

Sterculia is a genus of about 200 tree species found throughout the tropics, some utilized for their timber, gums, and edible seeds, and a few cultivated as ornamentals. The name *Sterculia* is from the Latin word meaning dung, referring to the typically bad smell (to humans) of the flowers.

Sterculia foetida Linnaeus

DISTINGUISHABLE by the spreading tree habit, alternate, deeply palmately lobed leaves crowded at the branch tips, and racemes of crimson, five-lobed, foul-smelling flowers.

Sterculia foetida, skunk tree, sometimes called Indian almond, is native from India to northern Australia but is widely if not commonly cultivated in the tropics as a shade tree and as a novelty because of its malodorous flowers. When these cover the tree during flowering, the odor can be a drawback. The tree is often deciduous in areas with a dry climate. The seeds are reportedly poisonous. TREE to 20 m high (66 ft). LEAVES simple, alternate, 10–30 cm long (4–12 in), deeply palmately

Sterculia foetida

cut into 5 to 11 obovate to oblanceolate, attenuate lobes 7–20 cm long (3–8 in), usually crowded at the ends of the branches. FLOWERS frequently throughout the year; flowers many, borne in clusters of terminal panicles. Corolla none but the cup-shaped calyx petal-like, 1.5–2 cm long (⅝–¾ in), crimson, often with yellow markings, offensive smelling. FRUIT comprised of one to five red follicles containing 10 to 15 large black seeds. PROPAGATE by seeds or cuttings. Moist but well-drained soils in sunny places are preferred. Because of its large, spreading habit, it is not recommended for small yards.

Strelitzia STRELITZIACEAE

Strelitzia comprises four large, palm-like herbaceous species and one hybrid. The genus is southern African. It and the two other genera of the family Strelitziaceae, *Ravenala* and *Phenakospermum,* were formerly included in the banana family Musaceae, to which they are closely related. Strelitzias are cultivated for their inflorescences, and the two most widely cultivated species are included here.

Strelitzia nicolai Regel & Körnicke

DISTINGUISHABLE by the palm-like habit, distinct trunk, banana-leaf-like foliage in a fan-like arrangement, and dark, boat-like bracts enclosing the prominent flowers that have five lanceolate white tepals and one blue, spear-shaped one. It is similar to *Ravenala madagascariensis* but differs in having fewer boat-shaped bracts, reddish brown to purple rather than green, and the petiole distinctly shorter than the blade.

Strelitzia nicolai, bird-of-paradise tree or giant bird-of-paradise and sometimes called simply bird-of-paradise like its sister, *S. reginae,* is native to South Africa but is widely cultivated for its palm-like habit and flowers. **Shrub** to 5 m high (16½ ft) or more, clump forming with a distinct trunk. **Leaves** simple, two-ranked in a fan-like arrangement, blade oblong, usually 75–200 × 25–60 cm (30–80 × 10–24 in) on a petiole shorter than the blade, gray-green. **Flowers** continuously through the year; flowers several, borne erect within three to five reddish brown to purple, waxy white, boat-like bracts 20–40 cm long (8–16 in) on a short stalk clustered in the leaf

Strelitzia nicolai

axils. Corolla irregular, of six free unequal tepals 10–22 cm long (4–9 in), one light blue and spear-shaped, the others white and lanceolate. **Fruit** a capsule containing several seeds, each with a red aril at the base. **Propagate** by seeds or suckers. Moist but well-drained soils in sunny places are preferred. It is usually grown outdoors by itself to form clumps of banana-leaf-like foliage that gives a tropical look to the landscape, often beside pools since it produces little leaf litter. It makes an excellent potted plant that is also grown in temperate climates in the greenhouse. The leaves tend to get shredded if not protected from the wind.

Strelitzia reginae Banks

Distinguishable by the stemless herbaceous habit, leaves in a fan-like arrangement, and boat-shaped bracts enclosing the flowers that have five orange lanceolate tepals and one blue, spear-shaped one.

Strelitzia reginae, bird-of-paradise, named after the colorful New Guinea bird, sometimes called crane flower or crane's bill, is native to southern Africa but is grown throughout the tropics and subtropics for its orange and blue flowers. The remarkable inflorescences, which make it one of the most easily recognizable tropical plants, are harvested commercially for cut flowers. The inflorescence looks like the head of an exotic bird with a crest of orange flowers and a blue head and bill. In their native habitat these attract the birds needed for its specialized pollination mechanism. The birds alight on the spathe and flower, which causes the stamens to protrude and spread pollen on the breast feathers. One orange flower comes out each day so that the inflorescence looks more beautiful each day while this is occurring. **HERB**, stemless, erect, to 1.5 m high (5 ft). **LEAVES** simple, two-ranked in a fan-like arrangement, blade lanceolate, erect to ascending, usually 22–50 × 5–15 cm (9–20 × 2–6 in) on a longer petiole, gray-green with a yellow midvein.

Strelitzia reginae

FLOWERS continuously through the year; flowers about six, arising from one or two horizontal, folded, boat-shaped, green or purplish, red-edged bracts 10–22 cm long (4–9 in) atop a stalk bearing sheathing bracts. Corolla irregular, of six free, unequal tepals 7–13 cm long (3–5 in), one light blue and spear-shaped, the others orange and narrowly elliptic with an attenuate tip. **FRUIT** a capsule containing several seeds, each with a red aril at the base. **PROPAGATE** by division of rooted suckers or by seeds. Moist but well-drained soils in sunny places are preferred. Full sun produces optimal flowering, and partial shade produces more attractive leaves. It is often planted in borders and gardens, often beside pools since it produces little leaf litter.

Strobilanthes ACANTHACEAE

Strobilanthes is a genus of about 250 tropical Asian herb and shrub species, some utilized as a source of dyes, and some cultivated as ornamentals for their colorful flowers or leaves.

Strobilanthes dyerianus Masters

Synonym, *Perilepta dyeriana* (Masters) Bremekamp. **DISTINGUISHABLE** by the herbaceous habit and opposite leaves marked with pink to purple between the veins on the upper surface, purple on the lower.

Strobilanthes dyerianus, Persian shield, sometimes called purple strobilanthes, is native to Myanmar (Burma) but is widely if not commonly cultivated in the tropics for its iridescent foliage with silver to purple markings on the upper surface and purple below. **HERB**, perennial, to 1.8 m high (6 ft) but usually much less. **LEAVES** simple, opposite in unequally sized pairs, blade elliptic, usually 4–20 cm long (1⅝–8 in), subsessile, with pink to purple between the veins on the upper side, purple on the lower. **FLOWERS** infrequently during the year; flowers many, borne in terminal spikes, each flower with a round, pubescent bract below it. Corolla of fused petals, bell-shaped, 2.5–3 cm long (1–1¼ in), five-lobed, violet. **FRUIT** a spindle-shaped capsule, infrequently formed in cultivation. **PROPAGATE** by cuttings. Fertile, moist, but well-drained soils in

Strobilanthes dyerianus

partially shaded places are preferred. It is often grown in planters, in pots, in mass plantings, or mixed with other ornamentals and is also popular as an indoor plant in cooler climates.

Strongylodon FABACEAE

Strongylodon is a genus of 20 liana species ranging from Madagascar to Hawaii, one of which is cultivated as an ornamental.

Strongylodon macrobotrys A. Gray

DISTINGUISHABLE by the liana habit, alternate trifoliate leaves, and hanging seasonal racemes of bluish green, butterfly-like flowers.

Strongylodon macrobotrys, jade vine, sometimes called emerald creeper, is native to the Philippines but is widely if not commonly cultivated for its large, spectacular masses of blue-green to jade-colored flowers, among the rarest flower colors in the plant world. In Hawaii and elsewhere

where the flowers are used for leis and other decorations. **LIANA**, often forming dense masses with stems to 18 m long (59 ft). **LEAVES** trifoliate, alternate, leaflet blade lanceolate or ovate to oblong, 9–17 cm long (3½–7 in). **FLOWERS** mostly in spring and early summer; flowers many, borne in dense, hanging racemes to 3 m long (10 ft) or more. Corolla papilionaceous, of four free unequal petals, the two largest, the standard and the curved keel, usually 4–8 cm long (1⅝–3½ in), blue-green to jade green. **FRUIT** a cylindrical pod 4–6 cm long (1⅝–2½ in). **PROPAGATE** by scarified seeds, but seeds are viable for only 2 weeks, which is responsible for its having been brought

Strongylodon macrobotrys

into cultivation only more recently. Fertile, moist, but well-drained soils in partially shaded places are preferred. It is often grown on trellises and fences, which its rampant growth can soon overwhelm. Trellises or arbors with enough room for the large inflorescences to hang are recommended.

Syngonium ARACEAE

Syngonium is a genus of about 33 climbing tropical American species, several of which, called arrowhead vines, are cultivated as ornamentals.

Syngonium podophyllum Schott

Sometimes misidentified as *Syngonium angustatum* Schott. DISTINGUISHABLE by the creeping or climbing habit, milky sap, doubly palmate leaves, and spathe-and-spadix inflorescence. The very similar *S. angustatum* differs in having smaller juvenile leaves to 6 cm long (2½ in) and the veins on the upper surface marked with gray-green, but the two species seem to intergrade.

Syngonium podophyllum is an arrowhead vine native from Mexico to Brazil but is widely planted for its attractive, tropical-looking foliage. LIANA with adventitious roots at the nodes, sap milky. LEAVES doubly palmately compound but juvenile leaves arrowhead-shaped and simple, alternate, adult blade irregularly divided into three to ten ovate to elliptic leaflets, the largest 15–35 cm long (6–14 in), juvenile leaves 7–14 cm long (3–6 in). FLOWERS anytime during the year; flowers many, tightly packed in several axillary, erect, white spadices 4–9

Syngonium podophyllum

cm long (1⅝–3½ in), each surrounded by a longer greenish white to yellow spathe attached below. **Fruit** a compound group of brown to black berries. **Propagate** by division or cuttings. Fertile, moist, but well-drained soils in shaded places are preferred. It is often grown as a ground cover in the tropics, and in the greenhouse or as a houseplant in temperate climates. Several cultivars have been named.

Tabebuia BIGNONIACEAE

Tabebuia comprises about 100 tropical American shrub and tree species, many cultivated for their flowers or harvested for their valuable timber. There is much confusion about the correct names of the species in the genus, with many synonyms. Three ornamental species are included here and two others are mentioned.

Tabebuia aurea (Manso) Bentham & J. D. Hooker ex S. Moore

Tabebuia aurea

Synonym, *Tabebuia argentea* (Bureau & K. Schumann) Britton, and called *T. caraiba* (Martius) Bureau by some authors. **Distinguishable** by the tree habit, opposite, palmately compound leaves, leaflets silvery on the lower surface, and panicles of bell-shaped yellow flowers.

Tabebuia aurea, silver trumpet tree, is native to central South America, Brazil and Paraguay, but is widely cultivated for its yellow flowers. **Tree** to 8 m high (26 ft) or more, evergreen. **Leaves** palmately compound, opposite, leaflets three to seven, blades narrowly oblong to elliptic, 4–23 cm long (1⅝–9 in), leathery, silvery to dull green on the lower surface. **FLOWERS** most of the year in the tropics; flowers many, borne in a short terminal panicle. Corolla of fused petals, bell-shaped, 5–7 cm long (2–3 in) with five rounded lobes, bright yellow. **FRUIT** a narrowly cylindrical capsule 10–15 cm long (4–6 in) filled with winged seeds. **PROPAGATE** by cuttings, air layering, or seeds. Fertile, moist, but well-drained soils in sunny to partially shaded places are preferred. It is neither as spectacular nor as seasonal as *T. donnell-smithii* but is commonly grown by itself or as a small street tree.

Tabebuia donnell-smithii Rose

Synonyms, *Cybistax donnell-smithii* (Rose) Siebert and *Rosadendron donnell-smithii* (Rose) Miranda. **DISTINGUISHABLE** by the tree habit, opposite, palmately lobed leaves, toothed leaf margins, and dense clusters of bell-shaped yellow flowers that cover the tree during the seasonal flowering. The similar *Tabebuia aurea* differs in having narrower, more leathery leaflets and in producing flowers through most of the year rather than seasonally.

Tabebuia donnell-smithii, prima vera, sometimes called gold tree, is native to tropical America but is widely cultivated as an ornamental for its flowers. Some authors consider the species as belonging to *Cybistax,* a genus of three tropical American species. The wood is valued commercially for making furniture. **TREE** to 20 m high (66 ft), deciduous. **LEAVES** palmately compound, opposite, leaflets five to seven, thin, blades broadly oblong to obovate, 8–22 cm long (3½–9 in), gray-green pubescent on the lower surface, margins toothed. **FLOWERS** mostly in winter to early summer with individual trees

Tabebuia donnell-smithii

Tabebuia donnell-smithii, an attractive specimen tree during its seasonal flowering period

flowering once or twice for a short period during this time; flowers many, borne in dense, erect terminal panicles. Corolla of fused petals, bell-shaped, 5–7.5 cm long (2–3 in) with five rounded lobes, bright yellow. FRUIT a narrow cylindrical capsule 15–25 cm long (6–10 in) filled with winged seeds. PROPAGATE by cuttings or seeds. Fertile, well-drained soils in hot, sunny places are preferred. It is often planted alone as a specimen plant or as a street tree. The periodic flowering is spectacular with yellow blossoms covering the entire tree after all or some of the leaves have fallen.

Tabebuia heterophylla (A. P. de Candolle) Britton

Synonym, *Tabebuia pentaphylla* (Linnaeus) Hemsley, and sometimes misidentified as *T. pallida* (Linnaeus) Hemsley, a species with simple leaves. DISTINGUISHABLE by the tree habit, opposite, palmately compound leaves, terminal clusters of bell-shaped pink to lavender or white flowers, and a cylindrical capsule filled with winged seeds. The

similar *T. rosea* (Bertoloni) A. P. de Candolle, often misidentified as *T. pentaphylla,* differs in having generally larger, more coarsely veined elliptic leaflets with a sharply pointed, extended tip. Another cultivated species, *T. impetiginosa* (A. P. de Candolle) Standley, differs in having pubescent inflorescences and lower leaf surfaces.

Tabebuia heterophylla, pink tecoma, sometimes called pink trumpet tree or white cedar, is native to tropical America but is widely cultivated for its pink flowers. TREE to 15 m high (50 ft) or more, semideciduous in some climates. LEAVES palmately compound, opposite, leaflets three to five, blades

Tabebuia heterophylla, leaflets with rounded tips and fine veins

elliptic to obovate or oblanceolate, 4–18 cm long (1⅝–7 in), leathery, blunt. **FLOWERS** continuously through the year, most pronounced in dry areas; flowers one to several, borne in terminal clusters. Corolla of fused petals, bell-shaped, 6–9 cm long (2½–3½ in) with five rounded lobes at the tip, pink or lavender, rarely white, with a pale yellow throat. **FRUIT** a narrow cylindrical capsule 7–16 cm long (3–6 in), opening along two seams to release the numerous winged seeds. **PROPAGATE** by seeds or air layering. Fertile, moist, but well-drained soils in sunny to partially shaded places are preferred. It is one of the most common and widespread species of its genus and is planted alone as a specimen tree in gardens or as a street tree. It can spread rapidly by means of its winged seeds and sometimes becomes naturalized and troublesome. Unlike some of the other common ornamental trees of the genus, it flowers throughout the year.

Tabebuia rosea, leaflets more coarsely veined, acuminate

Tabebuia impetiginosa with pubescent inflorescences and lower leaflet surfaces

Tabernaemontana Apocynaceae

Tabernaemontana is a widespread tropical genus of about 100 tree and shrub species, some utilized locally for medicines, dyes, and as a source of rubber, and some cultivated as ornamentals for their attractive flowers.

Tabernaemontana divaricata (Linnaeus) R. Brown

Synonyms, *Ervatamia coronaria* (Jacquin) Stapf, a name used by some authors, and *E. divaricata* (Linnaeus) Burkill. DISTINGUISHABLE by the shrubby habit, milky sap, conspicuous white flowers with five unequally sided lobes, or double-flowered, and sometimes a yellow throat.

Tabernaemontana divaricata, crape jasmine, is sometimes called crape or paper gardenia. The common names are misnomers since the plant is related neither to *Jasminum* nor *Gardenia* though the flowers are sim-

Tabernaemontana divaricata

Tabernaemontana divaricata 'Flore Pleno', double-flowered

ilar to those of *Jasminum* spp. and *G. augusta* but not as fragrant, and the milky sap serves to distinguish it from the other two genera. It is probably native to northern India but is widely cultivated in the tropics and subtropics for its white flowers and dark, glossy green foliage. In its native range the wood is sometimes burned for incense, the fruits used to make a dye, and various parts employed for native remedies. **SHRUB** to 2 m high (6½ ft) with milky sap. **LEAVES** simple, opposite, elliptic to oblanceolate, 6–16 cm long (2½–6 in), tip attenuate, surfaces dark glossy green. **FLOWERS** continuously through the year; flowers several, borne in clusters at the tips of the stems. Corolla of fused petals, salverform, 3.5–4.5 cm long (1⅜–1¾ in) with five or six crape-like, rounded lobes forming a spreading limb 3–6 cm in diameter (1¼–2½ in), usually double-flowered, white, sometimes with a yellow throat. **FRUIT** consisting of two spreading orange pods. **PROPAGATE** by cuttings or seeds. Fertile, moist, but well-drained soils in sunny to partially shaded places are preferred. It is often planted as a foundation or shrubby border plant. Two kinds are seen, one with a normal corolla, and a more frequently cultivated, double-flowered 'Flore Pleno'.

Tacca TACCACEAE

Tacca is a genus of eight to ten stemless perennial herbaceous species ranging from Asia to the Pacific islands, some cultivated for their edible tubers, especially *T. leontopetaloides* (Linnaeus) Kuntze, the Polynesian arrowroot but not related to true arrowroot, *Maranta arundinacea,* and one cultivated as an ornamental for its unusual flowers.

Tacca chantrieri André

DISTINGUISHABLE by the stemless herbaceous habit, leaves that are large, basal, and lanceolate to oblong, and dark green to black flowers with many long, filamentous bracts.

Tacca chantrieri, bat flower, sometimes called cat's whiskers, is native to Myanmar (Burma) and Thailand but is widely if not commonly cultivated as a novelty because of its unusual, black, bat-like flowers. The black color resulted in the ominous name devil flower. These flowers have an odor reminiscent of rotting meat, attracting the flies needed for pollination. **HERB**, nearly stemless, to 70 cm high (28 in), growing from a rhizome. **LEAVES** simple, basal, erect, blade oblong to lanceolate, 25–55 cm long (10–22 in), dark green above, paler below. **FLOWERS** anytime during the year; flowers many, borne among two pairs of green to black ovate involucral bracts and many filamentous floral bracts, in umbels atop a hollow leafless scape to 70 cm long (28 in). Corolla with fused petals, divided into six ovate to lanceolate tepals 1–2 cm long (⅜–¾ in) in two whorls, olive green to

Tacca chantrieri

black. **FRUIT** ellipsoidal, berry-like, six-ribbed, 1.5–4 cm long (⅝–1⅝ in). **PROPAGATE** by seeds or division. Moist but well-drained soils in partially shaded places are preferred. The plant is often grown by itself as a specimen plant or in borders in the tropics, and in the greenhouse in temperate climates.

Tagetes ASTERACEAE

Tagetes is a genus of 30 to 50 annual or perennial herb species found mostly in hot, dry areas of tropical and subtropical America. The ornamental ones are often divided into four groups, including the African marigolds and French marigolds.

Tagetes erecta Linnaeus

DISTINGUISHABLE by the opposite, gland-dotted, simple to deeply pinnately lobed leaves, and orange to yellow petal-like florets borne in a

Tagetes, one of many cultivars involving *T. erecta* and possibly other species of *Tagetes* through hybridization

head on an inflated stalk. A similar cultivated garden ornamental, *Tagetes patula* Linnaeus, French marigold, has smaller flower heads.

Tagetes erecta is an African marigold native to Mexico, not Africa, but is widely cultivated in gardens for its orange flower heads, often in borders or mass plantings. The flower heads have been used to produce a yellow dye in Mexico. **Herb**, annual, erect, to 1 m high (3¼ ft) with strongly scented, gland-dotted foliage. **Leaves** simple to nearly pinnately compound, alternate to opposite on the same plant, blade 5–20 cm long (2–8 in) but progressively shorter upward, deeply pinnately cut into 4 to 15 pairs of narrowly elliptic lobes with toothed margins. **Flowers** continuously through the year after maturity; flowers in large, terminal, bell-shaped heads on a long stalk inflated at the top and surrounded by a cup-like series of bracts. Ray florets several in one series or double-flowered, with an obovate corolla limb usually 1–4 cm long (⅜–1⅝ in), orange to yellow. Disk florets many, sometimes modified and petal-like, yellow to orange. **Fruit** a narrow achene with scales on top. **Propagate** by achenes. It is drought resistant and adaptable to most conditions but well-drained soils in sunny places are preferred. Numerous cultivars, possibly involving hybridization with other species, have been named.

Tamarindus FABACEAE

Tamarindus is a genus with a single species cultivated as an ornamental and food plant.

Tamarindus indica Linnaeus

Tamarindus indica

DISTINGUISHABLE by the large tree habit, drooping branches, alternate, pinnately compound leaves, hanging racemes of five-lobed, yellow to cream-colored flowers with red or purple veins, and a mealy brown, sausage-shaped pod.

Tamarindus indica, tamarind, is possibly native to Africa but has been cultivated so long in tropical Asia to Africa that its origin is uncertain. The fruit pulp is used to make beverages, jams, and chutneys. The seeds and flowers are eaten in India and elsewhere, and the wood is sometimes used for timber. **TREE** to 20 m high (66 ft) or more with somewhat drooping branches. **LEAVES** even-pinnately compound, alternate, leaflets in 9 to 21 pairs, blades oblong, 1–3 cm long (⅜–1¼ in), notched to rounded at the tip. **FLOWERS** mostly in spring to fall; flowers many, borne in terminal and upper axillary racemes. Corolla of five free unequal petals, two scale-like, the other three oblanceolate, 1–1.8 cm long (⅜–¾ in), yellow to cream-colored with red or purple veins. **FRUIT** a velvety, reddish brown, thick, oblong or sausage-shaped pod usually 5–15 cm long (2–6 in), somewhat constricted between the seeds and not splitting. **PROPAGATE** by seeds or cuttings. Fertile soils in sunny places are preferred. It is a favorite fruit tree in Asia and Africa and is widely planted by itself as a specimen tree or as a park or street tree.

Tapeinochilos ZINGIBERACEAE

Tapeinochilos is a genus of 15 rhizomatous perennial species ranging from Malaysia to Australia that is sometimes combined with other genera into a separate family Costaceae. At least 1 species is cultivated as an ornamental.

Tapeinochilos ananassae (Hasskarl) K. Schumann

Tapeinochilos ananassae

DISTINGUISHABLE by the subshrub habit, cane-like stems, spirally arranged leaves, waxy red, pineapple-like spike, and orange flowers.

Tapeinochilos ananassae, pineapple ginger, sometimes called Indonesian wax ginger, is native from Malaysia to Australia but is widely cultivated for its red bracts and orange flowers. Its inflorescence looks like a bright red plastic pineapple, *Ananas comosus.* **SUBSHRUB**, coarse, erect, to 2.5 m high (8¼ ft), with cane-like stems growing from a rhizome. **LEAVES** simple, alternate, spirally arranged, subsessile atop a sheath, blade oblanceolate to elliptic, usually 10–30 × 3–8 cm (4–12 × 1¼–3½ in). **FLOWERS** continuously through the year; flowers many, borne among densely packed, overlapping, recurved, red bracts in an ovoid, pineapple-like spike 10–30 cm long (4–12 in) atop a stem, leafless or with terminal leafy bracts, 15–100 cm high (6–40 in). Corolla with fused tepals 2–3 cm long (¾–1¼ in) divided about halfway into three subequal lobes, yellow-orange, with a cup-shaped, yellow-orange labellum. **FRUIT** a capsule. **PROPAGATE** by root division. Fertile, moist, but well-drained soils in shaded or partially shaded places are preferred. It is often grown as a border plant in the tropics and in the greenhouse in temperate climates.

Tecoma BIGNONIACEAE

Tecoma is a genus of 12 to 15 tree and shrub species found from the southeastern United States to Argentina, with one in Africa, some cultivated as ornamentals for their showy flowers.

Tecoma stans (Linnaeus) A. L. Jussieu ex Kunth

Synonym, *Stenolobium stans* (Linnaeus) Seemann. DISTINGUISHABLE by the shrubby habit, opposite, pinnately compound leaves, toothed leaf margins, racemes of bell-shaped yellow flowers, and cylindrical capsule filled with winged seeds. The flowers are very similar to those of *Tabebuia* spp. but the shrubby habit and pinnately compound leaves of *Tecoma stans* serve to distinguish it from most of the common species of that genus.

Tecoma stans yellow elder, sometimes called yellow bells, is native to the West Indies or tropical America but is widely cultivated for its yellow flowers, and it is the official flower of the U.S. Virgin Islands and the Bahamas. In some places it is reported to be used medicinally as a diuretic. SHRUB or small tree to 5 m high (16½ ft) or more. LEAVES odd-pinnately compound, opposite, leaflets mostly five to seven, blades ovate to lanceolate, 2–15 cm long (¾–6 in), margins toothed. FLOWERS continuously through the year; flowers many, borne in upper axillary and terminal racemes. Corolla of fused petals, bell-shaped, 3.5–6 cm long (1⅜–2½ in) with five rounded lobes, bright yellow. FRUIT a narrow cylindrical capsule 10–20 cm long (4–8 in), opening along two seams to release the winged seeds. PROPAGATE by seeds or cuttings. Fertile, moist, but well-drained soils in sunny places are preferred. It is often grown by itself as a specimen plant

Tecoma stans

rather than in hedges. Pruning after flowering is advisable to achieve a bushier habit. It sometimes becomes naturalized and spreads by means of its windborne seeds.

Tecomanthe BIGNONIACEAE

Tecomanthe is a genus of five liana species ranging from New Zealand to Malaysia. The name *Tecomanthe* is derived from *Tecoma,* a related genus, and the Greek word meaning flower.

Tecomanthe dendrophila (Blume) K. Schumann

DISTINGUISHABLE by the opposite, pinnately compound leaves, five leaflets, and large, rose-colored flowers appearing in spring.

Tecomanthe dendrophila is a vine or shrub that lacks a well-known common name other than that of the genus. It is native from Indonesia to the Solomon Islands but is widely if not commonly cultivated for its

Tecomanthe dendrophila

glossy green leaves and large, rose-colored flowers. LIANA or VINE-LIKE SHRUB with purple young stems and older stems marked by conspicuous white dots, the lenticels. LEAVES pinnately compound, opposite, leaflets five, oblong to elliptic, 6–13 cm long (2½–5 in), glossy green, with a conspicuous acuminate tip. FLOWERS seasonally, mostly in spring, January to March in the northern hemisphere; flowers as many as 20 in short, dense, umbel-like fascicles formed on old wood. Corolla of fused petals, funnel-shaped, slightly two-lipped, 7–11 cm long (3–4½ in), rose-colored, red-lined inside, with five lighter colored triangular lobes. FRUIT a linear two-valved woody capsule 17–30 cm long (7–12 in). **PROPAGATE** by cuttings. Fertile, moist, well-drained soils in sunny or partially shaded places are preferred. It is often planted on fences or trellises, which can be covered by its rampant growth. The flowers, while attractive, are seasonal and absent for most of the year.

Tecomaria BIGNONIACEAE

Tecomaria has a single species that some authors include in the genus *Tecoma,* from which the name of the genus is derived.

Tecomaria capensis (Thunberg) Spach

Synonym, *Tecoma capensis* (Thunberg) Lindley, a name used by some authors. **DISTINGUISHABLE** by the vine-like or shrubby habit, opposite, pinnately compound leaves, toothed leaf margins, and short racemes or panicles of orange, two-lipped, funnel-shaped flowers. The similar *Pyrostegia venusta* differs in having two or three leaflets with entire margins.

Tecomaria capensis, Cape honeysuckle, is native to South Africa, the Cape in the common name referring to the Cape of Good Hope, but honeysuckle is a misnomer since it is not related to honeysuckle, *Lonicera* spp. of the family Caprifoliaceae. It is widely cultivated in the tropics and subtropics for its orange flowers and attractive leaves. **VINE-LIKE SHRUB** or shrub. **LEAVES** odd-pinnately compound, opposite, leaflets five to nine, blades ovate to round, 1–4 cm long (⅜–1⅝ in) with toothed margins. **FLOWERS** continuously through the year; flow-

Tecomaria capensis

ers several, borne in short terminal racemes or narrow panicles. Corolla of fused petals, funnel-shaped, curved, 4–6 cm long (1⅝–2½ in), two-lipped with five oblong spreading lobes, bright orange or scarlet. **Fruit** a narrow linear capsule 7–18 cm long (3–7 in), containing many winged seeds. **Propagate** by seeds, cuttings, or air layering. Fertile, moist, but well-drained soils in sunny places are preferred. It is often grown in planters or hedges and is sometimes trained over arches and trellises to produce a screen. Periodic pruning is needed to hold its rampant growth in check.

Telosma ASCLEPIADACEAE

Telosma is a genus of ten vine species of the Old World tropics, at least one of which is cultivated as an ornamental.

Telosma cordata (N. L. Burman) Merrill

Telosma cordata

Distinguishable by the viny habit, clear sap, opposite, heart-shaped leaves, and short-stalked axillary umbels of five-lobed, two-toned yellow flowers.

Telosma cordata, fragrant telosma, called pakalana in Hawaii, is native from India to Southeast Asia but is widely if not commonly cultivated in the tropics for its flowers, sometimes used in leis. Its soft, heart-shaped leaves make it look like a morning glory, *Ipomoea* spp., but the flowers are distinctly not like those of morning glories. The leaves and flowers are eaten throughout its native range. **Vine** with slender branches and clear sap. **Leaves** simple, opposite, blade heart-

shaped, 4–12 cm long (1⅝–5 in) with a rounded notch at the base.
FLOWERS mostly in spring to fall; flowers several, in short-stalked axillary umbels. Corolla of fused petals, 1.3–2 cm long (½–¾ in) divided less than halfway into five rounded yellow lobes, lighter yellow inside. FRUIT a cylindrical, pod-like follicle 10–14 cm long (4–6 in). PROPAGATE by cuttings or seeds. Moist but well-drained soils in sunny places are preferred. It is often grown on trellises or fences.

Thevetia APOCYNACEAE

Thevetia is a genus of eight species found from Mexico to Paraguay. Several are cultivated as ornamentals for their attractive flowers. Some authors consider all but one of the species as belonging to a separate genus, *Cascabela*.

Thevetia peruviana K. Schumann

Synonyms, *Cascabela thevetia* (Linnaeus) Lippold, a name used by some authors, and *Thevetia neriifolia* A. L. Jussieu ex Steudel. DISTINGUISHABLE by the small tree habit, milky sap, spirally arranged linear leaves, flowers that are large, yellow, and funnel-shaped, and green fruit containing a large, hard-shelled seed. A similar species, *T. thevetioides* (Kunth) K. Schumann [synonym, *C. thevetioides* (Kunth) Lippold], differs in having leaves that are downy beneath and secondary veins that are conspicuous.

Thevetia peruviana, yellow oleander, sometimes called be-still tree or lucky nut, is not in the oleander genus *Nerium* though both genera are mem-

Thevetia peruviana

bers of the same family, Apocynaceae. It is native to hot, dry places in tropical America but is widely cultivated for its yellow flowers or as a novelty because of its hard seeds, thought in some places to be a good-luck charm. All parts of the plant, including the large hard seed, are poisonous and can be fatal if ingested by humans or livestock. **TREE** to 6 m high (20 ft) or more with milky sap. **LEAVES** simple, alternate, spirally arranged, blade linear, 8–16 cm long (3½–6 in) with the margins slightly rolled under. **FLOWERS** continuously through the year; flowers several, borne in short terminal clusters. Corolla of fused petals, funnel-shaped with a limb of five spreading, rounded lobes 4–7 × 3–4 cm (1⅝–3 × 1¼–1⅝ in), yellow or sometimes peach-colored. **FRUIT** a black, somewhat triangular drupe 2.5–4 cm across (1–1⅝ in) with a single, large, hard seed inside. **PROPAGATE** by seeds or cuttings. Fertile, well-drained soils in sunny or partially shaded places are preferred but full sun produces optimal flowering. It is often planted in rows to make a dense, living fence and sometimes becomes naturalized.

Thunbergia ACANTHACEAE

Thunbergia comprises 100 to 200 vine and shrub species widely distributed in the Old World tropics, many of which, often called clockvines, are cultivated for their large flowers. Six of the most common and attractive ornamental species are included here.

Thunbergia alata Bojer ex Sims

DISTINGUISHABLE by the viny habit, opposite, arrowhead-shaped leaves with a winged petiole, and flowers that are solitary, long-stalked, and typically with a funnel-shaped orange corolla with a dark throat.

Thunbergia alata, black-eyed Susan, is native to tropical East Africa but is widely cultivated for its flowers. The contrasting orange lobes and typically dark purple throat make the flowers particularly appealing. The dark throat is the origin of the vine's common name. **VINE**, annual in cooler climates or perennial, herbaceous, twining. **LEAVES** simple, opposite, blade ovate to arrowhead-shaped, 3.5–10 cm long (1⅜–4 in) with the petiole narrowly winged nearly to the base. FLOWERS continuously through the year; flowers solitary and axillary, long stalked with a pair of leafy bracts below. Corolla of fused petals, funnel-shaped, tube 1.7–2.4 cm long (¾–⅞ in), with a spreading five-lobed limb 3.2–4.5 cm across (1¼–1¾ in), orange or sometimes white ('Alba') with a purple or white ('Bakeri') center. FRUIT a subglobose woody capsule with an extended terminal beak. PROPAGATE by cuttings or seeds. Well-drained soils in sunny places are preferred. It is usually grown on fences and trellises and often becomes naturalized as a minor weed, which does not readily spread, however.

Thunbergia alata, orange with dark throat; 'Bakeri', orange with white throat; and 'Alba'

Thunbergia erecta

(Bentham) T. Anderson

DISTINGUISHABLE by the shrubby habit, opposite leaves, and flowers that are solitary, funnel-shaped, and blue to purple with a yellow throat. A similar species, *Thunbergia affinis* S. Moore, differs most obviously in having slightly larger flowers, a larger calyx 10 mm long (⅜ in) versus 3–6 mm (about ⅛–¼ in), and persistent bracteoles.

Thunbergia erecta, king's mantle,

Thunbergia erecta

sometimes called bush thunbergia or bush clockvine, is native to tropical West Africa but is widely if not commonly cultivated for its flowers colored an exquisite purple, rarely white. The common name, king's mantle, probably refers to the purple, sepia color that was sometimes the official color of royalty in the Mediterranean region. **SHRUB** to 2 m high (6½ ft). **LEAVES** simple, opposite, arranged in one plane, blade ovate, 2–7 cm long (¾–3 in). **FLOWERS** continuously through the year; flowers solitary and axillary with a pair of leafy deciduous bracts below. Corolla of fused petals, narrowly bell-shaped, 5–8 cm long (2–3½ in) with a spreading five-lobed limb 4–6 cm across (1⅝–2½ in), blue to purple, yellow within. **FRUIT** a subglobose capsule with an extended terminal beak but infrequently formed in cultivation. **PROPAGATE** by cuttings. Fertile, moist, but well-drained soils in sunny places are preferred. It is often grown as a specimen plant, in mixed beds, or as a low border plant. With heavy pruning it can become a creeping or mat-forming plant but this inhibits flowering.

Thunbergia fragrans

Thunbergia fragrans Roxburgh

DISTINGUISHABLE by the viny habit, opposite, arrowhead-shaped leaves, flowers that are solitary or paired, long-stalked, white, and funnel-shaped, and a globose capsule with a beaked tip.

Thunbergia fragrans, sweet clockvine, sometimes called white clockvine, is native from India to Southeast Asia but is widely cultivated in the tropics and subtropics for its white flowers. **VINE**, herbaceous, twining. **LEAVES** simple, opposite, blade ovate to arrowhead-shaped, usually 5–12 cm long (2–5 in). **FLOWERS** continuously through the year; flowers solitary or paired, axillary on a long stalk with a pair of leafy bracts below, not fragrant. Corolla of fused petals, salverform, tube 2–3 cm long (¾–1¼ in), with a spreading five-lobed limb 4–6 cm across (1⅝–2½ in), white. **FRUIT** a subglobose capsule with an extended terminal beak to 2 cm long (¾ in). **PROPAGATE** by cuttings or seeds. Moist but well-drained soils in sunny places are preferred. It is often grown in the greenhouse or as a ground cover in subtropical climates but is possibly more frequently found as a minor weed than as an ornamental, though it does not readily spread. Its white flowers are not as attractive as most of the other ornamental thunbergias.

Thunbergia grandiflora (Roxburgh ex Rottler) Roxburgh

DISTINGUISHABLE by the liana habit, leaves that are opposite, broad, and somewhat lobed, hanging racemes of large white to violet flowers, and a subglobose capsule with a beaked tip. It differs from *Thunbergia laurifolia,* which some authors consider to be a variety of *T. grandiflora,* by its broader leaves.

Thunbergia grandiflora, skyflower vine, also called Bengal clockvine, Bengal trumpet, and blue trumpet vine, is native to India but is widely cultivated for its large violet or white flowers. **LI-ANA**, climbing, sprawling, or creeping. **LEAVES** simple, opposite, blade broadly ovate to heart-shaped, 8–24 × 9–16 cm (3½–9 × 3½–6 in), margins somewhat lobed. **FLOWERS** continuously through the year in the tropics but from spring to fall in cooler climates; flowers many, borne in terminal and upper axillary racemes with a pair of leafy bracts below each flower. Corolla of fused petals, bell-shaped, two-lipped, tube 3–4.5 cm long (1¼–1¾

Thunbergia grandiflora

in), yellowish, with a spreading five-lobed limb 7–10 cm across (3–4 in), pale violet to bluish purple or occasionally white. FRUIT a subglobose capsule with an extended terminal beak but infrequently formed in cultivation. PROPAGATE by cuttings. Fertile, moist, but well-drained soils in sunny or partially shaded places are preferred. It produces a vigorous growth and is often planted on trellises or bowers, which it decorates with its large, hanging inflorescences.

Thunbergia laurifolia   Lindley

DISTINGUISHABLE by the liana habit, leaves that are opposite, ovate, and somewhat lobed, hanging racemes of large white to violet flowers, and a subglobose capsule with a beaked tip. Some authors consider it to be a variety of *Thunbergia grandiflora,* which has quite different, broader leaves, but the flowers by themselves are hard to distinguish.

Thunbergia laurifolia, laurel-leaved clockvine, sometimes called laurel-leaved thunbergia, is native to Myanmar (Burma) and Malaysia but is widely cultivated for its large white flowers and is infrequently naturalized. LIANA, sprawling or climbing. LEAVES simple, opposite, blade ovate to elliptic or lanceolate, 6–24 × 4–9 cm (2½–9 × 1⅝–3½ in), margins slightly lobed. FLOWERS continuously through the year in the tropics; flowers many, borne in hanging, upper axillary and terminal racemes, each flower with a pair of basal, leaf-like bracts 4.5–5.5 cm long (1¾–2¼ in). Corolla of fused petals, bell-shaped, two-lipped, tube 3–4.5 cm long (1¼–1¾ in), with a spreading five-lobed limb 7–9 cm

Thunbergia laurifolia

across (3–3½ in), pale blue or violet with a white center, sometimes all white. FRUIT a subglobose capsule with an extended terminal beak 2–3 cm long (¾–1¼ in). PROPAGATE by seeds or cuttings. Fertile, moist, but well-drained soils in partially shaded places are preferred. Because of its vigorous growth it is often grown on fences, trellises, and bowers.

Thunbergia mysorensis (Wight) T. Anderson

DISTINGUISHABLE by the liana habit, leaves that are opposite and three-veined from the base, and hanging racemes of bright yellow flowers arising between paired purple to red bracts.

Thunbergia mysorensis, Mysore clockvine, is native to India, where the state of Mysore is located, but is widely if not commonly cultivated elsewhere for its hanging racemes of orange and purple flowers. LIANA, climbing into trees or on trellises in cultivation. LEAVES simple, oppo-site, blade lanceolate to ovate, 10–18 cm long (4–7 in) with three distinct veins from the base, margins wavy. FLOWERS continuously through the year; flowers many, borne in long, hanging, terminal racemes, each flower enclosed within a pair of ovate purple to red bracts. Corolla of fused petals, two-lipped, 5.5–7 cm long (2¼–3 in), bright yellow, with pro-truding stamens hairy near the tip. FRUIT a capsule but infrequently formed in cul-tivation. PROPAGATE by cuttings. Fertile, well-drained soils in sunny places are preferred. It is often grown on trellises or bowers, which show the flowers most ef-fectively. It is less common and wide-spread than the other, less ornamental liana thunbergias noted here.

Thunbergia mysorensis

Tibouchina MELASTOMATACEAE

Tibouchina is a genus of 300 to 350 tropical American shrub and sub-shrub species, many of which are cultivated as ornamentals for their beautiful flowers.

Tibouchina urvilleana (A. P. de Candolle) Cogniaux

Often misidentified as *Tibouchina semidecandra* (Schrank & Martius) Cogniaux, a different species not commonly in cultivation. DISTINGUISHABLE by the shrubby habit, opposite fuzzy leaves three- to seven-veined from the base, and panicles of five-parted, pink to purple flowers with ten stamens having conspicuously bent filaments.

    Tibouchina urvilleana, glory bush, sometimes called lasiandra, is native to Brazil but is widely cultivated for its large purple flowers. SHRUB to 4 m high (13 ft) or more with quadrangular fuzzy stems. LEAVES simple, opposite, blade ovate, 5–20 cm long (2–8 in), three- to seven-veined from the base, fuzzy on both surfaces. FLOWERS continuously through the year; flowers several, in small terminal panicles. Corolla of five free, obovate, pink to purple petals 3–6 cm long (1¼–2½ in), with ten purplish stamens with curved anthers. FRUIT an ovoid capsule 1.2–1.6 cm long (½–⅝ in). PROPAGATE by seeds, cuttings, or air layering. Fertile, moist, but well-drained soils in sunny places are preferred. It is often grown by itself as a specimen plant or in hedges. In some areas it has become a naturalized pest and should not be introduced to areas where it is not already found.

Tibouchina urvilleana

Tillandsia BROMELIACEAE

Tillandsia is a genus of more than 400 tropical American herbaceous species, most epiphytic with rosette leaves, and many cultivated as ornamentals.

Tillandsia usneoides (Linnaeus) Linnaeus

DISTINGUISHABLE by the hanging, epiphytic habit, stems that are stringy and gray, and gray linear leaves.

Tillandsia usneoides, Spanish moss, sometimes called Florida moss or old-man's beard, is not a moss nor is it Spanish. It is native from Florida to Argentina and is widely cultivated for its distinctive appearance, superficially similar to but entirely unrelated to the pendulous lichens, *Usnea* spp., and not at all similar to its cousin the pineapple, *Ananas comosus.* The plant is harvested in some places and used for packing material and stuffing for furniture, and it is a favorite for bird nests. **EPIPHYTE** with curled, hanging stems to 6 m long (20 ft), about 1 mm in diameter (about ⅟₃₂ in), lacking roots but absorbing water and nutrients from water dripping over it. **LEAVES** simple, alternate and clustered at regular intervals, linear, 2.5–7.5 cm long (1–3 in), gray, fuzzy. **FLOWERS** rarely; flowers solitary, sessile in the leaf axils but infrequently forming. Corolla of three yellow tepals 4–7 mm long (about ¼ in). **FRUIT** a small capsule, infrequently forming. **PROPAGATE** by division, simply breaking the stems, or offsets. Moist, partially shaded places are preferred. It is often planted in hanging

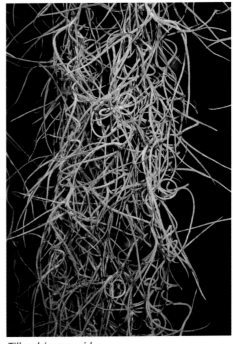

Tillandsia usneoides

baskets or to festoon trees, outdoors in the tropics and subtropics and in greenhouses or conservatories in temperate climates.

Tithonia ASTERACEAE

Tithonia comprises about ten herb, shrub, or small tree species found in Mexico and Central America, some cultivated for their flowers. Two of the most common ornamental species are included here.

Tithonia diversifolia (Hemsley) A. Gray

DISTINGUISHABLE by the subshrub habit, leaves that are large, mostly alternate, and palmately lobed, and sunflower-like heads of yellow ray and disk florets. It differs from the similar *Helianthus annuus* in having lobed leaves and all-yellow ray florets instead of the latter being tipped with black.

Tithonia diversifolia

Tithonia diversifolia, tree marigold, is native to eastern Mexico and Central America but is widely cultivated for its flower heads, very similar to those of sunflowers, *Helianthus* spp. SUBSHRUB, branching, to 4 m high (13 ft). LEAVES simple, mostly alternate, blade generally obovate to round in outline but palmately three- to five-lobed at least on the lower part of plant, 8–25 cm long (3½–10 in). FLOWERS continuously through the year; flowers in large terminal heads 7–14 cm in diameter (3–6 in) surrounded by three or four series of ovate bracts. Ray florets 7 to 21, 3–7 cm long (1¼–3 in), bright yellow. Disk florets many, yellow. FRUIT a wedge-shaped achene 4–6 mm long (about ¼ in) with two unequal awns on top. PROPAGATE by achenes. Well-drained soils in sunny places are preferred. It is often planted in hedges, occasionally by itself as a specimen plant, but it sometimes escapes from cultivation and has become naturalized in some places, Fiji, Hawaii, and Kenya, for example.

Tithonia rotundifolia (Miller) S. F. Blake

DISTINGUISHABLE by the subshrub habit, leaves that are stiffly hairy and alternate, and sunflower-like heads of petal-like orange ray florets and yellow disk florets, borne on swollen stalks.

Tithonia rotundifolia, Mexican sunflower, is native to Mexico but is widely cultivated for its orange flower heads. SUBSHRUB, branching, to 1.5 m high (5 ft). LEAVES simple, alternate, blade ovate to deltoid, usually 5–12 cm long (2–5 in) with a long-attenuate base, hispid on the upper surface. FLOWERS continuously through the year; flowers in large terminal heads borne on pubescent, thickened stalks, each head surrounded by two series of ovate bracts. Ray florets mostly 10 to 14, obovate to elliptic, 1.5–3.3 cm long (⅝–1¼ in), reddish orange to yellow-orange. Disk florets many, yellow. FRUIT a wedge-shaped achene with several terminal awns and scales. PROPAGATE by achenes. The plant is easy to grow since it is drought and heat resistant but well-drained soils in sunny places are preferred. It is one of the most colorful sunflowers and is often planted as a large garden ornamental as well as being used for cut flowers. Several cultivars, all with red to orange flower heads, have been named.

Tithonia rotundifolia

Torenia SCROPHULARIACEAE

Torenia is a genus of 40 to 50 herbaceous species of the Old World tropics, several of which are cultivated as ornamentals for their attractive flowers.

Torenia fournieri Linden ex Fournier

DISTINGUISHABLE by the herbaceous habit, four-angled stems, opposite ovate leaves, and two-lipped pale purple flowers with dark purple lobes and a yellow spot on the lower lip.

    Torenia fournieri, wishbone flower, sometimes called blue wings, is native to Vietnam but is widely cultivated for its purple and yellow flowers, particularly attractive because of the combination of colors. HERB, annual or perennial, weak stemmed, to 50 cm high (20 in) with four-angled stems. LEAVES simple, opposite, blade ovate to oblong, 2.5–6.5 cm long (1–2⅝ in) with toothed margins. FLOWERS anytime during the year after maturity; flowers solitary and axillary, upper ones in a terminal raceme. Corolla with fused petals, two-lipped, 2.8–4 cm long (1⅛–1⅝ in), 2.5–4 cm across (1–1⅝ in), pale purple with dark purple on the inside margins, with a yellow spot on the lower lip. FRUIT a narrowly ovoid capsule. PROPAGATE by seeds. Fertile, moist soils in partially shaded places are preferred. It is often grown in borders in gardens in the tropics, and in temperate climates as an annual in gardens, greenhouses, and as a houseplant.

Torenia fournieri

Tradescantia COMMELINACEAE

Tradescantia comprises 65 species native from tropical to warm temperate North and South America. Many are cultivated for their ornamental form, flowers, and leaves, often as houseplants or in the greenhouse. Species are typically self-sterile, thus plants formed from the same clone cannot produce seeds. Some authors break the genus up into several smaller ones. Three widely cultivated ornamental species are included here.

Tradescantia pallida (Rose) D. Hunt

Synonym, *Setcreasea purpurea* B. K. Boom, a name used by many authors. **DISTINGUISHABLE** by the weak-stemmed, herbaceous habit, ovate purple leaves lacking a midrib, and pink flowers enclosed within folded, boat-shaped bracts.

Tradescantia pallida, purple heart, sometimes called purple tradescantia, is native to Mexico but is widely cultivated in the tropics and subtropics for its attractive purple foliage. Some authors put the species into the genus *Setcreasea,* comprising nine species native to tropical and subtropical North America. **HERB**, weak stemmed, with purple stems to 20 cm high (8 in), rooting at the lower nodes. **LEAVES** simple, alternate, spirally arranged, blade ovate to elliptic or lanceolate, 5–20 cm long (2–8 in), purple, green in the nonornamental plant, lacking a midrib. **FLOWERS** anytime during the year; flowers several, borne within a pair of unequal, divergent, terminal, purple,

Tradescantia pallida

folded, boat-shaped bracts 3–7 cm long (1¼–3 in). Corolla of three free, elliptic tepals 1.4–2 cm long (½–¾ in), pink. **FRUIT** a narrowly ellipsoidal capsule. **PROPAGATE** by stem cuttings or division. Fertile, moist, but well-drained soils in partially shaded places are preferred but the deepest colors develop in full sunlight. It is often grown in borders or as a ground cover in the tropics and in temperate climates as a potted plant in greenhouses, conservatories, or as a houseplant. Trimming the stems promotes the best form as a ground cover. The most common cultivar is called 'Purpurea' or 'Purple Heart'.

Tradescantia spathacea Swartz

Synonyms, *Rhoeo discolor* L'Héritier and *R. spathacea* (Swartz) Stearn. Some authors recognize a single-species genus *Rhoeo* and use the latter name. **DISTINGUISHABLE** by the coarse, clump-forming herbaceous habit, narrowly lanceolate leaves purple on the lower surface and lacking a midrib, and small white flowers enclosed within purple, folded, boat-shaped bracts

Tradescantia spathacea

Tradescantia spathacea oyster plant, also often called Moses in his boat or cradle or variations thereon, or boat lily or rhoeo, is native to Central America and the West Indies but is widely cultivated in warm regions because of its attractive, purple foliage. A colorful, all-purple cultivated form is particularly common in Central America, where the coloring extracted from the leaves was used in cosmetics. **HERB**, short stemmed, creeping, rosette and clump forming, to 60 cm high (24 in). **LEAVES** simple, alternate in a tight spiral, blade narrowly lanceolate, usually

20–35 × 2–6 cm (8–14 × ¾–2 ½ in), usually purple on the lower surface. **FLOWERS** anytime during the year; flowers several, enclosed within a pair of axillary, subsessile, purple, folded, boat-shaped bracts 2–4 cm long (¾–1⅝ in). Corolla of six free, ovate tepals 5–7 mm long (about ¼ in), white. **FRUIT** a three-celled capsule. **PROPAGATE** by cuttings, division, or seeds, unless seeds were mixed from various sources. Moist but well-drained soils in partially shaded places are preferred. It is a hardy, easily grown species that often escapes from cultivation and can grow even on rocks and rock walls. It is usually grown as dense ground cover (especially 'Dwarf'), for edging, or in planters. 'Concolor' is a cultivar with all-green leaves.

Tradescantia zebrina Bosse

Synonym, *Zebrina pendula* Schnizlein, a name used by many authors. **DISTINGUISHABLE** by the weak-stemmed, trailing habit, ovate, colorfully striped leaves lacking a midrib, and small, pinkish, three-parted flowers enclosed within folded, boat-shaped bracts.

Tradescantia zebrina, wandering Jew, is probably native to Mexico and perhaps elsewhere in the Caribbean region but is widely cultivated in warm regions for its colorful foliage. **HERB**, trailing, prostrate, rooting at the nodes, with weak, purple stems. **LEAVES** simple, sessile, alternate, blade ovate to elliptic, 2–7 cm long (¾–3 in), somewhat succulent, green or purple with two parallel, lengthwise, white or silvery bands, purple on the lower surface. **FLOWERS** anytime during the year; flowers one or two at a time

Tradescantia zebrina

borne within two unequal, folded, boat-shaped bracts 1–4 cm long (⅜–1⅝ in). Corolla with fused tepals, tube 7–10 mm long (¼–⅜ in) with three ovate segments 6–9 mm long (¼–⅜ in), pink or magenta. **Fruit** a small capsule, infrequently formed in cultivation. **Propagate** by stem cuttings or division. Moist but well-drained soils in sunny or partially shaded places are preferred. It needs some sun for optimal leaf color but bright sun may lead to bleaching. It is grown indoors or outdoors, often as a potted plant or ground cover, sometimes escaping from cultivation and becoming somewhat naturalized. Several cultivars have been named, including 'Perpusii', with wine-colored leaves.

Trimezia IRIDACEAE

Trimezia, a genus of five tropical American rhizomatous perennial species, some called walking irises. Some are useful as laxatives and one is cultivated for its flowers.

Trimezia martinicensis (Jacquin) Herbert

Trimezia martinicensis

Distinguishable by the linear leaves in a fan-like arrangement, terminal clusters of short-lived flowers on a one-leaved stalk, and three short and three longer yellow tepals with brown spots at the base.

Trimezia martinicensis is native to the Caribbean area but is widely grown in the tropics, often in borders, for its yellow flowers. It gets the name walking iris from its habit of developing plantlets on the inflorescence, which eventually droops to touch the ground, where the plantlets take root. It sometimes escapes from cultivation and becomes naturalized. **Herb**, perennial, erect, to 80 cm high (32 in), arising from a bulb-like tuber. **LEAVES** simple, basal, erect, equitant and fan-like, blade linear, 20–60 × 1.5–4 cm (8–24 × ⅝–1⅝ in), dull green. **FLOWERS** anytime during the year; flowers four to six, lasting only a few hours, borne in terminal clusters atop a stem bearing a single leaf in the middle. Corolla with fused tepals, deeply divided into six segments, the outer three oblanceolate, 1.8–3.6 cm long (¾–1⅜ in), pale yellow with brown spots at the base, the inner ones shorter, recurved, darker yellow and white with brown spots. **FRUIT** an obovate capsule 1.5–3 cm long (⅝–1¼ in). **PROPAGATE** by division, offsets, or seeds. Moist but well-drained soils in partially shaded places are preferred.

Triphasia RUTACEAE

Triphasia is a genus of three shrub or small tree species ranging from Southeast Asia to the Philippines, two of which are cultivated as ornamentals.

Triphasia trifolia (N. L. Burman) P. Wilson

DISTINGUISHABLE by the shrubby habit, paired axillary spines, alternate, trifoliate leaves, small axillary flowers, and juicy red berry.

Triphasia trifolia, limeberry, is native to somewhere in the range of the genus, Southeast Asia to the Philippines, but is widely cultivated in the tropics as an ornamental and for its edible fruits, usually made into preserves, particularly in China. The fruits are also used in some places by children to paint their fingernails. In some areas, such as Guam, it is common to abundant in forested areas on limestone where it has become naturalized. **SHRUB** or small tree to 4 m high (13 ft)

Triphasia trifolia

with paired axillary spines. **LEAVES** trifoliate, alternate, leaflet blades ovate to nearly round, the terminal one 2.5–5 cm long (1–2 in), the lateral ones smaller, margins crenate, tips notched, surfaces marked with tiny glands. **FLOWERS** anytime during the year; flowers solitary, axillary. Corolla of three free, oblanceolate, white petals 1–1.5 cm long (⅜–⅝ in). **FRUIT** a subglobose to ellipsoidal, juicy, red berry 1–1.7 cm long (⅜–¾ in). **PROPAGATE** by seeds or cuttings. Dry, rocky, often calcareous soils in sunny to partially shaded places are preferred. It is often planted in hedges but the thorny stems are a drawback unless the hedge is designed with this in mind.

Tristellateia MALPIGHIACEAE

Tristellateia is a genus of 20 to 22 liana species ranging from Africa to New Caledonia but concentrated in Madagascar, at least one of which is cultivated as an ornamental for its attractive flowers.

Tristellateia australasiae A. Richard

Tristellateia australasiae

DISTINGUISHABLE by the liana habit, opposite leaves with marginal glands at the base, and racemes of yellow flowers with five stalked petals and ten red-stalked stamens. It is very similar to *Galphimia gracilis* but is a liana rather than a shrub.

Tristellateia australasiae, bagnit, sometimes called shower-of-gold climber among other names, is native from Southeast Asia to New Caledonia but is widely if not commonly cultivated in the tropics for its inflorescence of yellow flowers. **LIANA**, climbing into trees or on trellises. **LEAVES** simple, opposite, blade ovate to lanceolate, 5–12 cm long

(2–5 in), leathery, dark glossy green, usually with two marginal glands at the base. **FLOWERS** continuously through the year; flowers many, borne in short axillary and terminal racemes. Corolla of five free, narrowly shovel-shaped, clawed, yellow petals 8–15 mm long (¼–⅝ in), surrounding the ten red-stalked stamens. **FRUIT** a three-parted capsule, each part like a seven-rayed star, infrequently formed in cultivation. **PROPAGATE** by cuttings or seeds. Fertile, moist soils in sunny to partially shaded places are preferred. It is often grown on fences, arches, or trellises, which it can easily cover with its rampant growth.

Tropaeolum TROPAEOLACEAE

Tropaeolum is a genus of about 86 species found in Central and South America, many grown as ornamentals, some cultivated as food plants (edible flowers, pods, leaves, or tubers) and some as ornamentals.

Tropaeolum majus Linnaeus

DISTINGUISHABLE by the herbaceous habit, round leaves stalked in the middle of the blade, and funnel-shaped, five-parted, typically orange flowers with a long spur.

Tropaeolum majus, nasturtium (or nasties as some people humorously call the plants), is native to Peru. It is sometimes called garden nasturtium or Indian cress but is unrelated to *Nasturtium*, a cress genus that is a member of the mustard family Brassicaceae (Cruciferae). It is cultivated for its attractive, colorful flowers, the leaves are edible, and the seeds are sometimes used as a spice. **HERB**, annual or longer lived, weak stemmed, glabrous,

Tropaeolum majus

to 40 cm high (16 in) or sometimes much more. LEAVES simple, alternate, blade generally round, 3–15 cm in diameter (1¼–6 in), peltate on a long petiole, margin wavy. FLOWERS anytime during the year; flowers solitary on a long axillary stalk with a long spur on the calyx. Corolla of five unequal free petals, funnel-shaped, petals mostly 2–4 cm long (¾–1⅝ in), usually orange but sometimes yellow, red, brown, purple, or other colors. FRUIT a three-lobed schizocarp 9–12 mm long (⅜–½ in). PROPAGATE by seeds. Relatively infertile, moist, but well-drained soils in sunny places are preferred, but the plant is somewhat drought resistant. It is grown in gardens or as a border plant in the tropics and as a potted plant indoors in cold climates. The plants do best in cooler climates or at higher elevations in the tropics. Many of the numerous cultivars identified with this species are actually hybrids between *T. majus* and one or two other species of the genus.

Tulbaghia AMARYLLIDACEAE

Tulbaghia is a genus of 22 to 24 herbaceous species found in Africa and sometimes put into the family Alliaceae, considered part of the family Liliaceae by many authors. Some are cultivated as ornamentals for their delicate, sometimes fragrant flowers.

Tulbaghia violacea

Tulbaghia violacea Harvey

DISTINGUISHABLE by the underground corm, linear, garlic-like leaves, and terminal umbels of small pink flowers with six spreading tepal lobes.

Tulbaghia violacea, society garlic, is native to South Africa but is widely cultivated for its attractive pink flowers. HERB, perennial, to 90 cm high (36 in), clump forming, arising from an underground corm. LEAVES simple, basal, linear, mostly 10–50 × 0.5–1 cm (4–20 × ¼–⅜ in), lacking a midrib, smelling like onions, green or variegated with longitudinal white lines. FLOWERS continuously through the year; flowers 10 to 16 borne in an umbel atop a leafless stalk to 80 cm long (32 in). Corolla with fused tepals, funnel-shaped, 1.6–2.5 cm long (⅝–1 in) divided about halfway into six lanceolate segments, with a corona of three lobes from the inner tepal segments, lilac with a darker median line. FRUIT an ovoid capsule. PROPAGATE by division of the corm, or by seeds. Moist but well-drained soils in sunny places are preferred. It is often planted in borders or in rock gardens in the tropics, and in pots in greenhouses and conservatories in temperate climates. 'Variegata' has variegated leaves.

Turnera TURNERACEAE

Turnera is a genus of 50–100 herb and shrub species found in tropical and subtropical America, one of which is cultivated as an ornamental.

Turnera ulmifolia Linnaeus

DISTINGUISHABLE by the subshrub habit, alternate leaves, toothed leaf margins, and large, yellow, five-parted flowers that close in the afternoon.

Turnera ulmifolia, yellow alder, unrelated to the alder genus *Alnus* in the birch family Betulaceae, is native to tropical America but is widely cultivated for its large yellow flowers and occasionally becomes naturalized. The flowers typically open in the early morning but by midday are closed, at least in dry climates. SUBSHRUB, coarse, to 1.5 m high (5 ft). LEAVES simple, alternate, blade lanceolate or ovate to

Turnera ulmifolia

elliptic, 4–13 cm long (1⅝–5 in) with coarsely toothed margins and a pair of glands at the top of the petiole. **FLOWERS** continuously through the year; flowers solitary, axillary. Corolla of five free, obovate, yellow petals 2.5–4 cm long (1–1⅝ in). **FRUIT** a many-seeded ovoid capsule. **PROPAGATE** by seeds. Moist but well-drained soils in sunny places are preferred. It is usually grown by itself as a specimen plant in gardens rather than in hedges.

Veitchia ARECACEAE

Veitchia is a genus of 18 palm species found from the Philippines to Fiji, some cultivated as ornamentals.

Veitchia merrillii (Beccari) H. E. Moore

DISTINGUISHABLE by the medium-sized palm habit, distinct glossy green crownshaft, gray, pinnately compound leaves, and plentiful red drupes. A related species from Fiji, *Veitchia joannis* H. Wendland, differs in being a much larger palm, to 30 m (100 ft) with longer fruits to 6 cm long (2½ in) and having about nine leaves at a time.

    Veitchia merrillii, Manila palm, sometimes called Christmas palm, is native to the island of Palawan in the Philippines but is widely cultivated elsewhere as an ornamental palm because of its attractive form and bright red fruits, sometimes used as Christmas decorations. **PALM** to 6 m high (20 ft), monoecious, trunk solitary and distinctly ringed, with a glossy green crownshaft. **LEAVES** 12 to 15 at a time, somewhat drooping with an ash-colored sheath, pinnately compound, alternate, blades narrowly oblong with as many as 50 pairs of pinnae with squared or toothed tips, the basal pinnae often long and hanging. **FLOWERS** mostly in spring to fall, fruiting in winter; flowers many, borne in ash-colored panicles to 70 cm long (28 in) attached just below the crownshaft. Corolla of three cream-colored petals 3–5 mm long (about ⅛–¼ in). **FRUIT** an attractive red ovoid drupe to 3 cm long (1¼ in) with the seed marked by a network of grooves. **PROPAGATE** by seeds, which are, however, slow to germinate. Moist but well-drained soils in sunny places are

Veitchia merrillii

preferred. It is often planted along walkways, borders, and streets though it is rather short for the latter purpose, and in temperate climates it is grown in the greenhouse or as a houseplant.

Warszewiczia RUBIACEAE

Warszewiczia is a tropical American genus of four shrub species, one of which is cultivated as an ornamental for its attractive inflorescences. The name *Warszewiczia* commemorates Józef Warscewicz, 1812–1826, Polish-Lithuanian plant collector.

Warszewiczia coccinea (Vahl) Klotzsch

DISTINGUISHABLE by the large shrubby habit, opposite leaves, interpetiolar stipules, and dense panicles bearing numerous red bracts and small yellow flowers.

Warszewiczia coccinea, wild poinsettia, a misnomer since it does not belong to the poinsettia genus *Euphorbia* or the family Euphorbiaceae,

Warszewiczia coccinea

is widely but not commonly cultivated in the tropics for its dense inflorescences of red flowers that cover the branches of the tree. SHRUB to 5 m high (16½ ft) or more with interpetiolar stipules. LEAVES simple, opposite, blade oblong, 15–60 cm long (6–24 in). FLOWERS continuously through the year; flowers many, borne in a terminal panicle of cymes with the calyx lobe of a flower enlarged into a red, oblong to elliptic, petal-like bract, two in 'David Auyong', usually 4–8 cm long (1⅝–3½ in) on the lower part of the panicle and shorter upward. Corolla with fused petals, funnel-shaped, tube 3–5 mm long (about ⅛–¼ in), deeply split into five lobes 4–5 mm long (about ¼ in), yellow. **FRUIT** a small capsule. **PROPAGATE** by cuttings or seeds. Moist but well-drained soils in sunny places are preferred. It is usually planted alone as a colorful specimen plant. The most common cultivar, 'David Auyong', has doubled bracts, giving the plant a denser inflorescence.

Wedelia ASTERACEAE

Wedelia is a genus of about 70 herb and shrub species found in the Old World and New World tropics but some authors limit the genus to only a few tropical American species. Several are cultivated as ornamentals.

Wedelia trilobata (Linnaeus) Hitchcock

DISTINGUISHABLE by the creeping habit, opposite, strongly veined leaves with toothed or lobed margins, and long-stalked flower heads of yellow ray and disk florets.

Wedelia trilobata, which lacks a widely recognized common name other than that of the genus, is native to tropical America but is widely cultivated for its yellow flower heads. **HERB**, perennial, creeping, rooting at the nodes, often with purple tinted stems. **LEAVES** simple, opposite, blade obovate to ovate, 2–9 cm long (¾–3½ in) with irregularly toothed or lobed margins. **FLOWERS** continuously through the year; flowers many, borne in solitary, long-stalked heads and surrounded by two to four series of bracts. Ray florets mostly 8 to 13, oblanceolate, 6–15 mm long (¼–⅝ in), yellow. Disk florets numerous, darker yellow than the ray florets. **FRUIT** an achene 4–5 mm long (about ¼ in) with a few scales on top but not

Wedelia trilobata

fertile. **PROPAGATE** by cuttings. Moist soils in partially shaded places are preferred. It is usually planted as a ground cover since it is able to crowd out nearly all other herbaceous species. It also does well in coastal situations and in large planters, and can be grown in elevated containers so that its flowering stems hang down in yellow cascades. Though it is sterile and does not set viable seed, it is a weed in many places, spreading widely by being cut and the cuttings discarded, and locally by creeping and rooting at the nodes.

Xiphidium HAEMODORACEAE

Xiphidium is a genus with a single species.

Xiphidium caeruleum Aublet

DISTINGUISHABLE by the equitant, *Iris*-like leaves lacking a midrib, and large, spreading inflorescences of small, white, lily-like flowers on long branches.

Xiphidium caeruleum

This species, which lacks a widely recognized common name other than that of the genus, is native to the Caribbean area but is occasionally cultivated in the tropics for its small white flowers. **HERB** to 1 m high (3¼ ft), arising from creeping rhizomes. **LEAVES** simple, alternate, equitant, blade linear-lanceolate, 35–60 × 3–6 cm (14–24 × 1¼–2½ in), glabrous, with a long-acuminate apex. **FLOWERS** continuously through the year; flowers many, borne in two rows on the curving branches of a terminal panicle to 36 cm long (14 in) with plantlets sometimes produced in the axils. Corolla with fused tepals, united at the base,

5–8 mm long (about ¼ in), deeply divided into six lanceolate to elliptic segments, white. **Fruit** a subglobose capsule, infrequently formed in cultivation. **Propagate** by division or plantlets. Moist but well-drained soils in sunny places are preferred. It is most often grown in gardens or as a border plant.

Yucca AGAVACEAE

Yucca comprises 30 to 40 shrubby or tree-like species native to warm temperate North America, some cultivated as ornamentals. The genus includes the Joshua tree, *Yucca brevifoia* Engelmann, of the Mojave Desert of the southwestern United States. Some are utilized for fiber or edible parts, and some are cultivated as ornamentals.

Yucca gloriosa Linnaeus

Distinguishable by the basal rosette sword-like leaves, sharp leaf tip, dark leaf margins, and large, dense panicles of large white flowers. It differs from *Agave* species by its narrower leaves and much shorter, more compact inflorescence.

Yucca gloriosa, Spanish dagger or bayonet, is native to the southeastern United States, from South Carolina to Florida, but is widely cultivated in warm temperate to tropical regions for its attractive appearance and the large inflorescences that periodically form. **Shrub-like** to 2.5 m high (8¼ ft) or more when flowering, straight or rarely branched. **Leaves** simple, mostly basal, spirally arranged, blade linear-lanceolate, sessile, usually 30–80 ×

Yucca gloriosa

3–7 cm (12–32 × 1¼–3 in), blue-green when young, maturing to dark green, margins dark, entire or with a few spines, tip sharp. **FLOWERS** intermittently during the year in warm climates. Pollination by hand may be necessary for seed set. Flowers many, drooping, fragrant at night, borne in a large terminal panicle. Corolla of six free elliptic tepals 3–5 cm long (1¼–2 in), greenish white to reddish. **FRUIT** a cylindrical capsule, infrequently formed in cultivation. **PROPAGATE** by seeds or division. Well-drained soils in sunny places are preferred. It is often grown as a potted plant, especially in temperate climates, or in water-conserving gardens. 'Variegata' has variegated leaves.

Zephyranthes AMARYLLIDACEAE

Zephyranthes comprises 71 bulb-forming, herbaceous perennial species found in tropical to warm temperate North and South America. Many zephyr lilies are cultivated as garden ornamentals or potted plants for their variously colored flowers. Two of the most common ornamental species are included here. The name *Zephyranthes* is from the Greek words meaning west wind and flower.

Zephyranthes citrina Baker

Synonym, *Zephyranthes eggersiana* Urban. **DISTINGUISHABLE** by the underground bulbs, leaves that are linear, erect, and basal, and bright yellow, six-parted flowers atop a leafless stalk. Two similar, white-flowered zephyr lilies are often cultivated. *Zephyranthes candida* Herbert, white zephyr lily, has the perianth, starting above the ovary, 3–4.5 cm long (1¼–1¾ in) and the stamens and style less than half as long as the tepals. *Zephyranthes atamasco* Herbert, atamasco lily, has the perianth 6.5–7.5 cm long (2⅝–3 in), the stamens more than half as long as the perianth, and the style nearly as long as the perianth.

    Zephyranthes citrina, yellow zephyr lily, sometimes called yellow rain lily, is native to Guyana but is widely cultivated in the tropics for its yellow flowers. **HERB**, scapose, to 40 cm high (16 in), clump forming, arising from an underground bulb. **LEAVES** simple, basal, linear, to 30 cm

Zephyranthes citrina with yellow flowers

Zephyranthes candida with white flowers

long (12 in) or more and 2–3 mm wide (about ¹⁄₁₆–⅛ in). FLOWERS any-time during the year; flowers solitary, borne above a bract 2–2.5 cm long (¾–1 in) on a leafless scape 10–40 cm long (4–16 in). Corolla with fused tepals, funnel-shaped, 3.5–4.5 cm long (1⅜–1¾ in) above the ovary, the tube 1–1.3 cm long (⅜–½ in), the tepal segments six, elliptic, 1–1.3 cm wide (⅜–½ in), yellow, green at the base. FRUIT a three-lobed capsule. PROPAGATE by offsets. Fertile, well-drained soils in sunny places are preferred. It is often grown in borders or in planters in the tropics, and as a potted plant in the greenhouse in temperate climates.

Zephyranthes rosea (Sprengel) Lindley

DISTINGUISHABLE by leaves that are erect, linear, basal, and solitary, and terminal, pink, six-parted flowers atop a leafless stem. A similar pink-flowered species, *Zephyranthes grandiflora* Lindley, differs in having larger tepal segments 4–6 × 1–2 cm long (1⅝–2½ × ⅜–¾ in) and the bract longer than the pedicel.

Zephyranthes rosea

Zephyranthes rosea, pink zephyr lily, is native to Cuba but is widely cultivated for its pink flowers. **HERB,** scapose, to 20 cm high (8 in), clump forming, arising from an underground bulb. **LEAVES** simple, basal, linear, to 20 cm long (8 in) and 3–7 mm wide (about ⅛–¼ in) but often shorter if grazed or mowed in lawns. **FLOWERS** anytime during the year; flowers solitary, borne on a pedicel 2.5–4 cm long (1–1⅝ in) above a sheathing bract on a leafless scape to 20 cm long (8 in). Corolla with fused tepals, funnel-shaped, 3–4.5 cm long (1¼–1¾ in) above the ovary, the tube short, green, the tepal segments six, oblanceolate, 3–4 cm long (1¼–1⅝ in), rose-colored, whitish at the base. **FRUIT** a three-lobed capsule. **PROPAGATE** by offsets or seeds. Fertile, moist, but well-drained soils in sunny places are preferred. It is usually grown as an herbaceous border or in planters in the tropics, where it often escapes and becomes naturalized as an admittedly attractive weed in lawns, and as a potted plant in the greenhouse in temperate climates.

Zingiber ZINGIBERACEAE

Zingiber is a genus of 80 species of herbs with aromatic rhizomes, ranging from eastern Asia to northern Australia. Some are cultivated as condiments, including the commercial ginger, *Z. officinale* Roscoe, and some as ornamentals for their attractive inflorescences.

Zingiber spectabile Griffith

DISTINGUISHABLE by the ginger-like leaves, ovoid, beehive-like spike of overlapping yellowish bracts with the tips curled, and yellow and purple flowers borne among the bracts.

Zingiber spectabile, beehive ginger, is native to Malaysia but is widely if not commonly cultivated for its inflorescence. One look at its inflorescence is all that is needed to know how it got its common name. **HERB** to 3 m high (10 ft) or more, arising from a fleshy, creeping rhizome. **LEAVES** simple, alternate, two-ranked, subsessile, blade narrowly elliptic, 20–50 cm long (8–20 in). **FLOWERS** intermittently during the year but mostly in summer and fall; flowers many, borne among yellowish ovate bracts with rounded, curled tips in a dense, ovoid to

Zingiber spectabile

cylindrical spike 15–30 cm long (6–12 in) on a leafless scape to 1 m high (3¼ ft). Corolla with fused petals, unequally three-lobed, yellowish, usually 3–4 cm long (1¼–1⅝ in) with an obovate, two-lobed, petal-like labellum about 3 cm long (1¼ in), purple spotted with yellow, and with a single stamen. **FRUIT** a three-angled capsule enclosed within the bracts. **PROPAGATE** by division. Moist but well-drained soils in partially shaded places are preferred. The inflorescence looks especially attractive in cut flower arrangements.

Zinnia ASTERACEAE

Zinnia is a genus of 11 to 22 herb and shrub species found from the southern United States to Chile. Several species and many hybrids are cultivated as ornamentals for their attractive flower heads.

Zinnia violacea Cavanilles
Synonym, *Zinnia elegans* Jacquin. **DISTINGUISHABLE** by the opposite

Zinnia violacea

sessile leaves three- to five-veined from the base, and ovoid flower heads of variously colored ray and disk florets.

Zinnia violacea, which lacks a widely recognized common name other than that of the genus, is native to Mexico but is a garden favorite throughout tropical and temperate areas for its large, variously colored flower heads. Most garden plants are believed to be hybrids involving *Z. violacea* and other species of the genus. **HERB**, annual, coarse, to 60 cm high (24 in). **LEAVES** simple, opposite, blade ovate to elliptic, 2–10 cm long (¾–4 in), subsessile, surface palmately three- to five-veined. **FLOWERS** anytime during the year after maturity; flowers in solitary, long-stalked, terminal, ovoid heads 4–8 cm in diameter (1⅝–3½ in) surrounded by three or four series of nearly round bracts. Ray florets numerous, obovate to oblanceolate, 1.5–4 cm long (⅝–1⅝ in), variously colored, violet, purple, orange, yellow, or white, sometimes entirely covered by the disk florets. Disk florets many, variously colored, often yellow. **FRUIT** a flattened narrow achene. **PROPAGATE** by achenes. Fertile moist soils in sunny places are preferred. It is often grown as a garden plant in borders or as a potted plant. Many cultivars, differing in color and shape of the heads, have been named. A common one with small heads is 'Thumbelina'. Though sometimes escaping and becoming naturalized, zinnia is not reported to be a problem weed.

Twenty Common Plant Families

Twenty of the most common families of tropical ornamental plants are described here, which include about two-thirds of all the plants in this book. All are flowering plants, Angiospermae. Angiosperms are divided into two groups, Dicotyledonae and Monocotyledonae. Dicotyledons or dicots have a pair of embryonic seed leaves or cotyledons, mostly netted or pinnate, feather-like venation, and flower parts mostly in multiples of four or five. Moncotyledons or monocots have a single seed leaf, mostly parallel leaf venation, and flower parts mostly in multiples of three.

Dicotyledons

Acanthaceae

The acanthus family Acanthaceae comprises about 346 genera with 4300 herb, shrub, vine, and some tree species centered in the tropics. Because of the noticeable flowers, bracts, or leaves of the species, it is one of the most important tropical ornamental families, ranking second in this book in number of species. Members of the family can often be recognized by their shrubby or viny habit, opposite leaves, colorful or green inflorescence bracts, two-lipped flowers, and two-celled capsule that splits open along two seams. Twenty-four species in 13 genera are featured here—*Aphelandra, Asystasia, Barleria, Crossandra, Grapto-*

phyllum, Hemigraphis, Justicia, Odontonema, Pachystachys, Pseuderanthemum, Sanchezia, Strobilanthes, and *Thunbergia.*

Amaranthaceae

The amaranth family Amaranthaceae comprises 65 to 71 genera with about 800 perennial and annual herb and shrub species found throughout tropical to temperate regions. It includes many weedy species, some used for grains and edible greens, *Amaranthus cruentus,* the amaranth, for example, and some as ornamentals. Members of the family can often be recognized by their mostly herbaceous habit, alternate or opposite leaves, racemes or spikes typically with membranous bracts below tiny, inconspicuous flowers, and dry, one-seeded, nonsplitting fruit called a utricle that often contains a single shiny black seed. Six species in five genera are featured here—*Alternanthera, Amaranthus, Celosia, Gomphrena,* and *Iresine.*

Apocynaceae

The dogbane family Apocynaceae comprises about 215 genera with 2100 vine, shrub, and less frequently, herb and tree species found throughout the world but especially in the tropics. It includes many ornamentals with large flowers, and many of the species are poisonous, hence the name dogbane. Members of the family can usually be recognized by their opposite leaves, milky sap, flowers with the fused petals typically overlapping in the bud, and single style and stigma. Fourteen species in 11 genera are featured here—*Adenium, Allamanda, Beaumontia, Carissa, Catharanthus, Mandevilla, Nerium, Plumeria, Stemmadenia, Tabernaemontana,* and *Thevetia.*

Asclepiadaceae

The milkweed family Asclepiadaceae comprises about 350 genera with 2850 herb, vine, and rarely, shrub and tree species found throughout the world, particularly in Africa. Some of them are noxious weeds that contain a latex poisonous to livestock, and many are grown as ornamentals. The most famous plants in the family are the milkweeds that serve as a food source for the monarch butterfly. Members of the family may be recognized by their opposite leaves, milky sap, stamens fused into a column around the two styles that share one stigma, and pollen stuck together into specialized sacs called pollinia. The family is most easily confused with Apocynaceae, whose members have a single style with its own stigma. Seven species in seven genera are featured here—*Asclepias, Calotropis, Cryptostegia, Hoya, Stapelia, Stephanotis,* and *Telosma.*

Asteraceae

The aster or sunflower family Asteraceae, also known as Compositae, is the largest family of flowering plants and comprises approximately 1300 genera with 21,000 herb, shrub, vine, and rarely, tree species distributed throughout the world. Economically, it includes many weeds, some species with edible leaves or seeds (*Cynara scolymus,* artichoke; *Helianthus annuus,* sunflower seeds and oil; *Lactuca sativa,* lettuce), some that are used as condiments (*Cichorium endivia,* endive; *C. intybus,* chicory), and many that are important ornamentals. This is one of the most easily recognized families. Its members are characterized by sessile, stalkless flowers in short dense spikes called heads, usually surrounded by a ring of bracts. The flowers of the head of many species are of two kinds, ray florets with a strap-shaped corolla that looks like a petal of an individual fl ower at the edge and disk florets with tubular corollas at the center. Seventeen species in 14 genera are featured here—*Aster, Centratherum, Chrysanthemum, Cosmos, Coreopsis, Dahlia, Gaillardia, Gerbera, Helianthus, Solidago, Tagetes, Tithonia, Wedelia,* and *Zinnia.*

Bignoniaceae

The catalpa family Bignoniaceae comprises about 112 genera with 725 tree, shrub, vine, and rarely, herb species found mostly in the tropics, especially in South America. Some species are important for their timber but the most important economic species are ornamentals. Members of the family may be recognized by their tree, shrub, or vine habit, leaves that are opposite and often pinnately compound, colorful two-lipped flowers, and capsule fruits frequently containing winged seeds. Sixteen species in 14 genera are featured here—*Catalpa, Crescentia, Jacaranda, Kigelia, Macfadyena, Mansoa, Parmentiera, Podranea, Pyrostegia, Spathodea, Tabebuia, Tecoma, Tecomanthe,* and *Tecomaria.*

Convolvulaceae

The morning glory family Convolvulaceae comprises about 58 genera with 1650 woody and herbaceous vine species found throughout the world, especially in the tropics. Nearly a third of these belong to the genus *Ipomoea.* The family is economically important because of its many weedy species, one edible species (*I. batatas,* sweet potato), and many ornamentals. Members of the family may be recognized by their viny habit, leaves that are alternate and often heart-shaped, petals fused into a bell- or wheel-shaped corolla, and fruit typically a four-seeded capsule. Many of the species have milky sap. Seven species in four genera are featured here—*Argyreia, Evolvulus, Ipomoea,* and *Merremia.*

Euphorbiaceae

The spurge family Euphorbiaceae comprises about 300 to 320 genera with 7500 to 8000 herb, shrub, and tree species found throughout tropical, subtropical, and temperate regions. The family is commercially important for rubber *(Hevea brasiliensis),* cassava *(Manihot esculenta),* timber, various medicines, and many ornamentals, the latter mostly as succulent novelties or for colorful foliage since the flowers are often small and inconspicuous. Many species are serious weeds because they often contain a poisonous latex. The family is quite heterogeneous but its members may often be recognized by their simple, alternate or opposite leaves, often milky sap, unisexual flowers in a distinctive inflorescence, the cyathium, three styles or style lobes, and the fruit often a schizocarp splitting at maturity into three one-seeded segments. Nineteen species in seven genera are featured here—*Acalypha, Breynia, Codiaeum, Euphorbia, Jatropha, Manihot,* and *Pedilanthus.*

Fabaceae

The pea family Fabaceae, also known as Leguminosae, comprises about 667 genera with 16,400 to 18,000 tree, shrub, herb, vine, and liana species found throughout the world. The family is split by many authors into three families, Mimosaceae, Caesalpiniaceae, and Papilionaceae, which when considered as subfamilies are Mimosoideae (numerous stamens and relatively small petals), Caesalpinioideae (mostly with distinct petals and up to ten free stamens), and Papilionoideae (mostly with butterfly-like, papilionaceous flowers with modified unequal petals and ten stamens often fused together). Despite this diversity, members of the family may often be recognized by their alternate leaves often trifoliate or pinnately compound, often butterfly-like flowers, and fruit typically a pod splitting open along two seams. In addition to the many ornamentals, the family Fabaceae comprises more species than any other in this book, including many edible plants (various genera, beans; *Arachis hypogaea,* peanut; *Glycine max,* soy bean; *Pisum sativum,* pea), fodder plants (*Medicago sativa,* alfalfa; *Trifolium* spp., clover), and tropical timbers, not to mention species used for dyes, oils, and resins. The roots of most species contain nitrogen-fixing bacteria that are important for replenishing soil fertility. Thirty-two species in 24 genera are featured here—*Acacia, Albizia, Amherstia, Bauhinia, Brownea, Caesalpinia, Calliandra, Cassia, Clitoria, Colvillea, Delonix, Enterolobium, Erythrina, Gliricidia, Parkinsonia, Peltophorum, Pithecellobium, Pterocarpus, Samanea, Saraca, Senna, Sesbania, Strongylodon,* and *Tamarindus.*

Malvaceae

The mallow family Malvaceae comprises about 55 to as many as 116 genera with 100 to 2300 shrub, annual and perennial herb, and some tree species found throughout the tropics and subtropics, with some in temperate regions. It is economically important for fiber plants (*Gossypium* spp., cotton), food plants (*Abelmoschus esculentus,* okra; *A. manihot,* tree spinach), and especially, ornamental plants. Members of the family can usually be recognized by their alternate, often palmately lobed leaves, corolla of five free petals, and numerous stamens fused into a staminal column around an elongated style. Nine species in four genera are featured here—*Abelmoschus, Gossypium, Hibiscus,* and *Malvaviscus.*

Rubiaceae

The coffee family Rubiaceae comprises about 500 to 630 genera with 6500 to perhaps as many as 10,400 herb, vine, and tree species that are mostly but not entirely found in the tropics and subtropics. In addition to the numerous ornamental species, the family includes important tropical crops such as *Cinchona* spp., quinine; *Coffea* spp., coffee; and *Psychotria ipecacuanha,* ipecac. Members of the family may be recognized by their opposite simple leaves, interpetiolar stipules of the paired leaves connected together around the node, and corolla of fused petals with an inferior ovary, that is, the corolla and calyx are attached on top of the ovary. Twelve species in seven genera are featured here—*Gardenia, Hamelia, Ixora, Mussaenda, Pentas, Rondeletia,* and *Warszewiczia.*

Solanaceae

The nightshade family Solanaceae comprises about 90 genera with 2600 species found throughout the world, especially South America, which has 25 endemic genera. The family is economically important for its edible plants (*Capsicum annuum,* chili peppers; *Lycopersicon esculentum,* tomato; *Solanum tuberosum,* potato), drug plants, (*Datura* spp., producing scopolamine, for example), and many ornamentals and weeds. Members of the family may be recognized by their alternate, usually simple leaves, common presence of star-shaped, stellate hairs on the foliage, five-lobed regular corolla (not two-lipped or unequally lobed), and fruit usually a berry. Eight species in six genera are featured here—*Brugmansia, Brunfelsia, Cestrum, Datura, Solandra,* and *Solanum.*

Verbenaceae

The verbena family Verbenaceae comprises about 91 genera with 1900 herb, shrub, tree, and vine species found throughout the world but concentrated in the tropics. It includes many ornamentals cultivated for their flowers, and some trees (teak, *Tecoma grandis,* for example) harvested for their timber. Members of the family may be recognized by their mostly woody habit, common presence of four-angled stems, opposite and simple leaves, typically five-lobed, two-lipped corolla, typically four stamens, and fruit a drupe or composed of four nutlets. The family is very similar to the mint family Lamiaceae or Labiatae, which consistently has an ovary divided into four parts. Sixteen species in nine genera are featured here—*Citharexylum, Clerodendrum, Congea, Duranta, Holmskioldia, Lantana, Petraea, Phyla,* and *Stachytarpheta.*

Monocotyledons

Agavaceae

The agave family Agavaceae comprises 18 to 20 genera with 410 to 580 woody or arborescent, often succulent plants found throughout the tropics and subtropics, particularly in dry regions. Members of the family have often been included in the Liliaceae or Amaryllidaceae but differ in being mostly woody or subwoody plants with fibrous leaves besides having other, less obvious characteristics. They are economically important for a few things such as medicines (*Aloe vera,* aloe), fibers (*Agave sisalana,* sisal), and beverages (*Agave* spp., tequila) but are most useful as ornamentals. Ten species in seven genera are featured here—*Agave, Aloe, Cordyline, Dracaena, Polianthes, Sansevieria,* and *Yucca.*

Amaryllidaceae

The amaryllis family Amaryllidaceae comprises 85 genera with 1100 herbaceous species found throughout the tropics and subtropics of the world. Members of the family are often included in the Liliaceae, from which they differ mostly in having the flowers borne in umbels. Most of the economically important species are ornamentals. Members of the family may be distinguished by their rhizomes, corms, or bulbs, mostly linear leaves, often prominent flower parts, and inflorescences of umbels. Fifteen species in 11 genera are featured here—*Agapanthus, Clivia, Crinum, Eucharis, Hippeastrum, Hymenocallis, Molineria, Proiphys, Scadoxus, Tulbaghia,* and *Zephyranthes.*

Araceae

The arum family Araceae comprises about 106 genera with about 2950 corm-bearing herbs, vines, scrambling shrubs, and rarely, true epiphytes and free-floating species found throughout the tropics and subtropics, with a few in temperate regions. Members of the family can usually be recognized by their unisexual flowers, lacking both corolla and calyx, borne in an inflorescence consisting of a cylinder of sessile, unisexual flowers called a spadix enveloped, at the base at least, by an often colorful bract called a spathe. Many species are cultivated for their edible corms (taro, *Colocasia esculenta,* for example) and others as ornamentals for their leaves or growth form. Ten species in ten genera are featured here—*Aglaonema, Alocasia, Anthurium, Caladium, Dieffenbachia, Epipremnum, Monstera, Philodendron, Spathiphyllum,* and *Syngonium.*

Arecaceae

The palm family Arecaceae, also known as Palmae, comprises about 198 genera with 2650 palm species found throughout the tropics and warm temperate regions. It includes many commercially important species such as coconut *(Cocos nucifera),* oil palm *(Elaeis guineensis),* sago palm *(Metroxylon sagu),* and date palm *(Phoenix dactylifera)* as food plants, some climbing species important for their stems (various genera of rattans), and hundreds of ornamental species. It is one of the major ornamental groups of plants, and societies and journals are dedicated to the study and propagation of palms. Members of the family may usually be recognized by their woody habit, leaves (fronds) that are large and pinnate or palmately lobed or compound, and dense inflorescences of many inconspicuous flowers. Of these hundreds of species, eight of the most common ones in eight genera are featured here—*Caryota, Chrysalidocarpus, Livistona, Phoenix, Pritchardia, Rhapis, Roystonea,* and *Veitchia.*

Liliaceae

The lily family Liliaceae comprises nearly 200 genera with 3000 mostly herb species but estimates range much higher if families such as Agavaceae and Amaryllidaceae among others are included in it. Conversely, it is a smaller family if some members are removed to separate families such as Alliaceae or Asparagaceae. Some species are economically important for food (*Allium* spp., onion, garlic, and leek) but the family is most important for numerous and popular ornamentals such as tulips *(Tulipa),* lilies *(Lilium),* and hyacinths *(Hyacinthus).* Members of the family may be recognized by their mostly herbaceous habit, flowers with six subequal tepals (the calyx and corolla often being indistinguishable), and inflorescences of panicles or racemes. Six species in five genera are featured here—*Asparagus, Chlorophytum, Gloriosa, Hemerocallis,* and *Ophiopogon.*

Orchidaceae

The orchid family Orchidaceae comprises 800 to 1000 genera with 15,000 to 20,000 epiphytic or terrestrial herbs or, rarely, lianas found throughout the world. It is commercially very important for cut flowers and potted plants. Many of the horticultural orchids are hybrids that can readily be made using hand pollination, even between genera, making orchid taxonomy difficult. One species, *Vanilla planifolia,* vanilla, is valuable as a flavoring. Members of the family can usually be recognized by their herbaceous, sometimes epiphytic habit, three unequal, petal-like sepals, three petals, one of which, the labellum or lip, is three-lobed, and the fused structure called the column, composed of the stigma and one anther with two to eight packets called pollinia that contain the pollen. Although thousands of orchids are cultivated, with the number constantly increasing through hybridization, most orchids are grown by specialists and relatively few are commonly grown by the casual gardener. Five of the most common orchids in five genera are featured here—*Arachnis, Arundina, Epidendrum, Papilionanthe,* and *Spathoglottis*.

Zingiberaceae

The ginger family Zingiberaceae comprises 48 to 53 genera with about 1300 mostly rhizomatous, perennial herb species found throughout the tropics, especially the islands and mainland of southeastern Asia, an area that used to be called Indo-Malaya. Some species are utilized as spices (*Elettaria cardamomum,* cardamom; *Zingiber officinale,* ginger), some for their aromatic flowers (*Hedychium coronarium,* white ginger; *H. flavescens,* yellow ginger), and many as ornamentals because of their attractive flowers. Members of the family can be recognized by their typically large herbaceous habit, leaves having parallel veins from a midrib, and flowers having a single fertile stamen and three petal-like staminodes or sterile stamens, the middle and usually larger one, the labellum, typically prominent and sometimes even looking like an entire corolla. Some authors put four of the genera into a separate family, Costaceae, partly by virtue of their spirally arranged rather than two-ranked leaves. Twelve species in seven genera are featured here—*Alpinia, Costus, Curcuma, Etlingera, Hedychium, Tapeinochilos,* and *Zingiber*.

Identification Key

A key is used to help in the identification of plants. It is composed of pairs of opposing descriptive statements called couplets or leads. Select the one that best fits the plant. For example, the first choice is 1, Plants with flowers, versus 1′, Plants without flowers and with cones (gymnosperms). If the plant has flowers, go to the next numbered couplet, 2 versus 2′; if the plant has cones, the plants are described in the accompanying table (then turn to the main text and photograph). If it seems as though you have reached a dead-end where the couplets do not offer appropriate choices or the plant you are trying to identify does not fit the description in the table or the text, either start over at the beginning of the key or work backwards through it, checking the choices. In each couplet, the preceding couplet that led there is indicated in parentheses, for example, 10 (4′), meaning return to couplet 4 versus 4′ if couplet 10 seems to be a dead-end. Some species are keyed out in more than one place to facilitate identification.

In the tables, plants have been grouped alphabetically first by flower color—red, orange, yellow, green, cream and white, blue, lavender and purple—with pink either at the beginning or the end of the table, depending on the particular circumstances. Other characteristics are given to help distinguish plants in a given group. Please turn to the main entries and photographs to confirm identifications.

1   Plants with flowers. 2
1′   Plants without flowers and with cones (gymnosperms):

PLANT	SEEDS	OTHER CHARACTERISTICS
Araucaria heterophylla	1 per scale in pine-like cone	leaves awl-shaped; large pine-like tree
Cycas circinalis	4–10 on spoon-shaped scales	leaves pinnately compound; palm-like tree

2 (1)   Leaves with netted venation and flower parts usually in fours and fives (dicots). 3
2′   Leaves with parallel venation and flower parts usually in multiples of three (monocots) . . 28

3 (2)   Plant a tree or shrub. 4
3′   Plant a vine or herb 17

4 (3)   Plant a tree, large, woody, not usually branching at the base. 5
4′   Plant a shrub or subshrub, woody or subwoody, erect, usually branching from the base . . 10

5 (4)   Leaves compound, divided into leaflets. 6
5′   Leaves simple. 8

6 (5)   Leaves alternately arranged 7
6′   Leaves oppositely arranged:

PLANT	FLOWER COLOR	OTHER CHARACTERISTICS
Spathodea campanulata	orange to yellow	flowers large, calyx boat-shaped
Tabebuia aurea	yellow	tree, leaf margins entire
Tabebuia donnell-smithii	yellow	tree, leaf margins toothed
Tecoma stans	yellow	shrub or small tree
Sambucus mexicana	white	shrub or small tree; flowers many, tiny
Parmentiera cereifera	greenish	fruits gourd-like; flowers solitary on stems
Guaiacum officinale	blue	petals free, 5; fruits yellow
Jacaranda mimosifolia	lavender	leaves pinnately compound
Tabebuia heterophylla	lavender to white	leaves palmately compound
Kigelia africana	purple inside	fruits hanging, sausage-like; flowers large

7   Leaves palmately divided, or trifoliate:

PLANT	FLOWER COLOR	OTHER CHARACTERISTICS
Calliandra haematocephala	red or white	flowers powder-puff-like
Erythrina crista-galli	red	leaves trifoliate; flowering year-round
Erythrina variegata	red	leaves trifoliate; flowering in winter
Schefflera actinophylla	red	leaves palmately compound; petioles sheathing
Schefflera arboricola	yellow	leaves palmately divided; petioles sheathing
Triphasia trifolia	white	leaves trifoliate; tree or shrub; stems thorny

7′   Leaves pinnately or bipinnately divided:

PLANT	FLOWER COLOR	OTHER CHARACTERISTICS
Cassia grandis	pink to white	stipule awl-shaped; lower leaf surface fuzzy
Cassia javanica	pink to white	stipule 2-lobed; leaves mostly glabrous
Cassia ×*nealii*	pink, yellow, white	flowers seasonally abundant; no fruits
Gliricidia sepium	rose pink	flowers seasonal, butterfly-like
Amherstia nobilis	red to pink	inflorescence bracts large, red to pink
Brownea macrophylla	red	flowers in heads on trunks and branches
Delonix regia	red	petals showy, one with a white blotch
Quassia amara	red	petioles winged; flowers cone-shaped
Saraca indica	red	flower 4-lobed with a red stalk
Samanea saman	red and white	petals inconspicuous; stamens showy
Colvillea racemosa	orange	seasonal hanging, cone-shaped racemes
Grevillea robusta	orange	leaves woolly white; leaflets lobed
Cassia fistula	yellow	petals showy, 5; pods long, cylindrical
Parkinsonia aculeata	yellow	stems and trunk spiny, green; appears leafless
Peltophorum pterocarpum	yellow	pods oblong, red-brown; petals frilly-edged
Pterocarpus indicus	yellow	pods flat, winged; flowers butterfly-like
Senna surattensis	yellow	petals showy, 5; pods flattened
Tamarindus indica	cream	pods mealy brown, sausage-shaped
Albizia lebbeck	white	heads powder-puff-like; pods woody
Enterolobium cyclocarpum	white	fruits dark, ear-shaped; flowers small
Filicium decipiens	white	foliage fern-like; small seasonal flowers in spring
Harpullia pendula	white	capsule 2-lobed with 2 large black seeds
Murraya paniculata	white	usually shrubby; flower clusters very fragrant
Pithecellobium dulce	white	thorny tree; pods twisted, pith-filled
Sesbania grandiflora	white or red	flowers large, butterfly-like
Melia azedarach	lavender	fruits yellow; leaves bipinnately compound

8 (5′) Leaves alternately arranged or, rarely, absent 9
8′   Leaves oppositely arranged or clustered:

PLANT	FLOWER COLOR	OTHER CHARACTERISTICS
Callistemon citrinus	red	leaf veins parallel; bottlebrush inflorescence
Punica granatum	red	large red edible fruit or showy flowers
Catalpa longissima	white	flowers 2-lipped; fruit long, linear
Citharexylum spp.	white	long racemes of tiny flowers; fruit globose
Clerodendrum quadriloculare	white	corolla tubular; lower leaf surface purple
Clusia rosea	white	leaves leathery; capsule crab-shaped when open
Crescentia cujete	white	fruits gourd-like; flowers solitary on stems
Eucalyptus deglupta	white stamens	stamens many; bark multicolored
Fagraea berteroana	white to pale orange	corolla long-tubed; fruit large, orange

PLANT	FLOWER COLOR	OTHER CHARACTERISTICS
Melaleuca quinquenervia	white	bark papery; bottlebrush inflorescence
Stemmadenia litoralis	white	sap milky; corolla always 5-lobed
Tabernaemontana divaricata	white	sap milky; corolla often doubled
Lagerstroemia speciosa	purplish to white	flowers seasonal, crape-like

9 (8)   Sap milky:

PLANT	FLOWER COLOR	OTHER CHARACTERISTICS
Thevetia peruviana	yellow	leaves linear; fruit with 1 large hard seed
Chrysophyllum oliviforme	greenish	lower leaf surfaces velvety, copper-colored
Plumeria obtusa	white	leaves blunt-tipped, glossy
Plumeria rubra	white to pink or yellow	leaves acute-tipped, dull-surfaced
Ficus spp.	tiny, enclosed	fruits round; stem tip with a sheathing cap
Euphorbia lactea	inconspicuous, rare	spiny succulent white-striped stem; leafless

9′   Sap clear:

PLANT	FLOWER COLOR	OTHER CHARACTERISTICS
Bauhinia monandra	pink to white	leaves 2-lobed; petals long-stalked
Bixa orellana	pink	capsule bristly, filled with red seeds
Sterculia foetida	red-purple	leaves palmately lobed, flowers fetid
Bauhinia galpinii	red	leaves 2-lobed; petals long-stalked
Brachychiton acerifolius	red	leaves lobed, deciduous; flowers seasonal
Couroupita guianensis	red	fruits on short basal branches, cannonball-like
Cordia sebestena	orange	corolla funnel-shaped, crape-like
Acacia confusa	yellow	leaves narrow, parallel-veined
Bauhinia tomentosa	yellow	leaves 2-lobed; flowers hardly open
Cananga odorata	yellow	leaves in 1 plane; flowers very fragrant
Cochlospermum vitifolium	yellow	leaves palmate; flowers large, seasonal
Hibiscus tiliaceus	yellow	leaves heart-shaped; petals purple at base
Brugmansia ×*candida*	white	flowers large, hanging; leaves downy
Elaeocarpus grandis	white	leaves aging red; fruits blue, marble-like
Coccoloba uvifera	green	leaves round, red-veined from base
Salix babylonica	green	branches drooping; flowers inconspicuous

10 (4′) Leaves simple **11**
10′   Leaves compound, divided into leaflets:

PLANT	FLOWER COLOR	OTHER CHARACTERISTICS
Caesalpinia pulcherrima	red and/or yellow	stems thorny; stamens long, showy
Calliandra spp.	red to white	powder-puff-like flowers of showy stamens
Leea guineensis	red to purple	leaves divided 2–3 times, often purple

PLANT	FLOWER COLOR	OTHER CHARACTERISTICS
Quassia amara	red	petioles winged; flowers cone-shaped
Rosa ×damascena	red to white	stems thorny; flowers with many petals
Schefflera arboricola	yellow	leaves palmately divided; petioles sheathing
Senna alata	yellow	bracts orange to yellow; fruits black, winged
Senna surattensis	yellow	petals showy, 5; pods flattened
Tecoma stans	yellow	leaves opposite; flowers bell-shaped
Jasminum grandiflorum	white	leaves opposite; stamens 2
Murraya paniculata	white	flowers in clusters, strongly aromatic
Nandina domestica	white	leaves opposite, divided 2–3 times
Sambucus mexicana	white	shrub or small tree; flowers many, tiny
Triphasia trifolia	white	tree or shrub; leaves trifoliate; stems thorny
Polyscias spp.	green to white	petiole base sheathing; leaves often variegated

11 (10) Sap milky 12
11′   Sap clear 13

12 (11) Leaves oppositely arranged:

PLANT	FLOWER COLOR	OTHER CHARACTERISTICS
Adenium obesum	red	stems swollen
Asclepias curassavica	red with orange	subshrub; seeds silky
Allamanda cathartica	yellow	scandent shrub; leaves whorled, glossy
Allamanda schottii	yellow	scandent shrub; leaves whorled, fuzzy
Beaumontia multiflora	white	scandent shrub; flowers big
Calotropis gigantea	white to purplish	leaves opposite, surface powdery white
Carissa macrocarpa	white	thorns branched; fruit red
Euphorbia leucocephala	white bracts	covered with bracts seasonally
Stemmadenia litoralis	white	tree to small shrub; not thorny
Allamanda blanchetii	purplish	leaves whorled; flowers bell-shaped
Catharanthus roseus	purplish or white	leaves opposite; subshrub
Cryptostegia grandiflora	purplish	leaves opposite; flowers bell-shaped
Euphorbia cotinifolia	inconspicuous	foliage purple

12′   Leaves alternately arranged or absent:

PLANT	FLOWER COLOR	OTHER CHARACTERISTICS
Euphorbia milii	red bracts	thorny shrub, often low-growing
Euphorbia pulcherrima	red to white bracts	bracts large, showy, seasonal
Pedilanthus tithymaloides	red	stems zigzag; flowers cone-shaped
Manihot esculenta	green to white	leaves deeply lobed, variegated
Ipomoea fistulosa	purplish	flowers large, showy, funnel-shaped
Euphorbia lactea	inconspicuous	spiny succulent; stems white-striped; leafless
Euphorbia neriifolia	inconspicuous	succulent spiny shrub; stems often leafless

PLANT	FLOWER COLOR	OTHER CHARACTERISTICS
Euphorbia tirucalli	inconspicuous	nearly leafless; stems pencil-like, green
Ficus pumila	inconspicuous	creeper on walls and rocks; fruits fig-like

13 (11′) Leaves alternately arranged or basal, clustered at the base 14
13′   Leaves oppositely arranged, whorled, absent, or tiny 16

14 (13) Leaves or bracts not colorful but leaves may be white-variegated 15
14′   Leaves or bracts colorful:

PLANT	FLOWER COLOR	OTHER CHARACTERISTICS
Acalypha spp.	greenish	leaves large, colorful; margin toothed
Breynia disticha	purplish	leaves small, oval, colorful; margin smooth
Bougainvillea spp.	various	bracts colorful; stems thorny; viny shrub
Codiaeum variegatum	inconspicuous	leaves variously shaped and colored

15 (14) Leaf margins toothed or lobed:

PLANT	FLOWER COLOR	OTHER CHARACTERISTICS
Abelmoschus rugosus	red	staminal tube drooping; flower center white
Acalypha hispida	red	inflorescences cattail-like
Bauhinia galpinii	red	leaves 2-lobed; petals long-stalked
Hibiscus rosa-sinensis	red and other colors	stamens fused into tube; petals not lobed
Hibiscus schizopetalus	red	stamens fused into tube; petals lobed
Jatropha multifida	red	leaves deeply palmately lobed
Malvaviscus penduliflorus	red	stamens fused into tube; flowers closed
Pelargonium ×hortorum	red	subshrub; leaves round, margin round-toothed
Tithonia rotundifolia	orange	sunflower-like; inflorescence stalk swollen
Gossypium barbadense	yellow	stamens fused into tube; cotton fruits
Helianthus annuus	yellow	sunflower; leaves green, margin toothed
Helianthus argophyllus	yellow	sunflower; leaves silvery, margin toothed
Ochna thomasiana	yellow	fruits black on a red disk; many stamens
Solidago nemoralis	yellow	tall and narrow; panicles of tiny flowers
Tithonia diversifolia	yellow	sunflower-like; leaves deeply lobed
Turnera ulmifolia	yellow	petals 5, bright yellow; stamens free
Hibiscus sabdariffa	pale yellow	stamens fused into tube; leaves 3-lobed
Jatropha curcas	yellowish	flowers tiny; fruits globose, 3-seeded
Datura metel	white or other colors	flowers large, solitary; fruits spiny
Hibiscus mutabilis	white to pink	stamens fused into tube; leaves fuzzy
Grewia occidentalis	purplish	petals and longer sepals similarly colored
Hibiscus syriacus	purple and other colors	stamens fused into tube

PLANT	FLOWER COLOR	OTHER CHARACTERISTICS
Jatropha integerrima	rose	separate male and female flowers on same plant

15′   Leaf margins smooth, or leafless:

PLANT	FLOWER COLOR	OTHER CHARACTERISTICS
Bixa orellana	pink	capsules spiny, filled with red seeds
Jatropha podagrica	red	leaves with petiole attached inside margin
Opuntia cochinellifera	red	cactus; leafless; flattened succulent stems
Pedilanthus tithymaloides	red	stems zigzag; flowers cone-shaped
Artabotrys hexapetalus	yellow	hook-like structure on flower stalk
Cestrum nocturnum	pale yellow	flowers tubular with erect corolla lobes
Brugmansia ×*candida*	white	flowers large, hanging; leaves downy
Brunfelsia americana	white	flowers long-tubed, fragrant
Cestrum diurnum	white	flowers tubular with lobes bent back
Datura metel	white or other colors	flowers large, solitary; fruits spiny
Pittosporum tobira	white but rare	leaves obovate; surface convex, not flat
Rhaphiolepis umbellata	white to pink	leaves leathery; corolla of 5 free petals
Evolvulus glomeratus	blue and white	corolla wheel-shaped; low plant
Plumbago auriculata	pale blue	flowers long-tubed with sticky calyx
Brunfelsia pauciflora	purplish to white	flowers fading from purplish to white

16 (13′) Leaves or flower bracts colorful:

PLANT	FLOWER COLOR	OTHER CHARACTERISTICS
Medinilla magnifica	pink	bracts below inflorescence large, pink
Aphelandra sinclairiana	pink to rose	bracts orange, ovate, densely overlapping
Aphelandra aurantiaca	red	bracts green; leaves pale-veined
Warszewiczia coccinea	red bracts	flowers small, yellow; bracts large, showy
Mussaenda erythrophylla	yellow	1 large, bright red, leaf-like calyx lobe
Mussaenda philippica	yellow	5 large, white, showy calyx lobes
Mussaenda 'Queen Sirikit'	yellow	5 pink, showy calyx lobes
Sanchezia speciosa	yellow to orange	leaves yellow-veined; flower bracts red
Clerodendrum quadriloculare	white	leaves purple beneath; corolla tubular
Congea griffithiana	white	bracts pink; velvety lower-leaf surface
Justicia brandegeeana	white	bracts red, leaf-like; corolla 2-lipped
Pachystachys lutea	white	bracts orange, showy, ovate, overlapping
Pseuderanthemum bicolor	white and purplish	leaves dark purple; flowers often mottled
Pseuderanthemum carruthersii	white and purplish	leaves purple or yellow; flowers mottled
Justicia betonica	purplish	bracts white, green-veined; flowers 2-lipped
Strobilanthes dyerianus	purplish	leaves with iridescent purple markings
Graptophyllum pictum	purple-red	leaves variegated; corolla strongly 2-lipped
Iresine herbstii	inconspicuous, white	leaves red-variegated; leaf tip notched

16'   Leaves or flower bracts not colorful:

PLANT	FLOWER COLOR	OTHER CHARACTERISTICS
Callistemon citrinus	red	leaf veins parallel; bottlebrush inflorescence
Clerodendrum buchananii	red	panicles loose; stamens protruding
Clerodendrum paniculatum	red	panicles cone-shaped; stamens protruding
Clerodendrum thomsonae	red	calyx purple or white; stamens protruding
Holmskioldia sanguinea	red	calyx red, saucer-like; flowers 2-lipped
Ixora casei	red	corolla tubular, 4-lobed; leaves 10–20 cm (4–8 in) long
Ixora coccinea	red or yellow	corolla tubular, 4-lobed; leaves less than 10 cm (4 in) long
Lantana camara	red, orange, etc.	heads hemispheric, flowers multicolored
Nerium oleander	red to white	leaves whorled; corolla funnel-shaped
Odontonema tubiforme	red	corolla tubular, 5-lobed; panicles terminal
Pachystachys spicata	red	spikes terminal; flowers showy, 2-lipped
Quisqualis indica	red or pink	flowers 5-lobed, long, tubular
Rondeletia odorata	red with orange	corolla 5-lobed, orange in center
Russelia equisetiformis	red	stems nearly leafless; flowers tubular
Hamelia patens	orange	corolla tubular with 5 short, erect lobes
Galphimia gracilis	yellow	petals stalked; stamens red
Ixora coccinea	yellow or red	corolla tubular, 4-lobed; leaves less than 10 cm (4 in) long
Lantana camara	orange, red, etc.	heads hemispheric with differently colored flowers
Barleria cristata	white or purplish	bracts green-fringed; flowers funnel-shaped
Clerodendrum indicum	white	flowers long, tubular; unbranching shrub
Clerodendrum wallichii	white	racemes hanging; stamens long, protruding
Eugenia uniflora	white	flowers tiny with many stamens; fruit red, lobed
Gardenia augusta	white	flowers large, usually with many lobes
Gardenia taitenis	white	flowers large, 6- to 8-lobed; calyx winged
Hiptage benghalensis	white and yellow	fruits winged; petals fringed
Homalocladium platycladum	white	leafless; stems strap-shaped; flowers tiny
Ixora finlaysoniana	white	flowers long, tubular, 4-lobed
Jasminum laurifolium	white	flowers 9- to 11-lobed, lobes spreading; 2 stamens in throat
Jasminum multiflorum	white	flowers 6- to 9-lobed; 2 stamens in throat; leaves fuzzy
Jasminum sambac	white	flowers 4- to 9-lobed; 2 stamens in throat
Lawsonia inermis	white	petals 4, stalked, wrinkled; 8 longer stamens
Ligustrum japonicum	white	flowers small; 2 protruding stamens
Nerium oleander	white to red	leaves whorled; filament fringe on corolla
Clerodendrum myricoides	blue	flowers 2-toned blue; stamens long, protruding

PLANT	FLOWER COLOR	OTHER CHARACTERISTICS
Duranta erecta	pale blue or white	racemes drooping; fruits golden
Barleria cristata	purplish or white	bracts green-fringed; flowers funnel-shaped
Cuphea hyssopifolia	purplish or white	flowers small; low, spreading shrub
Justicia carnea	purplish to pink	spikes dense, terminal; flowers 2-lipped
Lagerstroemia indica	purplish	petals stalked, crape-like
Lantana camara	purplish, yellow, etc.	heads hemispheric, flowers multicolored
Leucophyllum frutescens	purplish	leaves ash-colored; corolla funnel-shaped
Petraea volubilis	purplish	flowers 2-toned purplish; leaf surface sandpaper-like
Thunbergia erecta	deep purple	leaves in 1 plane; corolla yellow inside
Tibouchina urvilleana	purplish	petals free; filaments bent; calyx bristly
Lantana montevidensis	pink	flowers in heads; 2-lipped
Malpighia coccigera	pink	petals 5, stalked; leaf margin spine-tipped
Ocimum tenuiflorum	pink to lavender	stems square; flowers tiny; stamens protruding
Stachytarpheta mutabilis	pink	flowers in long, rattail-like spikes
Portulacaria afra	rarely formed	stems red; leaves succulent, jade-like

17 (3′) Plant a vine, creeping or climbing, herbaceous or woody, or weak-stemmed shrub . . .18
17′   Plant an herb or subshrub, generally small, not woody 23

18 (17) Leaves compound, divided into leaflets 19
18′   Leaves simple or absent 21

19 (18) Leaves oppositely arranged 20
19′   Leaves alternately arranged:

PLANT	FLOWER COLOR	OTHER CHARACTERISTICS
Ipomoea quamoclit	red	leaves finely pinnately dissected
Strongylodon macrobotrys	green to blue-green	leaves trifoliate; flowers in large racemes
Clitoria ternatea	blue to purple	leaves trifoliate; flowers showy, butterfly-like
Solanum seaforthianum	blue to purple	leaves pinnately compound; flowers 5-lobed

20 (19) Tendrils present at ends of leaves:

PLANT	FLOWER COLOR	OTHER CHARACTERISTICS
Pyrostegia venusta	orange	corolla tubular
Macfadyena unguis-cati	yellow	corolla funnel-shaped
Mansoa hymenaea	purplish	foliage garlic-scented

20′   Tendrils not present:

PLANT	FLOWER COLOR	OTHER CHARACTERISTICS
Podranea ricasoliana	pink, red-veined	leaf margin entire
Tecomanthe dendrophila	rose	flower clusters dense, in spring only

PLANT	FLOWER COLOR	OTHER CHARACTERISTICS
Tecomaria capensis	orange	leaf margin toothed
Jasminum grandiflorum	white	corolla tubular with a spreading limb

21 (18′) Leaves oppositely arranged, in pairs; or whorled, three or more together at a node
(the point of attachment) 22

21′   Leaves alternately arranged:

PLANT	FLOWER COLOR	OTHER CHARACTERISTICS
Antigonon leptopus	pink	bracts pink; tendrils at inflorescence tip
Ipomoea horsfalliae	red	leaves palmately lobed
Ipomoea quamoclit	red	leaves finely pinnately dissected
Artabotrys hexapetalus	yellow	hook-like structure on flower stalk
Merremia tuberosa	yellow	leaves heart-shaped; calyx woody
Solandra maxima	yellow	corolla large, funnel-shaped, purple-lined
Telosma cordata	yellow	leaves heart-shaped; corolla 2-toned yellow
Tristellateia australasiae	yellow	petals 5, free; glands at base of leaf
Hiptage benghalensis	white and yellow	shrub-like; petals fringed; fruits winged
Hylocereus undatus	white	spiny, leafless; stems 5-angled
Lonicera japonica	white to yellow	flowers deeply split, paired; stamens long
Argyreia nervosa	purplish	stems and lower leaf surfaces woolly
Aristolochia littoralis	dark purple	corolla-like calyx tubular, curved
Ipomoea cairica	purplish	leaves palmately lobed
Bougainvillea spp.	various	bracts colorful; stems thorny; viny shrub

22 (21) Sap milky:

PLANT	FLOWER COLOR	OTHER CHARACTERISTICS
Allamanda cathartica	yellow	leaves glossy, whorled
Allamanda schottii	yellow	leaves fuzzy, whorled
Hoya australis	cream	flowers waxy, arranged in umbels
Beaumontia multiflora	white	corolla large, spreading
Stephanotis floribunda	white	corolla tubular
Allamanda blanchetii	purplish	leaves whorled
Cryptostegia grandiflora	purplish	leaves opposite; liana or shrub
Mandevilla ×*amabilis*	pink	leaves opposite; herbaceous vine

22′   Sap clear:

PLANT	FLOWER COLOR	OTHER CHARACTERISTICS
Thunbergia alata	orange	herbaceous; corolla throat dark purple
Thunbergia mysorensis	orange	liana; bracts paired, showy purple
Thunbergia fragrans	white	herbaceous; flowers solitary, long-stalked
Thunbergia grandiflora	pale violet or white	liana; leaves relatively broad
Thunbergia laurifolia	pale violet or white	liana; leaves relatively narrow

23 (17′) Leaves simple or absent 24
23′   Leaves compound, divided into leaflets:

PLANT	FLOWER COLOR	OTHER CHARACTERISTICS
Kalanchoe pinnata	red	succulent; flowers hanging, tubular
Coreopsis tinctoria	yellow	leaves finely dissected; ray base dark
Cleome speciosa	white	leaves palmately divided; stamens long
Cosmos bipinnatus	various	ray florets showy; leaves finely dissected
Dahlia ×*hortensis*	various	ray florets showy, many; stems hollow

24 (23) Leaves alternately arranged; basal, clustered at the base; or absent 25
24′   Leaves oppositely arranged, in pairs; or whorled, three or more at the point of
attachment (the node) 26

25 (24) Flowers in heads, plant in the sunflower family Asteraceae:

PLANT	FLOWER COLOR	OTHER CHARACTERISTICS
Gaillardia pulchella	yellow and red	ray florets yellow-toothed at tip
Helianthus annuus	yellow	sunflower; ray florets dark-tipped
Helianthus argophyllus	yellow	sunflower; leaves silvery
Tagetes erecta	yellow to orange	leaves deeply pinnately lobed; florets showy
Tithonia rotundifolia	orange	stalks of heads inflated; florets showy, many
Centratherum punctatum	purplish	florets of two lengths
Aster laevis	pink to blue-violet	aster flower heads; leaves spoon-shaped
Chrysanthemum ×*morifolium*	various	ray florets many; leaves downy
Gerbera jamesonii	various	leaves basal; heads showy, long-stalked

25′   Flowers not in heads, plant not in the sunflower family Asteraceae:

PLANT	FLOWER COLOR	OTHER CHARACTERISTICS
Abelmoschus rugosus	red	staminal tube drooping; flower center white
Euphorbia cyathophora	red bracts	sap milky; leaves often notched
Kalanchoe blossfeldiana	red or yellow	leaves succulent; margins red, scalloped
Tropaeolum majus	orange	petiole attached to middle of leaf blade
Hippobroma longiflora	white	leaves basal, toothed; sap milky
Amaranthus tricolor	green	leaves colorful; seeds shiny black
Peperomia obtusifolia	green	spikes of tiny inconspicuous flowers
Portulaca grandiflora	purplish	succulent; leaves linear; stamens many
Stapelia gigantea	purplish to yellow	stems leafless, purple, ridged; flowers large
Evolvulus glomeratus	blue and white	plant low, spreading; flowers wheel-shaped
Nymphaea capensis	blue to pink	plant aquatic, leaves floating; petals many
Heliotropium amplexicaule	blue-violet	flowers in coiled cymes
Begonia ×*semperflorens-cultorum*	pink or white	fruits winged; leaf margin toothed

PLANT	FLOWER COLOR	OTHER CHARACTERISTICS
Oxalis debilis	pink	leaves long-stalked, trifoliate
Celosia argentea	various bract colors	inflorescences variously shaped; flowers tiny
Impatiens spp.	various	flowers spurred, 2-lipped
Portulaca oleracea 'Wildfire'	various	succulent; leaves obovate; stamens many

26 (24′) Flowers not in heads, plant not in the sunflower family Asteraceae 27
26′   Flowers in heads, plant in the sunflower family Asteraceae:

PLANT	FLOWER COLOR	OTHER CHARACTERISTICS
Cosmos sulphureus	yellow-orange	ray florets toothed at tip, 5–8
Wedelia trilobata	yellow	plant prostrate; ray florets 8–13
Zinnia violacea	purplish, etc.	heads with many showy ray and disk florets

27 (26) Leaves colorful, not just green:

PLANT	FLOWER COLOR	OTHER CHARACTERISTICS
Episcia cupreata	red	plant prostrate; leaves attractively colored
Pilea cadierei	green	flowers inconspicuous; silver leaf markings
Alternanthera brasiliana	white	foliage purple; bracts forming white heads
Alternanthera tenella	white	plant low-growing; leaves variegated
Hemigraphis alternata	white	plant prostrate; foliage purple
Iresine herbstii	white, inconspicuous	leaves red-variegated, notched at tip
Solenostemon scutellarioides	blue to purple	stems square; leaves toothed, often showy

27′   Leaves green:

PLANT	FLOWER COLOR	OTHER CHARACTERISTICS
Asclepias curassavica	red and orange	subshrub; sap milky; seeds silky
Crossandra infundibuliformis	red and orange	spikes dense, terminal; corolla appearing one-sided
Cuphea ignea	red	flower tubular, purple or white at tip
Kalanchoe pinnata	red	succulent; flowers hanging, 4-lobed
Kalanchoe tubiflora	red or orange, rarely white	succulent; leaves mottled, cylindrical; margins purplish
Salvia splendens	red, pink, or purple	stems square; calyx matching red, pink, or purple
Chrysothemis pulchella	orange	calyx red, winged; leaves rough-surfaced
Orthosiphon aristatus	white	stems square; stamens long, protruding
Pilea spp.	green	flowers inconspicuous
Hydrangea macrophylla	blue to pink	heads large, dense, of 2 types of flowers
Plectranthus amboinicus	pale blue to pink	leaves succulent, fuzzy, fragrant
Angelonia spp.	purplish and/or white	leaves narrow, toothed, sticky
Asystasia gangetica	purplish and white	scrambling herb; corolla lobes 5, rounded

PLANT	FLOWER COLOR	OTHER CHARACTERISTICS
Asystasia salicifolia	purplish	flowers bell-shaped; leaves narrow, elliptic
Catharanthus roseus	purplish or white	subshrub; sap milky
Dissotis rotundifolia	purplish	petals free; filaments bent, yellow
Gloxinia perennis	purplish	leaves heart-shaped; flowers bell-shaped
Mirabilis jalapa	purple or yellow	flowers funnel-shaped, opening in afternoon
Otacanthus caeruleus	purplish	flowers 2-lipped, white in the center
Pentas lanceolata	purplish to white	flowers clustered, 5-lobed; foliage fuzzy
Salvia splendens	purple, red, or pink	stems square; calyx matching purple, red, or pink
Torenia fournieri	purple, 2-toned	flower purple and lavender with yellow spot
Gomphrena globosa	pink or white bracts	heads globose, of colored bracts
Phyla nodiflora	pink to white	plant prostrate; flowers in long-stalked heads
Portulaca oleracea 'Wildfire'	various	succulent; flowers with 5 petals

28 (2′)   Plant with distinctly leafy stem, not an orchid 29
28′   Plant with large or small basal leaves 31

29 (28) Plant a palm, palm-like, or banana-like 30
29′   Plant not a palm, palm-like, or banana-like:

PLANT	FLOWER COLOR	OTHER CHARACTERISTICS
Alpinia zerumbet	pink outside	flowers red and yellow inside
Cordyline fruticosa	pink to white	stems ringed; leaves often colorful.
Curcuma zedoaria	pink bracts	spikes dense, on short, leafless stalk
Alpinia purpurata	red to white bracts	racemes of showy red, white, or pink bracts
Costus malortianus	red and yellow	sessile ovoid spikes of green bracts
Etlingera elatior	red or pink	inflorescences large, torch-like, red or pink
Costus woodsonii	orange	ovoid spikes of overlapping red bracts
Tapeinochilos ananassae	orange	inflorescences red, pineapple-like
Hedychium flavescens	pale yellow	stamen 1, long, protruding, pale yellow
Hedychium gardnerianum	yellow	stamen 1, long, protruding, red
Zingiber spectabile	yellow and purple	inflorescences beehive-like; bracts curled
Alpinia vittata	white	leaves white-variegated
Carludovica palmata	white	no trunk; basal palm-like pleated leaves
Costus speciosus	white	flower crape-like; bracts red
Dracaena spp.	white	often tree-like; leaves often variegated
Hedychium coronarium	white	stamen 1, long, protruding, white
Pandanus tectorius	white (male)	leaf margin thorny; fruit pineapple-like
Aglaonema commutatum	pale green	erect herb; leaves colorful
Arundo donax	green	large grass; leaves often variegated
Bambusa vulgaris	green but rare	bamboo; stems often yellow
Pennisetum macrostachyum	green to purple	large grass; leaves and spikes purple
Dichorisandra thrysiflora	deep violet	plant erect; flowers white in center

30 (29) Leaves compound, divided into leaflets, or deeply lobed:

PLANT	LEAVES	OTHER CHARACTERISTICS
Caryota mitis	pinnately compound	clump-forming palm; leaves doubly divided
Chrysalidocarpus lutescens	pinnately compound	clump-forming palm; petioles yellowish
Phoenix dactylifera	pinnately compound	trunk with conspicuous leaf scars
Roystonea regia	pinnately compound	solitary large palm; middle of trunk swollen
Veitchia merrillii	pinnately compound	solitary small palm; leaves gray-green
Carludovica palmata	palmately lobed	no trunk; basal palm-like pleated leaves
Livistona chinensis	palmately lobed	solitary palm; leaflet tip long and drooping
Pritchardia pacifica	palmately lobed	solitary palm; leaflet tip stiff and short
Rhapis excelsa	palmately lobed	clump-forming small palm; rarely flowering

30′   Leaves simple:

PLANT	FLOWER COLOR	OTHER CHARACTERISTICS
Musa uranoscopus	red or pink bracts	showy red bracts in terminal racemes
Ravenala madagascariensis	white to yellow	flowers in 7–12 green, boat-shaped bracts
Strelitzia nicolai	white and blue	flowers in 3–5 dark, boat-shaped bracts

31 (28′) Leaf blade strap-shaped, usually without a distinct petiole 32
31′   Leaf blade distinct from petiole 34

32 (31) Leaves not in two opposite rows 33
32′   Leaves in two opposite rows:

PLANT	FLOWER COLOR	OTHER CHARACTERISTICS
Belamcanda chinensis	light red-orange	tepals spotted with red; leaf edges fused
Clivia miniata	orange	flowers funnel-shaped, in umbels
Crocosmia ×crocosmiiflora	orange	tepals red at base; panicle branches zigzag
Arachnis ×maingayi	pale yellow	spider-like orchid flowers mottled with red
Hemerocallis lilio-asphodelus	yellow	flowers large, funnel-shaped, in tall panicles
Dietes bicolor	yellow, dark spot at base	stems erect; leaves *Iris*-like
Trimezia martinicensis	yellow, spotted brown	stems drooping; plantlets forming at nodes
Xiphidium caeruleum	white	panicles with curving branches; flowers small
Neomarica caerulea	pale blue to white	panicle with folded leaf-like stalk
Agapanthus praecox	purplish to white	flowers large, showy, in long-stalked umbels
Arundina graminifolia	purplish and white	tall orchid; leaves linear lanceolate

33 (32) Leaves basal, spirally arranged:

PLANT	FLOWER COLOR	OTHER CHARACTERISTICS
Crinum augustum	pink	umbels of large flowers; stamen bases free
Tulbaghia violacea	pink	small herb; flowers small, in umbels
Zephyranthes rosea	pink	flowers solitary, terminal; leaves grass-like
Aloe vera	red to yellow	leaf margin soft-spiny; leaves gray or mottled
Hippeastrum reticulatum	red and white	umbels of large, funnel-like flowers
Zephyranthes citrina	yellow	flowers solitary, terminal; leaves grass-like
Chlorophytum comosum	white	plant creeping; leaves often white-striped
Crinum spp.	white	umbels of large flowers; stamen bases free
Hymenocallis pedalis	white	flowers spider-like; stamen bases fused
Polianthes tuberosa	white	panicles tall, narrow; flowers showy, fragrant
Yucca gloriosa	white	leaves narrow, spine-tipped; leaf margin dark
Agave americana	greenish yellow	leaves large, spiny-edged; tipped by black spine
Agave attenuata	greenish yellow	leaves large, gray; panicles large, drooping
Cyperus involucratus	green	sedge with leaf-like bracts in a tight spiral
Sansevieria trifasciata	greenish white	leaves erect, leathery, mottled or variegated

33' Leaves grass-like, tiny, cylindrical, or absent:

PLANT	FLOWER COLOR	OTHER CHARACTERISTICS
Papilionanthe 'Agnes Joaquim'	pink	tall orchid with cylindrical leaves
Asparagus densiflorus	white	branches spirally arranged; leaves linear
Asparagus setaceus	white	branches in 1 plane; leaves tiny, linear
Cyperus involucratus	green	sedge with leaf-like bracts in a tight spiral
Cyperus papyrus	green	sedge tall, leafless; spikelets on filaments
Ophiopogon japonicus	rarely formed	turf-forming; grass-like leaves brown at tip
Tillandsia usneoides	rarely formed	thin, hanging stems and gray linear leaves

34 (31') Flowers in a spike enclosed in a sheathing bract, the spathe:

PLANT	FLOWER COLOR	OTHER CHARACTERISTICS
Anthurium andraeanum	red to white	spathe showy, waxy; spadix yellow
Caladium bicolor	whitish	stemless; leaves colorful, arrowhead-shaped
Philodendron bipinnatifidum	white inside	large herb; leaves large, deeply dissected
Spathiphyllum wallisii	white	spathe attractive, glossy; spadix white
Syngonium podophyllum	white	creeper; adult leaves bipalmately compound
Aglaonema commutatum	pale green	erect herb; leaves colorful
Carludovica palmata	green	no trunk; basal palm-like pleated leaves
Monstera deliciosa	green	leaves large, with holes and notched margin
Alocasia cucullata	bluish green	clump-forming herb; leaves heart-shaped
Dieffenbachia maculata	rarely formed	plant erect; leaves usually flecked with white
Epipremnum pinnatum	rarely formed	vine; leaves usually white-variegated

34′   Flowers not in a spike with sheathing bract:

PLANT	FLOWER COLOR	OTHER CHARACTERISTICS
Scadoxus multiflorus	pink to red	heads large; stamens and linear tepals showy
Canna spp.	red or yellow	plant erect; flowers showy; capsules warty
Gloriosa superba	red	vine with tendril-tipped leaves
Heliconia spp.	red, orange, or green	bracts large, showy red to orange, boat-like
Molineria capitulata	yellow	leaves palm-like; flowers on leafless stalk
Strelitzia reginae	orange and blue	flowers arising from 1 boat-like bract
Eucharis amazonica	white	leaves heart-shaped; spikes 3- to 7-flowered
Maranta arundinacea	white	leaves large, variegated
Proiphys amboinensis	white	leaves elliptic; spikes 3- to 7-flowered
Tradescantia pallida	white	herb; foliage and boat-like bracts purple
Tradescantia spathacea	white	coarse herb; leaves purple on underside
Eichhornia crassipes	blue to blue-violet	floating aquatic plant; petioles swollen
Spathoglottis plicata	purple to pink	leaves pleated; flowers yellow in center
Tradescantia zebrina	pink to purplish	weak-stemmed creeper with striped leaves
Tacca chantrieri	dark green to black	flowers bat-like with long, filamentous bracts
Epidendrum ×*obrienianum*	various	leaves sessile; orchid with fringed labellum

Glossary

Achene. A small, dry, one-seeded fruit, not splitting, with the seed fused to the ovary, typical of the grass family Poaceae and sunflower family Asteraceae.

Acuminate. Tapering to a concave-sided, narrow, protracted point.

Acute. Tapering to a sharp but not drawn-out point. Compare attenuate.

Adventitious roots. Roots developing from the sides of stems or trunks rather than at the bottom.

Air layering. A propagation method involving making a cut on a branch, packing moist material such as sphagnum moss, Spanish moss *(Tillandsia usneoides),* or vermiculite around it, and enclosing it in plastic wrapping to keep in the moisture. This procedure promotes root growth, producing a stem with adventitious roots, and the rooted stem is then cut off and planted in soil.

Alternate. Arrangement of leaves one to a node. Compare opposite.

Annual. A plant that completes its life cycle, from seed, to seedling, to adult plant, and through flower and fruit back to seed, within a year. Compare biennial and perennial.

Anther. The pollen sac of a stamen, attached to the top of a filament.

Appressed. Lying flat against a surface, as in appressed hairs.

Areole. Cushion from which spines arise in members of the cactus family Cactaceae.

Aroid. A member of the taro family Araceae.

Attenuate. Tapering gradually to form a long, straight-sided tip. Compare acute.

Awn. A slender, bristle-like appendage usually at the tip of a structure, especially on grass spikelets.

Axil (axillary). The angle at a node between the stem and the upper leaf surface. The axillary bud found here may develop into a branch or inflorescence.

Banner. The uppermost, typically broad petal of a papilionaceous flower.

Basal. Originating at the base.

Berry. A fleshy fruit formed by a single flower and containing more than one seed.

Biennial. A plant that grows from seed, to seedling, to a vegetative stage in the first year of its life, often dying back and overwintering as a root or bulb, and then resumes growth to become an adult plant, and through flower and fruit completing its life cycle back to seed in its second year. Compare annual and perennial.

Bipinnate (bipinnately compound). Twice pinnate, said of compound leaves with the first division being further pinnately divided.

Blade. The expanded part of a leaf, usually attached to the stem by a petiole.

Bract. A reduced or modified leaf attached below a flower or inflorescence. A bracteole is a secondary bract.

Bulb. A short underground stem with leaves modified for food storage, as in onions. Compare rhizome, tuber.

Bulbil. A bulb-like structure formed in the axils of some plants, which can simply be cut off and planted as a propagation method. Compare offshoots and suckers.

Calyx. The outer, usually green whorl of a flower that encloses the corolla, stamens, and the female part of the flower, composed of sepals or, when fused, of calyx lobes. In flowers lacking a corolla, the sepals or calyx are sometimes petal-like.

Capsule. A dry, splitting fruit with two or more seed-containing compartments, locules, or cells, opening along seams between the valves. Compare follicle and pod.

Chaffy. Describing dry, thin, membranous structures, as in chaffy bracts.

Clone (clonal). A group of genetically identical plants resulting from vegetative (nonsexual) reproduction.

Composite. A member of the sunflower family Asteraceae. A composite flower head is the typical inflorescence of composites, looking like a flower but composed of small flowers often of two types, petal-like ray florets on the margin and disk florets in the center.

Compound leaf. A leaf divided into several parts, leaflets. See pinnate (and bipinnate, even-pinnate, odd-pinnate, and tripinnate) and palmate (and trifoliate).

Corm. A bulb-like underground stem enclosed by dry, scale-like leaves.

Corolla. The inner, usually colored whorl of a flower, composed of free or fused petals, or sometimes absent.

Corona. A set of small petal-like appendages on the corolla of some flowers.

Corymb. A flat-topped, short, broad inflorescence with the center flower the youngest.

Crenate. Scalloped, as the margins of leaves with round teeth.

Crownshaft. A smooth, pillar-like extension of the trunk of some palms.

Cultivar. A horticultural variety, usually reproduced vegetatively. Designated with single quotation marks, for example, 'Queen Sirikit'.

Cuttings. A propagation method in which cut sections of stems are simply stuck in the ground and watered, or chemicals may be applied to the cut end to promote growth. Compare division.

Cyathium (plural, cyathia). A cup-like, highly reduced inflorescence found in some members of the spurge family Euphorbiaceae.

Cyme (cymose). A compound inflorescence with the oldest flowers at the end or center. Compare panicle.

Dicot. A member of the Dicotyledonae, one of the two divisions of flowering plants and characterized by seeds with two seed leaves and flower parts usually in multiples of four or five.

Dioecious. Referring to plants that have separate male and female flowers on different plants; literally, two houses. Compare monoecious.

Disk floret. The small kind of flower typically lacking a strap-shaped corolla and found at the center of most composite flower heads. Compare ray floret and composite.

Distichous. Describing leaves arranged in two rows, one on each side of the stem.

Division. A propagation method in which a plant is simply divided into two, for example, a rhizome with or without leaves is cut off the main plant and replanted. Compare cuttings.

Double-flowered. Having a corolla with twice or more the normal number of petals.

Drupe. A fleshy fruit with a single hard-shelled seed, such as a mango or peach; a "stone fruit." A drupelet is a small drupe.

Elliptic. Shaped like an ellipse, referring to leaves that are much longer than wide and have the sides curving and not parallel to each other.

Entire. Smooth-edged, without teeth, usually referring to the margin of a leaf blade.

Epicalyx. A ring or whorl of bracts borne below the calyx of some flowers.

Epiphyte (epiphytic). A plant growing on another plant but not using the host plant for food.

Equitant. Describing leaves that are overlapping in two ranks, as in members of the iris family Iridaceae.

Even-pinnate (even-pinnately compound). Said of pinnately compound leaves with an even number of leaflets, that is, without a terminal leaflet.

f. Abbreviation for form.

Fascicle. A condensed cluster, said of leaves or flowers.

Filament. The stalk of a stamen, atop which is the anther.

Filiform. Linear and filament-like in shape.

Floret. A small flower. See disk floret, ray floret, and composite.

Follicle. A dry, splitting fruit containing a single seed-containing compartment, locule, or cell, opening along one seam. Compare capsule and pod.

Form. The lowest taxonomic rank, abbreviated f., usually differentiating variation in some single characteristic such as color.

Glabrous. Said of a surface lacking hairs or pubescence; hairless and smooth.

Head. A type of inflorescence with sessile flowers attached to a single point. Compare composite and umbel.

Hispid. Having short stiff hairs.

Hypanthium. A cup-like structure formed by fusion of the lower parts of the corolla, calyx, and stamens, found in some flowers.

Inflorescence. A cluster of flowers or the mode or arrangement of flowers on a plant.

Internode. The portion of a stem between the nodes, which are the points of attachment of leaves.

Interpetiolar stipule. Stipules of opposite leaves that fuse together and extend all the way around a node, as in the coffee family Rubiaceae.

Involucre (involucral). A whorl of leaves or bracts close to the base of an inflorescence.

Keel. The specialized petal of a papilionaceous flower that encloses the stamens.

Labellum. A modified, usually large and showy petal found in members of the orchid family Orchidaceae and ginger family Zingiberaceae.

Lanceolate. Lance-shaped in outline, several times longer than wide with the widest portion toward the base of a leaf. Compare oblanceolate.

Leaf. A lateral structure of a plant, usually borne on a stem and composed of a blade and petiole.

Leaflet. A division of a compound leaf.

Lenticel. A corky area sometimes found on the surface of stems, appearing as a dot or oval, used for aeration of the internal tissues.

Liana. A climbing woody vine. Compare strangler.

Limb. The expanded upper portion of some flowers, as opposed to the lower tube or tubular portion.

Midvein. The main vein of a leaf that is a continuation of the veins in the petiole. From it arise the secondary veins.

Monocot. A member of the Monocotyledonae, one of the two divisions of flowering plants and characterized by seeds with a single seed leaf and flower parts usually in multiples of three.

Monoecious. Referring to plants that have separate male and female flowers on the same plant; literally, one house. Compare dioecious.

Node. Point of attachment of a leaf on a stem. See internode.

Nutlet. A small, dry lobe of a divided fruit.

Ob- . A prefix referring to reverse condition, for example, oblanceolate means reverse lance-shaped, broader toward the point than the base.

Obcordate. Heart-shaped but broadest toward the tip rather than the base.

Oblanceolate. Reverse lance-shaped in outline, broader toward the point than the base.

Oblique. Unequally sided, as at the bases of some leaves.

Oblong. A rectangular shape with rounded ends and parallel long sides.

Obovate. Reverse egg-shaped in outline, broad and rounded at the tip and tapering toward the base.

Odd-pinnate (odd-pinnately compound). Said of pinnately compound leaves with an odd number of leaflets, that is, with a terminal leaflet.

Offshoot. Referring to a propagation method used for some plants that produce smaller plantlets (the offshoots) on the branches and that can simply be cut off and planted. Compare bulbils and suckers.

Opposite. Arrangement of leaves paired two to a node. Compare alternate and whorled.

Ovary. The part of a flower enclosing the ovules, developing into the fruit, which bears the seeds.

Ovate. Egg-shaped in outline, broad and rounded at the base and tapering toward the tip.

Palmate (palmately compound). Lobed or divided in a hand-like fashion, usually in reference to compound leaves or veins. Compare pinnate.

Panicle (paniculate). A compound inflorescence with a main axis and racemose branches, with the youngest flowers toward the tip. Compare cyme.

Papilionaceous. Butterfly-like, said of flowers of some members of the pea family Fabaceae. The flower is typically composed of an expanded banner, a keel enclosing the stamens, and a pair of lateral petals called wings.

Parallel venation. Leaf venation arrangement in which the veins lie parallel to each other, as in most monocots.

Pedicel. The stalk of a flower in an inflorescence.

Peduncle. The stalk of a solitary flower or of an inflorescence or cluster of flowers.

Peltate. Said of a leaf blade with the petiole attached inside the leaf margin rather at the edge.

Perennial. A plant that has an indefinite life span, taking more than a year to grow from seed, to seedling, to adult plant, which continues to flower and fruit for varying periods of time. Perennials may be herbaceous, perhaps dying back periodically to their root, rhizome, or bulb before resuming growth, or woody trees, shrubs, or vines. Compare annual and biennial.

Perianth. Collective term for the calyx and corolla.

Petal. A division of a corolla, usually three in monocots, or four or five in dicots.

Petiole. The stalk of a leaf. Leaves without a petiole are referred to as being sessile.

Pinna (plural, pinnae). The first division of a compound leaf. In bipinnate leaves the pinna is further divided into leaflets.

Pinnate (pinnately compound). Lobed or divided in feather-like fashion, usually in reference to compound leaves (bipinnate, even-pinnate, odd-pinnate, tripinnate). Compare palmate.

Plicate. Folded, said of leaves with folds or pleats in the blade.

Pod. A dry, splitting fruit with a single seed-containing compartment, locule, or cell, opening along two sutures. Compare capsule and follicle.

Pubescent. Hairy, covered with hairs, which are the pubescence.

Raceme (racemose). A simple, unbranched inflorescence bearing stalked flowers on a single main axis, the rachis, with the youngest ones at the top. It is like a spike, which differs in having sessile flowers.

Rachis. The main axis of a compound leaf or an inflorescence.

Ray floret. The small kind of flower with a strap-shaped corolla found at the margin of most composite flower heads. Compare disk floret.

Recurved. Curved back.

Reflexed. Bent back.

Revolute. Having the margins rolled toward the lower surface, said of leaves.

Rhizomatous. Forming a rhizome.

Rhizome. An underground stem, usually with nodes and buds. Compare bulb, tuber.

Rosette. A tight spiral of basal leaves.

Rotate. Wheel-shaped, said of a corolla. Compare salverform.

Salverform. A corolla with a narrow tube and an abruptly spreading limb at the top. Compare rotate.

Scabrous. Having a rough surface, usually from short stiff hairs or small scales.

Scandent. Said of shrubs that have weak stems that can climb like those of vines.

Scape (scapose). An inflorescence borne on a long, leafless stalk.

Scarified. Cut or otherwise abraded, said of some seeds that need this mechanical treatment in order to germinate.

Schizocarp. A dry fruit splitting apart at maturity into one-seeded segments.

Secondary veins. Veins that arise from the midvein of a leaf.

Sepal. A division of a calyx, usually three in monocots, or four or five in dicots.

Serrate. Having a saw-toothed margin, said of leaves.

Sessile. Lacking a stalk, often said of leaves lacking petioles or flowers lacking pedicels or peduncles.

Sheath. The tubular structure at the base of a leaf of members of the grass family Poaceae, typically surrounding the stem.

Simple leaf. See leaf.

Solitary flower. Flower occurring by itself, not with others in an inflorescence.

sp. (plural, spp.). Abbreviation for species.

Spadix (plural, spadices). An inflorescence spike with a fleshy axis, often associated with a bract called a spathe, in aroids, members of the taro family Araceae.

Spathe. A large, solitary bract attached at the base of the spadix in the inflorescence of an aroid, a member of the taro family Araceae.

Species (plural, species). A taxonomic rank, abbreviated sp. (plural, spp.), defined as members of a morphologically similar, interbreeding or potentially interbreeding population that share a common ancestry and usually are reproductively isolated from other species.

Spike. A simple, unbranched inflorescence bearing sessile flowers on a single main axis, the rachis, with the youngest ones at the top. It is like a raceme, which differs in having stalked flowers.

Spikelet. The inflorescence of a member of the grass family Poaceae or sedge family Cyperaceae, comprising small green flowers and membranous scales.

Stamen. The male part of a flower comprising a stalk, the filament, and pollen sac, the anther.

Staminal column. Column formed by fused stamens.

Staminode. A stamen that has lost its anther and is thus not used for reproduction; a sterile stamen.

Stellate. Star-shaped, said of branched hairs with radiating arms.

Stigma. The pollen-receptive tip of a style in the female part of a flower.

Stipule (stipular). One of a pair of appendages found at the base of some leaves. Compare interpetiolar stipule.

Strangler. A type of tree (banyans, *Ficus* spp., for example) that grows on another tree called a host, which is eventually surrounded and strangled by prevention of further growth. Compare liana.

Style. The stalk of the female part of a flower connecting the ovary with the stigma.

Sub-. A prefix meaning less than, for example, subequal means not quite equal.

Subsessile. Nearly stalkless.

Subspecies. A taxonomic rank, abbreviated subsp., below species and above variety and form. Some botanists equate subspecies with variety.

Suckers. A propagation method used for some plants that produce smaller plants at the base, termed suckers, which can simply be cut off and planted. Compare bulbils and offshoots.

Syconium. The inflorescence of the fig genus *Ficus* in which the flowers are entirely enclosed within a fruit-like structure.

Syncarp. A fruit formed from the fusion of several to many flowers sharing a common axis.

Tendril. A thread-like structure that grasps other plants or objects and clings to them for support.

Tepal. The collective term for sepals and petals when they are similar to each other in a flower.

Trifoliate. Describing a compound leaf with three leaflets. Some authors prefer the term trifoliolate.

Tripinnate (tripinnately compound). Thrice pinnate, said of compound leaves with the first division being further bipinnately divided.

Triploid. A plant that has three sets of chromosomes rather than the normal two, formed from some hybridizations.

Tube. The narrower lower portion of some flowers, as opposed to the expanded upper limb.

Tuber (tuberous). A swollen, underground, root-like stem. Compare bulb, rhizome.

Umbel. A flat- or round-topped inflorescence with the stalks of the flowers all arising from one point.

Unisexual. Said of flowers lacking either stamens or an ovary.

Utricle. A dry, one-seeded, often inflated seed, often opening by a lid.

Variety. A taxonomic rank, abbreviated var., below species and subspecies and above form. Some botanists equate variety with subspecies.

Venation. The arrangement of veins in a leaf. See parallel venation.

Whorled. Arrangement of leaves more than two to a node. Compare opposite.

Wing. One of a pair of petals found in papilionaceous flowers.

Winged. Having flattened, often wide ridges, the wings; said of stems, petioles, or fruits.

Index

Common plant names are cross-referenced to the scientific names by which the entries in the book are organized. Keep in mind that some common names are in fact the scientific names, and such names are not repeated below. Examples of such names are aloe vera *(Aloe vera)*, gardenia *(Gardenia)*, jacaranda *(Jacaranda)*, and yucca *(Yucca)*. Synonyms are also cross-referenced to the accepted scientific names, and family names are cross-referenced to their genera.